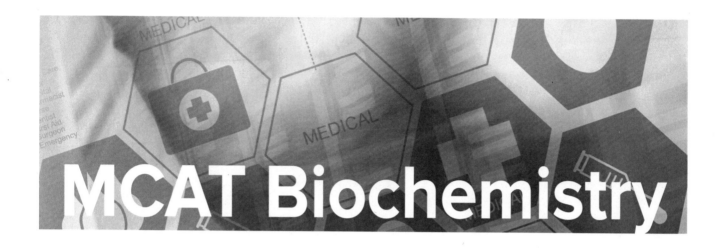

# MCAT Biochemistry

# CONTENT REVIEW AND PRACTICE PASSAGES

# NextStep
TEST PREP nextsteptestprep.com

Printed in the United States of America

Second Printing, 2018

ISBN 978-1-944-935-18-4

Next Step Test Prep, LLC
4256 N Ravenswood Ave
Suite 207
Chicago IL 60613

www.nextsteptestprep.com

Revision Number: 1.2 (2018-04-01)

# FREE ONLINE FULL LENGTH MCAT

Want to see how you would do on the MCAT
and understand where you need to focus your prep?

**TAKE OUR FREE MCAT DIAGNOSTIC EXAM**
and **FREE FULL LENGTH**
Timed practice that simulates Test Day and provides
comprehensive analysis, reporting, and in-depth explanations.

Included with this free account is the first lesson
in Next Step's online course, a free sample
from our science QBank, and more!

All of these resources are provided free to students who have
purchased a Next Step book. Register for your free account at:

http://nextsteptestprep.com/mcat-diagnostic

This page left intentionally blank.

# STOP! READ ME FIRST!

The book you're holding is one of Next Step's six MCAT review books and contains both concise content review and questions to practice applying your content knowledge. In order to get the most out of this book, we strongly recommend that you follow a few simple steps:

**1.** Register for a free MCAT bundle at http://nextsteptestprep.com/mcat-diagnostic and begin your prep by taking the MCAT Diagnostic and Science Content Diagnostic to assess your strengths and weaknesses.

**2.** Begin working through the Next Step Review set starting with the Verbal, Quantitative, and Research Methods book. Complete this entire book at the start of your prep.

**3.** Use the Study Plan generator in your free account at nextstepmcat.com to generate a day-by-day study plan to take you through the rest of the Next Step Books.

**4.** Begin working through the rest of the Next Step MCAT review books, including this one. To get the most value out of these books, use spaced repetition to ensure complete mastery of the material. A spaced repetition approach would look something like this:

>I. Begin by skimming through the chapter to familiarize yourself with the key terms and content in the book. Then go back and read the chapter carefully.

>II. Sleep on it! Solidifying those long term memories requires sleep.

>III. Come back to the chapter **the next day**, re-skim it and then **complete the questions at the end of the chapter**. Carefully read all of the explanations, even for the questions you got right.

>IV. Take notes in your Lessons Learned Journal from the chapter. For a full explanation on what a Lessons Learned Journal is, watch Lesson 1 included in the free online bundle at nextstepmcat.com.

>IV. Sleep on it!

>V. Two days later, come back, briefly re-skim the chapter, re-do the questions at the end of the chapter, and review your Lessons Learned Journal.

Mastering the MCAT requires more than just a good set of books. You'll want to continue your prep with the most representative practice tests available. Your free bundle includes Next Step Full Length #1. After you've completed that, you can upgrade your account to include additional practice exams.

Finally, if you would like more extensive help, including daily live office hours with Next Step's senior faculty, contact us for more information about our online course. You can reach us at 888-530-NEXT or mcat@nextsteptestprep.com.

| Group→ / Period↓ | 1 | 2 | 3 | 4 | 5 | 6 | 7 | 8 | 9 | 10 | 11 | 12 | 13 | 14 | 15 | 16 | 17 | 18 |
|---|---|---|---|---|---|---|---|---|---|---|---|---|---|---|---|---|---|---|
| 1 | 1 H | | | | | | | | | | | | | | | | | 2 He |
| 2 | 3 Li | 4 Be | | | | | | | | | | | 5 B | 6 C | 7 N | 8 O | 9 F | 10 Ne |
| 3 | 11 Na | 12 Mg | | | | | | | | | | | 13 Al | 14 Si | 15 P | 16 S | 17 Cl | 18 Ar |
| 4 | 19 K | 20 Ca | 21 Sc | 22 Ti | 23 V | 24 Cr | 25 Mn | 26 Fe | 27 Co | 28 Ni | 29 Cu | 30 Zn | 31 Ga | 32 Ge | 33 As | 34 Se | 35 Br | 36 Kr |
| 5 | 37 Rb | 38 Sr | 39 Y | 40 Zr | 41 Nb | 42 Mo | 43 Tc | 44 Ru | 45 Rh | 46 Pd | 47 Ag | 48 Cd | 49 In | 50 Sn | 51 Sb | 52 Te | 53 I | 54 Xe |
| 6 | 55 Cs | 56 Ba | 57 La * | 72 Hf | 73 Ta | 74 W | 75 Re | 76 Os | 77 Ir | 78 Pt | 79 Au | 80 Hg | 81 Tl | 82 Pb | 83 Bi | 84 Po | 85 At | 86 Rn |
| 7 | 87 Fr | 88 Ra | 89 Ac ** | 104 Rf | 105 Db | 106 Sg | 107 Bh | 108 Hs | 109 Mt | 110 Ds | 111 Rg | 112 Cn | 113 Nh | 114 Fl | 115 Mc | 116 Lv | 117 Ts | 118 Og |

| * | 58 Ce | 59 Pr | 60 Nd | 61 Pm | 62 Sm | 63 Eu | 64 Gd | 65 Tb | 66 Dy | 67 Ho | 68 Er | 69 Tm | 70 Yb | 71 Lu |
|---|---|---|---|---|---|---|---|---|---|---|---|---|---|---|
| ** | 90 Th | 91 Pa | 92 U | 93 Np | 94 Pu | 95 Am | 96 Cm | 97 Bk | 98 Cf | 99 Es | 100 Fm | 101 Md | 102 No | 103 Lr |

# TABLE OF CONTENTS

This page left intentionally blank.

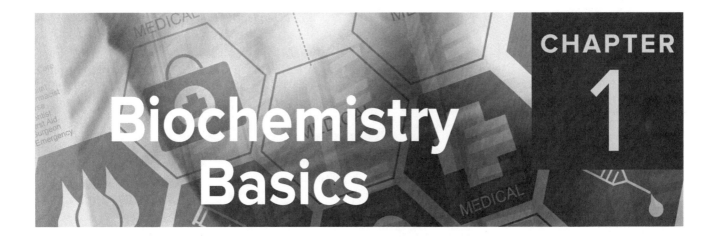

# CHAPTER 1

# Biochemistry Basics

## 0. Introduction

In this textbook, we'll be focusing on biochemistry, which is arguably at the core of MCAT competency, both because it directly comprises approximately 25% of both the Chemical and Physical Foundations section and the Biological and Biochemical Foundations section, and because it is at the intersection of chemistry/organic chemistry and biology. In particular, a solid understanding of biochemistry will help you take your understanding of biology to the level necessary to truly excel on the MCAT.

Nonetheless, biochemistry is often considered one of the most challenging subjects for the MCAT. There are three essential steps to success in MCAT biochemistry: (1) learning the details, (2) putting the details in a bigger picture, and (3) learning how to apply your biochemistry knowledge to passage-based questions. Point (3) is where practice tests—and carefully reviewing them—come in, while the goal of content review is to help with points (1) and (2).

There's simply no way around the fact that succeeding on MCAT biochemistry requires a solid mastery of the factual material, which includes the memorization of hundreds of facts about chemical structures, reactions, and pathways. In that sense, it's definitely important that you respect the subject and invest the time and energy necessary to become familiar with this entire array of facts. However, it's probably not a major surprise to hear that you need to master the factual material to succeed on the MCAT. The more subtle mistake that students can make is to focus *entirely* on the facts, or to focus on them as isolated pieces of knowledge, without putting them in a bigger picture.

When studying biomolecules, the "bigger picture" can involve understanding the range of functions that a type of molecule (e.g., proteins, nucleic acids, carbohydrates, etc.) has in the body, as well as understanding the biochemical logic behind the reactions. For pathways, the bigger picture includes knowing where the process takes place, what purpose it serves, and what the inputs and outputs are. A solid knowledge of just those aspects of a given process can help you answer some questions correctly, and will also help you contextualize further details involving specific steps and regulation.

In the rest of this chapter, we'll explore a few high-level themes that recur throughout biochemistry. Thinking in these terms even before you jump into the detailed material will help you study more efficiently, in a way that will be optimally tailored to the requirements of the MCAT. In general, it's also simply easier to remember details if you

> > **CONNECTIONS** < <

**Chapter 1 of Biology**

can connect them to a set of deeper principles, rather than approaching them in isolation. For this reason, we recommend that you read through this chapter first, but also that you come back and quickly review it *after* completing the rest of the textbook. It may also be useful to review Chapter 1 of the Biology textbook, which contains a general review of biomolecules.

# 1. Charge and Redox Chemistry in Biochemistry

In a very real sense, all of biochemistry (as well as all of organic chemistry, and most of general chemistry) is a story about how our body does cool things by shuffling electrons around. This point can easily be lost in the thicket of terminology, but simply following the electrons can be a very useful way of making sense of structures and mechanisms, and electron transfer processes also play a major role in the bioenergetics of metabolism. Electrons (and therefore charge) also help make sense of how biochemical properties contribute to biological function, as we will discuss more in section 2 of this chapter. In this section, we'll review some examples of how charge can help shed light on familiar biochemical facts. This is not a comprehensive presentation of every phenomenon in biochemistry that involves charge; instead, the goal is to present some of the most important examples and to illustrate the principle of how thinking about charge can help organize your knowledge of biochemistry.

An excellent example of how charge is a useful lens through which to approach biochemical structures is provided by the broad topic of proteins, which includes amino acids, enzymes, non-enzymatic proteins, and protein analytical techniques. Charge shapes the behavior of proteins at all levels. At the smallest level, charge (in combination with steric considerations) shapes the behavior of amino acid residues, which are the building blocks of proteins. On the level of a protein as a whole, charge plays a major role in secondary, tertiary, and quaternary structure. On an even higher level of organization, proteins generally interact with each other through non-covalent (that is, non-binding) interactions in the cell; these interactions are generally shaped by a combination of charge and sterics.

Nucleic acids furnish another excellent example of how paying careful attention to charge helps make sense of various phenomena involving biomolecules. Hydrogen bonds, which are due to interactions between partial positive and negative charges, between nucleobases on opposite strands of DNA and RNA molecules contribute to the stability of the double helix structure. One of the facts about DNA that you will need to memorize is that guanine-cytosine (G-C) pairs have three hydrogen bonds, while adenine-thymine (A-T) pairs have only two. This means that DNA strands that are rich in G-C pairs are more stable and resistant to heat, a fact that is directly due to the presence of more charge-based interactions, which in turn boils down once again to "follow the electrons." DNA structure is also stabilized by hydrophobic base stacking interactions between nucleobases, and this also reflects properties of charge; namely, the fact that the rings of nucleobases are relatively homogenous in terms of charge, and therefore non-polar. As we will discuss more below in section 2, the fact that the backbone of DNA is negatively charged has important functional implications as well.

**Figure 1.** Base pair interactions in DNA.

Charge is also helpful to understand some major principles of bioenergetics. One example of this is the use of ATP as the predominant intracellular form of energy. The reason why ATP is useful as a form of energy is because its hydrolysis into ADP and an inorganic phosphate group is highly energetically favorable. A major reason for this is because in ATP, three phosphate groups with strong negative charges (a total of four negative charges) are adjacent to each other, meaning that ATP stores potential energy that can be used to drive less favorable reactions forward.

**Figure 2.** Structure of ATP at physiological pH.

Moreover, charge plays a major role in the formation of ATP itself, via the electrochemical gradient that is formed in the mitochondria in the electron transport chain. Protons build up in the intermembrane space of the mitochondria, and that proton gradient is used to power the formation of ATP by ATP synthase.

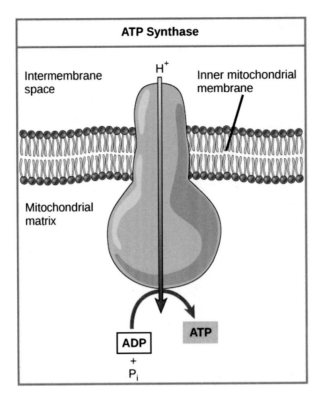

**Figure 3.** Proton gradient/proton pump.

Note the important connection to physics here, in that charge differentials can be used to store energy. For this reason, much of metabolism (how cells produce energy) ultimately boils down to an intricate system of transferring electrons from one place to another. This is accomplished through reduction/oxidation (redox) reactions. Although redox reactions are most familiar for many students in the context of electrochemistry, batteries, and electric cells, they are also ubiquitous in biochemistry, precisely because many metabolic pathways (most notably energy-producing pathways) ultimately have the goal of moving electrons from one place to another.

For this reason, it's important to be able to recognize redox reactions that occur in organic molecules. Table 1 below summarizes various definitions and examples of redox reactions, ranging from general chemistry to biochemistry.

| REDUCTION | OXIDATION |
|---|---|
| Gain of an electron | Loss of an electron |
| Decreased oxidation state | Increased oxidation state |
| Formation of a C–H bond (e.g., alkene → alkane) | Loss of a C–H bond (e.g., alkane → alkene) |
| Loss of a C–O or C–N bond (or any bond between carbon and an electronegative atom) | Gain of a C–O or C–N bond (or any bond between carbon and an electronegative atom) |
| Common reactions: alkyne > alkene > alkane carboxylic acid > aldehyde/ketone > alcohol | Common reactions: Alkane > alkene > alkyne alcohol > aldehyde/ketone > carboxylic acid |
| Common reduced biomolecules: NADH FADH$_2$ Glucose Fatty acid alkane units | Common oxidized biomolecules: NAD$^+$ FAD 6 CO$_2$ Acetyl CoA > CO$_2$ |

**Table 1.** Reduction and oxidation in organic chemistry and biochemistry.

While it's definitely important to understand the principles of redox reactions as applied to biochemistry, it's also a good idea to just memorize how certain common biomolecules fit into the redox paradigm. In particular, you should memorize the fact that NADH and FADH$_2$ are the reduced forms of the electron carriers and that NAD$^+$ and FAD are the corresponding oxidized forms. You may be surprised to see glucose and fatty acid alkane units listed as reduced biomolecules, but it's true. Recall that glucose contains five hydroxyl groups and one carbonyl group, making it quite reduced in the context of oxygen-containing organic chemicals, and alkanes are the most reduced hydrocarbons. The way that we produce energy from carbohydrates and fatty acids is by oxidizing them and shunting the electrons that are obtained by oxidizing them into the formation of the electrochemical gradient that we discussed above.

Later in this book, we will spend three full chapters discussing these metabolic pathways, so you will have plenty of opportunities to learn about them in more depth. Nonetheless, they all share a basic architecture: energy-generating pathways are long, multi-step, carefully regulated processes in which our cells take electrons from one place (in a nutrient molecule) and move them through the electron transport chain so that we can make ATP.

## MCAT STRATEGY > > >

A common mnemonic for oxidation and reduction is OIL RIG: oxidation is loss, reduction is gain. This is useful, but it's also worth making a special separate effort to study how oxidation and reduction apply in biochemical contexts.

## MCAT STRATEGY > > >

Take a minute and make sure you clearly understand the idea that energy is produced from biomolecules by stripping them of electrons and sending those electrons through the electron transport chain to create an electrochemical gradient. This is the unified principle that ties together the pathways discussed in detail in chapters 7, 8, and 9, and it is surprisingly easy to overlook. If you are comfortable with this principle in advance, you will have a much easier time mastering the details of metabolism.

# 2. Structure and Function

One of the best habits that you can develop while studying for the MCAT is taking every opportunity possible to link chemical structure to biological function. Questions linking the structure of biochemicals to their function in the organism are a mainstay of the MCAT; you are highly likely to get several questions on Test Day on this general theme, and they are worth special attention because they may initially be different from the memorization-based questions that you may have frequently encountered in your coursework. However, once you get the hang of thinking in this way, such questions can become quite predictable.

## MCAT STRATEGY > > >

The basic idea here is that to succeed on the test, you need to learn how to think like the test. This is an area where taking and analyzing practice exams/sections even before your content review is done can be very helpful, because active practice will help you develop and solidify test-like thinking habits.

Proteins are a perennial MCAT favorite for questions linking biochemical structure and physiological properties. Most protein-protein and protein-ligand interactions are noncovalent, meaning that they are generally driven by a combination of steric interactions (i.e., interactions shaped by size) and charge-driven interactions, as discussed above in section 1. Many questions on this topic fall into two major categories: (1) how could the function of a protein be *altered*, and (2) how could the function of a protein or a ligand be *simulated*. These are essentially two sides of the same coin, because both types of question require the application of the same principles of sterics and charge-driven interactions, with the only real difference being whether you're trying to find a protein/substrate with properties that are similar to or different from the properties of the protein that you are presented with. Below we list some especially common contexts in which the MCAT can test structure-function relationships in proteins.

> Enzymes. The active site on an enzyme tends to be very specific for its substrate. Therefore, substituting an amino acid residue in the active site with another amino acid that has different properties (hydrophobic vs. hydrophilic, positively charged vs. negatively charged, etc.) is very likely to disrupt enzyme function. In contrast, if you're asked to determine what will make a good substrate for a given active site, you'll want to look for a combination of amino acid properties that will result in attractive interactions (for example, hydrophobic residues are likely to attract each other, as are positively and negatively charged residues).

> Transmembrane proteins. Transmembrane proteins are characterized by central membrane-spanning domains and intracellular/extracellular domains. Due to the lipid bilayer structure of the plasma membrane, the membrane-spanning domains tend to be richer in hydrophobic amino acid residues, whereas the intracellular/extracellular domains tend to be richer in hydrophilic residues, because they face aqueous environments.

> Protein folding. The three-dimensional structure of proteins is determined by a process known as protein folding, which is surprisingly difficult to predict precisely. Protein folding is largely affected by the tertiary structure of proteins, a term that refers to structural features caused by interactions between the side chains of amino acids. These interactions can involve covalent bonding (most notably disulfide bond formation between two cysteine residues), but often involve non-covalent interactions shaped by polarity and charge. The MCAT might ask you to predict how the tertiary structure of a protein (or its folding) would be affected by an amino acid substitution. As with the active sites of enzymes, substituting an amino acid residue with one that has different polarity-related properties will be more likely to affect the three-dimensional form of a protein, whereas substituting an amino acid with one that has similar polarity-related properties would be more likely to preserve the three-dimensional structure with minimal alteration.

Another example of an important structure-function relationship is provided by the plasma membrane itself, which is primarily composed of phospholipids that have a polar head and a nonpolar tail. This structural property contributes to the formation of a bilayer membrane, in which the polar phosphate heads face the intracellular and extracellular environments, which are both aqueous solutions, while the nonpolar tails remain inside the membrane. This occurs because the clustering of nonpolar structures together is entropically favorable. In addition to phospholipids, the presence of cholesterol and lipid rafts within the plasma membrane help contribute to the fluidity of the membrane at lower temperatures and to its stability at higher temperatures. The resulting bilayer membrane is permeable to very small uncharged molecules and to lipid-soluble molecules, but not to hydrophilic molecules of any appreciable size. Such molecules require transporters. This is tremendously useful for the body because transporters can be regulated to a much greater extent than diffusion processes can be, meaning that the lipid bilayer structure that results from entropically favorable interactions between phospholipids ultimately allows the body to perform the physiologically essential task of closely regulating what goes into and out of the cell.

**Figure 4.** Bilayer membrane.

The different types of hormones in the endocrine system constitute another excellent example of how chemical structure affects physiological function. In a sense, this example combines the various points we've touched on so far, because it has to do with the different ways that lipids and proteins interact with the cell membrane. Hormones are signaling molecules that travel through the circulatory system to induce various effects on their target tissues, and play a major role in regulating homeostasis and mediating the body's response to various stimuli. Most hormones fall into one of two categories: peptide hormones and steroid hormones (there are also a few amino acid-derived hormones; see Chapter 6 of the Biology textbook for more details). As the name implies, peptide hormones are composed of chains of amino acids, while steroid hormones are lipids derived from cholesterol (a hormone with a characteristic four-ring structure).

> > CONNECTIONS < <

Chapter 6 of Biology

As described above, the structure of the plasma membrane means that it is permeable to nonpolar molecules, such as steroid hormones. Therefore, steroid hormones can diffuse into the cell, and ultimately exert their effect by interacting with nuclear receptors that regulate gene transcription. In contrast, peptide hormones are polar, and must interact with their target cells via membrane-bound receptors. The membrane-bound receptors then engage secondary messenger systems within the cell, which can amplify a signal within a very short amount of time. A consequence of the different mechanisms of peptide versus steroid hormones is that they tend to exert different types of effects on the body. The mechanisms of peptide hormones are suitable for hormones that induce quick, dramatic changes in response to a stimulus of some sort (classic examples include insulin and glucagon, which regulate blood sugar levels). In contrast, because the effects of steroid hormones are induced by changes in gene expression, they tend to have longer-onset, longer-lasting effects, with classic examples including the effects of the sex hormones estrogen and testosterone on sexual maturation and the development of secondary sex characteristics during puberty.

Note what we've done in this discussion: we've linked some very low-level properties of molecules (polar vs. nonpolar) to a non-obvious conclusion about how the body tends to respond to different kind of stimuli, as mediated by different interactions with the plasma membrane. In a passage dealing with the endocrine system, you could be given questions that range across this entire spectrum, jumping from chemical properties of hormones to their systemic effects and regulations. Training yourself to think in this way while studying will both directly help prepare you for such passages and indirectly help prepare you for any other surprises that you might encounter on Test Day by ensuring that your study process links the little details with the big picture.

Another interesting example of structure-function relationships involving charge is how histone modifications can impact DNA expression. DNA is a highly negatively-charged molecule due to the phosphate groups present in its backbone, and histones are proteins that function as a sort of scaffolding that packages DNA. The interactions between DNA and histones are non-covalent. As such, histones tend to be rich in positive (basic) amino acid residues, because the attraction between positive and negative charges is a large part of why DNA sticks to histones. However, histones can be modified by the covalent addition of a range of structures, such as methyl groups, phosphate groups, and acetyl groups. Acetylation of lysine is a particularly important and relatively well-understood modification of histones. The addition of an acetyl group to the basic N of lysine's side group removes its positive charge. By doing so, it weakens the interaction between a histone and the DNA that it organizes. When repeated over several lysine units, the cumulative effect of acetylation is to loosen the DNA, creating more space for transcription factors to actively transcribe the DNA. Therefore, histone acetylation is associated with upregulated gene expression. This is another example of how higher-level physiological processes (the regulation of gene expression) can at least partially be explained via very low-level, nitty-gritty chemical properties. As with the other examples that we've seen, this is a prime example of test-like thinking that illustrates some of the ways in which the MCAT likes to test biochemistry.

> > **CONNECTIONS** < <

Chapter 10 of Biochemistry and Chapter 5 of Biology

## 3. Principles of Regulation

A key aspect of taking your MCAT expertise to the next level is not just studying the inputs, outputs, and steps of a pathway, but understanding how the pathway is regulated. You can think about this on two levels: first, by focusing on individual steps in the pathway that are especially important and tightly regulated; and second, by focusing on how the pathway as a whole is regulated in the larger context of other, related pathways and/or physiological impacts.

As an example of how to understand why individual steps are regulated, let's consider glycolysis. There are three major steps of glycolysis that are regulated:

> Step 1: glucose → glucose 6-phosphate (G6P). This is the first step, in which a phosphate group is transferred from an ATP molecule to a glucose molecule (representing the first investment of ATP).
> Step 3: fructose 6-phosphate → fructose 1,6-bisphosphate (F1,6BP). This is the committed step of glycolysis, and like step 1, involves the transfer of a phosphate group from an ATP molecule.
> Step 10: phosphoenolpyruvate (PEP) → pyruvate. This is the final step, in which a phosphate group is transferred to an ADP molecule to produce ATP and pyruvate.

At this point, we should ask ourselves a simple-seeming question: what is it about these steps that makes them special targets for regulation? A common factor between all three is that they involve the investment or production of energy in the form of ATP. Since investing ATP in a pathway is quite important, it makes sense that these steps would be targets for regulation; regarding step 10, it is also generally common for the final step of a pathway to be regulated as a way for the cell to modulate the concentration of the pathway's final product, which is often the starting point for another pathway.

Steps 1 and 3 illustrate another important principle: highly endergonic (or energetically unfavorable) reactions tend to be tightly regulated because they need "help" of some sort to happen. Both steps 1 and 3 involve the energetically unfavorable step of phosphorylating a carbohydrate. This step is coupled to the energetically highly favorable hydrolysis of ATP to ADP. In fact, you can think of this coupling in very literal terms as the carbohydrate molecule simply taking a phosphate group from ATP, which really 'wants' to donate it.

**MCAT STRATEGY > > >**

An important point here to note for your study process is that it is often very productive to ask simple-sounding questions, like *why*. Students often feel ashamed of asking their peers, instructors, or tutors questions that sound simple, but in reality, simple questions don't always have easy answers, and can be very useful ways of digging into the material in depth in a way that will set you up for MCAT success.

It is also helpful to get an intuitive sense of what these reactions *do*, because understanding what they accomplish will help you to understand why they're regulated. In glycolysis, step 1 is important because it sequesters glucose within the cell. Glucose transporters will not transport glucose 6-phosphate back out of the cell, so the first phosphorylation step essentially sets aside the glucose molecule for other uses. There are two especially important points to understand about step 3. First, because glucose 6-phosphate can be shunted into other pathways like glycogenesis, it has to be double-phosphorylated to be committed to glycolysis. Second, recall that the next step of glycolysis involves splitting up the six-carbon carbohydrate to two three-carbon molecules that will eventually become pyruvate. The chemical logic only works if each of the daughter molecules gets a phosphate group, so it makes sense that forming a doubly-phosphorylated fructose derivative is the step immediately before cleavage.

**> > CONNECTIONS < <**

Chapter 7 of Biochemistry

Don't worry if you don't feel like you fully understand glycolysis after reading this. Chapter 7 reviews the steps of glycolysis in depth. The point of this discussion is, instead, to illustrate the kinds of questions that you should ask when studying regulatory steps of a pathway. You want to develop a degree of gut-level familiarity with the important steps, understand why they matter, and visualize how they are regulated.

On a higher level, it is also necessary to study regulation in the context of how a pathway fits into the bigger metabolic picture of the cell.

One of the fundamental principles you should be aware of is that of negative feedback. In a negative feedback system, a step of a pathway is inhibited either by its immediate product or by a product further downstream in the pathway. The effect of a negative feedback loop is generally to help the body maintain homeostasis by preventing a process from accelerating out of control and generating too much of a product to be useful. Negative feedback will apply to virtually every pathway you study, and you should make a point to observe where negative feedback takes place, and what triggers it. For example, multiple steps in glycolysis and the citric acid cycle are inhibited by ATP, which is both a direct product of glycolysis and (in much greater quantities) a product of the electron transport chain, which is 'fed' by glycolysis and the citric acid cycle in cells that conduct aerobic metabolism. The negative feedback provided by ATP isn't just random; it provides a way for a cell to say "hey, I have enough energy now – stop it!" Whenever possible, try to see how negative feedback within a cycle is reflective of intracellular conditions. This will help you learn to predict whether pathways will be upregulated or downregulated in response to the availability of various substrates, external stimuli, or pathogenic changes in the body – all of which the MCAT may test, especially in passage-based questions.

As a parenthetical note, you should be aware that positive feedback loops do exist, but they are rare physiologically and even rarer in metabolic pathways. The major example of positive feedback that you should be aware of for the MCAT is how in women undergoing labor, oxytocin stimulates uterine contractions, which in turn stimulate oxytocin release, resulting in a progress that culminates in childbirth. Note, though, that this is not a metabolic pathway. Researchers have identified positive feedback circuits in cell signaling and regulatory pathways under various conditions; you should be aware of this as a theoretical possibility in case you are presented with it in a passage, but there are no specific examples that you absolutely must be aware of.

The next question you should ask about how a pathway is regulated is how it fits into the larger context of the cell and the body. Some questions to ask as you study include:

> Where does the initial substrate of a pathway come from? How does that help you understand what the pathway does and how it is regulated?
> What ultimately happens to the products of a given pathway? Does that help you to understand what upregulates or downregulates the pathway in terms of intracellular requirements?
> Is a pathway affected by hormonal signaling? If so, pair your study of the pathway with your study of the hormones in question. A classic example of this is provided by the opposing pair of insulin and glucagon. Insulin reduces blood glucose levels by promoting glucose uptake by the cells. It also upregulates glycogen synthesis and lipid synthesis, because the cell has to do something with its new glucose reserves. Concomitantly, it decreases gluconeogenesis in hepatic cells, because the body does not need to release more glucose into the bloodstream at that point. In contrast, glucagon is released when the body needs more blood glucose, so it has the effect of promoting glycogen breakdown and gluconeogenesis in hepatic cells. In hepatic cells, it also has the effect of downregulating glycolysis, which helps ensure that available reserves of glucose are shunted towards release into the bloodstream. Studying insulin/glucagon together with the pathways that they affect will help you understand both topics better and prepare you for passage-based questions on the MCAT.

As mentioned in the beginning of this chapter, there's no way around the fact that you have to master a considerable amount of factual material to succeed with MCAT biochemistry. An important element of success is striving to see the biochemistry material that you must learn as parts of the large, interwoven, fascinating system that is the human body rather than as a collection of discrete facts. This is both because doing so will help you remember the material better and because biochemistry is often tested on the MCAT in the context of passages that will present you with novel information and ask you to apply your pre-existing knowledge to solve a problem that you may never have thought about before. The earlier in your study process that you can build the mental habits that will set you up for success with such problems, the better off you will be.

In particular, three principles are especially helpful, as we've discussed in this chapter: (1) follow the electrons and look for how charge helps explain various interactions, (2) look for how structure affects function, and (3) work to understand both low-level and high-level regulation.

# 4. Must-Knows

> Biochemistry is a major topic on the MCAT, and a challenging one! More so than for many other subjects, it's worth investing some time thinking about *how* to study biochemistry, both in terms of your own process and in terms of unifying themes.
> Three major unifying themes in biochemistry:
>   – Follow the electrons.
>   – Structure affects function.
>   – Pathways are carefully regulated.
> "Following the electrons" is equivalent to analyzing processes in terms of how they are affected by charge.
>   – Charge shapes the behavior of proteins at all levels, from individual amino acid residues to secondary, tertiary, and even quaternary structure.
>   – Hydrogen bonding is due to polarity/charge, and hydrogen bonding patterns of base pairs helps contribute to the stability of DNA structure (as well as hydrophobic base pair stacking interactions).
>   – Redox reactions power metabolism.
>     • OIL RIG: oxidation is loss (of electrons), reduction is gain (of electrons)
>     • Basic principle: pathways are multi-step processes that strip electrons from nutrient molecules via redox reactions and shunt those electrons to the electron transport chain, where they are used to set up an electrochemical gradient that powers ATP synthase.
> Structure affects function: a basic principle that you should incorporate into your MCAT studying.
>   – Proteins: charge and steric properties contribute to protein function.
>   – Plasma membrane: lipid bilayer formed by amphipathic lipids sets the stage for complex and well-regulated phenomena regulating the influx/efflux of substances into and out of the cell.
>     • Endocrine system: peptide hormones = polar, interact with receptors on cell membrane, generate short-lasting but intense effects; steroid hormones = nonpolar, diffuse through cell membrane, bind nuclear receptors to affect DNA transcription, generate longer-onset and longer-lasting effects.
>   – Histones and DNA expression: positively charged histone proteins interact with negatively charged backbones of DNA molecules. Acetylation of lysine residues on histones reduces the positive charge, meaning that they interact more loosely with DNA, providing access to transcription factors and promoting DNA expression.
> Regulation
>   – Important to understand the regulated steps of a pathway and how they fit into the bigger picture.
>   – Negative feedback: a step of a pathway is inhibited either by its immediate product or by a product that is further downstream in the pathway.
>   – Some important questions to ask about all pathways: (1) Where does its substrate come from? (2) What happens to its products? (3) Is it under the control of hormonal signaling?

## Practice Passage

Thiols are important in redox-mediated or regulated processes in the eukaryotic cell, yet the identity and levels of the various thiols can vary widely. Cysteine is among the most conserved amino acids in the human body. Figure 1 shows a closely related but much less common amino acid, selenocysteine (sec), which also exhibits chemistry similar to cysteine, but its reactivity is distinct due to the different intrinsic chemistry of Se versus S and is enhanced at physiological pH due to its more highly stabilized deprotonated form. This residue is distinct from the 20 common amino acids and is encoded by TGA, which requires special sec-charged tRNAs.

**Figure 1.** Selenocysteine

In an attempt to gauge the effects of Sec on protein folding, researchers performed an optical assay to determine the positions of the residue in the selenoprotein GPX1 and to identify amphiphilic sec biomarkers. However, the low specificity of this label-free assay technique requires mass spectrometry in order for proper analysis to take place. As an alternative, they used a labeled immunosorbent assay. In labeled assays, the target molecule is immobilized on the surface of a biosensor and then probed with an analyte, typically an antibody, coupled to a label (Figure 2).

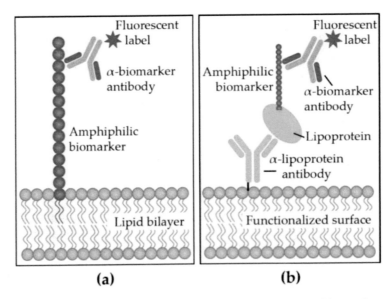

**Figure 2.** Immunoassay strategies to detect lipid and amphiphilic biomarkers using (a) membrane insertion or (b) lipoprotein capture

The physical and chemical properties of residues are inherently critical to their functional attributes, yet there is controversy even over whether some residues should be considered hydrophobic or not. An important reason that many scales rank residues as hydrophobic is their degree of burial. Researchers hypothesized that the presence of sec alters residue burial, so an experiment was performed to examine the relative degree of burial of five amino acids found on GPX1. Figure 3 shows the measured percentage of burial for each component atom of C234, G387, A56, D703, and M551.

**Figure 3.** Exposure of component atoms in amino acids on GPX1 (Note: Below each point, the positions along the molecule, including the side chain, are reported.)

*Adapted from Kubicek-Sutherland, J., et al. 2017. "Detection of Lipid and Amphiphilic Biomarkers for Disease Diagnostics." Biosensors 7, no. 3: 25 under CCBY 4.0*

1. The lipoprotein capture technique performed in the experiment is most similar to which ELISA technique?
   A. Direct assay
   B. Capture assay
   C. Indirect assay
   D. Competitive assay

2. The oxidation state of critical cofactors plays an important role in regulating cell metabolism. Which of the following correctly describes the relationship between oxidation state and cellular process?
   A. An increased $NAD^+$/NADH ratio will drive fatty-acid synthesis.
   B. An increased $FADH_2$/FAD ratio will drive ATP hydrolysis.
   C. A decreased $FADH_2$/FAD ratio will increase the activity of ATP synthase.
   D. A decreased NADH/$NAD^+$ ratio will drive fatty-acid oxidation.

3. If 40 ml of Tollens' reagent is added to the carbohydrate mixture discussed in the passage, which of the monosaccharides will NOT react?
   A. Glucose
   B. Galactose
   C. Fructose
   D. Ribose

4. In the absence of the special selenocysteine-charged tRNAs, which translational outcome will result?
   A. Pro
   B. Stop
   C. Start
   D. Asn

5. Based on the data in Figure 3, which residue on the protein will be found farthest from the cytoplasmic environment?
   A. C234
   B. G387
   C. A56
   D. D703

6. The metabolism of which biomolecule is least likely to directly increase aerobic respiration in the cell?
    A. Proline
    B. Cytosine
    C. A short-chain fatty acid
    D. Glycogen

7. A researcher designing an upcoming immunosorbent assay presents a list of molecules to use as a label for their experiments. Which molecule was most likely rejected for use as a label?
    A. Fluorescein isothiocyanate
    B. $^{131}I$
    C. Albumin
    D. Horseradish peroxidase

## Practice Passage Explanations

Thiols are important in redox-mediated or regulated processes in the eukaryotic cell, yet the identity and levels of the various thiols can vary widely. Cysteine is among the most conserved amino acids in the human body. Figure 1 shows a closely related but much less common amino acid, selenocysteine (sec), which also exhibits chemistry similar to cysteine, but its reactivity is distinct due to the different intrinsic chemistry of Se versus S and is enhanced at physiological pH due to its more highly stabilized deprotonated form. This residue is distinct from the 20 common amino acids and is encoded by TGA, which requires special sec-charged tRNAs.

*Key terms: thiols, selenocysteine, TGA, sec-charged tRNA*

*Contrast: sec more acidic than sys*

*Cause and effect: S → Se change in residue leads to chemical, physiological changes (tRNA)*

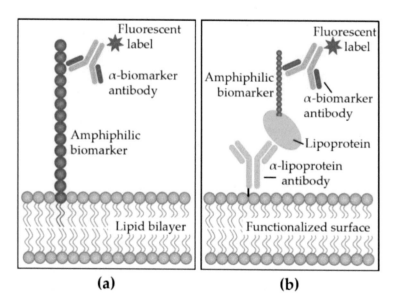

**Figure 1.** Selenocysteine

In an attempt to gauge the effects of Sec on protein folding, researchers performed an optical assay to determine the positions of the residue in the selenoprotein GPX1 and to identify amphiphilic sec biomarkers. However, the low specificity of this label-free assay technique requires mass spectrometry in order for proper analysis to take place. As an alternative, they used a labeled immunosorbent assay. In labeled assays, the target molecule is immobilized on the surface of a biosensor and then probed with an analyte, typically an antibody, coupled to a label (Figure 2).

*Key terms: selenoprotein, GPX1, biomarkers, immunosorbent assay*

*Cause and effect: sec may affect protein-folding → assay to find sec on GPX1*

**Figure 2.** Immunoassay strategies to detect lipid and amphiphilic biomarkers using (a) membrane insertion or (b) lipoprotein capture

*Figure 2 shows and example of direct (a) and indirect (b) assay*

The physical and chemical properties of residues are inherently critical to their functional attributes, yet there is controversy even over whether some residues should be considered hydrophobic or not. An important reason that many scales rank residues as hydrophobic is their degree of burial. Researchers hypothesized that the presence of sec alters residue burial, so an experiment was performed to examine the relative degree of burial of five amino acids found on GPX1. Figure 3 shows the measured percentage of burial for each component atom of C234, G387, A56, D703, and M551.

*Key terms: physical/chemical properties, residue burial*

*Cause and effect: greater residue burial in protein → hydrophobic rating; %-burial of 5 AAS*

**Figure 3.** Exposure of component atoms in amino acids on GPX1 (Note: Below each point, the positions along the molecule, including the side chain, are reported.)

*Figure 3 shows the relative lengths of each AA, along with its degree of burial (associated with hydrophobicity)*

Adapted from Kubicek-Sutherland, J., et al. 2017. "Detection of Lipid and Amphiphilic Biomarkers for Disease Diagnostics." Biosensors 7, no. 3: 25 under CCBY 4.0

1. B is correct. ELISAs can be performed with a number of modifications to the procedure. The antigen may be detected directly (labeled primary antibody), indirectly (labeled secondary antibody), or by capture or "sandwich" assay where the analyte is bound between two antibodies – the capture antibody and the detection antibody.

   D. Competitive ELISA is often used when the target antigen is small and has only one epitope. This method consists of labeling purified antigen instead of the antibody. Unlabeled antigen from samples and the labeled antigen compete for binding to the capture antibody.

2. D is correct. Catabolism of molecules like fatty acids is generally used to produce energy (e.g. ATP → ADP + P$_i$). Anabolism describes construction of molecules, like fatty acids, which requires energy. Reduced cofactors can be oxidized in the electron transport chain to fuel energy-consuming anabolic processes like fatty acid synthesis. A higher NAD$^+$/NADH ratio would drive catabolism because having more of the oxidized form in the cell signals an energy need. A lower NAD$^+$/NADH ratio would drive fatty acid synthesis because having more of the reduced form in the cell can eventually provide the ATP required for synthesis. Thus, a low NADH/NAD$^+$ means energy is needed, and fatty acids will be oxidized to eventually produce ATP.
   C. ATP synthase is the ATP-generating enzyme coupled to the electron transport chain, and is responsible for directly producing ATP.

3. C is correct. Tollens' reagent is an oxidizing agent commonly used to determine the presence of aldehydes and some ketone functional groups. Aldehydes are much more reactive to oxidation than ketones, so a ketose is unlikely to react to the addition of the oxidizing agent. Fructose is a common ketose monosaccharide (and a glucose isomer) we should be familiar with for Test Day. The remaining molecules are all aldoses.

4. B is correct. You are not expected to know the amino-acid specific codons for the exam (other than stop and start). The first paragraph tells us the code for selenocysteine is TGA. The equivalent RNA sequence would be UGA. In standard genetic code, there are three different stop codons: UAG, UAA and UGA (RNA); TAG, TAA, and TGA (DNA). Without the special selenocysteine-charged tRNA, this will send a signal to stop translation.

5. A is correct. Farthest from the outside environment means the amino acid which is the most buried beneath the surface of the protein. Examining Figure 3, we see that the residue with the greatest degree of burial is represented by the light-colored circles, and peaks around 80% burial for its carbonyl carbon. The figure shows that this amino acid has just 1 carbon in it side chain, followed by one more atom in the γ position (the α-C is adjacent to the carbonyl C, and is present on all amino acids). This means we need an amino acid with a 2-atom side chain. Only cysteine (C) fits this description.
   B. Glycine has no side chain attached to its α-carbon and has no signal beyond that position.
   C. Alanine has just a single methyl group attached to its α-carbon and has nothing beyond a β signal.
   D. Aspartic acid has a two-carbon carboxylic acid attached to its α-carbon, so it has up to a δ signal.

6. B is correct. Aerobic respiration in the cell consists the citric acid cycle, which is fed by glycolysis as well as other pathways, and the electron transport chain. The pyrimidines cytosine and uracil can be metabolized, but by doing so they are converted into beta-alanine and later to malonyl-CoA, which is needed for fatty acid synthesis.
   A. If glycogen is exhausted, glucose can be made from some amino acids via gluconeogenesis. Proline is a glucogenic amino acid.
   C. Fatty acids such as 3-ketoacyl-CoA can be broken down via beta-oxidation to produce two carbon units which are then fed into the citric acid cycle via acetyl CoA.
   D. Glycogen can be broken down into glucose, which can directly enter glycolysis.

7. C is correct. Detection or visualization of the antigen of interest in immunoassays may require labeling or conjugation of the antibodies with another molecule. These are commonly fluorophores (A), enzymes (D), radioisotopes (B) or biotin. These labeling agents can be conjugated either to a primary antibody (direct assay) or to a secondary antibody (indirect assay). While small polypeptides may also be used, a large protein like albumin is not likely to be chosen as it would be ineffective and inefficient as a label.

## Independent Questions

1. Which class of protein is the largest group of targets for drug therapies and often consists of two hydrophilic portions and one hydrophobic portion?
   A. Globular proteins
   B. Fibrous proteins
   C. Transmembrane proteins
   D. Monotopic proteins

2. Which of the following choices lists two electron carriers in their reduced forms?
   A. $NAD^+$ and FAD
   B. NADH and $FADH_2$
   C. $NAD^+$ and $FADH_2$
   D. NADH and FAD

3. Which of the following is a primary determiner of polypeptide tertiary structure?
   A. Hydrogen bonding between O and N atoms of the polypeptide backbone
   B. Covalent peptide bonds
   C. Ionic interactions between amino acid side chains
   D. Covalent bonds between carboxylic acid groups and amino groups

4. All of the following are expected to be attracted to positively-charged species EXCEPT:
   A. ATP.
   B. ADP.
   C. the backbone of a nucleic acid.
   D. testosterone.

5. Histone deacetylase is an enzyme that removes acetyl groups from histone proteins. Which of the following is the most likely effect of the activation of histone deacetylase?
   A. The rate of transcription of the affected DNA will decrease.
   B. The affected histones will become less positively charged.
   C. The affected histones will become more negatively charged.
   D. DNA-histone attractions will become weaker.

6. The hydrolysis of ATP to form ADP and phosphate:
   I. is highly endergonic.
   II. is often coupled with energetically unfavorable reactions.
   III. releases energy due in part to the negatively-charged nature of ATP's phosphate groups.
   A. I only
   B. I and II only
   C. II and III only
   D. I, II, and III

7. Which of the following is true of insulin?
   A. It is a steroid hormone that promotes a decrease in blood glucose levels.
   B. It is a steroid hormone that promotes an increase in blood glucose levels.
   C. It is a peptide hormone that promotes a decrease in blood glucose levels.
   D. It is a peptide hormone that promotes an increase in blood glucose levels.

8. A certain signaling molecule binds its receptor in the nucleus, causing transcription of a particular gene to increase. This signaling molecule most likely:
   A. exerts its physiological effects rapidly and for a short duration.
   B. promotes a second-messenger cascade within the target cell.
   C. is highly water-soluble.
   D. has a nonpolar fused-ring structure.

# Independent Question Explanations

1. C is correct. Transmembrane proteins generally consist of a hydrophobic portion within the lipid bilayer and two hydrophilic portions that face the cytosol and extracellular space. These proteins are highly physiologically important and actually provide about 50% of drug targets. Monotopic proteins are similar; however, they are anchored to only one side of the membrane.

2. B is correct. The reduced form of these two electron carriers are NADH and $FADH_2$. Remember, reduction often involves the gain of bonds to hydrogen, and it always involves a decrease in oxidation state. In contrast, the oxidized forms are $NAD^+$ and FAD.

3. C is correct. As you read in this chapter, charge plays an important role in the determination of protein folding. Ionic interactions are based on the attraction between positive and negative charges, and ionic interactions between side chains help determine tertiary structure. Option A relates to secondary structure, as you will learn. Choices B and D are equivalent, so both can be eliminated, but note that covalent peptide bonds are found between carboxylic acid groups and amino groups and determine a protein's primary structure.

4. D is correct. Opposite charges attract; thus, negatively-charged molecules are attracted to positively-charged ones. Since this is a NOT question, we are looking for the lone option that does not carry a negative charge. ATP, ADP, and the backbone of DNA or RNA all contain phosphate groups, which are highly negatively charged. In contrast, testosterone is a steroid hormone; it is not charged at all, as evidenced by the fact that it can pass through the plasma membrane and is thus nonpolar.

5. A is correct. Histones are typically positively charged, which attracts them to the negatively-charged DNA backbone. The addition of acetyl groups, however, removes the positive charge on lysine residues. Here, the opposite is happening; acetyl groups are being removed by the deacetylase enzyme, causing the histone to become *more* positively charged (eliminate options B and C). This causes DNA to be more tightly attracted to the histone (eliminate choice D), limiting the ability of transcription factors to access the DNA. This will decrease the rate at which the DNA is transcribed (choice A is correct).

6. C is correct. ATP hydrolysis is extremely energetically favorable, or exergonic (eliminate Roman numeral I), as it releases a great deal of energy. For this reason, ATP hydrolysis is often coupled with unfavorable, or endergonic, reactions to help them proceed. The cleavage of the phosphodiester bonds in ATP is exergonic in part because the molecule itself is unstable due to the close proximity of ATP's multiple negative phosphate groups.

7. C is correct. Insulin is a peptide hormone, meaning that it is composed of amino acids (in contrast, steroid hormones like estrogen and testosterone are nonpolar and are derived from cholesterol). Insulin promotes the uptake of glucose by cells, causing the concentration of glucose in the bloodstream to decrease.

8. D is correct. Steroid hormones are signaling molecules that bind their receptors in the nucleus and impact transcription. These molecules are nonpolar and are derived from cholesterol, meaning they tend to share cholesterol's fused-ring hydrocarbon structure. Alternatively, we can use process of elimination. Peptide hormones are short-acting (eliminate choice A), promote second-messenger cascades (eliminate choice B), and are soluble in water (eliminate choice C). These traits are not true of steroid hormones.

This page left intentionally blank.

# Amino Acids and Proteins

## 0. Introduction

In this chapter, we will focus on amino acids and proteins. These are core MCAT biochemistry topics, because in a very real sense, proteins are the building blocks of the body, and amino acids are the building blocks of proteins. We will start with a careful review of the structure and properties of amino acids, which is an absolutely essential set of prerequisite information for understanding how proteins carry out their various functions within the body, and then proceed to a discussion of how amino acids fit together to generate various levels of protein structure. We will then discuss the acid-base chemistry of proteins and certain specific reactions involving proteins that you should be aware of for the MCAT.

## 1. Amino Acid Structure and Properties

Amino acids are defined by having both an amine ($-NH_2$) functional group and a carboxylic acid ($-COOH$) functional group. Theoretically, this could refer to a wide range of structures—you could add an $-NH_2$ group and an $-COOH$ group to some large organic, cyclic compound and call it an "amino acid"—but for the MCAT, amino acids refer specifically to 20 amino acids that are coded for by specific codons and are used by the body to build proteins. Chemically, these amino acids are known as α-amino acids because they have a single carbon at the α position from the carbonyl carbon in the $-COOH$ group (recall from organic chemistry that we can refer to carbons as α-carbons, β-carbons, γ-carbons, and so on, depending on their distance from the carbonyl carbon).

Figure 1 shows the generic structure of an amino acid. Note the central α-carbon that has four substituents: $-NH_2$, $-COOH$, $-H$, and $-R$. The $-R$ group is known as the side chain of the amino acid, and differences in the side chain are what contributes to different properties in individual amino acids (that is to say, all other substituents are invariant). Since the α-carbon has four different substituents (except for the amino acid glycine, in which case the side chain is $-H$), it is a chiral center. As a rule, naturally occurring amino acids that play a major role in our body are all L-amino acids. D-amino acids exist in a few eukaryotic organisms and are abundant in bacteria, and some suggestions have been made that they may play some signaling role in the body. However, whenever you see an amino acid on the MCAT, you should assume that its orientation is L. In terms of R/S notation, which is based on the actual chemical structure rather than on the rotation of plane-polarized light, most amino acids are S, with the exceptions of cysteine, which is R, and glycine, which is not chiral.

**Figure 1.** Generic structure of an amino acid.

Side chains are classified in multiple ways, some of which overlap with each other (for example, an amino acid can be both nonpolar and aromatic). The simplest way of classifying amino acids is into four groups: nonpolar, polar uncharged, negatively charged (at physiological pH), and positively charged (at physiological pH). The best way to learn the amino acids is *not* simply just to review and memorize a table with structures and properties, but rather to familiarize yourself all of them individually – that is, to learn something special about each one. Each amino acid has a three-letter abbreviation, which is usually fairly intuitive, and a one-letter abbreviation, which may or may not be intuitive. You are absolutely expected to know both sets of abbreviations for the MCAT, and you should be able to recognize the structure of each amino acid. Also note that the average molecular weight of an amino acid is 110 Da.

## Nonpolar amino acids

*Group 1: Nonpolar amino acids with aliphatic hydrocarbon chains*

> Glycine (Gly, G). Glycine is the simplest amino acid, with a side chain of –H (◀H). For this reason, it is the only non-chiral amino acid. It was discovered in 1820, before we had a comprehensive understanding of amino acids, and was named "glycine" (the same root as in *glyco*lysis) because it has a slightly sweet taste.

> Alanine (Ala, A). Alanine is the next step up in terms of complexity of the side chain, which is a simple methyl group (–CH$_3$, ◀). It is often used on the MCAT as the canonical example of a simple, small, nonpolar amino acid.

> Valine (Val, V). As we keep adding carbons to the side chains, our next step is valine, which is generated by adding not one, but *two* methyl groups to the end of alanine's side chain, resulting in a side chain of –CH(CH$_3$)$_2$. Its side chain is also referred to as an isopropyl group. A notable fact about valine is that its substitution for glutamic acid in hemoglobin causes sickle-cell disease, which is a canonical, MCAT-relevant example of how protein structure and function are related. Its side chain is:

> Leucine (Leu, L). Leucine is very similar to valine, but with an extra carbon added in the side chain before the tertiary carbon at the end (–CH$_2$CH(CH$_3$)$_2$). Animals, including humans, cannot synthesize leucine on our own, so we must obtain it from our diet, making it an essential amino acid. In fact, leucine can be used as a food additive, to enhance flavor. Its side chain is:

> Isoleucine (Ile, I). As the name implies, isoleucine is similar to leucine. The main difference between them is the location of the tertiary carbon; in isoleucine, it is one position closer to the amino acid, such that the

structure of the R group is $CH(CH_3)CH_2CH_3$. Similarly to leucine, isoleucine is an essential amino acid that we must obtain from our diet. The best way to remember isoleucine is that it's like leucine, but different. The structure of its side chain is:

## Group 2: Nonpolar amino acids with more "interesting" structures

> Methionine (Met, M). Methionine is noteworthy because it's one of the two amino acids that contains a sulfur (with the other being cysteine). However, it is still considered nonpolar because in it, sulfur only bonds with carbon, and the C–S bond is nonpolar, with an electronegativity difference of only 0.03. Methionine is an essential amino acid that is present in especially high quantities in eggs, and has been found to be involved in angiogenesis and DNA methylation. Its side chain is $-CH_2CH_2SCH_3$:

> Proline (Pro, P). Proline is remarkable because it is the only amino acid that has a cyclic component that links back with the amino acid itself—the N in the amine group in the amino acid is actually part of the proline side chain. As such, it has a remarkable ability to break up the secondary structure of proteins by introducing so-called "proline kinks" (more about that in section 2). Its side chain is:

> Phenylalanine (Phe, F). This is the first of the aromatic amino acids that we will cover, and its R group is a simple benzene ring attached to a methyl group. Note that this is the first case we've seen where the single-letter abbreviation doesn't correspond to the first letter of its name – instead, here it refers to how the first syllable of its name *sounds*. Its presence must be strictly controlled in the diet of individuals with phenylketonuria, or a congenital malfunction of the enzyme necessary to convert phenylalanine into tyrosine. It is also present in the artificial sweetener aspartame. Its side chain is:

> Tyrosine (Tyr, Y). This is another aromatic amino acid, which differs from phenylalanine in that tyrosine has a hydroxyl (–OH) group. Tyrosine is another amino acid, like phenylalanine, for which the one-letter abbreviation reflects how it sounds more than how it is spelled. It may be surprising that tyrosine is considered a nonpolar amino acid, since the C–OH bond is indeed polar. In fact, for this reason, tyrosine is significantly more water-soluble than phenylalanine. However, in terms of its behavior within proteins, the polar C–OH bond is considered to be 'outweighed' by the large, sterically bulky, hydrophobic aromatic ring, making its overall behavior more nonpolar. Tyrosine is the precursor for many biologically important signaling molecules, such as dopamine, epinephrine, and norepinephrine. Its side chain is:

> Tryptophan (Trp, W): Tryptophan is the third aromatic amino acid, and is notable for actually having two rings in its side chain, one of which is a heterocyclic ring containing an amine group. This is the first of the amino acids we've seen for which the one-letter abbreviation is essentially just a random piece of information that you need to remember. It is the precursor of serotonin and melatonin. The incorrect belief that tryptophan is especially common in turkey has been used to "explain" the "turkey coma" that people often experience after Thanksgiving dinner. The side chain of tryptophan is shown below:

## Polar uncharged amino acids

> Serine (Ser, S). Serine is one of the two amino acids with an alcohol functional group on the side chain. The side chain of serine is quite simple: $-CH_2OH$. The terminal $-OH$ group is fairly susceptible to undergoing covalent modifications, meaning that serine is often a target for phosphorylation and other processes involved in post-translation modification and signaling. It can be produced physiologically by glycine, meaning that we do not specifically have to consume it in our diet. Its side chain is:

> Threonine (Thr, T). Threonine is, along with serine, the other amino acid with a simple alcohol functional group. The side chain of threonine contains one extra carbon in comparison with serine, meaning that the $-OH$ group is secondary in threonine. The formula for its side chain is $CH(OH)CH_3$. Like serine, it can be a target for phosphorylation, but unlike serine, we have to obtain threonine from our diet. Its side chain is shown below:

> Asparagine (Asn, N). Asparagine is one of two amino acids that are amides. The formula for its side chain is $-CH_2C(=O)NH_2$. Note that the single-letter abbreviation for asparagine is not especially intuitive, and is focused on the end of the name of the compound. You might be able to remember it by keeping in mind that asparagine (N) is the amino acid that starts with an "asp" but ends in an amide group, which has an N. An interesting fact about asparagine is that it reacts with reducing sugars (including fructose and glucose) in baked and fried foods to form a potentially carcinogenic compound known as acrylamide. The side chain of asparagine is shown below:

> Glutamine (Gln, Q). Glutamine is the second amino acid, along with asparagine, that has an amide side chain. Its structure is very similar to that of asparagine, with the main difference that it has a longer hydrocarbon chain leading up the amide group: its side chain formula is $-CH_2CH_2C(=O)NH_2$. Note that

the three-letter abbreviation of glutamine contains an "n" that is reminiscent of the fact that it contains an –$NH_2$ in the amide group, while its one-letter abbreviation is largely just random. An interesting fact about glutamine is that it is the most common free amino acid in the human blood, and it is involved in a wide range of metabolic reactions, the details of which go beyond the scope of the MCAT. Its side chain is:

> Cysteine (Cys, C). Along with methionine, cysteine is the other amino acid that contains sulfur. Its structure is similar to that of serine, but with a thiol (–SH) group instead of a hydroxyl group. Interestingly, the S–H bond only has an electronegativity difference of 0.38, but it is considered to be polar for the purposes of amino acid classifications because it can participate in hydrogen bonding. Cysteine is an extremely important amino acid because two cysteine residues can form covalent disulfide bonds, which is an important component of tertiary structure (as discussed in section 2). Its side chain is given below:

## Positively-charged (basic) amino acids

> Arginine (Arg, R). Arginine has a side chain composed of an alkyl chain followed by a guanidium group: –$NHC(NH_2^+)NH_2$. Its three-letter abbreviation is pretty intuitive, while its one-letter abbreviation reflects pronunciation, not spelling. It is remarkable because it has three nitrogens in its side chain, including one that is double-bonded to a carbon. This positive charge can be resonance-stabilized, making arginine the most basic of all of the amino acids. It is involved in the synthesis of several important biomolecules and plays a role in regulating blood pressure. Its side chain is:

> Histidine (His, H). Histidine is notable because it is the only positively charged (basic) amino acid that has a cyclic (and moreover, aromatic) side chain. Although it is generally classified as a positively-charged amino acid, the deprotonated version of the side chain is actually prevalent at physiological pH. The $pK_a$ of the side chain NH is 6.04, which means that it can serve as a buffer at pH levels slightly more acidic than physiological pH. In other words, histidine is meaningfully basic, and "basic" and "positively-charged" are often used as synonyms. Its side chain is:

> Lysine (Lys, K). Lysine is structurally the simplest positively-charged amino acid, with a side chain consisting of an alkyl chain that terminates in a primary amine: –$CH_2CH_2CH_2CH_2NH_3^+$. The primary amine at the end of the chain is fairly reactive, and is the target of many covalent modifications, such as methylation and acetylation. For this reason, lysine often appears in MCAT passages/questions. Note, however, that its one-letter abbreviation is not particularly intuitive. Its side chain is:

## Negatively charged (acidic) amino acids

> Aspartic acid (aspartate) (Asp, D). Aspartic acid is one of the two negatively charged (acidic) amino acids, and has a side chain that is $-CH_2COOH$ in its protonated form (corresponding to aspartic acid) and $-CH_2COO^-$ in its deprotonated form (aspartate), which is overwhelmingly dominant at physiological pH. Along with phenylalanine, aspartic acid is a component of the artificial sweetener aspartame. Note that the three-letter abbreviation is straightforward, but the one-letter abbreviation is largely random. Its side chain is:

> Glutamic acid (glutamate) (Glu, E). Glutamic acid (glutamate) is structurally quite similar to aspartic acid/aspartate, except that it has an additional carbon in its side chain, which is: $-CH_2CH_2COOH$ in its protonated form (glutamic acid) and $-CH_2CH_2COO^-$ in its deprotonated form (glutamate). Interestingly, glutamate is both a structural component of proteins and an important neurotransmitter. Similarly to aspartic acid/aspartate, the single-letter abbreviation is largely random, but it is at least helpful that the two acidic/negatively-charged amino acids both have abbreviations that are next to each other in the alphabet (D and E). Its side chain is shown below:

Studying the structures of the amino acids and how they are classified can be overwhelming at times, but some patterns exist that can help you in this process. Both of the negatively-charged/acidic amino acids have carboxylic acid side chains, with the only difference between them being the length of the alkyl chain connecting the –COOH group to the α-carbon. The positively-charged/basic amino acids all have a nitrogen atom on the side chain that can serve as the locus of a positive charge; besides that, they have three notably distinct side chains. The polar uncharged amino acids have side chains with three different functional groups: (1) hydroxyl (serine, threonine); (2) thiol (cysteine); and (3) amide (asparagine, glutamine). The nonpolar amino acids are the largest group, but can still be divided into three main categories: (1) aromatic (phenylalanine, tyrosine, and tryptophan); (2) aliphatic/hydrocarbon (glycine, alanine, valine, leucine, and isoleucine); and (3) others (methionine, which contains a sulfur in a thioether group, and proline, which

### MCAT STRATEGY > > >

If you search online for 'amino acid mnemonics' you'll find many results, but it's not something we recommend focusing on. Although it may not be tested in depth on every MCAT, amino acid properties are core MCAT content to the point that it's worth really becoming familiar with each amino acid, instead of relying on the somewhat more superficial tool of mnemonics.

has a unique cyclic side chain incorporating the skeleton of the amino acid itself).

To a great extent, the properties of proteins—or of specific active sites on proteins—are due to the properties of the amino acids that are present at specific locations. Recall that proteins are synthesized by transfer RNA (tRNA) based on mRNA transcripts that are, in turn, derived from DNA sequences. Therefore, a mutation in DNA might mean that a different amino acid is incorporated into a protein, which can in turn have a profound effect on its behavior. The MCAT will expect you to be able to connect the dots, so to speak, between mutations and protein function, and knowing the amino acids thoroughly is a key component of that skill.

Table 1 below summarizes the side chains of amino acids and their properties, as well as their pKa values (for more about this, see section 4).

## > > CONNECTIONS < <

Biology chapter 3

## MCAT STRATEGY > > >

Don't rush to memorize Table 1 before carefully working through the material presented above at greater length! You should strive for your knowledge of amino acids to be relatively deep and long-term, not based on hasty memorization of a table. Doing so demands an up-front investment of time, but it will pay off in terms of timing, confidence, and accuracy on Test Day.

| | Name | Side chain | pK$_a$ values<br>pK$_{a1}$ = COOH<br>pK$_{a2}$ = NH$_2$<br>pK$_{aR}$ = R | pI |
|---|---|---|---|---|
| Nonpolar | Glycine (Gly, G) | | pK$_{a1}$ = 2.34<br>pK$_{a2}$ = 9.58 | 5.97 |
| | Alanine (Ala, A) | | pK$_{a1}$ = 2.33<br>pK$_{a2}$ = 9.71 | 6.00 |
| | Valine (Val, V) | | pK$_{a1}$ = 2.27<br>pK$_{a2}$ = 9.52 | 5.96 |
| | Isoleucine (Ile, I) | | pK$_{a1}$ = 2.26<br>pK$_{a2}$ = 9.60 | 6.02 |
| | Leucine (Leu, L) | | pK$_{a1}$ = 2.32<br>pK$_{a2}$ = 9.58 | 5.98 |
| | Methionine (Met, M) | | pK$_{a1}$ = 2.16<br>pK$_{a2}$ = 9.08 | 5.74 |
| | Proline (Pro, P) | | pK$_{a1}$ = 1.95<br>pK$_{a2}$ = 10.47 | 6.30 |
| | Phenylalanine (Phe, F) | | pK$_{a1}$ = 2.18<br>pK$_{a2}$ = 9.09 | 5.48 |
| | Tyrosine (Tyr, Y) | | pK$_{a1}$ = 2.24<br>pK$_{a2}$ = 9.04<br>pK$_{aR}$ = 10.10 | 5.66 |
| | Tryptophan (Trp, W) | | pK$_{a1}$ = 2.38<br>pK$_{a2}$ = 9.34 | 5.89 |

| Polar uncharged | Serine (Ser, S) | | $pK_{a1} = 2.13$ $pK_{a2} = 9.05$ | 5.68 |
|---|---|---|---|---|
| | Threonine (Thr, T) | | $pK_{a1} = 2.20$ $pK_{a2} = 8.96$ | 5.60 |
| | Asparagine (Asn, N) | | $pK_{a1} = 2.16$ $pK_{a2} = 8.76$ | 5.41 |
| | Glutamine (Gln, Q) | | $pK_{a1} = 2.18$ $pK_{a2} = 9.00$ | 5.65 |
| | Cysteine (Cys, C) | | $pK_{a1} = 1.91$ $pK_{a2} = 10.28$ $pK_{aR} = 8.14$ | 5.07 |
| Positively charged (basic) | Arginine (Arg, R) | | $pK_{a1} = 2.03$ $pK_{a2} = 9.00$ $pK_{aR} = 12.10$ | 10.76 |
| | Histidine (His, H) | | $pK_{a1} = 1.70$ $pK_{a2} = 9.09$ $pK_{aR} = 6.04$ | 7.59 |
| | Lysine (Lys, K) | | $pK_{a1} = 2.15$ $pK_{a2} = 9.16$ $pK_{aR} = 10.67$ | 9.74 |
| Negatively charged (acidic) | Aspartic acid (aspartate) (Asp, D) | | $pK_{a1} = 1.95$ $pK_{a2} = 9.66$ $pK_{aR} = 3.71$ | 2.77 |
| | Glutamic acid (glutamate) (Glu, E) | | $pK_{a1} = 2.16$ $pK_{a2} = 9.58$ $pK_{aR} = 4.15$ | 3.22 |
| Special cases | | | | |
| Achiral: Gly | | Sulfur-containing: Cys, Met | | |
| Aromatic: Phe, Tyr, Trp | | Breaks up secondary structure: Pro | | |

# 2. Levels of Protein Structure

As we've stated before, amino acids are the building blocks of proteins. Amino acids are linked together by peptide bonds. We'll discuss peptide bonds in more depth in section 4, which focuses on important reactions that proteins participate in, but for the time being we should note that peptide bonds involve the formation of an amide via the condensation of the –COOH group of one amino acid with the –NH$_2$ group of another. Two amino acids joined together via a peptide bond are known as a dipeptide, three are known as a tripeptide, and four are known as a tetrapeptide. The term "oligopeptide" ("few" peptides) can refer to chains of up to 20 amino acids, after which point, the term "polypeptide" is used. Proteins can vary widely in size, but in eukaryotic cells, the size of proteins is typically on the order of hundreds or thousands of amino acid residues. Protein size can also be measured in molecular mass, usually using units of kilodaltons (kDa); the average size of proteins in human cells has been estimated to be on the order of 50 kDa.

Peptide chains can be written using three-letter or one-letter abbreviations (or illustrated structurally), but there is an important convention that you must be aware of. Peptide chains have an N-terminus (the terminal –NH$_2$ group) and a C-terminus (the terminal –COOH) group, and are always written from the N-terminus to the C-terminus. This order also corresponds to how proteins are actually synthesized in the ribosome. Figure 2 shows the structure of a simple oligopeptide, angiotensin II, and how it can be referred to using three-letter or single-letter abbreviations.

**Asp-Arg-Val-Tyr-Ile-His-Pro-Phe**

**DRVYIHPF**

**Figure 2.** Simple oligopeptide.

All proteins have three levels of structure, known as primary, secondary, and tertiary structure, and some proteins are characterized by the additional level of quaternary structure. For the MCAT, you should be aware of how these structures are defined, what kinds of interaction they involve, and how they can be disrupted.

Primary structure refers to the linear chain of amino acid residues that make up a protein. It corresponds to what tRNA translates from a given strand of mRNA. The primary structure of a protein is held together by covalent bonds—more specifically, the peptide bonds that link amino acid residues—and for that reason, the primary structure of a protein is quite resilient to various environmental conditions.

Secondary structure refers to local structures formed by the patterns of hydrogen bonding between the amino and carboxylic acid groups of the amino acid residues. Common motifs of secondary structure include alpha-helices and beta-pleated sheets. Proline is particularly well-known for breaking up secondary structures, introducing so-called "proline kinks" because of its unique side chain that actually incorporates its own amine group. A natural follow-up question would be to ask about which factors support the formation of various types of secondary structure. This question turns out to be quite complex. Some amino acid residues are known to favor helices over sheets and vice versa, but the details are challenging to predict, not least because proteins can have areas without well-defined secondary structures.

Tertiary structure, in turn, is defined as the three-dimensional structures that result from interactions among the side chains of the amino acid residues of a protein. Many of these interactions are non-covalent charge-driven interactions; for example, in an aqueous environment, hydrophobic residues will tend to cluster together towards the inside of globular proteins, whereas hydrophilic residues will tend to aggregate on the external surface. Charged residues interact with each other to form structures known as salt bridges. Tertiary structure also involves covalent bonding, as exemplified by the disulfide bonds that form between cysteine residues.

There are a few separate points about disulfide bonds worth noting. First, the formation of a disulfide bond is an oxidation reaction, because the net reaction involves the loss of two protons and two electrons. This is not just a random observation; understanding this is useful because it implies that the opposite reaction (breaking up a disulfide bond) is a reduction reaction. The term "reducing environment" is often used to refer to treatments that have the effect of breaking up disulfide bonds, with one common reagent being 2-mercaptoethanol. Third, since disulfide bonds are covalent interactions, they are relatively quite strong in comparison with the other non-covalent interactions that contribute to tertiary structure. This means that disulfide bonds play a disproportionate role in contributing to the tertiary structure of a protein.

Some proteins are additionally characterized by quaternary structure, which refers to larger structures generated by the assembly of protein subunits via non-covalent interactions. A protein with two subunits is known as a dimer, one with three units is known as a trimer, one with four units is known as a tetramer, and so on. Hemoglobin is a classic example of quaternary structure, as it is composed of four subunits (two alpha units and two beta units). This fact about hemoglobin is part of what allows it to exhibit cooperative binding; since each of the subunits of hemoglobin can bind one oxygen, hemoglobin as a whole can bind four, and the binding of the first oxygen alters the conformation of the other subunits in a way that facilitates oxygen binding.

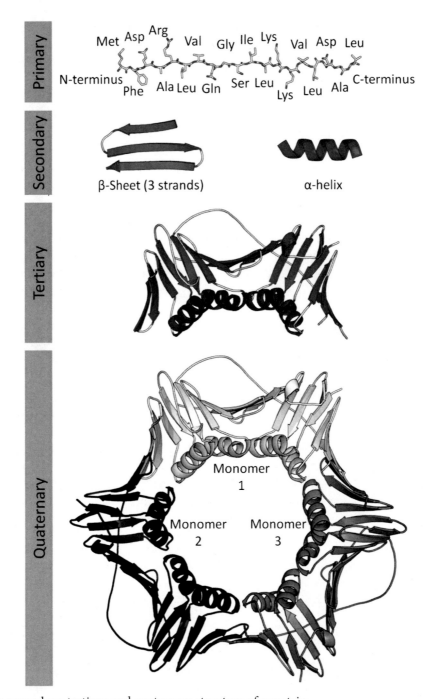

**Figure 3.** Primary, secondary, tertiary, and quaternary structure of a protein.

The basic characteristics of the various levels of protein structure are presented below in Table 2.

| | INTERACTIONS BETWEEN | CHEMICAL TYPE OF INTERACTION | EXAMPLES | NOTES |
|---|---|---|---|---|
| Primary | Adjacent amino acids in a linear order | Peptide bond | - | Refers to the linear string of amino acids; resistant to denaturation; cleaved by proteases |
| Secondary | Amine and carboxylic acid groups of amino acid residues | Hydrogen bonding | Alpha-helices, beta-sheets | Certain amino acid residues favor certain types of secondary structure, but details are complicated |
| Tertiary | Side chains | Hydrophilic interactions, hydrogen bonding, covalent bonds (disulfide bonds in Cys), salt bridges between charged residues | - | Heavily involved in protein folding; commonly disrupted by denaturing agents, refers to all interactions between side chains |
| Quaternary | Protein subunits | Noncovalent interactions | Four subunits of hemoglobin | Not present in all proteins |

**Table 2.** Levels of protein structure.

Protein folding refers to how the secondary structure and tertiary structure of a protein generate a three-dimensional structure. Protein folding is extremely difficult to predict, to the point that simulations of protein folding can require supercomputer-level resources, and the details of protein folding are a topic that goes beyond the scope of the MCAT. You do need to be familiar with the definitions of secondary and tertiary structure, as well as characteristic examples. In terms of protein folding as a whole, you should be aware of the general principle that the function of a protein in the cell directly depends on its three-dimensional structure, so that anything that disrupts that structure will be highly likely to disrupt the protein's function.

## MCAT STRATEGY > > >

Knowing the basic material in Table 2 is absolutely a must for the MCAT. In particular, students are often confused about the difference between the "interactions between" and "chemical type of interaction" columns, because textbooks are not always clear about what technically defines the different levels of structure. View Table 2 as a summary of must-knows about protein structure, with the other information in this section being a useful supplement.

Breaking up the non-primary structure of a protein is known as denaturation. Some common examples of denaturing agents include temperature, high and low pH extremes, solvents such as alcohol and acetone, detergents, and other solutes such as urea. Temperature simply destabilizes the non-primary three-dimensional structure of a protein, resulting in inactivation of a protein above a certain temperature. Most proteins in the human body are optimized to function around body temperature, or 37.6°C, while heat-stable proteins have evolved in organisms such as thermophilic bacteria. One such heat-resistant protein, known as *Taq* polymerase, plays a crucial role in making polymerase chain reaction (PCR) work effectively. Other denaturing agents interfere with the charge-based interactions that contribute to secondary and tertiary structure, such as hydrogen bonds and hydrophobic interactions. Reducing agents can break disulfide bonds.

An important point, though, is that denaturation is not permanent. The primary structure remains unaffected by denaturation, so once the denaturing conditions are removed, secondary, tertiary, and quaternary structures can freely reassemble.

**Figure 4.** Denaturation.

In contrast, enzymes known as proteases can break down the primary structure of proteins. A wide range of proteases exist, and many types of proteases are characterized by targeting specific amino acid residues in a protein. For example, serine proteases use the hydroxyl group of the serine in the mechanism of the reaction that cleaves the protein, usually via hydrolysis. A real-world example of a serine protease in the digestive system is the enzyme trypsin. An example of a digestive enzyme with a different mechanism is pepsin, which cleaves at the N-terminal side of aromatic amino acids. As is a common theme for the MCAT, you don't need to know the mechanisms of all of the proteases present in the digestive system, but you should know what a protease does, understand the difference between a denaturing agent and a protease, and understand that different proteases have different, and often very specific, mechanisms, because it is possible that you could be presented with the mechanism of a novel protease in a passage.

The thermodynamic concept of entropy is critical for understanding how protein folding takes place, and in particular for understanding why hydrophobic amino acid residues generally wind up clustered together on the inside of globular proteins in aqueous solution. This is a topic that students often find to be confusing, but the basic idea can be explained in fairly intuitive and concrete terms. All we need to do is to carefully compare what would happen if hydrophobic residues face the aqueous solution versus what would happen if hydrophilic residues face the aqueous solution, keeping in mind the polarity and excellent hydrogen-bonding properties of water.

If hydrophilic—that is, polar—residues are facing the aqueous solution, then water will be able to hydrogen-bond freely with those residues, meaning that it will have relatively high entropy, which is energetically favorable. In contrast, water molecules will not be able to hydrogen-bond effectively with nonpolar residues, and as a result will form a highly-ordered solvation shell to minimize interactions with those residues. This highly-ordered shell represents a decrease in entropy, which is energetically unfavorable. Thus, the three-dimensional structure of globular proteins in aqueous solution will minimize interactions between hydrophobic amino acid residues and water by incorporating them into the interior of the protein. A similar principle is at work in how phospholipids form a bilayer membrane with the hydrophobic alkyl tails in the interior of the membrane and the hydrophilic phosphate heads facing out.

# 3. Acid-Base Chemistry

Amino acids exhibit some interesting acid-base properties that are often tested on the MCAT. The carboxylic acid group of each amino acid is a weak acid (although usually a relatively strong weak acid), and the amine group is a weak base. Moreover, in acidic and basic amino acids (generally corresponding to the categories of negatively and positively charged amino acids at physiological pH, respectively), the side chain can contain a weak acid or weak base.

The main reason why we are interested in the acid-base properties of amino acids is because the charge pattern of amino acids will change in accordance with pH. Let's consider a simple amino acid, alanine, for which the side chain is not meaningfully acidic or basic. At an extremely low pH, both the carboxylic acid group and the amine group will be protonated (–COOH and $-NH_3^+$, respectively), resulting in a net charge for the amino acid as a whole of +1. At an extremely high pH, very few $H^+$ will be available, and both groups will be deprotonated (–COO⁻ and $-NH_2$, respectively), resulting in a net charge of –1.

What happens at an intermediate pH? Let's work through what we know about the relevant functional groups in simple terms. Carboxylic acids are, as the name suggests, acids, whereas amine groups are weakly basic. This means that carboxylic acid groups are relatively happy to give up their extra proton and exist as carboxylate ions (–COO⁻), even at relatively low pH values where there is a fair amount of $H^+$ present. Another way of looking at this would be to say that you have to have a huge amount of $H^+$ present to force the carboxylate ions to accept a proton. In contrast, amine groups like being protonated, which means that the pH has to be quite high (meaning that very few $H^+$ are present) for it to be willing to give up its proton. This, for intermediate pH ranges, the carboxylic acid will be deprotonated (–COO⁻) and the amine group will be protonated ($NH_3^+$), resulting in a net charge of zero. This is the case at physiological pH.

The form of an amino acid with a deprotonated carboxylic acid group (–COO⁻), a protonated amine group ($NH_3^+$), and a net charge of zero is known as a zwitterion. (More generally, the term refers to any electrically neutral molecule that contains positive and negative charges that balance out). As we will see in Chapter 5, zwitterions are important for protein analytic techniques, because molecules with a pure neutral charge are impervious to electrophoresis.

While it is important to understand qualitatively how an amino acid with a non-acidic/basic side chain, such as alanine, transitions from a net charge of +1 at low pH, to a charge of 0 as a zwitterion at intermediate pH, to a charge of –1 at high pH, we want to be more precise about the pH values involved. We will also want to extend our analysis to include amino acids with acidic or basic side chains. To do so, we need to incorporate a quantitative way of relating pH to the protonation state of an acidic/basic functional group. The Henderson-Hasselbalch equation is what we need. It states:

$$pH = pK_a + \log\left(\frac{[A^-]}{[HA]}\right)$$

In this equation, pH is our familiar measure of acidity (pH = –log[$H^+$]), pKa is the negative logarithm of the acid dissociation constant ($K_a$), and *HA* and *A⁻* are shorthand for representing the protonated and deprotonated forms of an acid, respectively.

Let's consider what happens when [*HA*] and [*A⁻*] are equal – that is, what happens when an acid is exactly halfway deprotonated. The ratio

## > > CONNECTIONS < <

Chapter 7 of Chemistry

of $[A^-]/[HA]$ will then equal 1, and log(1) = 0, so the term $\log\left(\frac{[A^-]}{[HA]}\right)$ will equal 0, such that pH = p$K_a$. Qualitatively, this means that the p$K_a$, which is a negative log-transformed measure of the strength of an acid, corresponds to the pH at which a given functional group is exactly half-protonated and half-deprotonated. Recall that lower p$K_a$ values correspond to stronger acids. This gives us another way to think about the relationship between pH and p$K_a$: namely, since strong acids really "like" giving up an H⁺ (i.e., being deprotonated), there must be a *ton* of H+ in solution—corresponding to a low pH—to prevent them from doing so. In contrast, bases "like" accepting an H⁺ (i.e., being protonated), so they won't start giving up protons until they are forced to by a high-pH environment.

Table 1 contains p$K_a$ values for all of the amino acids, where p$K_{a1}$ refers to the p$K_a$ of the carboxylic acid group, p$K_{a2}$ refers to that of the amine group, and p$K_{aR}$ refers to that of the side chain. You do *not* have to memorize the p$K_a$ values of all of the amino acids. Doing so is not even a good idea; if you have to do anything quantitative with p$K_a$ values, they will be provided to you. However, it's not a bad idea to review some general trends in p$K_a$ values, to help you develop some general intuitions about the acid-base properties of amino acids.

The carboxylic acid groups of amino acids tend to be quite acidic, with p$K_a$ values generally clustered around 2 or slightly higher. The amine groups show a bit more variance, but tend to be in the range of 9 to 9.5. This means that they are mildly basic. Things get a bit more complicated when we need to account for acidic and basic side chains. The acidic –COOH side groups of aspartic acid and glutamic acid have p$K_a$ values around 4, meaning that they are deprotonated (–COO⁻) at physiological pH. The side chains of arginine and lysine are quite basic, with p$K_a$ values above 10.5. This means that the side chains are actually more basic than the core amine group of the amino acid, and that they will "hold on" to their protons until being forced to give it up by extremely high pH values. Histidine is a bit tricky, because the p$K_a$ of its side chain is 6.04. This means that roughly 15% of histidine is positively charged at physiological pH. This contributes to some terminological uncertainty about histidine, as it is considered a "positively charged" amino acid although its deprotonated form predominates at physiological pH, and also reflects the fact that histidine can be used as a buffer at near-physiological pH values.

The isoelectric point (pI) corresponds to the pH where the average charge of an amino acid is exactly zero. For diprotic amino acids (i.e., those amino acids for which the side chain is neither acidic nor basic), the pI can straightforwardly be captured as the average of the two p$K_a$ values. For triprotic amino acids (i.e., those that have an acidic or basic side chain), the pI can be obtained by averaging the two acidic p$K_a$ values for acidic amino acids or the two basic p$K_a$ values for basic amino acids.

Since amino acids are acids, they can be titrated, and you should be familiar with the basic features of an amino acid titration curve. Consider Figure 5, which illustrates the titration curve of alanine, a simple diprotic amino acid. The sharp transition point at a pH of about 6 corresponds to the pI, and you can also identify two buffer regions centered at the p$K_a$ values of 2.35 and 9.87. You should be able to translate these regions of the titration curve into chemical structure and charge.

**Figure 5.** Labeled titration curve of alanine.

The titration curves of basic/positively-charged triprotic amino acids show three distinct $pK_a$ values, whereas for acidic/negatively-charged triprotic amino acids, the buffer regions corresponding to the acidic $pK_a$ values are difficult to visualize. Figure 6 summarizes and compares the titration curves of all amino acids; there is no need to memorize or to be able to replicate this figure, but you should be able to understand how to identify $pK_a$ values and pI values and be aware of some of the tendencies this chart illustrates in general terms.

**Figure 6.** Amino acid titration curves.

# 4. Amino Acid Reactions

Amino acids take part in some key reactions that you should be familiar with for the MCAT. The first set of key reactions has to do with how amino acids are joined together and broken apart.

As mentioned earlier in this chapter, amino acids are joined together when a bond forms between the carboxylic acid group of one amino acid and the amine group of another, resulting in an amide. This is technically a condensation reaction, as it results in the production of a water molecule. Figure 7 shows the formation of a peptide bond.

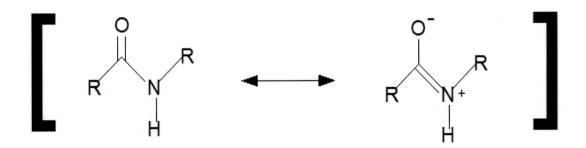

**Figure 7.** Formation of a peptide bond.

Peptide bonds are quite stable under intercellular conditions, and are characterized by resonance, as shown below in Figure 8.

**Figure 8.** Peptide bond resonance.

The resonance form shown on the right with the double C=N bond actually makes quite a significant contribution to the properties of peptide bonds. One consequence of this resonance structure is that peptide bonds are planar and do not rotate freely, which helps contribute to the structural stability of three-dimensional polypeptide structures.

Peptide bonds are broken through hydrolysis, which is simply the reverse of the condensation reaction through which a peptide bond is formed. The hydrolysis of peptide bonds is energetically favorable, but is extremely slow under physiological conditions. For this reason, the breaking of peptide bonds (i.e., the destruction of the primary structure of a protein) is generally accomplished by specific enzymes in living cells.

The MCAT also expects you to be aware of two classical reactions used to synthesize amino acids in laboratory conditions: the Strecker synthesis and the Gabriel synthesis.

The Strecker synthesis starts with an aldehyde, which is then reacted with KCN and $NH_4Cl$ to form an aminonitrile. The aminonitrile is then hydrolyzed in an acidic aqueous environment to form an amino acid. The general logic of the Strecker synthesis is shown below:

**Figure 9.** Strecker synthesis.

It's worth taking a little bit of a closer look at the Strecker synthesis, although as is often the case for biochemistry mechanisms on the MCAT, you should not memorize it, but just simply work through the logic of the process. You will not be asked to reproduce the mechanism from scratch, but if you are presented with the mechanism, you may be asked questions about specific steps or the logic of the process as a whole.

What was presented above as the first stage of the Strecker synthesis actually involves two steps. First, $NH4^+$ protonates the aldehyde oxygen and $NH_3$ adds to the carbonyl carbon. Second, the resulting hydroxyl group becomes protonated and leaves as water, allowing the cyanide ion to add to what used to be the carbonyl carbon. This generates the aminonitrile intermediate, as shown in Figure 10.

**Figure 10.** First stage of the Strecker synthesis.

The second stage of the Strecker synthesis takes place under acidic aqueous solutions, and essentially involves successive rounds of protonation and addition of $H_2O$ to the aminonitrile, until two –OH groups are added and a protonated $-NH_3^+$ group leaves as ammonia. It is shown below in Figure 11.

**Figure 11.** Second stage of the Strecker synthesis.

The logic of the Gabriel synthesis is quite different. The more general form of the Gabriel synthesis actually involves synthesizing amines; technically speaking, the form of the Gabriel synthesis that you need to be aware of for the MCAT is known as the Gabriel malonic ester synthesis. As the name suggests, the starting point is a malonic ester with a good leaving group (usually a halide, such as Br) attached to the alpha carbon. An $S_N2$ reaction then takes place with a nitrogen that is very carefully protected in the form of a bicyclic compound known as phthalimide. The reason for this is that $S_N2$ reactions with amines can easily get out of control. At this point, we get a large, unwieldy-looking intermediate. Note, though, that the skeleton of the malonic ester still has a –H at the alpha-carbon. This –H is slightly acidic, so treatment with a strong base will deprotonate and allow R–X (where R is the side group of the amino acid we're interested in synthesizing and X is usually a halide) to attach to the alpha carbon. We now have all the pieces we're interested in: R, N, and a COOH group (actually, two COOR groups that will eventually turn into a single COOH group) attached to a central carbon. We now just have to remove substituents. Hydrolysis under basic or acidic conditions will remove the phthalamide ring and convert the ester (COOR) groups to carboxylic acids (COOH), and then one round of decarboxylation through heat will remove the surplus COOH group, leaving us with our amino acid.

**Figure 12.** Gabriel malonic ester synthesis.

# 5. Must-Knows

> Generic structure of an amino acid: $-NH_2$, $-COOH$, $-H$, and $-R$
> Structural properties of amino acids:
> - <u>Nonpolar</u>: glycine (Gly, G), alanine (Ala, A), valine (Val, V), leucine (Leu, L), isoleucine (Ile, I), methionine (Met, M), proline (Pro, P), phenylalanine (Phe, F), tyrosine (Tyr, Y), tryptophan (Trp, W)
> - <u>Polar uncharged</u>: serine (Ser, S), threonine (Thr, T), asparagine (Asn, N), glutamine (Gln, Q), cysteine (Cys, C)
> - <u>Positively-charged (basic)</u>: arginine (Arg, R), histidine (His, H), lysine (Lys, K)
> - <u>Negatively charged (acidic)</u>: aspartic acid/aspartate (Asp, D), glutamic acid/glutamate (Glu, E)
> Special cases:
> - Glycine is achiral. Others are L.
> - Sulfur-containing: cysteine and methionine. Cysteine forms disulfide bonds, and the Cys-Cys dipeptide is known as cystine.
> - Aromatic: phenylalanine, tyrosine, tryptophan
> - Proline: has ring that incorporates $-NH_2$ of amino acid backbone, which causes 'kinks' that break up secondary structure of proteins.
> **Know all amino acid structures, abbreviations, and properties.**
> Peptide chains: written in direction from N-terminus to C-terminus, mirroring translation
> Levels of protein structure:
> - <u>Primary</u>: the linear chain of amino acids itself.
> - <u>Secondary</u>: hydrogen bonding between the amino and carboxylic acid groups of the amino acid residues; alpha-helices and beta-sheets.
> - <u>Tertiary</u>: three-dimensional structures that result from interactions among the side chains of the amino acid residues of a protein; hydrophobic interactions, hydrogen bonding, salt bridges, disulfide bonds.
> - <u>Quaternary</u>: larger structures generated by the assembly of protein subunits via non-covalent interactions; not all proteins; hemoglobin is a common example.
> Acid-base chemistry:
> - $pK_a \rightarrow pH$ at which a given functional group is exactly half-protonated and half-deprotonated.
> - In amino acids, $-COOH$ groups tend to have a $pK_a$ ~2, $-NH_2$ groups have a $pK_a$ of 9-9.5, and the $pK_a$ of $-R$ groups varies: ~4 for Asp and Glu, >10.5 for Arg and Lys, but 6.04 for His.
> - At physiological pH: $-COO^-$ (both in amino acids themselves and in side chains), terminal $-NH3^+$, and protonation state of side chain will depend on the residue.
> - pI (isoelectric point): the pH where the average charge of an amino acid is exactly zero.
> Peptide bonds:
> - Amide formed by condensation of $-COOH$ group of one amino acid and $-NH_2$ group of another; these are peptide bonds.
> - Peptide bonds: resonance-stabilized, planar, and are broken down by hydrolysis, usually catalyzed by enzymes.

This page left intentionally blank.

## Practice Passage

Alpha helices are an important part of the structure of most proteins. They form because of the structure of the amino acids in a protein. The functional groups of amino acids in proximity are able to form hydrogen bonds. When these hydrogen bonds consistently form between every fourth amino acid, the result is a right-handed helix. There are 3.6 residues per helical turn in an alpha helix and 5.4 Angstroms between consecutive turns.

Figure 1 shows a Wenxiang diagram, which can be used to show the relative two-dimensional location of amino acids as they bind with one another about the central axis. Each amino acid has a different propensity for being in an alpha helix, with alanine having the greatest propensity. Table 1 shows the relative propensities of the amino acids to be involved in an alpha helix. Energy values in the table represent the difference between the Gibbs free energy change of the hydrogen bond formation for each amino acid and the energy change for alanine.

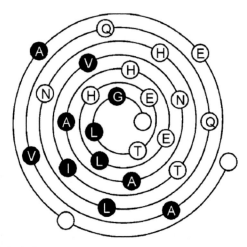

**Figure 1.** Wenxiang diagram of an alpha helix

There are two other forms of helices that can occur with some frequency. They are denoted the $3_{10}$ helix and the $\pi$-helix. Residues in a $3_{10}$ helix hydrogen bond every third amino acid, where every amino acid represents a 120° rotation in the helix. In a $\pi$-helix there are 4.1 residues per turn, and each amino acid corresponds to an 87° turn in the helix. Most importantly in a $\pi$-helix, the amino group of an amino acid H-bonds with the carbonyl group five residues earlier.

**Table 1.** Relative Propensities of Amino Acids to form α-Helical Hydrogen Bonds

| RESIDUE | ΔG° | RESIDUE | ΔG° |
|---------|-----|---------|-----|
| Alanine | 0 | Tyrosine | 0.52 |
| Arginine | 0.21 | Phenylalanine | 0.54 |
| Leucine | 0.21 | Histidine | 0.61 |
| Methionine | 0.23 | Valine | 0.61 |
| Lysine | 0.27 | Asparagine | 0.65 |
| Glutamine | 0.38 | Threonine | 0.66 |
| Glutamate | 0.39 | Cysteine | 0.68 |
| Isoleucine | 0.42 | Aspartate | 0.69 |
| Tryptophan | 0.49 | Glycine | 1 |
| Serine | 0.50 | Proline | 3.15 |

1. Alpha helices contribute to which of the following?
   A. Primary structure
   B. Secondary structure
   C. Tertiary structure
   D. Quaternary structure

2. Which exclusively ketogenic amino acid in Table 1 is most likely to be found in an α–helix?
   A. Lysine
   B. Leucine
   C. Histidine
   D. Proline

3. Starting from the center of Figure 1, which amino acid has hydrogen bonds to the first E?
   A. Asparagine
   B. Guanine
   C. Histidine
   D. Lysine

4. What is the best explanation for the finding that the substitution of pro residues on a protein can cause up to a 75% decrease in alpha helix formation compared with the native protein?
   A. The ring on proline causes too much strain to be bent sufficiently in the helix.
   B. The amine group from proline creates a more polar molecule than other amino acids.
   C. The aromatic portion of proline disrupts its ability to hydrogen bond.
   D. Proline is too large to properly engage in the necessary hydrogen bonding.

5. Which of the amino acids in the α–helix in Figure 1 is exclusively glucogenic?
   A. Glutamic acid
   B. Leucine

C. Lysine

D. Phenylalanine

6. Which of the following are most directly involved in the formation of the alpha helix backbone?
   A. The side hydrophobic groups on the amino acid side chains.
   B. The amine groups from one amino acid with the amine group of another.
   C. The carbonyl groups from one amino acid with the carbonyl group of another.
   D. The amine group from one amino acid with the carbonyl group of another.

7. In the π-helix shown below, how many complete turns will be found in the secondary structure?

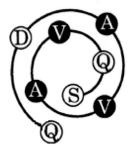

   A. 0
   B. 1
   C. 2
   D. 3

## Practice Passage Explanations

Alpha helices are an important part of the structure of most proteins. They form because of the structure of the amino acids in a protein. The functional groups of amino acids in proximity are able to form hydrogen bonds. When these hydrogen bonds consistently form between every fourth amino acid, the result is a right-handed helix. There are 3.6 residues per helical turn in an alpha helix and 5.4 Angstroms between consecutive turns.

*Key terms: alpha helices, proteins, amino acids, hydrogen bonds, every 4th, right-handed, 3.6 residues, 5.4 angstroms*

Figure 1 shows a Wenxiang diagram, which can be used to show the relative two-dimensional location of amino acids as they bind with one another about the central axis. Each amino acid has a different propensity for being in an alpha helix, with alanine having the greatest propensity. Table 1 shows the relative propensities of the amino acids to be involved in an alpha helix. Energy values in the table represent the difference between the Gibbs free energy change of the hydrogen bond formation for each amino acid and the energy change for alanine.

*Key terms: Wenxiang diagram, propensity, alanine, Gibbs free energy*

*Cause and effect: In this section we are told that not all amino acids have the same propensity toward participating in hydrogen bonding necessary for alpha helix formation. Alanine is the most likely to do so*

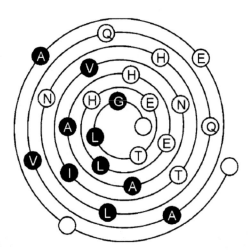

**Figure 1.** Wenxiang diagram of an alpha helix

*Figure 1 shows specific AA residues, save analysis for questions*

There are two other forms of helices that can occur with some frequency. They are denoted the $3_{10}$ helix and the π-helix. Residues in a $3_{10}$ helix hydrogen bond every third amino acid, where every amino acid represents a 120° rotation in the helix. In a π-helix there are 4.1 residues per turn, and each amino acid corresponds to an 87° turn in the helix. Most importantly in a π-helix, the amino group of an amino acid H-bonds with the carbonyl group five residues earlier.

*Key terms: $3_{10}$ helix, π-helix*

*Contrast: $3_{10}$ = H-bond every 3 AA (360°/120° = 3); π = H-bond every 5 AA (360°/90° = 4)*

**Table 1.** Relative Propensities of Amino Acids to form α-Helical Hydrogen Bonds

| RESIDUE | ΔG° | RESIDUE | ΔG° |
|---|---|---|---|
| Alanine | 0 | Tyrosine | 0.52 |
| Arginine | 0.21 | Phenylalanine | 0.54 |
| Leucine | 0.21 | Histidine | 0.61 |
| Methionine | 0.23 | Valine | 0.61 |
| Lysine | 0.27 | Asparagine | 0.65 |
| Glutamine | 0.38 | Threonine | 0.66 |
| Glutamate | 0.39 | Cysteine | 0.68 |
| Isoleucine | 0.42 | Aspartate | 0.69 |
| Tryptophan | 0.49 | Glycine | 1 |
| Serine | 0.50 | Proline | 3.15 |

*Table 1 shows us that compared with ala, pro is the least likely, arg/leu are the most likely*

1. B is correct. This question is asking us to recall what type of structures alpha helices are. Within the long protein chains, there are regions in which the chains are organized into regular structures known as alpha helices, which are secondary structures in proteins. These secondary structures are held together by hydrogen bonds. In an alpha helix, the protein chain is coiled like a loosely-coiled spring.
   A. This term is used to describe the order of the amino acids joined together to make the protein. The primary structure is usually shown using abbreviations for the amino acid residues.
   C. Tertiary structure of a protein is a description of the way the whole chain, including the secondary structures, folds itself into its final 3D shape.
   D. Quaternary protein structure involves the clustering of several individual peptide or protein chains into a final specific shape. A variety of bonding interactions including hydrogen bonding, salt bridges, and disulfide bonds hold the various chains into a particular geometry.

2. B is correct. This question is asking us to name a ketogenic amino acid. Ketogenic amino acids that yield acetyl-CoA or acetoacetyl-CoA, meaning they do NOT produce intermediates that can be converted to glucose. Lysine (K) and Leucine (L) are the only amino acids that are exclusively ketogenic. Of the two, leucine, at 0.21, is more likely to be a part of the helix compared to lysine (0.27).

3. C is correct. We are told in the passage that amino acids in an alpha helix are bound to every 4th amino acid. Looking at Figure 1, you can see that the first glutamic acid (E) is the fourth residue present. Counting four more residues outward along the spiral, we find a histidine (H) residue.

4. A is correct. This question requires us to remember the general structure of proline. Proline is the only amino acid whose amine group forms a ring. This means that it is unable to twist and turn with the same fluidity as other amino acids. Below is the structure of proline

   B. There is no charge on proline. It is less polar than some other charged amino acids.
   C. There is no aromatic portion of proline.
   D. Proline is smaller than other amino acids, such as phenylalanine, which can appear in alpha helices.

5. A is correct. Glucogenic amino acids are amino acids which, when metabolized, yield pyruvate or Krebs cycle intermediates, or that can be converted to glucose through gluconeogenesis. They are alanine (A), arginine (R), asparagine (N), aspartate (D), cysteine (C), glutamic acid (E), glycine (G), histidine (H), valine (V), methionine (M), proline (P), and serine (S).

6. D is correct. This question asks us to consider what two species on an amino acid will hydrogen bond with one another. The N-H bonds in the amine results in a partial positive charge on the H that can interact with the negative dipole on the O of the carbonyl group on another residue.
   A. Side group interactions contribute to tertiary structure, not alpha helices.
   B. The oxygen in carbonyl groups are both partially negative, and would be unlikely to be attracted to each other via hydrogen bonding. The carbonyl carbons are both electropositive, and would also repel.
   C. This will not occur because there will be no positive side of a dipole with which the negative O in a carbonyl can interact.

7. B is correct. We are told in the final paragraph that in a π-helix, there are 4.1 residues per turn. Thus with, 8 residues, we can fit 8/4.1. = 1.95, or 1 turn.

## Independent Questions

1. Which of the following statements is NOT true of disulfide bonds?
   A. They can be broken through exposure to certain reagents, including 2-mercaptoethanol.
   B. Like peptide bonds, they constitute covalent interactions.
   C. They can form between any two sulfur-containing amino acid residues.
   D. Their formation involves oxidation, while their breaking constitutes reduction.

2. Aromatic amino acids include all of the following EXCEPT:
   A. R.
   B. F.
   C. W.
   D. Y.

3. A certain globular protein is typically found in an aqueous environment in the body. In this protein, which of the following amino acid residues would you expect to be facing outside, towards the environment?
   A. Valine
   B. Isoleucine
   C. Threonine
   D. Tryptophan

4. A dipeptide is formed through the reaction of one amino acid with another to form a peptide bond. During this reaction, the nucleophile is:
   A. the amino terminal nitrogen of one of the amino acids.
   B. the side chain of one of the amino acids.
   C. the carboxylic acid terminal oxygen of one of the amino acids.
   D. a carbonyl carbon.

5. Which of the following is LEAST likely to be used to denature the higher-level structure of a protein?
   A. Heat
   B. Extreme pH
   C. An inorganic salt solution
   D. An enzymatic inhibitor

6. The $pK_a$ of the side chain of histidine is approximately 6. In a solution with a pH of 8, the side chain of histidine is most likely to be:
   A. protonated and charged.
   B. deprotonated and uncharged.
   C. deprotonated and charged.
   D. protonated and uncharged.

7. Assuming that the $pK_a$ of the side chain of histidine is approximately 6, which of the following is closest to the isoelectric point of this amino acid?
   A. 4
   B. 5.7
   C. 7.5
   D. 9

8. During the Gabriel synthesis of an amino acid, which of the steps listed below occurs?
   A. A malonic ester undergoes an $S_N1$ reaction.
   B. An unprotected amine attacks the carbonyl carbon of an ester.
   C. The oxygen atom of an aldehyde is protonated.
   D. Heat is used to remove an extra -COOH group.

# Independent Question Explanations

1. C is correct. Of the twenty standard amino acids, just two contain sulfur: cysteine and methionine. Disulfide bonds can form between two cysteine residues, but they cannot form between two methionine residues or between a cysteine and a methionine. The remaining statements are true. Formation of a disulfide bond occurs through oxidation, while breaking such a bond requires reduction; this can be accomplished using reducing agents like 2-mercaptoethanol. Both disulfide linkages and peptide bonds are covalent interactions.

2. A is correct. If you have not yet memorized the one- and three-letter abbreviations for all twenty standard amino acids, be sure to do so before Test Day! Arginine (R) is a basic amino acid and is not aromatic. Phenylalanine (F), tryptophan (W), and tyrosine (Y) are all aromatic.

3. C is correct. When the external environment is aqueous (and thus polar), hydrophilic amino acids generally face towards the cytosol or external environment, while hydrophobic residues comprise the inner core of the protein. Here, threonine is the only polar amino acid listed, so it is the option most likely to face the exterior of the protein, which interfaces with the aqueous polar environment.

4. A is correct. This question overlaps the information in this chapter with organic chemistry, which is precisely what a real MCAT question might do. However, even if our organic chemistry is rusty, we can still reason through this question. Peptide bonds form between the amino terminal of one amino acid and the carboxylic acid terminal of another. They do not directly involve side chains (eliminate choice B). Additionally, in the formation of a peptide bond, the amino terminal nitrogen of one amino acid attacks the carbonyl carbon of another. The -COOH terminal oxygen is not a direct part of this attack and instead is lost from the molecule as water (eliminate choice C). Finally, note that carbonyl carbons are classic electrophiles due to the electron withdrawing effect of the double-bonded carbonyl oxygen (eliminate choice D). Our answer is thus option A, which makes logical sense as it is the amino terminal nitrogen that does the attacking in peptide bond formation.

5. D is correct. Enzyme inhibitors prevent enzymes (which are almost always proteins) from functioning properly, but they do not typically denature the protein structure. All of the other answers are commonly used to directly disrupt the structures of proteins.

6. B is correct. When pH > $pK_a$, the group in question (whether side chain, carboxylic acid terminal, or amino terminal) will be deprotonated. Since the side chain of histidine contains an N-H (which is specifically part of an imidazole ring), it will be positively charged when it is protonated and uncharged when it is deprotonated. In this case, since it is deprotonated, it will be uncharged.

7. C is correct. To calculate isoelectric point, you must consider the $pK_a$ values of the amino acid in question. Histidine has a carboxylic acid group ($pK_a \sim 2$), an amino group ($pK_a \sim 9$), and its side chain ($pK_a \sim 6$). Note that we should *not* average all three of these values; instead, since histidine is a basic amino acid, we should average the two most basic $pK_a$s. $(6 + 9) / 2 = 7.5$.

8. D is correct. A final step in the Gabriel synthesis of an amino acid is the administration of heat to decarboxylate the molecule, removing an extra -COOH. Choice A is incorrect because the Gabriel synthesis involves an $S_N2$ mechanism, not $S_N1$. Option B is wrong because the amine in a Gabriel synthesis is protected, and choice C is something that occurs during the Strecker synthesis.

This page left intentionally blank.

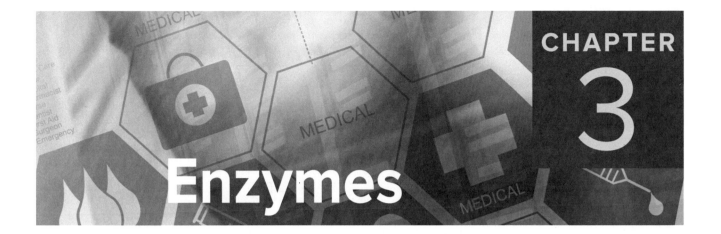

# CHAPTER 3

# Enzymes

## 0. Introduction

In this chapter, we move beyond structural descriptions of proteins to start exploring how proteins function in the body. Enzymes are one of the most important classes of protein function, so we will break this discussion into enzymes, which are covered in this chapter, and non-enzymatic protein functions, which are covered in chapter 4.

Enzymes are one of the highest-yield topics on the MCAT for several reasons. First, they are crucial for physiological function. Second, they can be thought of as an intersection point for multiple important topics for the MCAT: biochemical pathways, protein structure, normal and abnormal physiological function, kinetics, and even genetics, since mutations can lead to altered protein structures. Any time you see a topic that links biochemistry, biology, and general chemistry, be sure to pay special attention to it for the MCAT! Third, because enzymes are so important physiologically, they are relevant for many diseases and for pharmacological therapies, which may appear in passages. In other words, a thorough understanding of enzymes can be very helpful even for passages and questions that are not "about" enzymes, because enzymes may play a supporting role in the content that is being tested. For all of these reasons, to ensure success on the MCAT, it is important for you to have a thorough understanding of enzymes, enzyme kinetics, and enzyme regulation. This is an especially important chapter to know inside and out for Test Day.

## 1. Mechanisms

Enzymes are biological catalysts. This is a simple statement, but it has important implications. This means that enzymes speed up the rate of a reaction by reducing the activation energy ($E_a$), are sensitive to temperature and pH, and are specific for certain reactions or classes of reactions. Enzymes are not changed or consumed in the reaction, do not affect the equilibrium ($K_{eq}$) of a reaction, and do not affect any thermodynamic parameters of the reaction ($\Delta G$, $\Delta H$, and $\Delta S$). For this reason, enzymes cannot make an energetically unfavorable reaction into a favorable one. These points are summarized in Table 1.

| THINGS THAT ENZYMES DO | THINGS THAT ENZYMES DO NOT DO |
|---|---|
| Enzymes increase the rate of a reaction | Enzymes do NOT alter equilibrium |
| Enzymes reduce the activation energy ($E_a$) | Enzymes do NOT change $\Delta G$, $\Delta H$, or $\Delta S$ |
| Enzymes are sensitive to temperature and pH | Enzymes are NOT changed or consumed in a reaction |
| Enzymes are specific for certain reactions or classes of reactions | Enzymes CANNOT make an energetically unfavorable reaction into a favorable one |

**Table 1.** Things that enzymes do and do not do.

## MCAT STRATEGY > > >

These are familiar-sounding statements because they are repeated in the beginning of virtually all lectures and chapters about enzymes, but don't skim over them – dwell on this table and make your understanding of this material into a reflex. On Test Day, be sure not to fall for an answer choice that tries to convince you that an enzyme does something that it doesn't. The answer choice may not be phrased this directly, but any answer choice that implies that enzymes can alter the final equilibrium or energetic favorability of a reaction *must* be wrong.

Just as is the case for non-biological catalysts, the effect of an enzyme on a reaction can be shown in a reaction coordinate diagram. Figure 1 contrasts a catalyzed and an uncatalyzed reaction; as seen in this figure, the effect of an enzyme is to lower the activation energy ($E_a$), which can be thought of as lowering the energetic threshold that has to be crossed for a reaction to proceed. Once this threshold is crossed, the reaction proceeds more quickly – in fact, enzymes can cause reactions in the body to proceed *much* faster than they would otherwise, by factors of hundreds, thousands, or even $10^{17}$. Note that this also holds true for the reverse reaction; in fact, an enzyme *must* also speed up the reverse reaction in order to avoid affecting the equilibrium.

**Figure 1.** Reaction coordinate diagram for catalyzed and non-catalyzed reactions.

The substance that an enzyme operates on is known as a substrate. Enzymes and substrates interact at the active site of an enzyme, which can be divided into a binding site and a catalytic site. The catalytic site is the very specific place where a reaction is catalyzed, while the binding site is a larger area where the substrate interacts with the enzyme through intermolecular interactions (e.g., hydrogen bonding, dipole-dipole interactions, and London dispersion forces) in a way that positions the substrate properly relative to the catalytic site. When the substrate interacts with the active site of an enzyme, it forms what is known as the enzyme-substrate complex.

A crucial bit of terminology relating to the active site of an enzyme involves how enzymes are regulated (which is explored in more detail below). Regulatory elements that interact with an enzyme at its active site are known as orthosteric, whereas regulatory membranes that bind at some other site on the enzyme are known as allosteric. Another point of terminology to be aware of is that a substance that an enzyme interacts with can be referred to as a ligand, a term that encompasses both the substrate and regulatory molecules.

**Figure 2.** Active site on an enzyme (showing binding and catalytic sites).

**orthosteric regulation: at active site**

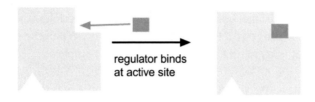

regulator binds
at active site

**allosteric regulation: at non-active site**

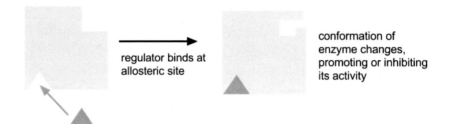

regulator binds at
allosteric site

conformation of
enzyme changes,
promoting or inhibiting
its activity

**Figure 3.** Allosteric vs. orthosteric regulation.

## MCAT STRATEGY > > >

Whenever possible, try to develop conceptual links between MCAT topics. For example, in the case of enzyme-substrate interactions, think about what factors might lead to alterations in enzyme function. Mutations are one such factor, because point mutations can lead to the incorporation of different amino acid residues at a specific location in a protein. If, for example, a hydrophobic amino acid residue replaces a hydrophilic residue at a crucial location in the active site, the ability of an enzyme to interact with a substrate could be seriously impeded.

As mentioned above, enzymes are highly specific for certain substrates. Two important models have been proposed to describe how enzymes interact with substrates: the lock and key theory and the induced fit model. As the name implies, the lock and key theory proposes that the active site of an enzyme and the substrate fit together like puzzle pieces, with no change in tertiary or quaternary structure. However, it eventually became clear that the lock and key theory was not sufficient to adequately explain enzyme-substrate interactions, leading to the development of the induced fit model. In the induced fit model, the enzyme and substrate are seen as affecting each other; the initial stages of binding induce conformational shifts that allow closer binding and more efficient catalysis.

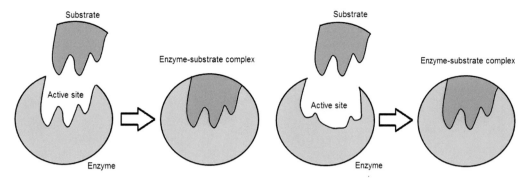

**Figure 4.** Lock and key (left) vs. induced fit (right) models.

## 2. Classification

The highest-level classification groups enzymes into six classes based on their mechanism. These classes are presented in Table 2.

| CATEGORY | MECHANISM | EXAMPLES |
|---|---|---|
| Oxidoreductases | Catalyze oxidation/reduction reactions | Alcohol dehydrogenase<br>Superoxide dismutase |
| Transferases | Transfer a functional group between molecules | Aspartate transaminase<br>Creatine kinase<br>DNA polymerase |
| Hydrolases | Catalyze hydrolysis | Angiotensin-converting enzyme<br>Pancreatic lipase<br>Lactase |
| Lyases | Cleave bonds through non-hydrolysis mechanisms | Pyruvate decarboxylase<br>Aconitase |
| Isomerases | Catalyze isomerization | Ribose-5-phosphate isomerase |
| Ligases | Join molecules together with covalent bonds | Aminoacyl tRNA synthetase<br>Glutamine synthetase<br>Pyruvate carboxylase |

**Table 2.** Major categories of enzymes.

As shown in Table 2, enzymes have the characteristic suffix "-ase." The names in the high-level categories in the left-most column in Table 2 follow the template "[mechanism]+ase." These high-level categories describe chemical mechanisms, not biological functionality, which is usually described by the specific name of the enzyme, as shown in the right-most column. Note that the "-ase" word in name of a specific enzyme is often not identical with the name of its high-level category. For example, although it is easy to tell that ribose-5-phosphate isomerase belongs to the category of isomerases, it may not be so obvious that pyruvate carboxylase belongs to the category of ligases. Understanding the general chemical function of an enzyme is the key to recognizing which category it belongs to:

pyruvate carboxylase adds a carboxylic acid functional group to pyruvate ($C_3H_3O_3^-$), converting it to oxaloacetate ($C_4H_3O_5^-$). Since this involves joining molecules together with covalent bonds, pyruvate carboxylase is a ligase.

## MCAT STRATEGY > > >

The naming pattern of high-level enzyme classifications is more obvious in some cases than others. For instance, it is quite intuitive that transferases involve transferring a functional group. The two categories that might be harder to remember are lyases and ligases. For lyases, think of the word "lysis" or breakdown. For ligases, think of the word "ligation" or "to ligate," meaning "to bind," or the biochemical term "ligand."

## MCAT STRATEGY > > >

It's especially important to remember the definitions of kinases and phosphatases because phosphorylation is a crucial physiological process. Among other functions, phosphorylation can activate or inactivate a protein, with potentially major downstream effects. For this reason, kinases (most famously, tyrosine kinase) have emerged as targets for anti-cancer drugs. For Test Day, you certainly don't have to be up to speed on recent advances in drug development, but it is important to be aware of the implications of phosphorylation, to be familiar with the associated terminology, and (ideally) not to be surprised if it comes up in a passage.

As the examples in Table 2 indicate, enzymes can have diverse names, but they almost all end in "-ase." When you see an unfamiliar enzyme name, you can generally conclude that the enzyme acts on or breaks down whatever comes before the "-ase" suffix. To illustrate this point through some of the examples in Table 2, superoxide dismutase converts the superoxide radical into molecular oxygen or hydrogen peroxide, pyruvate decarboxylase removes a carboxylic acid group from pyruvate, and glutamine synthetase synthesizes glutamine. Many enzyme names are intuitive, but there is one tricky piece of nomenclature that you should absolutely aware of on Test Day: phosphatases *remove* phosphate groups from a substrate, while kinases *add* phosphate groups in a process known as phosphorylation.

## 3. High-Level Regulation

For enzymes to work as needed in the body, they can't just catalyze a given reaction at a certain rate: their activity must be controlled so that a reaction happens at the right rate at the right time. As you can imagine, this becomes quite complicated in physiological contexts, but for the MCAT it is most important to be familiar with the basic principles of enzyme regulation.

Enzymes in a metabolic pathway are commonly regulated by downstream products of the pathway, which is a process known as feedback regulation. The pattern to be most familiar with for the MCAT is negative feedback, also known as feedback inhibition. Negative feedback functions to maintain homeostasis by ensuring that the products of a pathway remain at appropriate concentrations. In negative feedback, the downstream product of a pathway acts to inhibit the pathway itself – put more simply, the idea is that when we have enough of a product, then we don't need to produce more of it. This is shown schematically in Figure 5.

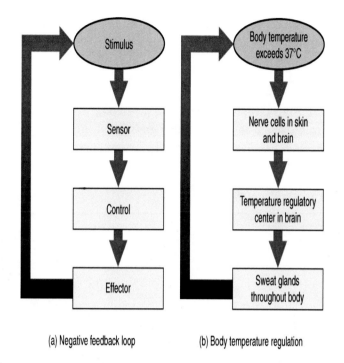

(a) Negative feedback loop          (b) Body temperature regulation

**Figure 5.** Negative feedback.

Examples of negative feedback are extremely abundant in metabolism, to the point that you should think of negative feedback as being the default high-level mechanism of enzyme regulation. One important example is in glycolysis, where phosphofructokinase (PFK-1) catalyzes the irreversible, rate-limiting step in which fructose-6-phosphate is phosphorylated to become fructose-1,6-bisphosphate. The products of glycolysis are pyruvate, NADH, and ATP, of which ATP has the most direct payoff in terms of energy. ATP, in turn, reduces the affinity of PFK-1 for its substrate, fructose-6-phosphate. This has the effect of downregulating the process of glycolysis in response to the presence of sufficient energy in the cell.

Positive feedback is less common but is nonetheless important to understand. An example of positive feedback in enzyme regulation is the formation of blood clots. This is a very complex process that is discussed more in Chapter 9 of the Biology textbook. Although it isn't crucial to understand the entire process in depth, the basic point with regard to enzyme regulation is that positive feedback in blood clot formation allows initial stages to be amplified such that clots can form quickly when necessary. Negative feedback is also at work in blood clot formation, however; positive feedback allows a quick response, while negative feedback ensures that the process doesn't spiral out of control.

Another pattern of regulation is known as feed-forward regulation, in which an enzyme is regulated by an upstream product of the pathway. Glycolysis also provides a valuable example of feed-forward regulation. In the final step of glycolysis, a phosphate group is transferred from phosphoenolpyruvate to ADP, resulting in ATP and pyruvate. This reaction is catalyzed by pyruvate kinase,

> > **CONNECTIONS** < <

**Chapter 9 of Biology**

**MCAT STRATEGY > > >**

The interplay between negative and positive feedback is also an important topic in the endocrine system. Although enzymes and hormones are technically different substances, the principle is basically the same. The MCAT rewards problem-solving and the ability to apply general principles to new situations, so be sure to focus on these commonalities and understand the different physiological effects of negative and positive feedback systems in both metabolism and the endocrine system.

which is activated by the glycolytic intermediate fructose-1,6-bisphosphate. Since fructose-1,6-bisphosphate is an upstream intermediate of glycolysis, this is a feed-forward mechanism.

A further concept to be aware of is cooperativity, which occurs when an enzyme has multiple active sites and binding at one active site facilitates binding at another. In more simple words, this means that it is hardest for an enzyme to bind its first ligand, easier to bind the second ligand, still easier to bind the third ligand, and so on. Although this occurs in enzymes, the most important example of cooperativity for the MCAT is hemoglobin, which is not technically an enzyme. Cooperativity characteristically results in a sigmoidal curve on graphs showing saturation (the percentage of active sites occupied) as a function of substrate concentration, as shown in Figure 6.

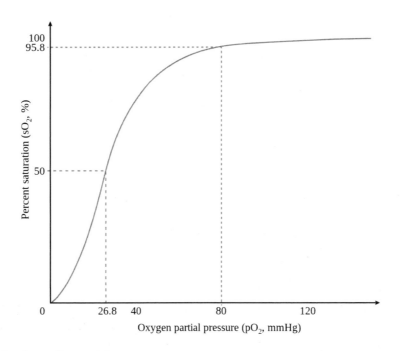

**Figure 6.** Cooperative binding of hemoglobin.

The degree of cooperativity in an enzyme or protein can be expressed using the Hill coefficient. A Hill coefficient value >1 results from positively cooperative binding, as described above, with higher values indicating greater cooperativity. A Hill coefficient value equal to 1 indicates non-cooperative binding, and a value <1 reflects negative cooperativity, in which binding of the first ligand reduces the enzyme's affinity for subsequent ligands.

# 4. Kinetics and Inhibition

One way that enzymes can be regulated is through inhibition – that is, a substance can interact with an enzyme in a way that prevents it from catalyzing the reaction it normally does. Understanding the effects of inhibitors requires a solid understanding of enzyme kinetics, which describes how enzymes affect the rate of a reaction and how that process is affected by other factors.

The Michaelis-Menten model of enzyme kinetics is crucial to understand for Test Day. Let's start by defining some terms through an example. Imagine that we have a test tube with 100 molecules of enzyme X, which catalyzes the reaction S → P (with S standing for "substrate" and P for "product"), and that all other conditions are appropriate for the reaction to occur (i.e., ideal temperature and pH). If we add 10 molecules of S, we can expect that they will all be converted to P quickly, since we have a lot of extra X floating around. To make the math easy, let's say that it takes 1 second for X to catalyze the reaction S → P; in this case, we have a reaction rate of 10 molecules of S per second (remember that the reaction rate is defined in terms of changes in the concentration of the substrate). If we add 50 molecules of S, we'll expect the reaction to go even faster, since we still have excess X – although not 5 times as fast, since we can expect some degree of delay to occur in terms of all the molecules of S finding their way to available molecules of X. Given this delay, perhaps our reaction rate will be 40 molecules of S per second.

Now let's ask ourselves: what happens if we keep adding S? Up to a certain point, the reaction rate will continue to increase, but not forever. The reason for this is simple: we only have 100 molecules of X. If we compare the reaction rate when we add 900 molecules of S to the rate when we add 1,000 molecules, we shouldn't expect there to be any significant difference – no matter how many molecules of S we add, only 100 can be converted to P at any given moment. If all the molecules of X are occupied, we say that X is saturated. The maximum rate of a reaction is known as $v_{max}$, where the $v$ is there to remind you of velocity. Don't forget, though, that like any other reaction rate, the units of $v_{max}$ are [substrate]/time.

Another crucial parameter to understand in Michaelis-Menten kinetics is the Michaelis constant, $K_m$. The definition of $K_m$ is deceptively simple: $K_m$ is the concentration of substrate that corresponds to half of $v_{max}$. This is derivable from the Michaelis-Menten equation (Equation 1) if $v$, the reaction rate, is set equal to half of $v_{max}$.

**Equation 1:**

$$v = \frac{v_{max}[S]}{K_m + [S]}$$

$K_m$ is important because it can be used as a measure of the affinity that an enzyme has for its substrate – that is, the phenomenon that some enzymes interact more readily with their substrates than others. This is a consideration that we neglected in our discussion of the sample reaction S → P above, but it is an important complication in real-world applications. The reason we can use $K_m$ this way is because it provides a measure of how much enzyme you need to get halfway to the saturation point. $K_m$ is not affected if you change the concentration of the substrate or enzyme, although it can be affected by inhibitors, as we will discuss in more depth below.

Figure 7 shows a sample Michaelis-Menten plot of enzyme kinetics with important parameters labeled. Study this plot thoroughly and make sure that you can explain what everything on it refers to.

## MCAT STRATEGY > > >

Students often get confused about $K_m$ because it looks like other important concepts in biochemistry and chemistry, like the equilibrium constant ($K_{eq}$) and the rate constant for reactions ($k$). $K_m$ is a different beast entirely. It is nothing more and nothing less than a specific concentration of substrate (or reactant) that happens to be useful for understanding enzymes. Sometimes students skip past this in a rush to memorize the effects of various types of inhibitors on $K_m$. This is important too, but it's worth pausing to make sure that you thoroughly understand the basics of what $K_m$ is about, because doing so will help you cope with any unexpectedly challenging problems or passages on Test Day.

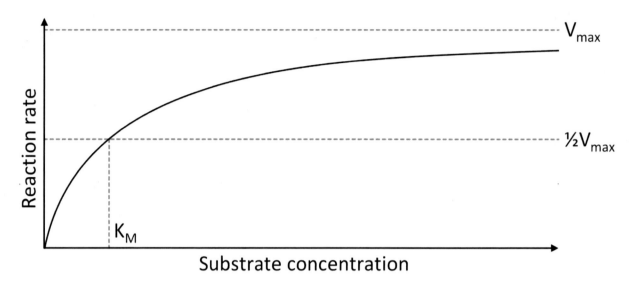

**Figure 7.** Michaelis-Menten plot showing $K_m$ and $v_{max}$.

In addition to Michaelis-Menten plots, you should be familiar with Lineweaver-Burk plots, which are a double-reciprocal transformation of Michaelis-Menten plots. What this means is that while Michaelis-Menten plots have $v_{max}$ on the y-axis and [S] on the x-axis—that is, they explore how reaction rate varies as a function of substrate concentration—Lineweaver-Burk plots have $1/v_{max}$ on the y-axis and $1/[S]$ on the x-axis. Figure 8 shows a Lineweaver-Burk plot with a Michaelis-Menten plot, with the values of $K_m$ and $v_{max}$ indicated.

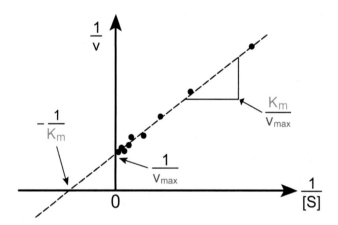

**Figure 8.** Lineweaver-Burk plot.

The most important aspect of Lineweaver-Burk plots is that they assign very specific graphical coordinates to the important parameters of $K_m$ and $v_{max}$. As seen in Figure 7, in a Lineweaver-Burk plot, the x-intercept is $-1/K_m$ and the y-intercept is $1/v_{max}$. This allows the easy graphical comparison of how inhibitors (discussed more below) affect these parameters. If $v_{max}$ is decreased, the y-intercept increases (moves further from the origin), and if $K_m$ is decreased, the x-intercept decreases (moves further from the origin). Table 3 presents a chain of logic that you can use to predict these changes, using sample values of $K_m$ and $v_{max}$ that do not have units and are designed to make the math easier to visualize.

| CHANGE | ORIGINAL VALUE OF PARAMETER | ORIGINAL VALUE OF INTERCEPT | NEW VALUE OF PARAMETER | NEW VALUE OF INTERCEPT | DID INTERCEPT INCREASE OR DECREASE? | DID INTERCEPT MOVE TOWARDS OR AWAY FROM ORIGIN? |
|---|---|---|---|---|---|---|
| Increase $K_m$ | 4 | −1/4 | 8 | −1/8 | Increase (became less negative) | Towards |
| Decrease $K_m$ | 4 | −1/4 | 2 | −1/2 | Decrease (became more negative) | Away |
| Increase $v_{max}$ | 10 | 1/10 | 20 | 1/20 | Decrease (became less positive) | Towards |
| Decrease $v_{max}$ | 10 | 1/10 | 5 | 1/5 | Increase (became more positive) | Away |

**Table 3.** Effect of changes in $K_m$ and $v_{max}$ on Lineweaver-Burk plots.

As the name suggests, inhibitors are substances that reduce the effective activity of enzymes. Inhibitors can be reversible or irreversible; reversible inhibitors interact with enzymes through noncovalent interactions such as hydrogen bonding, dipole-dipole interactions, and ionic interactions, while irreversible inhibitors (suicide inhibitors) covalently bind to enzymes. The MCAT will only expect you to know the details of reversible inhibitors, but it is worth being aware of irreversible inhibitors as a possibility.

> **MCAT STRATEGY > > >**
>
> On Test Day you can use logic like that in Table 3 to check your work on questions dealing with changes in $K_m$ and $v_{max}$, but investing in this work ahead of time is a good idea to ensure that you can do so confidently and accurately on Test Day.

Reversible inhibitors are classified based on how they interact with an enzyme. Different types of inhibitors have different effects on $K_m$ and $v_{max}$, and it is imperative for the MCAT to be familiar with these types on inhibitors, their effects, and how those effects are represented in Michaelis-Menten and Lineweaver-Burk plots.

Inhibitors that interact with the active site of an enzyme are known as competitive inhibitors, because they can be thought of as competing with the substrate. They do not affect $v_{max}$, because by adding additional substrate, they can be out-competed and their effect minimized. No matter how much of a competitive inhibitor is present, it is always possible to flood the system with substrate to the point that its effect becomes negligible. However, competitive inhibitors do affect $K_m$, precisely because their effects can be neutralized with extra substrate. Requiring more substrate to reach $v_{max}$ logically means requiring more substrate to reach half of $v_{max}$, which by definition means increasing $K_m$.

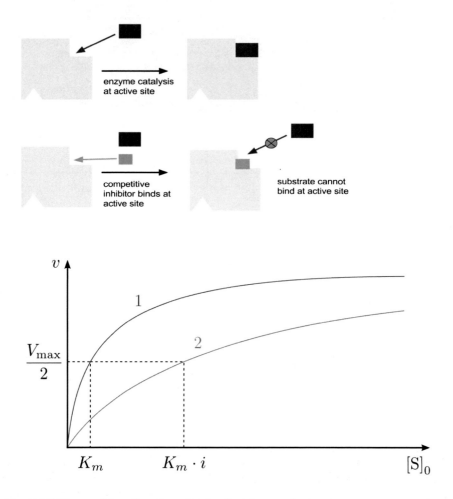

**Figure 9.** Competitive inhibition and its effects on a Michaelis-Menten plot.

In contrast, noncompetitive inhibitors interact with the enzyme allosterically – that is, at a site other than the active site. They are called noncompetitive because they can interact with an enzyme regardless of whether it has bound to a substrate. Noncompetitive inhibitors essentially prevent an enzyme from working, meaning that their effect is similar to reducing the concentration of enzyme that is present. This has the effect of reducing $v_{max}$. However, the molecules of enzyme that are not affected by the noncompetitive inhibitor remain functional. This means that $K_m$ stays the same.

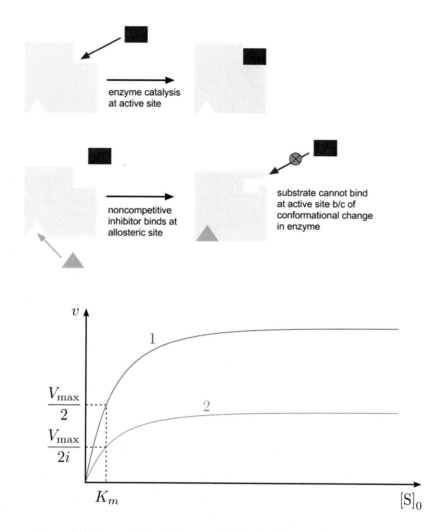

**Figure 10.** Noncompetitive inhibition and its effects on a Michaelis-Menten plot.

Next, uncompetitive inhibitors interact with the enzyme-substrate (E-S) complex at an allosteric site. In other words, they essentially prevent an enzyme from letting go of a substrate that it has bound. If an enzyme cannot release its substrate as efficiently, it is logical that the rate of the catalyzed reaction is reduced, meaning that $v_{max}$ is decreased. Uncompetitive inhibition also leads to a decrease of the apparent $K_m$ of a reaction because the stabilization of the E-S complex effectively means that the enzyme seems to have a greater affinity for the substrate.

## MCAT STRATEGY > > >

To be blunt, the names "noncompetitive" and "uncompetitive" are about as unhelpful as you can get in terms of distinguishing two very different mechanisms. It's imperative for you to distinguish between them, though, so any mnemonic you can create is worth considering. One possibility is using the letter *n* to remember that *nothing* happens at the active site in *noncompetitive* inhibition.

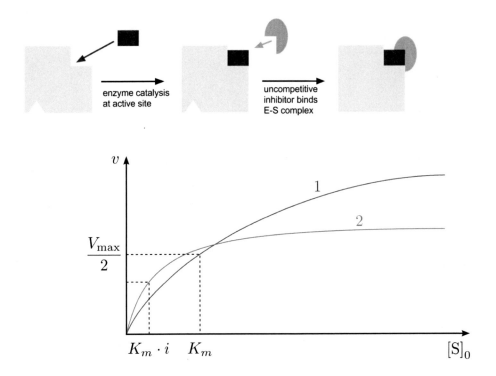

**Figure 11.** Uncompetitive inhibition and its effects on a Michaelis-Menten plot.

The final category of reversible inhibition is mixed inhibition, in which the inhibitor can either bind the free enzyme at an allosteric site or bind the E-S complex. In mixed inhibition, $v_{max}$ is always decreased; however, the effect on $K_m$ depends on the binding preference of a given inhibitor. If a mixed inhibitor prefers to bind the free enzyme at an active site, $K_m$ is increased. If a mixed inhibitor prefers to bind the E-S complex, its overall effect can be thought of as similar to that of an uncompetitive inhibitor, and $K_m$ will be decreased.

Table 4 summarizes the effects on various types of reversible inhibitors on $K_m$ and $v_{max}$, as well as their effects on the x- and y-intercepts of Lineweaver-Burk plots. Figure 13 graphically shows how each type of inhibition affects Michaelis-Menten and Lineweaver Burk plots.

| TYPE OF INHIBITION | WHERE DOES THE INTER-ACTION HAPPEN? | EFFECT ON $V_{MAX}$ | EFFECT ON $K_M$ | EFFECT ON X-INTERCEPT OF LINEWEAVER-BURK PLOTS | EFFECT ON Y-INTERCEPT OF LINEWEAVER-BURK PLOTS |
|---|---|---|---|---|---|
| Competitive | Active site | None | ↑ | ↑ (moves towards origin) | None |
| Noncompetitive | Allosteric site | ↓ | None | None | ↑ (moves away from origin) |
| Uncompetitive | E-S complex | ↓ | ↓ | ↓ (moves away from origin) | ↑ (moves away from origin) |
| Mixed | Allosteric site of free enzyme or E-S complex | ↓ | ↓ or ↑ | ↓ or ↑ (moves towards or away from origin) | ↑ (moves away from origin) |

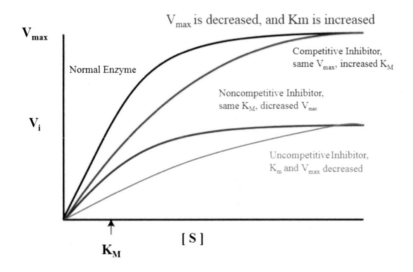

$V_{max}$ is decreased, and Km is increased

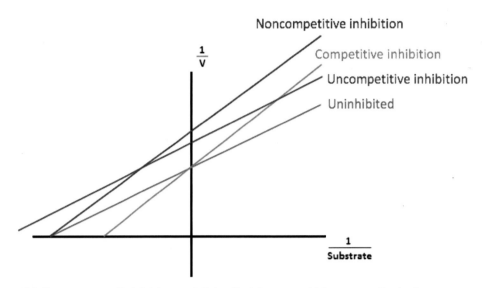

**Figure 12.** Effects of different types of inhibition on Michaelis-Menten and Lineweaver-Burk plots.

## 5. Other Mechanisms of Regulation

Some physiologically important mechanisms of enzyme regulation involve covalent bonds.

Phosphorylation refers to attaching a phosphate group to a protein and dephosphorylation refers to removing it. These processes are well-known for affecting the activity of an enzyme, although whether phosphorylation "activates" or "deactivates" an enzyme must be determined experimentally. Phosphorylation most commonly targets serine, threonine, and tyrosine, which all have –OH groups that a phosphate group can be attached to. Phosphorylation and dephosphorylation are catalyzed by kinases and phosphatases, respectively.

Glycosylation refers to the modification of enzymes (and, more generally, proteins) by carbohydrate moieties, with a broad range of effects that goes beyond the scope of the MCAT.

Finally, zymogens, also known as proenzymes, are inactive forms of enzymes that must be cleaved to become active. Zymogens can be recognized by the suffix –ogen, and common examples can be drawn from the digestive system. For example, trypsin is an enzyme involved in protein digestion that is released from the pancreas. To appreciate the importance of zymogens, consider what would happen if trypsin was secreted in its active form: the pancreas would digest itself! The secretion of zymogens followed by their cleavage into active enzymes at the physiologically appropriate time and location allows the tight regulation of processes that would be dangerous for the body if uncontrolled. This basic principle applies to other molecules as well, such as preprohormones that are cleaved to form prohormones, which are in turn cleaved to form hormones.

It can also sometimes be the case that an enzyme requires another chemical compound to be present in order for it to carry out its biological functionality. In general, such "helper" molecules are known as cofactors. Cofactors can be either inorganic (with some common examples including metal ions such as $Mg^{2+}$, $Zn^{2+}$, and $Cu^+$) or organic, and organic cofactors are sometimes known as coenzymes. Many coenzymes are vitamins or derivatives of vitamins, and they often contribute to the function of enzymes by carrying certain functional groups from one place to another in a reaction. Perhaps the most well-known example of this is coenzyme A, which transfers acyl groups from one place to another.

> > CONNECTIONS < <

Chapter 7 of Biology

Coenzymes that are tightly (or even covalently) bonded to their enzyme are known as prosthetic groups. A famous example of an organometallic prosthetic group is heme, which contains an iron ion in the center of a porphyrin ring, and is attached to oxygen-transport proteins such as hemoglobin and myoglobin.

Some additional terminology that you should be aware of has to do with whether a coenzyme/cofactor is present or not. A holoenzyme is an enzyme together with the coenzyme(s) and/or metal ions it needs to carry out its catalytic activity. In contrast, the term apoenzyme (or apoprotein) is used to refer to an enzyme without the coenzymes/cofactors it needs to function correctly.

# 6. Must-Knows

> Enzymes are biological catalysts. They lower the activation energy of a reaction, and affect rate, not equilibrium.
> Enzymes are absolutely crucial to biological function.
> Allosteric interactions occur at sites other than the active site.
> High-level enzyme classification:
  - Oxidoreductases catalyze oxidation/reduction reactions.
  - Transferases transfer a functional group between molecules.
  - Hydrolases catalyze hydrolysis.
  - Lyases cleave bonds through other mechanisms.
  - Isomerases catalyze isomerization.
  - Ligases join molecules with covalent bonds.
> Enzymes are often regulated by negative feedback, which works to maintain homeostasis. In negative feedback, the downstream product of a pathway inhibits upstream enzymes.
> Cooperativity: binding at the first active site facilitates binding at subsequent active sites.
  - Hemoglobin is a prototypical example, although it is not an enzyme.
> Michaelis-Menten kinetics:
  - Increasing substrate concentration increases reaction rate until saturation is reached.
  - $V_{max}$ is the maximum rate, and $K_m$ is the substrate concentration corresponding to half of $v_{max}$.
> Lineweaver-Burk plots are double-reciprocal transformations of Michaelis-Menten plots.
  - X-intercept is $-1/K_m$, y-intercept is $1/v_{max}$.
> Types of reversible inhibition
  - Competitive: inhibitor binds at active site; $v_{max}$ unchanged, $K_m$ increased.
  - Noncompetitive: inhibitor binds at allosteric site; $v_{max}$ decreased, $K_m$ unchanged.
  - Uncompetitive: inhibitor binds enzyme-substrate complex; $v_{max}$ decreased, $K_m$ decreased.
  - Mixed: inhibitor either binds free enzyme allosterically or enzyme-substrate complex; $v_{max}$ decreased, $K_m$ either increased or decreased

## Practice Passage

Both glucose and galactose enter glycolysis through a common intermediate, glucose-6-phosphate (G-6-P). Glucose is acted upon either by hexokinase or by one of its isoforms to yield G-6-P in a single step. The multi-step conversion of galactose to glucose-6-phosphate requires the action of several enzymes.

When cancer cells are forced to switch from glucose to galactose for metabolism, the cells exhibit moderately elevated lactic acid production, but similar growth rates. It has been hypothesized that tumor mitochondria are either defective or less able to compete with glycolytic enzymes for common intermediates. Nearly all imported hexoses enter glycolysis, but few are oxidatively phosphorylated. To investigate mitochondrial changes in tumor cells, three experiments were performed on cultured cells established from rat hepatoma cell lines.

*Experiment 1*

$^{14}C$-labeled hexose transport in hepatoma cells was measured for 30 minutes at physiological temperature and pH for $^{14}C$-glucose, $^{14}C$-galactose, and 3-O-methyl-$^{14}C$-glucose (a non-metabolized sugar derivative). Transport rates for the three sugars were found to be nearly identical. However, measurements made in a repeat experiment taken after 120 minutes showed glucose uptake exceeded galactose uptake 10 to 1.

*Experiment 2*

Hexokinase specific activity was determined for control rat liver homogenates, regenerating rat liver homogenates and hepatoma cells at various G-6-P concentrations. The glucose concentration for the hepatoma cells was 0.5 mM, while that for control and regenerating liver was 13 mM. The hexokinase activity of liver homogenate at 0.5 mM was negligible. Hexokinase activity was found to be approximately constant and elevated more than 20-fold in hepatoma cells versus activities found in both control and regenerating rat liver at G-6-P concentrations of up to 0.6 mM. Mutant versions of hexokinase were then produced and their kinetic profiles were determined (Table 1).

**Table 1**

| ENZYME | $K_M$ | $K_{CAT}$ |
|--------|-------|-----------|
| 48-R | 250 mM | $4.9×10^6$ |
| 986-S | 0.05 mM | $2.8×10^3$ |
| 13-I | 108 mM | $9.8×10^4$ |
| 56-J | 60 mM | $1.5×10^5$ |

*Experiment 3*

Mitochondrial respiration rates in isolated hepatoma cells were measured using an oxygen electron in a closed container. Increased glucose significantly stimulated the respiration of coupled hepatoma mitochondria, a result that should be obtained only if the hexokinase reaction consumed mitochondria-synthesized ATP. Glucose-stimulated respiration of hepatoma cells was found to lack inhibition by G-6-P up to 0.6 mM. However, when added, glucose was unable to stimulate respiration of mitochondria from control and regenerating rat liver.

1. SGLT proteins found in the plasma membrane of the same cells import glucose against its concentration from the tubular filtrate into the cell while exporting sodium down its concentration gradient. This is an example of which form of solute transport?
    A. Primary active transport

B. Symport

C. Secondary active transport

D. Facilitated diffusion

2. A test of the respiratory response by regenerating rat liver to glucose stimulation was most likely included in Experiment 3 in order to:

A. determine whether high activity levels of mitochondria-bound hexokinase are present in the neoplastic state.

B. show that enhanced hexokinase response to glucose in hepatoma cells is not a property of the tissue of origin.

C. test whether glucose-stimulated hexokinase activity is also a function of rapidly dividing normal liver cells.

D. demonstrate that glucose is unable to stimulate the respiration of control rat liver.

3. Which of the following, if true, would most strongly challenge a conclusion from the experiments presented in the passage?

A. Transport rates of $^{14}C$-ribose exceed those of $^{14}C$-glucose or $^{14}C$-galactose.

B. Tumor mitochondria, when included in samples of normal mitochondria, significantly increase oxygen consumption due to their own basal rate of respiration.

C. Non-specific trapping of hexoses equally decreases the real hexose transport rate for both glucose and galactose versus that which was measured spectrophotometrically.

D. Enzyme activity measured in control and regenerating rat liver is exerted by the enzyme glucokinase.

4. Glucokinase regulatory protein (GKPR) is a fully competitive inhibitor of glucokinase. According to the Michaelis-Menten description of enzyme kinetics, what effect does the presence of GKPR have on the glucokinase kinetics?

A. $K_m$ increases and $V_{max}$ is unchanged

B. $K_m$ decreases and $V_{max}$ is unchanged

C. $K_m$ is unchanged and $V_{max}$ increases

D. $K_m$ is unchanged and $V_{max}$ decreases

5. If the complete oxidation of glucose to carbon dioxide and water has a $\Delta G° = $ -686 kcal/mol, what is the free energy change of the catalyzed glycolysis and Krebs cycle reactions that complete this process *in vivo*?

A. -750 kcal/mol

B. -686 kcal/mol

C. 0 kcal/mol

D. +686 kcal/mol

6. Researchers have developed a new anti-cancer drug, thought to be an uncompetitive inhibitor of hexokinase. When will this drug have the strongest effect on tumorigenesis?

A. High [glucose] and low [galactose]

B. Low [glucose] and low [galactose]

C. High [glucose] and high [galactose]

D. Low [glucose] and high [galactose]

7. Which of the tested enzymes is the most efficient at converting glucose into G-6-P?

A. 48-R

B. 986-S

C. 13-I

D. 56-J

## Practice Passage Explanations

Both glucose and galactose enter glycolysis through a common intermediate, glucose-6-phosphate (G-6-P). Glucose is acted upon either by hexokinase or by one of its isoforms to yield G-6-P in a single step. The multi-step conversion of galactose to glucose-6-phosphate requires the action of several enzymes.

*Key terms: glucose, galactose, glucose-6-phosphate (G-6-P), hexokinase*

*Cause and effect: glucose/galactose both enter glycolysis as G-6-P; glucose = 1 enzyme, galac = multi-step*

When cancer cells are forced to switch from glucose to galactose for metabolism, the cells exhibit moderately elevated lactic acid production, but similar growth rates. It has been hypothesized that tumor mitochondria are either defective or less able to compete with glycolytic enzymes for common intermediates. Nearly all imported hexoses enter glycolysis, but few are oxidatively phosphorylated. To investigate mitochondrial changes in tumor cells, three experiments were performed on cultured cells established from rat hepatoma cell lines.

*Key terms: lactic acid, hepatoma cells, mitochondria, anaerobic*

*Cause and effect: cancer cells switch glucose to galactose → ↑ lactic acid, similar growth; mito dysfunction or inability to outcompete glycolytic enzymes for common intermediates may be responsible*

*Experiment 1*

$^{14}$C-labeled hexose transport in hepatoma cells was measured for 30 minutes at physiological temperature and pH for $^{14}$C-glucose, $^{14}$C-galactose, and 3-O-methyl-$^{14}$C-glucose (a non-metabolized sugar derivative). Transport rates for the three sugars were found to be nearly identical. However, measurements made in a repeat experiment taken after 120 minutes showed glucose uptake exceeded galactose uptake 10 to 1.

*Key terms: $^{14}$C-labeled sugars, transport rates*

*Cause and effect: 30 min → $^{14}$C labeled hexoses were approximately equal; 120 min → glucose/galactose = 10*

*Experiment 2*

Hexokinase specific activity was determined for control rat liver homogenates, regenerating rat liver homogenates and hepatoma cells at various G-6-P concentrations. The glucose concentration for the hepatoma cells was 0.5 mM, while that for control and regenerating liver was 13 mM. The hexokinase activity of liver homogenate at 0.5 mM was negligible. Hexokinase activity was found to be approximately constant and elevated more than 20-fold in hepatoma cells versus activities found in both control and regenerating rat liver at G-6-P concentrations of up to 0.6 mM. Mutant versions of hexokinase were then produced and their kinetic profiles were determined (Table 1).

*Key terms: hexokinase activity, liver homogenates*

*Cause and effect: hexokinase at varied [G-6-P] → HK activity at [G-6-P] ≤ 0.6 mM was elevated 20-fold compared to control and regenerating liver samples*

**Table 1**

| ENZYME | $K_M$ | $K_{CAT}$ |
|--------|-------|-----------|
| 48-R | 250 mM | $4.9 \times 10^6$ |
| 986-S | 0.05 mM | $2.8 \times 10^3$ |
| 13-I | 108 mM | $9.8 \times 10^4$ |
| 56-J | 60 mM | $1.5 \times 10^5$ |

*Experiment 3*

Mitochondrial respiration rates in isolated hepatoma cells were measured using an oxygen electron in a closed container. Increased glucose significantly stimulated the respiration of coupled hepatoma mitochondria, a result that should be obtained only if the hexokinase reaction consumed mitochondria-synthesized ATP. Glucose-stimulated respiration of hepatoma cells was found to lack inhibition by G-6-P up to 0.6 mM. However, when added, glucose was unable to stimulate respiration of mitochondria from control and regenerating rat liver.

*Cause and effect: more glucose stimulated respiration in the coupled mitochondria because the hexokinase reaction consumed mitochondria-synthesized ATP; this process was inhibited by G-6-P; glucose unable to ↑respiration of mitochondria in control and regenerating rat liver, but ↑ in cancer; this indicates coupling of glycolysis and mitochondrial aerobic respiration*

1.  C is correct. Secondary active transport (co-transport) requires the input of energy to transport molecules across a membrane, but unlike in primary active transport, there is no direct coupling of ATP. The electrochemical potential difference created by pumping ions from the cell via primary active transport, thereby establishing a concentration gradient, is allows a molecule to flow down its concentration gradient.
    A, B, D: SGLT proteins are specifically an example of secondary active transport antiport, in which two species are pumped in opposite directions across a membrane and down their concentration gradient. In the proximal tubule cells of the nephron, the $Na^+/K^+$ ATPase establishes the $Na^+$ gradient used in antiport via primary active transport. In symport, both molecules are transported across a membrane in the same direction. Facilitated diffusion is the passive transport of solute down a concentration gradient through specific transmembrane protein channels.

2.  C is correct. The tests in Experiment 3 determined that hexokinases of hepatoma cells are coupled to the oxidative phosphorylation system of mitochondria, and that this coupling is characteristic of cells in the neoplastic (cancer) state. The inclusion of regenerating rat liver was intended as a control to show that this coupling is exclusively present in neoplastic cells.
    A, B, D: The inclusion of tumor mitochondria in Experiment 3 was intended to demonstrate Choice A. Testing the mitochondrial respiratory response of normal liver tissue was more specifically intended to test the statements made in choices B and D.

3.  B is correct. Experiment 3 demonstrates that oxygen consumption in the presence of glucose is increased in tumor mitochondria, but not in normal mitochondria. If that increase in oxygen consumption is due to basal levels of tumor mitochondrial respiration and not oxygen stimulation, then the finding that glycolysis and mitochondrial oxidative phosphorylation are coupled would be challenged.
    A, C, D: Experiment 1 tests and subsequently makes a claim regarding only the rate of hexose transport—ribose is a pentose sugar (choice A). Non-specific hexose trapping would decrease the measured transport rate for both glucose and galactose and not impact the validity of the claim made in Experiment 1 regarding their equal transport rates (choice C). If the levels of enzyme activity measured in control and regenerating rat liver, which are assumed in Experiment 2 to be due to hexokinase activity, are found to be due to glucokinase, rather than hexokinase, then the

claim made in 2 that the rate of hexokinase activity in tumor mitochondria is 20 times greater than in control and regenerating rat liver would represent a slight underestimate of the magnitude of the activity difference. However, the fundamental relationship between the activity levels would still be supported (choice D).

4. A is correct. Competitive inhibitors compete with substrate for the active site of enzymes. $V_{max}$ for such reactions is unchanged because at high [S], there is sufficient substrate to outcompete the inhibitor for the active site. At non-saturating [S] concentrations, competitive inhibitors interfere with the substrates ability to find and bind with the active site. This causes an increased $K_m$ value.

5. B is correct. While enzymes lower the activation energy and speed up reaction, they do not change the initial or final products and thus, cannot change the overall thermodynamics of a reaction.

6. C is correct. Uncompetitive inhibitors wait until the enzyme and substrate bind together to form the ES complex before they attach and inhibit the reaction. This reduction in the effective concentration of the ES complex increases the enzyme's apparent affinity for the substrate via Le Chatelier's principle ($\downarrow K_m$) and decreases the maximum enzyme activity ($\downarrow V_{max}$), as it takes longer for the substrate/product to leave the active site. As a result, uncompetitive inhibition works best when substrate concentration is high.

7. B is correct. For test day, we should know that the specificity constant (i.e. kinetic efficiency, $k_{cat}/K_m$) is a measure of how efficiently an enzyme converts substrates into products.
   A. Efficiency = $4.9 \times 10^6$ / 250 = 500/250 $\times 10^4$ = $2 \times 10^4$
   B. Efficiency = $2.8 \times 10^3$ / 0.05 = $3 \times 10^3 / 5 \times 10^{-2}$ = $0.6 \times 10^5$ = $6 \times 10^4$
   C. Efficiency = $9.9 \times 10^4$ / 108 = $1 \times 10^5 / 100$ = $1 \times 10^3$
   D. Efficiency = $1.5 \times 10^5$ / 60 = 15/60 $\times 10^4$ = $0.25 \times 10^4$ = $2.5 \times 10^3$

# Independent Questions

1. Which of the following is most likely true of an enzyme with a Hill coefficient of 2.8?
   A. It exhibits negative cooperativity.
   B. It is monomeric.
   C. A graph of its saturation versus substrate concentration is linear.
   D. It binds its second substrate molecule significantly more readily than its first.

2. The first step of glycolysis involves the phosphorylation of glucose by the enzyme hexokinase. This step requires the presence of magnesium cations. In this context, magnesium acts as a:
   A. cofactor.
   B. coenzyme.
   C. prosthetic group.
   D. apoenzyme.

3. An enzyme is subjected to an inhibitor with an unknown mechanism. Upon graphing the Lineweaver-Burk plots of the inhibited and uninhibited enzymes, researchers notice that the two plots share an x-intercept. The unknown inhibitor is most likely:
   A. competitive.
   B. noncompetitive.
   C. uncompetitive.
   D. either noncompetitive or uncompetitive.

4. Which type of inhibitor binds only to the enzyme-substrate complex, and how does this form of inhibition affect the kinetics of the enzyme in question?
   A. Uncompetitive; both $K_m$ and $V_{max}$ are reduced.
   B. Competitive; $K_m$ is reduced, while $V_{max}$ is not changed.
   C. Noncompetitive; $V_{max}$ is reduced, while $K_m$ is not changed.
   D. Uncompetitive; $V_{max}$ is reduced, while $K_m$ is not changed.

5. A biological molecule that catalyzes the transfer of a phosphate group onto its substrate is classified as which type of enzyme?
   A. Transferase
   B. Ligase
   C. Phosphatase
   D. Kinase

6. An allosteric enzyme changes its conformation when it binds an effector molecule at a site distinct from its active site. These enzymes are most likely to be prevalent in which pathways?
   A. Digestive pathways
   B. Metabolic regulatory pathways
   C. Feedback loops
   D. Cell growth and division pathways

7. A kinase is observed to act on a certain tetrapeptide. Of the following, which is most likely to represent the primary structure of this tetrapeptide?
   A. DEKH
   B. SYTF
   C. AGVL
   D. MCCI

8. Grapefruit juice is often listed as a contraindication for individuals on statins. This is the result of multiple studies that have shown that components of grapefruit juice covalently bind one or more enzymes involved in statin metabolism. Which of the following best describes this supposed "grapefruit juice effect"?
   A. Components of grapefruit juice inhibit the enzyme(s), thus increasing the bioavailability of the statin.
   B. Components of grapefruit juice inhibit the enzyme(s), thus decreasing the bioavailability of the statin.
   C. Components of grapefruit juice activate the enzyme(s), thus increasing the bioavailability of the statin.
   D. Components of grapefruit juice cleave the enzyme(s) from their precursors, which activates them.

## Independent Question Explanations

1. D is correct. A Hill coefficient greater than 1 reflects positive cooperativity (eliminating A), meaning that binding at one position or active site causes binding to take place more easily at the remaining active sites. The most famous example of positive cooperativity occurs in hemoglobin. Note that monomeric proteins contain only one subunit; since enzymes must contain multiple active sites or binding positions to display any form of cooperativity, it is more likely that the enzyme referenced in the question stem contains multiple subunits (eliminating B). Additionally, a graph of saturation versus substrate concentration for an enzyme that displays positive cooperativity would be sigmoidal, or S-shaped, not linear (eliminating C).

2. A is correct. Magnesium is a necessary cofactor for hexokinase. In fact, metal ions are very common examples of cofactors. The term "coenzyme" specifically refers to organic cofactors, and magnesium is inorganic (eliminate choice B). Prosthetic groups are cofactors that are tightly bonded to their enzymes, which is not the case here (eliminate choice C). Finally, "apoenzyme" refers to an enzyme without its required cofactor(s), making choice D incorrect as well.

3. B is correct. On a Lineweaver-Burk plot, the x-intercept represents $-1/K_m$. If the inhibited and uninhibited plots have the same x-intercept, they must also have the same $K_m$. Noncompetitive inhibitors do not alter $K_m$, so the unknown inhibitor is most likely noncompetitive. Competitive inhibitors increase $K_m$, while uncompetitive inhibitors decrease it.

4. A is correct. An uncompetitive inhibitor is an inhibitor of the enzyme-substrate (E-S) complex. This reduces the ability for the enzyme to catalyze the reaction, lowering $V_{max}$. Simultaneously, however, it seemingly increases the enzyme's affinity for its substrate, as E-S complexes are removed via inhibition. Thus, uncompetitive inhibition also reduces $K_m$. Also note that answer choice B gives the wrong relationship between competitive inhibition and $K_m/V_{max}$. In competitive inhibition km is increased.

5. D is correct. Kinases are responsible for transferring a high-energy phosphate group from a donor molecule (typically ATP) to the substrate. This reaction produces ADP along with the phosphorylated substrate molecule. Phosphatases do the opposite of this; they remove phosphate groups from their substrates (eliminating C). Ligases are enzymes that are responsible for binding together two smaller components (eliminating B). Finally, transferases transfer functional groups from one molecule to another, but kinase is a more specific answer here (eliminating A).

6. C is correct. While allosteric enzymes can play roles in each of the mentioned pathways, they are particularly important in feedback loops. Downstream products often inhibit an enzyme in an earlier step to prevent overproduction of the final product; this is seen in the production of serotonin, for example.

7. B is correct. Kinases phosphorylate their substrates. The amino acids most likely to become phosphorylated are those which contain an -OH group on their side chains. Specifically, these are serine (S), threonine (T), and tyrosine (Y), all of which are listed in choice B. None of the other choices contain any of these amino acids.

8. A is correct. Bergamottin, a component in grapefruit juice, covalently binds enzyme CYP3A4, which is responsible for metabolizing certain statins. This inhibits the enzyme and increases the systemic concentration of the statin, which can be dangerous. Choices B and C do not make sense, as the enzyme is described as playing a role in statin metabolism (breakdown). Thus, inhibiting the enzyme would *increase* statin bioavailability, while activating it would cause the statin to be broken down more rapidly and exhibit lower bioavailability. Nowhere is it indicated that the enzyme in question has a zymogen precursor, nor is it stated that the components of grapefruit juice lead to any cleavage.

# Non-Enzymatic Protein Functions

## CHAPTER 4

## 0. Introduction

Although enzymes are one of the most important classes of proteins, because enzyme function is crucial to life, proteins play a wide range of other roles throughout the body. In fact, since most biomolecules are relatively inert, proteins are responsible for most functional roles within the body; that is, whenever "stuff" is bumping up against and affecting other "stuff" in the body, it's a good bet that proteins are involved somehow. Much like the term "genome" refers to the set of genes in an organism, you may encounter the term "proteome," which refers to the range of proteins that a given cell or cell type expresses. The proteome is a way of capturing a cell's spectrum of activity, since it incorporates most of the functional components within a cell.

In this chapter, we will describe cytoskeletal proteins, followed by a discussion of motor proteins. We'll then step outside of the domain of individual cells to discuss proteins in the immune system, and then finally review their function in cell adhesion and biosignaling. This chapter covers a wider range of topics than the other chapters dealing with proteins in this textbook, but it is nonetheless important, both because it contains testable details and because the material in this chapter helps build important bridges between the physiological topics discussed in the Biology textbook and the more nitty-gritty biochemistry discussed in this textbook.

> ### MCAT STRATEGY > > >
>
> A recurring theme in studying biochemistry (and MCAT content more generally) is that it is often helpful to ask yourself how something actually *works* on a fundamental level. Many of the topics discussed in this chapter help explain how commonly-discussed biological phenomena work mechanically, so paying careful attention to the material in this chapter will help you take your biology knowledge to the next level.

## 1. Cytoskeletal Proteins

It can sometimes be easy to skip over the cytoskeleton when studying cellular biology, but the cytoskeleton plays a fundamental role in a range of biological processes. For this reason, the MCAT expects you to be familiar with the most important proteins that contribute to these functions.

Polymers of actin and tubulin constitute a significant portion of the cytoskeletal system, which provides the cell with its definitive shape and resistance to deformational force. The three principal types of protein filaments found in the cytoskeleton are microfilaments, microtubules, and intermediate filaments. Accessory proteins can regulate the function of the cytoskeletal system by binding to these three types of filamentous proteins.

Actin microfilaments in the cytoplasm are formed by the polymerization of G (globular) actin monomers into F-actin polymers in an ATP-dependent fashion. Microfilaments are composed of two strands of actin polymers, and play a role in cell motility (or movement), as well as endocytosis and exocytosis. Additionally, microfilaments contribute to the process of cell cleavage during division and to the ability of cells to contract. The actin components of microfilaments also interact with myosin as part of muscle contraction.

Intermediate filaments, as the name suggests, are intermediate in diameter between microfilaments and microtubules. They are a diverse family of proteins that provide structural support and are involved in cell-cell adhesion processes. Most intermediate filaments within the cell are located in the cytosol between the nuclear envelope and plasma membrane, allowing them to provide structural stability within the cytoplasm. They are formed by alpha-helical rod-like protein subunits with globular terminal domains. Keratin, which makes up our hair and nails, is a well-known example of an intermediate filament outside of the cell.

Microtubules are hollow cylinders composed of polymeric dimers of proteins known as alpha-tubulin and beta-tubulin. They are involved in the movement of chromosomes during cell division, in intracellular transport, in neutrophil and amoeboid motility, and in the formation of cilia and flagella. Microtubule formation is initiated at and organized in microtubule organizing centers (MTOCs). Common MTOCs include the centrosome and the basal bodies found in cilia and flagella. These MTOCs may or may not possess centrioles. The building blocks of microtubules are alpha- and beta-tubulin dimers, which polymerize end-to-end in protofilaments in a GTP-dependent process. Thirteen protofilaments bind laterally, forming a single microfilament structure that may be lengthened by the binding of additional protofilaments. In order for polymerization to occur, dimers must be present at a concentration at least equal to a minimum value that is known as the critical concentration.

> > CONNECTIONS < <

Chapter 2 in Biology

> > CONNECTIONS < <

Chapter 12 in Biology

MCAT STRATEGY > > >

Actin and keratin are the most important examples of microfilaments and intermediate filaments, respectively; however, you should be sure not just to know what category of protein they fall under, but also be sure to understand their function. Although you could get a question on Test Day testing the content in this section directly, it is more likely that the structural classification of actin and keratin would be folded into a larger context in which their function would be relevant.

**Figure 1.** Microfilaments, intermediate filaments, and microtubules.

## 2. Motor Proteins

Motor proteins, such as kinesin, dynein, and myosin, are structural proteins that generate mechanical force as a result of undergoing conformational changes. They play a major role in sperm motility, the movement of unicellular organisms, intercellular transport mechanisms, and in generating force during muscular contraction.

Kinesins are a class of ATPase motor proteins that are able to travel along the length of microtubule filaments. The hydrolysis of ATP provides the power required for them to move. Kinesin movement is closely associated with mitosis and meiosis, as well as the transport of cellular cargo, such as during axonal transport in neurons. Structurally, kinesins are heterotetramers, in which the motor domain subunits form a protein-protein dimer that binds two light chains. Each motor subunit contains a head that has separate binding sites for ATP and for a microtubule. The binding and hydrolysis of ATP, as well as the release of ADP, cause a conformational change in the microtubule-binding domains and the orientation of the other domains of the kinesin, resulting in unidirectional motion of the protein. Most kinesins transport cargo toward the periphery of the cell by "walking" towards the plus (+) end of a microtubule, which is referred to as anterograde transport.

In contrast, dyneins are motor proteins that carry cargo and "walk" toward the minus (–) end of a microtubule, which is usually oriented towards the center of the cell, in a form of transport referred to as retrograde transport. Dyneins fall into two groups: axonemal and cytoplasmic dyneins. Axonemal dyneins are also sometimes referred to as ciliary or flagellar dyneins, and they cause some sliding of the microtubules found in the structures of cilia and flagella. In contrast, cytoplasmic dyneins move progressively along a microtubule such that one stalk—a structural element connecting the globular head of a dynein to the microtubule along which it moves—is always attached to a microtubule. The functions of dyneins include transporting cellular cargo between vesicles, moving chromosomes and mitotic spindles during cell division, and transporting vesicles and organelles along neuronal axons toward the cell body in a process known as retrograde axoplasmic transport.

**Figure 2.** Kinesins and dyneins.

Myosins are another important molecular motor protein family of ATPases. They play a central role in actin-based muscular contraction in muscle, as well as in a wide range of other eukaryotic motility processes. Most myosin molecules contain head, neck, and tail domains. The head domains bind the actin of microfilaments and hydrolyze ATP to generate force and induce the movement of the protein along filaments, generally toward the so-called barbed (+) end. During skeletal muscle contraction, multiple myosin II molecules create force by a power stroke mechanism that makes use of the energy released by ATP hydrolysis. The power stroke mechanism is described in greater detail in Chapter 12 of the Biology textbook, but briefly, the power stroke occurs when myosin is tightly bound to actin. When inorganic phosphate is released from myosin following ATP hydrolysis, a conformational change occurs wherein actin is pulled toward myosin. The actin will remain attached until the subsequent binding of an ATP molecule triggers its release.

## MCAT STRATEGY > > >

The fact that kinesins, dyneins, and myosins are motor proteins can be remembered in a fairly straightforward way through their names. You can associate kinesins with kinetic energy, dyneins with being dynamic, and myosins with the motion of muscles (either because both *motion* and *muscle* also start with *m*, or because the prefix 'myo' is often used to describe phenomena related to muscles).

## Actin-myosin filaments

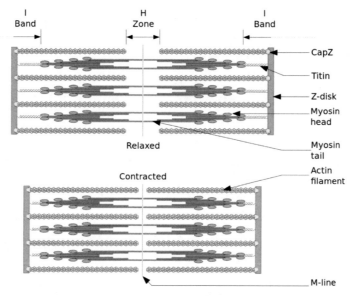

**Figure 3.** Actin and myosin mechanism.

## 3. Immune System

The immune system is a complex physiological system that protects the body from external threats, such as microbes. It is discussed in more depth in Chapter 11 of the Biology textbook, but in the context of biochemistry, it's important to note some of the specific roles played by proteins in the immune system.

> > **CONNECTIONS** < <

Chapter 12 of Biology

In particular, the adaptive immune system contains protein components known as antibodies, which are produced by the humoral subdivision of the immune system. As a review, the main function of antibodies is to bind with antigens, which are typically foreign objects that the body has targeted for elimination (although under some circumstances, elements of one's own body can serve as antigens, which is particularly common in autoimmune diseases). Antibody-antigen bonding triggers the immediate neutralization of the antigenic pathogen or toxin, the agglutination (precipitation) and phagocytosis of the antigen-antibody complex, or the opsonization (marking) of the pathogen for destruction by leukocytes.

> > **CONNECTIONS** < <

Chapter 11 of Biology

Antibodies are glycoproteins, and belong to the immunoglobulin superfamily. They irreversibly bind targets for which they are specific, with very high affinity. Each antibody contains a highly variable region where binding occurs that is specific for an epitope on an antigen (the term 'epitope' refers to the binding site on the antigen itself). This region of the antibody is known as the hypervariable region, and it allows for millions of antibodies with slightly different antigenic specificity to be produced. The enormous diversity of the hypervariable region is generated by random recombination and mutation of the gene segments encoding antigen-binding sites.

Antibodies can be found either extracellularly, in their soluble form, or anchored to mature B cells (also known as plasma cells), from which they are secreted. In its membrane-bound form attached to the surface of a B cell, an antibody is known as a B cell receptor (BCR). The basic unit of an antibody is an immunoglobulin (Ig) monomer containing a single Y-shaped Ig unit, but antibodies can be secreted as dimers (with two Ig units), tetramers (with four Ig units), or pentamers (with five Ig units). Each Ig unit is composed of two heavy chains and two light chains. The heavy chains correspond to the vertical component of the Y shape of the Ig unit and extend into the diagonal region, whereas the light chains are present only in the uppermost, diagonal part of the Y shape. Each heavy chain has two regions: the constant region, which is identical in all antibodies and contains a flexible hinge region, and a variable region, which differs in antibodies produced by different B cells, but is the same for all antibodies produced by a single B cell or its clone. Each heavy chain tends to weigh approximately 50 kDa, while light chains tend to weigh approximately 25 kDa apiece.

The structure of a single Ig unit is shown below in Figure 4, while Figure 5 shows some of the arrangements of Ig proteins that are present in different antibody types in the human immune system.

## MCAT STRATEGY > > >

It can be difficult to prioritize all the various pieces of information about antibodies. In descending order, here are the points to prioritize: (1) anti*bodies* are generated by your *body*, while antigens are protein motifs from outside the body (or, in the case of autoimmune diseases, from inside the body) that they target; (2) antibodies have a heavy chain and a light chain; and (3) the hypervariable region of antibodies is what allows them to be specific for a bewilderingly diverse range of antigens.

**Figure 4.** Antibody structure.

Monomer
IgD, IgE, IgG

Dimer
IgA

Pentamer
IgM

**Figure 5.** Antibodies in the human body.

Different antibodies contain different types of heavy chains and can be categorized accordingly. These different classes of antibodies, known as isotypes, play distinct roles in antigenic recognition and response as part of the immune system. For the MCAT, you should be generally aware of the different types of antibodies present in the human body and their main functions, as summarized below:

> IgA: Present in mucosal areas, such as the gut, respiratory tract, saliva, tears, breast milk, and the urogenital tract; it helps prevent colonization by pathogens.

> IgD: Principally acts as an antigen receptor on B cells that have not been exposed to antigens; it is involved in the activation of mast cells and basophils.

> IgE: Involved in allergies and anti-parasitic responses; IgE binds to allergens, causing histamine release from activated mast cells and basophils.

> IgG: Four forms of IgG provide most of the humoral immune response; it is the only antibody type that is capable of crossing the placenta and conferring passive immunity to a developing fetus.

> IgM: Responsible for mounting an immune response and eliminating pathogens in the early stages of the humoral response, before IgG levels increase; it is expressed on the surface of B cells as a monomer and is secreted by plasma cells as a pentamer.

Antibody diversity is further enhanced beyond differences in the hypervariable region by a process known as class switching. In class switching, antibody genes rearrange to modify the heavy chain of an antibody, thereby creating a different antibody that still retains the original antigen-specific variable region. Class switching enables a single hypervariable region specific for a particular epitope to rearrange in several different ways during the humoral immune response.

## CLINICAL CONNECTIONS > > >

The fact that IgM antibodies are secreted early in the immune response means that for some diseases, such as viral hepatitis, they can be used as a biomarker of an acute infection, as compared to a chronic infection that would be indicated by the presence of IgG antibodies.

The immune system is one of the most complicated systems in the body. As discussed in Chapter 11 of the Biology textbook, it can be very challenging to keep track of all of the terminology associated with the immune system, both because of the inherent complexity of the system and because our understanding of immunology has continually advanced over the last hundred years, meaning that many exceptions and complications have been discovered for what initially seemed like clear-cut classifications. (A classic example of this is that humoral immunity—as contrasted with cell-based immunity—is mediated by B cells). For the MCAT, however, your task is to master the fundamentals. In the context of studying antibodies in biochemistry (as compared to the physiological context of Chapter 11 in the Biology textbook), focus on understanding how antibodies are structured, how their structure contributes to their function, and being aware of the major different types.

# 4. Cell Adhesion

Another important non-enzymatic function of proteins is cell adhesion. In many presentations of human anatomy and physiology, it can be easy to overlook the basic question of how cells fit together and stay where they're supposed to be in the body, but in reality, cell adhesion processes both contribute to the functional stability of our bodies and to some important signaling processes. The molecules responsible for cell adhesion are known as cell adhesion molecules (CAMs). CAMs are associated with cytoskeletal elements, but also play the additional role of anchoring cells to one another and to the extracellular matrix (ECM). Adhesion molecules are often classified into three groups: selectins, cadherins, and integrins.

## MCAT STRATEGY > > >

This is one of those all-too-rare moments where the nomenclature can help you remember which is which: L-selectin is expressed in lymphocytes, P-selectin is expressed in platelets, and E-selectin is expressed in endothelial cells.

Selectins are a class of CAMs involved in the inflammatory response. Three types of selectins are found in humans: L-selectin, P-selectin, and E-selectin. L-selectin is expressed in lymphocytes, monocytes, and neutrophils. P-selectin is expressed in platelets and mediates their interaction with the endothelium of blood vessels, which express E-selectin.

Cadherins are calcium-dependent CAMs that play a role in the early stages of growth and development and can bind to the microfilaments of the cell's cytoplasm. They are typically expressed in cell-specific forms by different cells. They are transmembrane proteins, with a small cytoplasmic component that interfaces with the cell's microfilaments and a membrane-spanning region; the bulk of cadherins are located outside of the cell. Cadherins also form junctions known as adherens junctions. Adherens junctions help link cells to each other within tissues, and are technically defined by having a cytoplasmic side that is linked to actin filaments in the cytoskeleton of a cell.

Finally, integrins are a large family of transmembrane proteins that act both as adhesion molecules and as signaling molecules. You can think of them as *integrating* the functions of cell adhesion and biosignaling. The signaling functions of integrins are quite diverse and are the subject of ongoing research, but the details go beyond the scope of the MCAT.

There are three main types of cell junctions that you should be aware of: anchoring junctions, gap junctions, and tight junctions.

Anchoring junctions include the adherens junctions we mentioned above, which are associated with cadherins. The essential idea behind anchoring junctions is that they connect cytoskeletal components of the cell with other cells and/or the extracellular matrix, thereby contributing to the overall structural stability of tissues. As mentioned, adherens junctions involve cadherin-mediated connections between actin filaments and other cells and the extracellular matrix. Desmosomes also involve cadherin, but in this case cadherin connects intermediate filaments to other cells. Hemidesmosomes are junctions in which integrins connect the intermediate filaments of cells to the extracellular matrix.

Gap junctions are formed by connexin proteins, which connect cells in a way such that diffusion can take place between them, enabling communication, without involving direct contact between the cytoplasmic fluids of each cell. Gap junctions are relatively less common, but they play certain crucial roles within the body. The most important example for the MCAT is in cardiac muscle, where gap junctions allow cells to contract at the same time.

Finally, tight junctions are found in epithelial cells. As the name suggests, the cells in tight junctions are linked very closely to each other, preventing solutes from being able to move freely from one tissue into another. A classic example is the blood-brain barrier, where the epithelial cells in blood vessels in the brain form very tight junctions that allow the very close regulation of which substances from the bloodstream can enter the central nervous system. Among other substances, the blood-brain barrier blocks the diffusion of most drugs into the brain, which poses serious problems for researchers who are trying to develop drugs targeting neurological diseases. Some types of epithelial tissue have relatively few tight junction; these are known as leaky epithelia. Examples include some parts of the kidney. Moreover, tight junctions are fairly complex structurally, involving several different types of proteins. The details of the structure of tight junctions and of the distribution of leaky epithelia in the body go beyond the scope of the MCAT, but you should automatically associate tight junctions with epithelial cells and know that the blood-brain barrier is an example.

## 5. Biosignaling

The final non-enzymatic protein function that is important to review for the MCAT is biosignaling. This topic is closely connected with material from the nervous system and endocrine system, so you may find it helpful to quickly review the corresponding chapters from the Biology textbook before studying this section. Disordered signaling mechanisms are implicated in developmental disorders and diseases such as cancer, autoimmune disorders, and diabetes; for this reason, signaling mechanisms are the focus of intense ongoing biomedical research and may appear in passages on the MCAT.

As discussed in Chapter 7 of the Biology textbook on the endocrine system, cellular signaling mechanisms can be described using a potentially confusing set of terms that all end in '*–crine*': intracrine, autocrine, juxtacrine, paracrine, and endocrine. The difference between these terms essentially relates to the distance involved in the signaling process. Intracrine signals are produced by the target cell and stay within the target cell. Autocrine signals also are produced by and effect the same target cell, but they are secreted and affect the cell secreting the signal via its own receptors. Juxtacrine signals target cells in contact with the signaling cells. Paracrine signals target cells in the general vicinity of the cell that emits the signal, whereas endocrine signaling involves signaling molecules that travel through the circulatory system to reach their target cells.

> > **CONNECTIONS** < <

Chapters 6 and 7 of Biology

Signaling molecules are quite diverse. Three major functional categories exist: hormones, cytokines (signaling molecules of the immune system), and neurotransmitters. Structurally speaking, signaling molecules can belong to several chemical classes, including lipids, phospholipids, amino acids, proteins, glycoproteins, and gases (nitric oxide and carbon monoxide). Signaling molecules are discussed in more detail elsewhere in this textbook and the Biology textbook; in this section, we will primarily focus on the cellular machinery that allows cells to respond to signals that are received.

> > **CONNECTIONS** < <

Chapters 6, 7, and 11 of Biology and Chapter 9 of Biochemistry

The effects of signaling molecules on cells are mediated by receptors, which are pieces of protein machinery that can be thought of as "translating" the signal molecule into action. Receptors can be broadly divided into membrane receptors and nuclear receptors, depending on their location within the cell. In turn, membrane receptors can be divided into ion channel-linked receptors, enzyme-linked receptors, and G protein-coupled receptors.

Ion channel-linked receptors, also called ligand-gated ion channels, are cell membrane-bound receptors that act through synaptic signaling on electrically excitable cells. These membrane-spanning proteins undergo a conformational change when a ligand binds to them, such that a transmembrane pore is opened to allow the passage of a specific molecule. The ligands to which the receptor binds can be neurotransmitters or peptide hormones, and the molecules that pass through are often ions, such as sodium or potassium, which can alter the charge across the membranes. The ion channels, or pores, are opened only for a short time, after which the ligand dissociates from the receptor, making the receptor available for a new ligand to bind. Figure 6 shows a simple schematic of how ion channel-linked receptors function, where the triangles represent ligands and the ions are represented by circles.

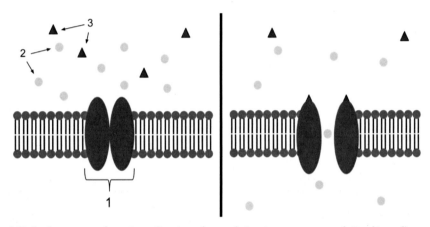

**Figure 6.** Ion channel-linked receptor function. (1 = ion channel; 2 = ion transported; 3 = ligand)

Enzyme-linked receptors are either enzymes themselves, or are directly associated with the enzymes that they activate. They are usually single-pass transmembrane receptors, with the enzymatic portion of the receptor being intracellular. The majority of enzyme-linked receptors are either protein kinases themselves or are associated with protein kinases. One prominent class of enzyme-linked receptors are receptor tyrosine kinases (RTKs), which are high-affinity cell surface receptors for many polypeptide growth factors and hormones, such as epidermal growth factor (EGF), platelet-derived growth factor (PDGF), and fibroblast growth factor (FGF). These receptors have been shown to be key regulators of normal cellular processes, while dysfunctions in RTKs have been implicated in the progression of many types of cancer.

Figure 7 shows the basic mechanism of how enzyme-linked receptors work. In the case of RTKs, extracellular ligand binding will typically cause or stabilize the dimerization of adjacent RTK monomers. This allows a tyrosine in the cytoplasmic portion of each receptor monomer to be trans-phosphorylated by its partner

## CLINICAL CONNECTIONS > > >

The development of drugs targeting tyrosine kinase receptors was a major leap forward in cancer therapy. In particular, the development of a drug known as imatinib, which received FDA approval in 2001, revolutionized the treatment of chronic myelogenous leukemia (CML).

receptor.

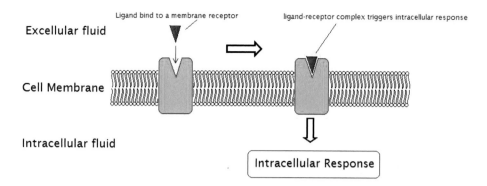

**Figure 7.** Enzyme-linked receptor mechanism.

In RTK receptors, the trans-phosphorylated tyrosine provides a phosphorylated binding site for adaptor proteins, which help couple the signal to further downstream signaling processes. For example, one of the signal transduction pathways that can be activated is known as the mitogen-activated protein kinase (MAPK) pathway, also known as the MAPK/ERK pathway. The MAPK protein is a protein kinase that can attach phosphate to target proteins such as transcription factors, thereby altering gene transcription and cell cycle progression. Many cellular proteins are activated downstream of growth factor receptors, such as EGFR, that initiate this signal transduction pathway.

G protein-coupled receptors (GPCRs) are our final class of membrane receptors, and comprise a large family of important receptor types. They have transmembrane domains and experience some form of conformational change after binding with a ligand. The ligands that bind and activate these receptors include light-sensitive compounds, molecules involved in odors, hormones, and neurotransmitters, and vary in size from small molecules to peptides to large proteins. When a GPCR undergoes a conformational change, it associates with and allosterically activates a G protein on the intracellular side of the membrane.

G proteins are known as heterotrimers, because they are composed of three distinct α, β, and γ subunits. When bound to GDP, G proteins are inactive, but they become activated by binding to GTP. The way that this happens is that an intracellular component of the G protein receptor facilitates the exchange of a molecule of GDP for GTP at the α-subunit of the G protein. Once this takes place, the α-subunit together with the bound GTP dissociates from the β and γ subunits. At this point, the subunits of the G protein *separately* interact with effectors in the cell, triggering downstream signaling processes. The α-subunit has a certain basal level of GTP hydrolysis activity, which means that it will eventually automatically regenerate GDP. Once GDP is regenerated, the G protein returns to its inactive state. The rate of GTP hydrolysis (i.e., G protein inactivation) can be accelerated by the actions of another family of allosteric modulating proteins, GTP-ase activating protein, also known as GAPs.

Figure 8 shows the basic logic of G protein-coupled receptor signaling.

## MCAT STRATEGY > > >

The MCAT does not specifically require you to know about the details of GTP-ase activating protein, but it is a useful example of how intricately various aspects of signaling can be regulated. Be prepared for a passage to describe multiple layers of regulation that you may not have heard about in detail before; part of the content review process in this section is for you to practice following the logic of regulation such that you can adapt to any such passages on Test Day.

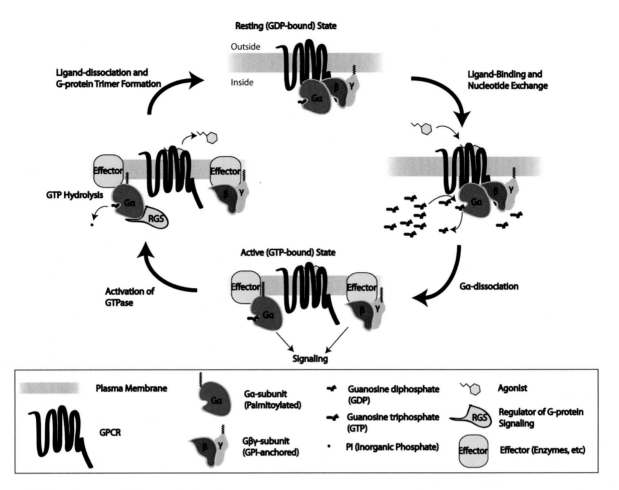

**Figure 8.** G protein-coupled receptor signaling.

G protein-coupled receptors are involved in multiple important and intricate intracellular signaling pathways. Two examples of secondary pathways are the cAMP-dependent (adenylyl cyclase) pathway and the inositol triphosphate ($IP_3$) pathway. cAMP stands for cyclic adenosine monophosphate, and is a secondary messenger that activates certain ion channels and an enzyme known as protein kinase A (PKA), which in turn affects cellular components involved in gene transcription and metabolism. $IP_3$, in contrast, involves an interesting mechanism. In its inactive form, it is coupled with the membrane-bound lipid diacylglycerol (DAG). When $IP_3$ is activated, it detaches from DAG and diffuses throughout the cell. $IP_3$ then triggers the release of intracellular calcium. Among other effects, intracellular calcium release activates protein kinase C (PKC), which exerts a diverse range of effects in the cell, ranging from constriction in muscle cells to glucose/glycogen metabolism in adipocytes and hepatocytes. Figure 9 shows the various steps of $IP_3$ signaling.

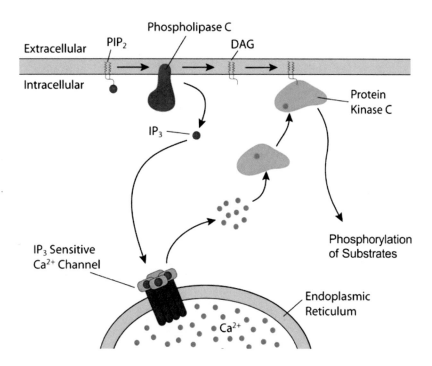

**Figure 9.** IP$_3$ signaling.

Finally, nuclear receptors are a class of proteins found within cells that are responsible for sensing steroid and thyroid hormones and certain other molecules. The ligands that bind to and activate nuclear receptors include lipophilic substances such as endogenous steroid hormones, thyroid hormone, vitamins A and D, and certain xenobiotics. This is an important point: peptides, proteins, and other hydrophobic signaling molecules must interact with the cell via membrane-bound receptors, whereas lipids can diffuse through the plasma membrane and move into the cell to interact with intracellular nuclear receptors. The basic function of nuclear receptors is to affect gene transcription.

Structurally, nuclear receptors have two main features. The ligand-binding domain binds with the signaling molecule. The DNA-binding domain, in contrast, is a highly conserved domain containing two characteristic 'zinc finger' elements that bind to specific DNA sequences known as hormone response elements (HREs). There are two major types of nuclear receptors. Type I nuclear receptors are located in the cytoplasm, where they bind with ligands before being translocated into the nucleus to exert their effects. This class includes androgen, estrogen, glucocorticoid, and progesterone receptors. Type II nuclear receptors are located in the nucleus, such that the hormone must enter the nucleus to bind with the receptor to modify DNA transcription. The best-known example of a type II nuclear receptor is thyroid hormone receptor.

Once a nuclear receptor binds an HRE sequence in DNA, it recruits other proteins known as transcription coregulators. These proteins facilitate or inhibit transcription via a range of mechanisms, including chromatin remodeling (i.e., making the target gene more or less accessible to transcription) via proteins such as histone deacetylases (HDACs), which strengthen the association of histones with DNA by making them more positively-charged, thereby repressing gene transcription.

# 6. Must-Knows

> Cytoskeletal proteins: help provide cell with its shape, resist force, and carry out vital functions both inside the cell and in terms of interactions with its environment.
>   – <u>Actin microfilaments</u> play a role in motility, cell cleavage, endocytosis/exocytosis, and muscle contraction.

- Intermediate filaments are larger than microfilaments but smaller than microtubules; provide structural support and other functions; major example = keratin.
- Microtubules: hollow cylinders composed of polymeric tubulin dimers. Contribute to chromosome movement during division and intracellular division.
- Motor proteins: generate mechanical forces via conformational changes.
  - Kinesins: move towards the (+) end of microtubules (towards periphery)
  - Dyneins: carry cargo towards (–) end of microtubules (towards center)
  - Myosin: involved in muscle contractions; use ATP to carry out a power stroke
- Antibodies: glycoproteins that recognize antigens (characteristic regions, usually of foreign objects/ substances)
  - Composed of at least one immunoglobulin (Ig) unit, each of which has two heavy chains and two light chains, forming a Y shape.
  - Several types exist; most important are IgM antibodies, which respond to acute infections, and IgG antibodies, which help confer lasting immunity.
- Cell adhesion: proteins involved include selectins, cadherins, and integrins.
  - Anchoring junctions involve cadherins; help keep cells/tissues in place.
  - Gap junctions: formed by connexin proteins, connect cells in a way such that diffusion/communication can take place between them.
  - Tight junctions: involve several types of proteins, are found in epithelial cells, and prevent solutes from being able to move freely from one tissue into another. Classic example = blood-brain barrier.
- Biosignaling:
  - Receptors cross the cell membrane and "translate" signal molecules into action.
  - Ion channel-linked receptors: also known as ligand-gated ion channels; change shape in response to binding with a ligand to open and let ions through.
  - Enzyme-linked receptors: either enzymes themselves, or are directly associated with the enzymes that they activate. Majority are protein kinases, and regulate many normal cellular processes.
  - G protein-coupled receptors: composed of three distinct α, β, and γ subunits. They become activated by binding with GTP. The α-subunit together with the bound GTP dissociates from the β and γ subunits, which interact with other signaling processes in the cell (secondary pathways).
  - Nuclear receptors: found within the cell (either in the nucleus or in the cytosol before traveling to the nucleus) and regulate gene transcription in response to binding with a signaling molecule (often a steroid hormone).
    - 'Zinc finger' elements are present in the DNA-binding domain.

This page left intentionally blank.

## Practice Passage

Aneuploidy is a common feature of cancer, with tumor cells typically harboring abnormal chromosome complements. In some contexts, aneuploidy has oncogenic effects. To investigate the role aneuploidy plays in tumorigenesis, scientists induced low-level aneuploidy across a large population of cells. The cells were exposed to increasing concentrations of GSK923295, an inhibitor targeting the mitotic kinesin Cenp-E, and cellular chromosome complements and Cenp-E activity were monitored. Figure 1 shows the activity of Cenp-E during the experiment.

**Figure 1.** GSK92395 inhibitory effect on Cenp-E function

Kinesins are cytoskeletal motor proteins that utilize the energy from ATP hydrolysis to perform mechanical work along microtubules. Mitotic kinesins are required for aspects of mitosis, including bipolar spindle assembly, chromosome alignment, chromosome segregation and cytokinesis. Since mitotic kinesins function exclusively during mitosis, compounds that specifically inhibit mitotic kinesins could affect only the proliferating cells, and thus are anticipated to be a new type of chemotherapeutic agents with better safety profiles.

Given that GSK92395 can bind to Cenp-E, suppress Cenp-E activity and induce multiple spindle formation in cancer cells another experiment was performed. Cells from two breast cancer cells lines were plated at $8{\times}10^4$ cells/ml in 96-well plates and treated with GSK92395 at the concentrations indicated in Figure 2. Cell viability as a function of inhibitor concentration was measured in cell lines MDA-MB-222 and MDA-MB-412.

**Figure 2.** Cell viability of breast cancer cell lines treated with GSK92395 (Note: **P < 0.01 versus corresponding control)

*Adapted from Bennett, A., et al. (2015). Cenp-E inhibitor GSK923295: Novel synthetic route and use as a tool to generate aneuploidy. Oncotarget, 6(25), 20921–20932 under CCBY*

1. Which of the following kinetic test results would indicate that GSK92395 is highly specific for the breast cancer cells it was tested with?
   A. Lower $k_{cat}$, lower $K_m$ compared to tests with normal cells.
   B. Higher $k_{cat}$, higher $K_m$ compared to tests with normal cells.
   C. High $k_{cat}$, lower $K_m$ compared to tests with normal cells.
   D. Lower $k_{cat}$, higher $K_m$ compared to tests with normal cells.

2. Analysis revealed that maximum Cenp-E activity was $10^4$ $s^{-1}$, according to the results in Figure 1, how much inhibitor is needed to change the activity to $5 \times 10^3$ $s^{-1}$?
   A. 0.6 μM
   B. 7 μM
   C. 30 μM
   D. 110 μM

3. Which of the following ratios would best indicate that Cenp-E has completed anaphase?
   A. ATP/ADP = 3
   B. ATP/ADP = 1.5
   C. ATP/ADP = 1
   D. ATP/ADP = 0.5

4. Which of the following is a primary difference between microtubules and actin filaments?
   A. Only actin filaments are capable of branched assembly.
   B. Only microtubules are part of epithelial cytoskeleton.
   C. Only actin filaments are assembled from nucleotide-bound subunits.
   D. Only microtubules have intrinsic structural polarity.

5. Which of the following structures is LEAST likely to be affected by GSK92395?
   A. Kinetochore
   B. Goldberg-Hogness box
   C. Spindle pole
   D. Centriole

6. One of the researchers concludes that GSK92395 influences cancer cell viability in a dose-dependent manner. Do the results of the experiment support this conclusion?
   A. Yes, because cancer cell death is positively correlated with GSK92395 concentration.
   B. No, because cancer cell viability is negatively correlated with GSK92395 concentration.
   C. No, because the effect of the inhibitor negatively correlates to inhibitor concentration.
   D. Yes, because the $IC_{50}$ values averaged approximately 18 μM of the inhibitor.

7. If researchers wished to determine if myosin were necessary for proper cell function, which motility function should be monitored in the experiment?
   A. Flagellar movement in spermatids
   B. Axoplasmic transport in sympathetic neurons
   C. Cleavage furrow formation in hepatocytes
   D. Ciliary movement in intestinal epithelia

# Practice Passage Explanations

Aneuploidy is a common feature of cancer, with tumor cells typically harboring abnormal chromosome complements. In some contexts, aneuploidy has oncogenic effects. To investigate the role aneuploidy plays in tumorigenesis, scientists induced low-level aneuploidy across a large population of cells. The cells were exposed to increasing concentrations of GSK923295, an inhibitor targeting the mitotic kinesin Cenp-E, and cellular chromosome complements and Cenp-E activity were monitored. Figure 1 shows the activity of Cenp-E during the experiment.

*Key terms: aneuploidy, kinesin, Cenp-E inhibitor, GSK92395*

**Figure 1.** GSK92395 inhibitory effect on Cenp-E function

*Figure 1 shows the exponential increase in [inhibitor] results in $I_{max} \sim 100\ \mu M$ and $I_{max}/2 \sim 7\ \mu M$*

Kinesins are cytoskeletal motor proteins that utilize the energy from ATP hydrolysis to perform mechanical work along microtubules. Mitotic kinesins are required for aspects of mitosis, including bipolar spindle assembly, chromosome alignment, chromosome segregation and cytokinesis. Since mitotic kinesins function exclusively during mitosis, compounds that specifically inhibit mitotic kinesins could affect only the proliferating cells, and thus are anticipated to be a new type of chemotherapeutic agents with better safety profiles.

*Key terms: mitotic kinesins, chemotherapeutic*

*Cause and effect: kinesins are responsible for microtubule structures of mitosis, and are elevated in cancer, good anti-cancer target*

Given that GSK92395 can bind to Cenp-E, suppress Cenp-E activity and induce multiple spindle formation in cancer cells another experiment was performed. Cells from two breast cancer cells lines were plated at $8\times10^4$ cells/ml in 96-well plates and treated with GSK92395 at the concentrations indicated in Figure 2. Cell viability as a function of inhibitor concentration was measured in cell lines MDA-MB-222 and MDA-MB-412.

*Key terms: spindle formation, breast cancer, cell viability, MDA-MB*

*Cause and effect: [GSK92395] vs. cancer cell viability measured*

**Figure 2.** Cell viability of breast cancer cell lines treated with GSK92395 (Note: **P < 0.01 versus corresponding control)

*Figure 2 shows that the anti-cancer cell effect of GSK92395 increases with the dose of the inhibitor*

*Adapted from Bennett, A., et al. (2015). Cenp-E inhibitor GSK923295: Novel synthetic route and use as a tool to generate aneuploidy. Oncotarget, 6(25), 20921–20932 under CCBY*

1. C is correct. A specific Cenp-E inhibitor should not only display its cytotoxicity against malignant cells, but also be less toxic toward normal cells. The specificity constant of the interaction between two molecules is $k_{cat}/K_m$. In order to maximize this value, we need a high $k_{cat}$ and a low $K_m$.

2. B is correct. This question asks for what concentration of the inhibitor, GSK92395, causes the Cenp-E activity to be reduced by half of its maximum value. This would be called the $IC_{50}$ of GSK92395. According to the figure, the activity reaches 50% of its maximum activity at around 7 μM GSK92395.

3. D is correct. The 2nd paragraph tells us that kinesins require ATP to carry out their motor activities. During anaphase, kinesins pull apart sister chromatids and drag them to separate poles of the dividing cell. This mechanical process will consume energy, and thus, we would expect minimum levels of ATP at the conclusion of this mechanical work.

4. A is correct. Actin filaments can be assembled into a branched pattern with the aid of an accessory protein complex. However, microtubule assembly can only produce single, straight microtubules, without branch points.
   B. Both actin and microtubules are components in the cytoskeleton of cells, including epithelial cells.
   D. Both actin and microtubules have intrinsic structural polarity because they are assembled from asymmetric subunits. Microtubules are made up of heterodimers of 2 kinds of tubulin, while actin is comprised of a monomeric globular protein with an asymmetric shape.
   C. The synthesis of microtubules and actin require that the subunits being added have a bound nucleoside triphosphate. GTP is used for tubulin, while ATP is used for actin.

5. B is correct. The 2nd paragraph tells us that GSK92395 inhibits the mitotic kinesin Cenp-E, and that these kinesis are responsible for microtubules structures of mitosis. The Goldberg-Hogness box, or TATA box, is a DNA sequence that indicates where a gene sequence can be read and decoded. It is a promoter sequence which specifies to other molecules where transcription begins.
   A. The kinetochore is a protein complex assembled at each centromere. This structure serves as the attachment site for spindle microtubules and the site at which motors generate forces to power chromosome movement.
   C. Spindle poles refers to the ends of a spindle, a specialized microtubule structure designed to attach and capture chromosomes in order to partition them evenly to each daughter cells.
   D. A centriole is made of 9 bundles of microtubules arranged in a ring. During mitosis, they radiate microtubules in star-shaped clusters known as asters, which act as guides for the alignment of the chromosomes as they separate later during the process of cell division.

6. A is correct. Examining Figure 2, we can see that as the inhibitor concentration increases, cancer cell viability decreases, which means cancer cell death increases as the drug is added. Thus, [GSK92395] and cell death is positively correlated while [GSK92395] and cell viability is negatively correlated. This would mean that the effect is indeed dose-dependent.
   C. The effect of an inhibitor should generally increase if there is more of the inhibitor present, and Figure 2 supports this conclusion.
   D. While this statement is supported by the data in Figure 2, it does not answer the question.

7. C is correct. Cleavage furrow formation, which aids the process of cytokinesis (daughter cell separation at the end of cell division), is based on the contraction of an array of actin filaments that are anchored to the plasma membrane. The sliding of actin filaments is induced by the action of the motor protein myosin, which splits the parent cell into 2 daughter cells.
   A, D: Both ciliary motility in epithelia and movement of the spermatid tail arise from microtubules and microtubule-associated motor proteins. Sperm motility is due to the movement of the sperm tail (a modified flagellum).
   B. Axoplasmic transport is the movement of membrane-bound organelles, mitochondria, lipids, synaptic vesicles, proteins, and other cell parts to and from a neuronal cell body, through the cytoplasm of the axon. This is handled by the action of microtubule-associated motor proteins kinesin (anterograde transport) or dynein (retrograde transport).

## Independent Questions

1. Non-enzymatic protein functions include all of the following EXCEPT:
   A. acting as part of the humoral immune system.
   B. adhering one cell to another.
   C. composing eukaryotic flagella.
   D. catalyzing biological reactions.

2. Kinesins are motor proteins that transport vesicles and organelles by traveling along:
   A. microtubules, which requires the hydrolysis of ATP.
   B. microtubules without the need for ATP.
   C. microfilaments, which requires the hydrolysis of ATP.
   D. microfilaments without the need for ATP.

3. Colchicine is extracted from the meadow saffron plant. It is used in the treatment of gout, but it can also cause many side effects, including gastrointestinal upset and neutropenia. Colchicine binds to tubulin and inhibits microtubule polymerization. From this information, which of the following is most likely true of colchicine?
   A. Colchicine interferes with the formation of the tight junctions that seal adjacent epithelial cells.
   B. Colchicine is a mitotic poison and prevents spindle formation.
   C. Colchicine interferes with actin and thus inhibits muscle contraction.
   D. Colchicine prevents the proper production of keratin, which is a necessary component of fingernails.

4. Proteins are important for cell-to-cell communication in the body. Which of the following incorrectly pairs a signaling mechanism with its description?
   A. Direct signaling occurs through gap junctions between neighboring cells.
   B. Paracrine signaling occurs between cells of different tissues and lasts for a long amount of time.
   C. Endocrine signaling occurs between distant cells and is mediated by hormones.
   D. Autocrine signals can bind to ligands on the same cell that secreted the signal.

5. Immunoglobulin M (IgM) is most commonly found in the form of a pentamer. In total, how many heavy and light chains are present in one IgM pentamer?
   A. Five heavy chains and five light chains
   B. Five heavy chains and ten light chains
   C. Ten heavy chains and ten light chains
   D. Twenty heavy chains and twenty light chains

6. Cadherins are classified as which of the following types of protein?
   A. Globular proteins
   B. Enzymes
   C. Transmembrane proteins
   D. Monotopic proteins

7. Dyneins would be expected to be most directly involved in which of the following processes?
   A. Retrograde cargo transport in neural axons
   B. Anterograde delivery of cellular vesicles
   C. Conduction of the power stroke during skeletal muscle contraction
   D. Passive movement of chromosomes during cell division

8. In a G protein-coupled receptor system, the G protein:
   A. is activated by the phosphorylation of GDP into GTP, and is inactivated by the hydrolysis of GTP.
   B. is activated by the phosphorylation of GDP into GTP, and is inactivated when GTP dissociates and is replaced by GDP.
   C. is activated when a GDP molecule is exchanged for a GTP molecule, and is inactivated by the hydrolysis of GTP.
   D. is activated when a GDP molecule is exchanged for a GTP molecule, and is inactivated when GTP dissociates and is replaced by GDP.

# Independent Question Explanations

1. D is correct. The question stem asks about *non-enzymatic* protein function. It is enzymes which catalyze biological reactions; thus, choice D is our "odd man out" and is correct. Option A is a function of non-enzymatic proteins, specifically antibodies. Choice B is also accomplished by non-enzymatic proteins. Finally we can rule out option C because eukaryotic flagella are composed of microtubules, which are proteins that do not play an enzymatic role.

2. A is correct. Motor proteins, which include dynein and kinesin, hydrolyze ATP to slide along microtubules with their bound cargo. Microfilaments form an intricate network that gives structure to the cell membrane and facilitates amoeboid movements, but they are not involved in vesicle traffic.

3. B is correct. Microtubule polymerization is an essential part of spindle formation, as microtubules make up the spindle fibers that connect to the centromere regions of chromosomes. Consequently, administration of colchicine results in mitotic interference, also known as mitotic poisoning. Microfilaments, not microtubules, are composed of actin (eliminating option C), and keratin is formed from intermediate filaments (eliminating option D). Finally, microtubules are involved in spindle formation, not forming tight junctions (eliminating option A).

4. B is correct. Paracrine signaling occurs between local cells (not cells of distinct tissues) and only lasts for a short amount of time. This is due to fast degradation of the paracrine ligands. The remaining statements are accurate descriptions.

5. C is correct. One immunoglobulin (Ig) subunit contains two heavy chains and two light chains. A pentamer contains five Ig subunits, so in total, one pentamer must contain ten heavy chains and ten light chains.

6. C is correct. Cadherins are cell adhesion molecules that comprise adherens junctions, which serve to connect cells to each other. As such, it makes logical sense that a cadherin should extend through the membrane of a cell and out into the surrounding environment. Transmembrane proteins are those which extend through the entire membrane of a cell. Globular proteins are spherical and tend to float freely, which is not the case of cadherins (eliminating choice A). Cadherins are not monotopic proteins, which connect only to one side of the plasma membrane (eliminating choice D).

7. A is correct. Dyneins are generally involved with the retrograde transport of cargo. (Retrograde transport is movement toward the center of the cell. This is the opposite of anterograde transport, which moves cargo toward the periphery/cell membrane.) Dynein activity requires ATP, so it is active rather than passive. The power stroke is more closely related to actin and myosin.

8. C is correct. This question is tricky! G proteins are activated when bound to GTP; this binding occurs when a GDP molecule is exchanged for GTP. Note that GDP is *not* simply phosphorylated; it is actually replaced by an entirely new GTP molecule (eliminate choices A and B). G proteins are rendered inactive by the hydrolysis of GTP (eliminate choice D), which is accomplished via an intrinsic GTPase activity.

This page left intentionally blank.

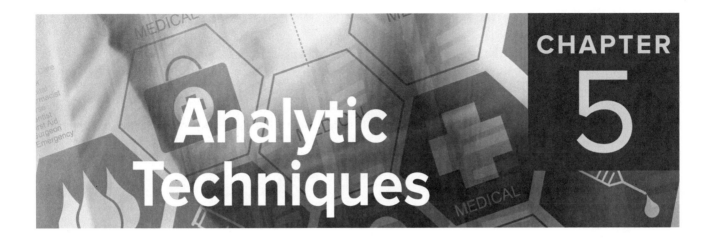

**CHAPTER 5**

# Analytic Techniques

## 0. Introduction

In this chapter, we'll review a range of analytic techniques that can be used to analyze amino acids, proteins, and other biologically and chemically relevant molecules. As anyone who has worked in a lab knows, it can be very difficult, practically speaking, to figure out what actually is *in* the clear aqueous solution or white powder that might be generated at the end of an experiment. When we read textbooks with elegantly labeled structures and diagrams, it can be easy to overlook how much work goes into isolating and analyzing the molecules that are present in a mixture of chemicals.

Sometimes analytic techniques are presented at the end of chemistry or biochemistry review materials as if they are an afterthought, but they are actually a core component of testable MCAT material. In particular, keep an eye out in this chapter for ways in which the use of analytic techniques to characterize or isolate a molecule depends on its structural features, because this is a lens through which the MCAT can test both your knowledge of analytic laboratory techniques and your knowledge of the structural properties of biomolecules.

The process of protein purification begins with the separation of the protein from the non-protein components of a mixture. This typically begins with the removal of biological materials by mechanically lysing a cell, followed by filtration and centrifugation in order to remove large insoluble particles. Centrifugation separates cellular contents according to differences in their mass and density. When a tube or other vessel containing a mixture of proteins (or cells and cellular components) is rotated rapidly, each particle experiences an inward acting force proportional to its mass. The net effect of spinning the sample in a centrifuge is that massive, small, and dense particles with greater inertia or less drag tend to move outward faster than less massive particles with less inertia or more drag in the liquid. In most cases, a pellet, enriched in the most massive/densest particles will form. Non-compacted particles remain in the supernatant liquid and may be separated from the pellet.

Proteins can then be separated individually, using some of the techniques described in this chapter, until only the protein of interest remains. If the protein target is tightly bound by a membrane, a detergent may be needed to solubilize the lipid membrane components and remove the protein. Proteins are purified through fractionation procedures, in which a series of treatments is performed, such that differences in the properties of a protein target and other proteins in solution can be taken advantage of to sequentially separate the substances until only the protein of interest remains.

An important distinction exists between preparative purifications, which are intended to produce a significant quantity of purified proteins for subsequent use, and analytical purifications, which produce a smaller amount of a protein intended for analytical purposes, such as identification, quantification, and functional studies. This difference is particularly important in real-world industrial applications, where a company may *have* to be able to produce/isolate a compound at scale in order to be successful.

In this chapter, we will first review some general analytical techniques including extraction, techniques that take advantage of solubility differences, and distillation. Then, we will discuss the principle of chromatography and review several of the most commonly-used variants of chromatography, which is a subject that is absolutely vital for MCAT success. Finally, we will review other protein analysis techniques, including the use of the isoelectric point, electrophoresis, quantitative analysis via spectrometry, and enantiomer separation.

# 1. Extraction and Solubility

A number of strategies can be employed to extract a protein from its surrounding environment, including cycles of freezing and thawing, mechanical agitation, filtration, or treatment with organic solvents. The appropriate choice of how vigorous a method to employ is made in light of the structural stability of the cell, as well as that of the protein target—that is, there is no one-size-fits-all method, and considerable work needs to be invested in figuring out the best technique for the desired extraction. After extraction, the proteins present can be separated from other cellular contents, including DNA and organelles, by ultracentrifugation. Once in solution, proteins become subject to the possibility of irreversible damage by agents and conditions to which they would not be exposed intracellularly. For this reason, proteins are often dissolved in buffers to maintain solution pH and are kept cold to avoid denaturation. Moreover, during the process of extracting proteins from tissue, proteases are released; these are normally carefully stored and regulated by the cell, but once the cell is mechanically broken down, they enter the environment. To avoid the proteolytic degradation of extracted proteins, binding agents that neutralize protease activity can be introduced, and to the extent that the temperature sensitivity of the protein extract allows, the temperature of the stored protein should be maintained outside the optimal range of the proteases. During long-term storage, additional care must be taken to prevent slow oxidation or microbial contamination. The most common precaution against these possibilities is to store proteins under an atmosphere of inert gas.

> > CONNECTIONS < <

Chapter 12 of Chemistry

MCAT STRATEGY > > >

When thinking about solubility, always remember that for organic compounds, "like dissolves like"—that is, hydrophobic substances will dissolve best in nonpolar solvents and hydrophilic substances will dissolve best in polar solvents—and that the hydrophilicity of substances can be manipulated by acid-base chemistry (i.e., selective protonaion and deprotonation).

In general, solubility can be leveraged to separate organic compounds in solutions with aqueous and hydrophobic layers, as discussed in Chapter 12 of the Chemistry and Organic Chemistry textbook. However, solubility can also be utilized in specific ways to selectively isolate proteins. The idea here is that the solubility of a given protein depends closely on the polarity, pH, temperature, and dissolved salt concentration.

In particular, the salt concentration can be leveraged. At first, as a salt is added to solution, protein solubility increases because the salt protects the charged groups of proteins from interacting with each other, which would contribute to them forming aggregations. By inhibiting aggregations, salt ions increase solubility; this effect is known as 'salting in.' However, as the salt concentration continues to rise, the dissolved salt ions begin to compete with the charged groups of proteins for solvent molecules. At high concentrations, there is meaningfully less bulk solvent available to solvate proteins and other solute

**102**  © 2018 Next Step Test Preparation, LLC. All rights reserved. Do not copy nor distribute without express consent.

molecules, decreasing protein solubility. This effect is referred to as 'salting out.' Because different proteins precipitate at different salt concentrations, adjusting the salt concentration (often via the addition of ammonium sulfate) to just below the concentration at which a target protein precipitates can separate out many unwanted proteins from solution. Fractionation by salting out is a useful technique because it often allows for the purification of a significant amount of protein.

# 2. Chromatography

Chromatography is a general term that refers to a range of laboratory techniques used to separate and/or identify the components of mixtures. The term chromatography itself is a bit of a historical relic; as you might be able to guess from the roots of the name, it means something like 'color writing.' The reason for this is that chromatography was initially developed in the context of separating different-colored components of plant materials, resulting in visually striking patterns of color.

There are several variants of chromatography that you need to be aware of for the MCAT, but the basic principle is always the same. The mixture containing the compound(s) of interest is introduced into a mobile phase that moves through a separate structure known as the stationary phase with which it interacts. The term 'elution' is used to describe how a mobile phase moves through a stationary phase. Differences in how substances interact with the stationary phase lead to differential retention. In particular, substances that don't interact strongly with the stationary phase will elute more quickly than substances that do.

One of the earliest chromatography methods was known as paper chromatography. In this method, filter paper is used as the stationary phase, and the mobile phase is a liquid solvent (also known as a developing solution) that contains the tested substance as a dissolved solute. The mobile phase is carried up the filter paper via capillary action. Thin layer chromatography, which you may remember from organic chemistry lab, uses a similar principle, but instead of paper, a different adsorbent—often silica—is used. TLC allows for better separations, faster run times, and a potentially wider variety of stationary phase polarities and properties than does paper chromatography. The development of a TLC plate is shown below in Figure 1.

> ## MCAT STRATEGY > > >
>
> The sheer variety of types of chromatography is one of the biggest obstacles for many students when approaching this topic for the MCAT. The key here is to understand that all forms of chromatography operate on the *same basic principle*. When studying a new variant of chromatography, or in the worst-case scenario, if you are presented with a form of chromatography on Test Day that you're not familiar with, focus on the basics: identify the stationary phase and figure out what kind of molecule (polar/nonpolar, small/large, positively/negatively charged, etc.) will interact with it most strongly. That kind of molecule will elute last. This will usually suffice to solve MCAT chromatography problems.

**Figure 1.** TLC plate development.

TLC is a useful technique for monitoring reaction progress and determining how many components a substance has (and their rough relative polarity), but it has limitations in terms of how precisely it can identify compounds.

One way to quantify the outcomes of TLC is known as the retention factor ($R_f$), which is a measure of how far up a substance in the mobile phase has traveled compared to how far the solvent has traveled (the so-called 'solvent front'). It is simply calculated as $R_f = \frac{distance\ traveled}{distance\ of\ solvent\ front}$. Essentially, $R_f$ is a very rough inverse measure of polarity; more polar compounds will interact more intensely with the stationary phase and therefore will not climb as high up the stationary phase as nonpolar compounds.

Figure 1 shows an example in which the different components of the test compound can be visualized as blue and red splotches, but it is often not the case that TLC results can be visualized so simply. The application of ultraviolet light and treatment with iodine are two common ways of visualizing TLC results.

One of the disadvantages of TLC is that it is only an analytical purification (and a fairly imprecise one at that)—that is, it can only be used to get a sense of what is in a mixture, but not to obtain purified samples of those components. This problem is addressed by column chromatography. There are multiple types of column chromatography, but the basic idea is that the stationary phase is not a rectangular sheet, but a column with a stopcock on the bottom that allows the content to be drained out. By successively draining the column into multiple receptacles, pure samples of the various components in the mobile phase can be obtained. The basic principle of column chromatography is illustrated in Figure 2; note how the red substance, which interacts the least with the stationary phase, elutes first, allowing it to be isolated.

**Figure 2.** Column chromatography.

One important example of column chromatography is high-performance liquid chromatography (HPLC). In HPLC, the mobile phase is passed under high pressure through a chromatographic matrix of solid absorbent, usually consisting of glass or plastic beads coated uniformly with chromatographic material. High-pressure transport generally increases the speed and resolution of the separation process in comparison to other forms of chromatography. HPLC relies on pumps to pressurize the liquid solvent passing through the solid absorbent of the column. The pressurized liquid—i.e., the mobile phase—is typically a mixture of solvents of differing polarities, commonly including various mixtures of water, alcohols, and acetonitrile. The composition and temperature of the solvent influence the electrostatic interactions that occur between sample components and the stationary phase, and for this reason, properly choosing the solvent is an important part of optimizing HPLC results.

The most commonly used method of HPLC is known as reverse-phase HPLC (RP-HPLC), which features a reversal of the polarity of the stationary phase and mobile phase traditionally found in HPLC and TLC. That is, in RP-HPLC, the stationary phase is nonpolar and the mobile phase is aqueous. One common nonpolar stationary phase is silica that has been surface-modified by attaching long-chain alkyl groups. In RP-HPLC, retention times are longer for less polar molecules, whereas polar molecules elute more rapidly because they will not 'want' to interact with the nonpolar stationary phase. Retention times can be increased by diluting the solvent with more water. This increases the relative polarity of the solvent, meaning that hydrophobic analytes in the mobile phase will 'want' even more to interact with the hydrophobic stationary phase.

Gas-liquid chromatography is another variation on chromatography, in which the stationary phase is liquid and the mobile phase is gas. The way this works is that the compounds of interest are in the gaseous phase and are mixed together with so-called 'carrier' gases (most commonly, helium and hydrogen) that bubble through the liquid stationary phase. As with other types of chromatography, the degree to which the substance of interest interacts with the stationary phase will affect how long it takes to move through the column. The temperature can be controlled by placing the column in an oven. Gas-liquid chromatography is a feasible way of analyzing substances that vaporize below approximately 300°C. Although it may seem like a counterintuitive system, gas-liquid chromatography is actually capable of highly sensitive analyses.

Another family of chromatography techniques involves making further optimizations to the stationary phase. In size-exclusion chromatography, gel beads containing pores, formed from the cross-linking of the polymer from which the beds are constructed, act as a molecular sieve. Figure 3 shows the principle of size-exclusion chromatography.

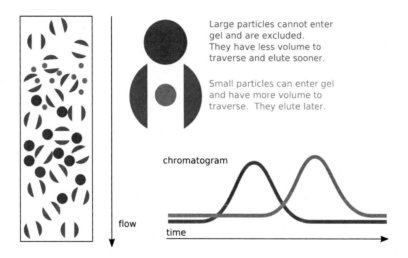

**Figure 3.** Size-exclusion chromatography.

The crucial thing to remember about size-exclusion chromatography is that large particles elute first. The basic reason for this is that small particles can interact more with the pores formed within the gel. More of the volume of the solvent is accessible to the small particles, because they can enter the pores within the gel. In contrast, the larger particles have access to less of the solvent volume, meaning that they can be thought of as 'bouncing' through the gel without much interaction.

Ion-exchange chromatography is similar, but relies on charge instead of size. The stationary phase is made of either an anion-exchange resin or a cation-exchange resin. The names of these compounds essentially tell you how they work, but you have to be careful: the names tell you their *function*, which is not the same as their *charge*. The point of an anion-exchange resin is to interact with negatively-charged compounds (anions), and in order to do so, it must be rich in *positively*-charged molecules. The most common anion exchanger is a matrix with diethylaminoethanol (DEAE) groups attached. Similarly, a cation-exchange resin has the goal of trapping positively-charged molecules, and in order to do so, it is rich in *negatively*-charged residues. The most common cation exchanger has a matrix with carboxymethyl (CM) groups attached.

Most proteins have both positively- and negatively-charged residues in normal pH ranges, so their interaction with ion-exchange chromatography stationary phases is complex. The binding affinity of proteins for the surface-modified resin of the stationary phase depends on the presence of other ions that compete with the protein to bind with the stationary phase, as well as on the pH-dependent net charge of the sample protein.

In ion-exchange chromatography, after a sample is added to the column, the column is washed. The length of retention for each resin-bound solute depends on the strength of its charge. The most weakly charged compounds will elute first, followed by those with successively stronger charges. Proteins that bind with very high affinity to the column can be eluted (removed) from the ion exchanger by treatment with an eluant (buffered rinse) that modifies the pH of the solution in a way that reduces the strength of the protein-stationary phase binding.

Affinity chromatography takes these techniques to the next level by embedding into the stationary phase molecules that are specific to the compound(s) of interest in the stationary phase. The ligand-protein binding used in affinity chromatography takes advantage of the capability that many proteins possess to bind tightly, but non-covalently, to ligands. This 'lock-and-key' fit between the ligand and its target compound means that when an impure protein solution is passed through such a chromatographic matrix, the desired protein binds the immobilized ligand, and all other substances are washed through the column with the buffer. The desired protein can then be recovered by changing the elution conditions to release the protein from the matrix. This technique is highly specific in comparison to the relatively crude techniques discussed above that rely on general physical/chemical characteristics.

An important subtype of affinity chromatography is known as immunoaffinity chromatography. In this technique, an antibody is attached to the matrix in order to purify solutions containing the protein against which the antibody binds. The bound protein is then eluted by washing the column with a solution containing high concentrations of unbound ligand or a solution of differing ionic strength.

## 3. Other Protein Analysis Techniques

In this section, we'll discuss some non-chromatography protein analysis techniques, starting with the basic concept of gel electrophoresis and its applications in SDS-PAGE and isoelectric focusing. We will then move on to quantitative analysis via spectrophotometric assays, and finish the chapter with a discussion of the analysis and separation of enantiomers. All of these techniques are ubiquitous in modern research and are very important to be familiar with for the MCAT.

Electrophoresis is a separatory technique that relies on the migration of charged particles in the presence of an electric field. It is usually conducted in polyacrylamide or agarose gels with characteristic pore sizes. This fact means that proteins can be separated according to two parameters: electrophoretic mobility, which is a function of its charge, and gel filtration, which is a function of its size or shape. Generally, the pH of the gel chosen is usually at or above 9, which exceeds the pI of virtually all proteins. At this pH, proteins will have an overall negative charge and will therefore move towards the positive pole (anode) of the gel. Molecules possessing a similar size and charge will move as a coherent band through the cell.

Following electrophoretic separation, bands may be visualized by exposing the gel to an agent that tightly binds proteins. One of the most popular protein stains is the anionic dye Coomassie Brilliant Blue, which non-specifically binds to proteins. Alternately, if the proteins

> **MCAT STRATEGY > > >**
>
> The fact that the anode is the positive pole in electrophoresis is often confusing to students, but the way to remember this is to recall that electrophoresis is like an electrolytic cell, not a galvanic cell. An external current is applied in electrophoresis; it's not like a spontaneously discharging battery.

separated are radioactive, the gel can be placed over X-ray film and, once developed, an autoradiograph displaying an identifiable banding pattern results. If an antibody to a separated protein target exists, it can be used to detect the presence of that protein specifically in a process known as western blotting or immunoblotting.

It's worth pausing here to note that gel electrophoresis can also be used to analyze fragments of nucleic acids (RNA and DNA); this is discussed in Chapter 5 of the Biology textbook.

> **> > CONNECTIONS < <**
>
> Chapter 5 of Biology

One particularly important gel electrophoretic technique is known as sodium dodecyl sulfate-polyacrylamide gel electrophoresis (whew, what a mouthful!) or SDS-PAGE. The takeaway point about SDS-PAGE is that it allows proteins to be sorted by their mass alone. It uses sodium dodecyl sulfate (SDS), which is a strong anionic detergent, to denature native proteins into their unfolded, unassociated polypeptide states. An interesting fact about SDS is that it imparts most proteins with an even distribution of charge per unit mass, because when the highly anionic SDS associates with the polypeptide backbone, the intrinsic charge of the polypeptide becomes negligible in comparison to the negative charges due to SDS. SDS denatures secondary and tertiary structure, except for disulfide bonds. Therefore, reducing agents such as dithiothreitol (DTT) and 2-mercaptoethanol (β-mercaptoethanol) are added to SDS-PAGE setups to reduce the disulfide linkages left intact by SDS-PAGE treatment. When SDS-PAGE is performed with a reductant, it is known as reducing SDS-PAGE.

Don't drown in the details here: the important point about SDS-PAGE (and especially reducing SDS-PAGE) is that it allows proteins to be separated only based on mass. More specifically, the electrophoretic mobility displayed by these proteins will be a linear function of the logarithms of their molecular weight.

Figure 4 shows an example of an SDS-PAGE analysis in which proteins were stained with Coomassie Brilliant Blue staining. Note that a molecular ladder is present on the left-hand side; this is essentially a calibration step in which proteins of known molecular weights are filtered through the gel to help interpret the results of the separation technique.

**Figure 4.** SDS-PAGE electrophoresis with Coomassie Brilliant Blue staining.

Isoelectric focusing is a related electrophoretic technique that separates proteins according to their isoelectric point (pI). Recall that the pI refers to the pH at which the net charge of a protein will be 0; this parameter varies across proteins, such that isoelectric focusing is a good way to separate proteins in a relatively specific manner. Isoelectric focusing requires the use of a gel that has a stable pH gradient. A protein that is in a region of the gel where the pH is below its pI will be positively charged and will migrate towards the negatively charged plate (the cathode). The protein will cease to migrate when it reaches the region of the gel where the pH of the gel equals the pI of the protein. At this point, the protein will stop migrating because the net charge of the protein will be 0, it will not experience any electric force. The proteins analyzed using isoelectric focusing will be separated based on the relative number of acidic and basic residues that they contain.

Two-dimensional gel electrophoresis combines isoelectric focusing followed by SDS-PAGE. This allows proteins to be separated by *both* charge and molecular weight, which greatly increases the specificity of the separation because it is quite unlikely that two proteins will happen to have identical properties in terms of charge and molecular weight. Figure 5 illustrates a sample of what two-dimensional electrophoresis looks like.

**Figure 5.** Two-dimensional gel electrophoresis.

Electrophoresis is useful in terms of visualizing and analyzing the proteins present in a mixture, but it is also often necessary to quantify the amount of proteins. Various types of assays exist to do this. One common principle is to use spectrometry. This is straightforward in reactions with colored or fluorescent substrates and/or products, and in reactions where that is not the case, the product of the reaction can be converted into another, more easily detected substance. Spectrometry operates on the principle of the Beer-Lambert law:

$$A = -\ln\left(\frac{I}{I_0}\right) = \varepsilon \ell c$$

In this law, $A$ is the solute's absorbance (also known as its optical density), $I$ is the transmitted intensity of a given wavelength of light, $I_0$ is the intensity of incident light at the given wavelength, $\varepsilon$ is a constant known as the molar absorptivity of the solute at the wavelength of light transmitted, $c$ is the concentration of the attenuating solute, and $\ell$ is the path length in centimeters of the transmitted light. Polypeptides absorb light strongly in the wavelength range of 200-400 nm (the ultraviolet [UV] range) because of the presence of residues containing aromatic side chains (Phe, Tyr, and Trp). Measuring absorbance at 280 nm, which is near the relative maximum of the UV absorbance curve for all three aromatic amino acids, can measure protein content during purification.

Immunochemical procedures are an alternative to spectrophotometric analysis. Immunoassays operate on the principle that antibodies cultured from antibody-producing cells recovered from the serum of an immunized source will bind with great specificity to a protein antigen of interest. A protein present in a mixture can be detected using a technique known as a radioimmunoassay (RIA); in an RIA, the concentration of protein can be assessed indirectly by measuring the extent to which the protein competes with a radioactively labeled standard for antibody binding sites.

A related and very important technique is known as the enzyme-linked immunosorbent assay (ELISA). In general, ELISA uses a solid-phase enzyme immunoassay that detects the presence of an antigen. In an ELISA procedure, a sample containing an unknown amount of antigen is applied to a solid-phase supporting structure. After the antigen contained in the sample becomes attached to the solid support, a specific detection antibody is applied to, and binds with, the antigen. The antibody is then covalently linked to an enzyme directly or through a secondary antibody that is conjugated with an enzyme. Between steps, the plate is often washed with a detergent to rinse unbound proteins or antibodies. Following addition of the enzyme's substrate, a reaction occurs that produces a visualizable signal. The intensity of this signal is related to the quantity of protein antigen present in the original sample.

For some purposes, ELISA has been supplemented and even replaced by polymerase chain reaction (PCR), which is a highly sensitive tool for amplifying certain sequences of DNA, but ELISA has traditionally been used for a range of diagnostic purposes, including for HIV and viral hepatitis. (Modern HIV testing also involves western blotting and rapid testing techniques, not just ELISA, but ELISA remains a cornerstone of diagnostic and analytical procedures).

The principle of ELISA is illustrated in Figure 6.

**Figure 6.** ELISA.

# 4. Must-Knows

> Protein analysis starts with separating protein from non-protein components of a mixture; typically through lysis, followed by filtration and centrifugation.

> Preparative purifications result in a significant quantity of proteins for subsequent use; analytical preparations produce a smaller amount.

> Solubility:
  - General principle of 'like dissolves like' can be manipulated.
  - Protein solubility is affected by polarity, pH, temperature, and salt concentration.
  - Salting in: as salt is added, solubility increases because salt separates charged residues of proteins from each other; but past a certain point, dissolved salt ions compete for solvent molecules, reducing solubility.

> Chromatography: mobile phase and stationary phase. Substance of interest is dissolved in mobile phase and passed over/through stationary phase. If a substance interacts more strongly with stationary phase, it will take longer to move through ('elute'). **This principle can be used to make sense of *all* chromatography techniques**.
  - Paper chromatography: mobile phase moves up filter paper via capillary action
  - Thin-layer chromatography (TLC): like paper chromatography, but stationary phase is usually silica
    - $R_f = \frac{distance\ traveled}{distance\ of\ solvent\ front}$; a rough measure of polarity
  - Column chromatography: stationary phase is in a column; different analytes will be eluted out at different times and can be collected in separate containers.
    - High-performance liquid chromatography (HPLC): mobile phase passed under high pressure through a matrix; normally a polar stationary phase and nonpolar mobile phase are used, but this is reversed in reverse-phase HPLC.
    - Gas-liquid chromatography: stationary phase is liquid; substance of interest is suspended in gaseous mobile phase.
  - Size-exclusion chromatography: gel beads contain pores and act as molecular sieve that catches up small particles, making them elute more slowly.
  - Ion-exchange chromatography: relies on charge interactions
    - Anion-exchange: gel contains cations that trap anions; anions elute last.
    - Cation-exchange: gel contains anions that trap cations; cations elute last.
  - Affinity chromatography: more specific (e.g., antibody-antigen) interactions

> Electrophoresis: a charge is applied across a gel and molecules migrate due to the applied voltage
  - Gel electrophoresis is also affected by size due to gel filtration properties
  - SDS-PAGE: SDS is an anionic detergent that results in an even distribution of charge per unit mass; this allows proteins to be separated by mass alone.
  - Isoelectric focusing: uses electrophoresis with a pH gradient to separate proteins by their pI (isoelectric point; the pH where a protein has a net charge of zero)
  - Western blotting: after electrophoresis, an antibody specific to the separated protein of interest is applied and visualized.

> Enzyme-linked immunosorbent assay: specific visualizable detection antibodies are used to find antigens.

## Practice Passage

The structure of a polypeptide was determined beginning with the identification of its constituent amino acids. A purified sample of the polypeptide was denatured and then hydrolyzed by a strong acid at 110°C for 24 hours. The individual amino acids released by the treatment were then separated by cation-exchange chromatography.

Following treatment with a series of eluting solutions, the separated amino acids contained in the eluate from the column were heated with ninhydrin—a reagent that forms the blue-purple compound Ruhemann's Purple with most amino acids, amines, and ammonia (Figure 1).

**Figure 1.** Ninhydrin and N-compound reaction mechanism

The amount of each amino acid present was then determined spectrophotometrically by measuring the amount of blue-purple light absorbed. The specific position of each amino acid in the polypeptide chain was also found. Edman reagent (phenylisothiocyanate) was used to label a terminal residue under mildly alkaline conditions, resulting in the formation of a phenylthiocarbamoyl. Under acidic conditions, the terminal amino acid of the polypeptide was cleaved, releasing free polypeptide and phenylthiohydantoin (PTH), an amino acid derivative that can be identified. Edman reagent was applied repeatedly, shortening the peptide bond obtained following each cycle. The steps of the Edman degradation are shown in Figure 2.

**Figure 2.** Edman degradation steps

There are limits on the length of polypeptides that can be sequenced by this method. Over time, the yield of PTH amino acid products decreases relative to the background level of PTH-amino acids. Repetitive yield is a measure of the percent of detectable material remaining after each turn of the cycle. Longer polypeptides can be sequenced from greater initial sample sizes and larger repetitive yields. They may also be cleaved by peptidase enzymes to create shorter polypeptides for sequencing.

1. If native Hrt-34 protein is run on SDS-PAGE and then a separate sample of Hrt-34 is subjected to 4 rounds of Edman degradation and run on a similar gel, how will the movement through the gel of the respective products compare?
   A. The Edman-degraded Hrt-34 will migrate four times as far as the native protein.
   B. The Edman-degraded Hrt-34 will migrate one-fourth as far as the native protein.
   C. The Edman-degraded Hrt-34 will migrate 5% further than the native protein.
   D. The Edman-degraded Hrt-34 will migrate further than the native protein.

2. Which of the following molecules is the product obtained at the end of the Edman degradation of the polypeptide $H_2N$-Ala-Gly-Arg-Met-COOH?
   A. PTH-Ala
   B. PTH-Gly
   C. PTH-Arg
   D. PTH-Met

3. What is most likely reason for the choice of eluant solutions used to recover free amino acids from the ion-exchange column made by the researchers?
   A. They are hydrophobic.
   B. They possess a characteristic salt concentration.
   C. They are capable of denaturing disulfide linkages.
   D. They contain digestive enzymes.

4. Experiments showed that protein unfolding in the presence of the denaturant proceeds in a unimolecular fashion, with rate constant, k. What are the units for k?
   A. $s^{-1}$
   B. $M \bullet s$
   C. $M^{-1} \bullet s^{-1}$
   D. $M \bullet s^{-1}$

5. Which of the following best describes the reaction shown in Figure 2 which forms the bond between phenylisothiocyanate and a polypeptide?
   A. Addition
   B. Dehydration
   C. Neutralization
   D. Elimination

6. Which of the following PAGE conditions would allow for the accurate determination of quaternary structure of a trimeric protein?
   A. Native gel
   B. SDS-PAGE
   C. Reducing gel
   D. Non-reducing gel

7. The kinetics of the ninhydrin reaction were shown to be first order with respect to 1,2,3-indantrione and α-amino acid molecules, and second order overall. The reaction rate was shown to vary with solution pH. The initial reaction rate was greatest when the product of which two concentrations was maximized? (Note: R = $C_8H_4O_2$)
   A. $[RC=O^+H]$, $[H_2NCHRCOO^-]$
   B. $[RC=O]$, $[H_3^+NCHRCOO^-]$
   C. $[RC=O^+H]$, $[H_3^+NCHRCOOH]$
   D. $[RC=O]$, $[H_2NCHRCOOH]$

## Practice Passage Explanations

The structure of a polypeptide was determined beginning with the identification of its constituent amino acids. A purified sample of the polypeptide was denatured and then hydrolyzed by a strong acid at 110°C for 24 hours. The individual amino acids released by the treatment were then separated by cation-exchange chromatography.

*Key terms: polypeptide, amino acids, cation-exchange chromatography, resins*

*Cause and effect: protein denature → hydrolysis → AA ID via (+) - exchange chromo; where + AA bind to, with differing affinities, (-) charged groups attached to resins applied along the column*

Following treatment with a series of eluting solutions, the separated amino acids contained in the eluate from the column were heated with ninhydrin—a reagent that forms the blue-purple compound Ruhemann's Purple with most amino acids, amines, and ammonia (Figure 1).

*Key terms: eluting solutions, ninhydrin, Ruhemann's Purple*

*Cause and effect: ninhydrin + AA → blue-purple Ruhemann's Purple*

**Figure 1.** Ninhydrin and N-compound reaction mechanism

*Figure 1 Ninhydrin dehydrates → reacts with α-amino acid → form a Schiff base → decarboxylation/hydration → 1° amine and aldehyde; amine condenses with a second molecule of ketone → Ruhemann's Purple*

The amount of each amino acid present was then determined spectrophotometrically by measuring the amount of blue-purple light absorbed. The specific position of each amino acid in the polypeptide chain was also found. Edman reagent (phenylisothiocyanate) was used to label a terminal residue under mildly alkaline conditions, resulting in the formation of a phenylthiocarbamoyl. Under acidic conditions, the terminal amino acid of the polypeptide was cleaved, releasing free polypeptide and phenylthiohydantoin (PTH), an amino acid derivative that can be identified. Edman reagent was applied repeatedly, shortening the peptide bond obtained following each cycle. The steps of the Edman degradation are shown in Figure 2.

*Key terms: terminal residue, PTH, Edman degradation, spectrophotometrically*

*Cause and effect: Edman degradation mechanism - N-terminal residues were labeled to form a phenylthiocarbamoyl → cleaved to release free polypeptide and PTH → PTH-amino acid derivative ID'd; cycle repeated, shortening peptide*

**Figure 2.** Edman degradation steps

*Figure 2 shows that phenylisothyiocyanate is coupled to a polypeptide; the coupled phenylthiocarbamyol is cleaved producing PTH and the shortened polypeptide; the PTH-amino acid derivative is separated from the shortened polypeptide, and the shortened polypeptide is recycled for further coupling*

There are limits on the length of polypeptides that can be sequenced by this method. Over time, the yield of PTH amino acid products decreases relative to the background level of PTH-amino acids. Repetitive yield is a measure of the percent of detectable material remaining after each turn of the cycle. Longer polypeptides can be sequenced from greater initial sample sizes and larger repetitive yields. They may also be cleaved by peptidase enzymes to create shorter polypeptides for sequencing.

*Key terms: limits on length, repetitive yield; peptidase*

*Cause and effect: repetitive yield = % of detectable material remaining after each turn of the cycle; longer polypeptides = sequenced from greater initial sample sizes and larger repetitive yields; peptides can also be cleaved by peptidases prior to sequencing*

1. D is correct. SDS acts to disrupt the molecular forces which allow proteins to take their native conformation. The detergent also creates a uniform (-) charge across the protein. The protein then migrates a distance through the gel which is inversely proportional to its molecular weight. Edman degradation shrinks the size of a polypeptide,

meaning the degraded protein will have a smaller molecular weight, and will migrate a greater distance. Because we do not know the exact size of Hrt-34, we cannot know the exact difference in migration distance.

2. D is correct. According to the passage, the first residue labeled by reaction with phenylisothiocyanate is a terminal one. Figure 2 indicates that the N-terminal amino residue is specifically the first removed. The N-terminal residue of the polypeptide shown, alanine (Ala), will be isolated first (choice A). Choice B will be the second residue isolated. Choice C will be the third residue isolated. Choice D will be the final residue isolated.

3. B is correct. According to the passage, free amino acids bind negatively charged resins. Treatment with an eluant of increasing ionic strength and pH, such as those with differing salt concentrations, could disrupt the ionic bonding between polypeptide and column anions by influencing the charge state of the polypeptides, decreasing their likelihood of existing in the charged, cationic state.
A, C, D: As the concentration of protonated amino acid decreases, so too does the concentration of amino acids capable of interacting with negatively charged substrate (Choice B). Hydrophobic wash would not directly lead to deprotonation of bound amino acids (Choice A). Neither digestive enzymes nor a denaturant would be relevant when considering free amino acids.

4. A is correct. If polypeptide unfolding proceeds via a unimolecular mechanism, the rate law for the reaction must be first order with respect to only the polypeptide and first order overall. The rate law for such a reaction is given by the expression:

$$R = k \, [\text{polypeptide}]$$

where R represents the rate of the reaction, given in units of M/s. Rearranging the expression to solve for k, you find k = R/[polypeptide].
B, C, D: In terms of unit, $k = ([M]/[s])/[M] = 1/s$ (choice A). Choice B is incorrect because all rate constants include an inverse time term. Choice C gives the units of a second order rate constant. Choice D gives the units for a zeroth order rate constant, the units of an overall rate expression.

5. A is correct. We need to look at Step 1 of Figure 2. The reaction of phenylisothiocyanate and the polypeptide is an addition reaction. In an addition reaction, the number of pi bonds declines, while the number of sigma bonds increases, as is the case in this reaction (Choice A).
B, C, D: A dehydration reaction (Choice B) involves the net loss of water. A neutralization reaction (Choice C) occurs between an acid and base to form a salt and, in many cases, water. An elimination reaction (Choice D), is the reverse of an addition reaction. During elimination, the number of pi bonds increases and the number of sigma bonds decreases.

6. C is correct. In order to determine quaternary (i.e. subunit) structure, the conditions must be able to target and then break up the links (e.g. disulfide links) holding quaternary structure together. Under reducing conditions interactions between polypeptides is disrupted. However, under non-reducing conditions, the interactions are preserved.
   A. Native gels means the proteins runs as it exists *in vivo*, meaning all of its protein structure remains intact.
   B. SDS is a detergent added to PAGE experiments in order to unwind and coat all proteins in the sample, ensuring a uniform negative charge across all of them, and allowing the proteins to be separated by size.

7. A is correct. The reaction between 1,2,3-indantrione and the α-amino acid begins with attack by the nitrogen of the α-amino acid's amino residue on a carbonyl carbon of 1,2,3-indantrione. The reaction requires an available lone pair on the amino nitrogen of the acid. No lone pair is available in the protonated, quaternary amino nitrogen shown in Choices B and C. The reaction rate will be maximized when the carbonyl oxygen of the carbonyl attacked in the reaction is activated to attack by protonation (choice A). Because of a more favorable resonance contributor in the protonated versus the unprotonated carbonyl, the electrophilicity of the carbonyl carbon, and the reaction rate, are increased when compared to the carbonyl carbon electrophilicity and reaction rate of the unprotonated carbonyl-oxygen (Choice D).

## Independent Questions

1. Isoelectric focusing is an electrophoretic technique that separates proteins based on isoelectric point (pI). Which of the following proteins would be expected to have the lowest pI, given no additional information?
   A. A protein with a higher-than-average lysine composition
   B. An enzyme with a lower-than-average valine composition
   C. An enzyme with a higher-than-average glutamic acid composition
   D. A protein with a lower-than-average aspartic acid composition

2. SDS-PAGE gels are routinely used to separate proteins. Which of the following describes how the application of SDS affects the structure of a protein?
   A. SDS disrupts secondary and tertiary protein structure and applies a uniform negative charge across the protein.
   B. SDS disrupts secondary and tertiary protein structure and applies a uniform positive charge across the protein.
   C. SDS denatures the protein's higher-level structure, allowing separation by charge.
   D. SDS disrupts the primary structure of the protein of interest, allowing separation by mass.

3. A research scientist has recently used *Escherichia coli* to overexpress a fusion protein, tagged with glutathione S-transferase (GST). Which of the following would be the most appropriate method to isolate the fusion protein?
   A. Filtration
   B. Mass spectrometry
   C. Size-exclusion chromatography
   D. Immunoaffinity

4. Which of the following statements is true regarding the impact of surrounding salt concentrations on protein solubility?
   A. "Salting in" increases protein solubility and is most effective when salt concentrations are already very high.
   B. "Salting in" increases protein solubility and is most effective when salt concentrations are not yet very high.
   C. "Salting out" is accomplished by lowering the salt concentration in a protein-containing solution.
   D. Protein solubility increases linearly with salt concentration along the entire range of possible concentrations.

5. A biochemist wishes to separate an enzyme into its subunits for further study. It is known that the complete enzyme has three catalytic subunits of similar sizes, as well as a single regulatory subunit that is much smaller than the catalytic subunits. After the biochemist purifies the enzyme and performs successful SDS-PAGE, the polyacrylamide gel will display:
   A. two bands, and the darker band will have migrated a greater distance.
   B. two bands, and the lighter band will have migrated a greater distance.
   C. a single band.
   D. four bands, all of which will have migrated different distances.

6. Of the following, which amino acid would contribute most to a protein's absorbance of light with a wavelength of 280 nm?
   A. Thr
   B. Asp
   C. Tyr
   D. Lys

7. A cation-exchange chromatography apparatus:
   A. contains a negatively-charged stationary phase, causing anions to elute faster than cations.
   B. contains a negatively-charged stationary phase, causing cations to elute faster than anions.
   C. contains a positively-charged stationary phase, causing anions to elute faster than cations.
   D. contains a positively-charged stationary phase, causing cations to elute faster than anions.

8. A tired research student is setting up an isoelectric focusing procedure. He accidentally adds a lysine-rich protein to the pH-gradient gel instead of his desired sample, which was largely composed of hydrophobic residues. How would this mistake impact his findings?
   A. The protein will be observed to move more rapidly toward the positively-charged pole.
   B. The protein will become stationary at a position farther from its isoelectric point.
   C. The protein will travel a greater distance toward the anode.
   D. The protein will become stationary at a position closer to the cathode.

## Independent Question Explanations

1. C is correct. Since acidic side chains have low $pK_a$ values, proteins rich in acidic residues are expected to have relatively low pI values due to the low pKa values of their side chains. Glutamic acid is an acidic residue. Note that the opposite is true for basic residues; a protein rich in lysine, for example, would have a relatively high pI assuming other factors are constant (choice A is incorrect). An low amount of acidic residues, like aspartic acid, would not contribute to a lower pI (eliminate choice D). An amino acid with uncharged side chains, like valine, would not be expected to have a low pI (eliminate choice B).

2. A is correct. We can use process of elimination to answer this question. SDS applies a uniform negative, not positive, charge along the protein (eliminate choice B). Additionally, SDS is used to allow separation by size or mass, not by charge (eliminate option C). Finally, SDS does not disrupt primary structure (eliminate choice D). We are left with choice A, which is an accurate description of the function of SDS.

3. D is correct. Immunoaffinity, also known as immunoaffinity chromatography, uses antibody-protein affinity to retain the desired substrate on the solid-phase matrix. In this case, the popular GST antibody is used to bind the GST-bound protein. We can also use process of elimination; filtration would not isolate the specific protein of interest, mass spectrometry would destroy the sample, and size-exclusion chromatography would fail to separate the GST-bound protein from other molecules of a similar size.

4. B is correct. "Salting in" refers to the addition of a salt to a solution that does not yet contain very high salt concentrations. The salt interacts with charged amino acid side chains, reducing the protein's ability to aggregate with other proteins. The net result is increased protein solubility, making choice B the correct answer. In contrast, when salt concentrations are already high, addition of more salt decreases protein solubility and is termed "salting out."

5. B is correct. SDS-PAGE separates proteins or protein subunits by size. Smaller proteins or subunits travel a greater distance through the polyacrylamide gel. Here, the darker band reflects the three catalytic subunits, which (as they have similar sizes) will be found at the same location on the gel and will thus appear as one dark band, rather than three lighter ones. The lighter band represents the single regulatory subunit. As this subunit is smaller than the others, its band will be observed farther along the gel.

6. C is correct. Tyrosine (Tyr) is an aromatic amino acid. The presence of residues with aromatic side chains causes a protein to absorb ultraviolet light, which ranges from 200-400 nm. Other aromatic amino acids include phenylalanine (Phe) and tryptophan (Trp).

7. A is correct. In cation-exchange chromatography, the stationary phase is designed to attract cations (positively-charged molecules). As such, the phase itself is anionic, or negatively- charged. Cations are attracted to this phase and are retained in the column, while anions (negatively-charged particles) elute through the column quickly.

8. D is correct. A protein rich in lysine (a basic amino acid) will have a higher isoelectric point (pI) than a protein largely formed from hydrophobic residues. A higher pI means the protein will tend to be more positively charged and will thus move closer to the negative end of the gel. In electrophoresis, the apparatus functions like an electrolytic cell, meaning that the anode is positive and the cathode is negative. The lysine-rich protein, which is positively charged at physiological pH, then, will move closer to the negatively-charged cathode. Note that in isoelectric focusing, a protein or amino acid always becomes stationary when it has reached the portion of the gel corresponding to its isoelectric point.

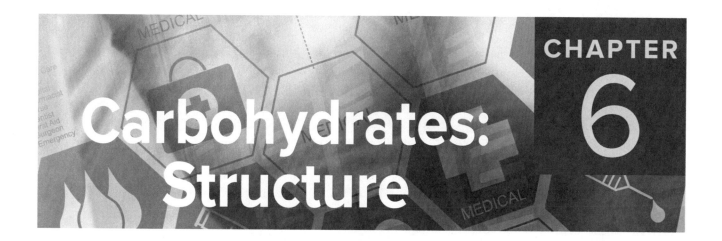

# CHAPTER 6

# Carbohydrates: Structure

## 0. Introduction

The function of carbohydrates in the body is primarily to provide energy (although, as we will see, fats can be an important energy source as well). In this chapter, we will focus on the structure of carbohydrates, while in the next two chapters, we will explore how carbohydrates are metabolized to provide energy.

Of the main classes of biomolecules (proteins, carbohydrates, lipids, and amino acids), studying the structure of carbohydrates poses some unique challenges. First, there's a wide range of carbohydrates that you have to be aware of, and they don't always differ in a structurally obvious way, like amino acids, which have notably different side chains. Second, carbohydrates exist both in linear forms and in ring forms. You have to be familiar with both, as well as with the interconversion between them. Moreover, several types of projections are used to visualize carbohydrate structure. Third, carbohydrates generally have multiple stereocenters, meaning that their stereochemistry is complex—and in fact, a separate system has been developed to analyze carbohydrate stereochemistry. Fourth, as if this wasn't enough, carbohydrates bond with each other to form chains, and you need to be aware of biologically relevant disaccharides and polysaccharides, *and* understand how they are formed.

> **MCAT STRATEGY > > >**
>
> The material in this chapter is challenging, but stay positive! If you invest the time in systematically learning this material, to the point where you can deploy it with confidence on Test Day, you will have a very real advantage.

In this chapter, we'll first focus on the overall structure and nomenclature of carbohydrates, and then discuss their cyclic form. Next, we'll review monosaccharides, disaccharides, and polysaccharides, and then we'll step back to thoroughly review the stereochemistry of carbohydrates. Finally, we'll review some of the important reactions of carbohydrates.

# 1. Overall Structure and Nomenclature

Carbohydrates get their name because they fit the formula $C_x(H_2O)_y$ – that is, they are composed of carbon and water. They contain a carbon backbone, a carbonyl group (C=O), and at least one hydroxyl group (–OH). If the molecule contains a terminal carbonyl group, it is known as an aldose (because it is an aldehyde), while if the carbonyl group is non-terminal, it is known as a ketose (because it is a ketone). Depending on the number of carbons, carbohydrates can be referred to as trioses (3 carbons), tetroses (4 carbons), pentoses (5 carbons), or hexoses (6 carbons). Some heptoses (7 carbons) exist as well, but are not relevant for the MCAT.

It is very unusual for carbohydrates to be referred to using IUPAC nomenclature. Instead, in most contexts, a common name (or a modification of a common name) is used. Many different monosaccharides exist, and the MCAT certainly does not expect you to be aware of all of them. However, there are a few (~5) biologically important monosaccharides that you should be able to recognize.

Glyceraldehyde is an important triose. It is the simplest aldose. Its structure is shown below in Figure 1, in two different projections. The projection on the left, which shows glyceraldehyde as having a straight backbone of carbon atoms, is known as a Fischer projection.

**Figure 1.** Glyceraldehyde.

Glyceraldehyde is significant for a few reasons. First, it is biologically relevant, because derivatives of glyceraldehyde are important intermediates in glycolysis. The six-carbon glucose molecule, after being converted into 1,6-fructose bisphosphate, is split in half to form glyceraldehyde 3-phosphate (GADP) and a compound known as dihydroxyacetone phosphate, which is itself then converted into GADP. GADP is therefore the basis for the second half of glycolysis, also known as the "payoff" phase.

> > **CONNECTIONS** < <

**Chapter 7 of Biochemistry**

Glyceraldehyde is also important historically and from the perspective of nomenclature. We'll talk more about this in section 4, which is devoted to stereochemistry, but the essential idea is that the stereochemistry of carbohydrates can be described based on whether the chiral carbon furthest from the carbonyl carbon is aligned in the same direction as D-glyceraldehyde (the form shown in Figure 1).

For the most part, tetroses and pentoses are not especially important from the point of view of MCAT biochemistry, although you should know that they exist. The one major exception is a pentose known as ribose, the structure of which is shown in Figure 2.

**Figure 2.** Ribose.

Ribose is mostly noteworthy because it is important in some key biochemical contexts. Most notably, it is one of the three structural components (along with nucleobases and phosphate groups) of nucleic acids. Ribonucleic acid (RNA) is formed with ribose itself, whereas its derivative, deoxyribose, is used to form deoxyribonucleic acid (DNA). As the name implies, deoxyribose is derived from ribose by the removal of an oxygen. More specifically, deoxyribose is missing the 2' hydroxyl group of ribose. Ribose—or, more precisely, ribose 5-phosphate—is also derived from glucose as part of the pentose phosphate pathway, from which it is used in nucleotide synthesis. The pentose phosphate pathway, which provides a bridge between carbohydrate metabolism and nucleic acids, is discussed in more detail in Chapter 7.

> > CONNECTIONS < <

Chapter 7 of Biochemistry

For the most part, in human metabolism, hexoses are where the action is. The most important hexose is glucose, which is the main source of energy for the body under normal circumstances. Glucose is an aldose, and its Fischer projection can easily be recognized because the hydroxyl group at C3 points in the opposite direction as the other hydroxyl groups. Another important hexose is fructose, which is present in many sources of food (glucose and fructose together form the disaccharide known as sucrose), and is metabolized by the liver. Considerable research has been carried out into the health effects of fructose, given its widespread use as a food additive in the form of high-fructose corn syrup. Structurally, fructose is notable because it is a ketose. Finally, galactose is found in dairy products and sugar beets. It is an aldose that can be rapidly converted to glucose. Its Fischer projection is characterized by having C3 and C4 point in one direction, while C2 and C5 point in another. The structures of glucose, fructose, and galactose are shown below in Figure 3.

**Figure 3.** Glucose, fructose, and galactose.

In Figure 3, the structure of glucose contains the conventional numbering of the carbons. C1 is the aldehyde carbon in aldoses, and this numbering scheme is carried over the ketoses. The ultimate rationale for this numbering scheme is connected to the Cahn-Ingold-Prelog priority rules, which state that a double bond counts as two equivalents of the given single bond. Therefore, in a molecule with one carbonyl (C=O) group and several carbons bonded to single hydroxyl (–OH) groups, the carbonyl carbon will have the highest priority.

## 2. Cyclic Carbohydrates

In physiological conditions, the linear structures we saw above in section 1 are fairly uncommon. Instead, pentoses and hexoses can exist in cyclic forms. The idea here is that the carbonyl carbon that forms the aldehyde or ketone group (C=O) in the carbohydrate can react with the hydroxyl (–OH) group of either C5 or C6 of the linear chain to form a hemiacetal or a hemiketal. This general reaction is shown below in Figure 4.

Aldehyde    Alcohol                     Hemiacetal

**Figure 4.** Formation of hemiacetals and hemiketals.

It is important to be able to visualize how the cyclic structures of carbohydrates correspond to the general schema of hemiacetal/hemiketal formation, because these functional groups are not necessarily the most familiar. Figure 5 below shows common cyclic forms of glucose and fructose with the carbon involved in forming the hemiacetal/hemiketal depicted with an arrow.

As can be seen in Figure 5, hexoses can form either six-membered rings or five-membered rings. This leads to another potential point of terminological confusion. Carbohydrates in six-membered rings are known as pyranoses, while those in five-membered rings are known as furanoses. These names are due to their similarities with cyclic ester compounds known as pyran and furan, which have six- and five-membered rings, respectively.

> **MCAT STRATEGY > > >**
>
> The best way to remember the difference between pyranoses and furanoses is that fructose tends to form a <u>five</u>-carbon <u>furanose</u> ring.

Aldohexoses such as glucose can form both pyranose and furanose rings, although the six-carbon pyranose rings tend to predominate. Ketohexoses such as fructose tend to form furanose rings, in which the C2 carbonyl carbon reacts with the C5 carbon. Thus, the structures seen in Figure 5 could also be labeled glucopyranose and fructofuranose.

**Figure 5.** Cyclic forms of glucose and fructose.

To review, a hemiacetal is defined as a carbon atom with the following substituents: –R, –OR, –OH, and –H. In the cyclic form of glucose shown in Figure 5, the –R group corresponds to the carbon ring of the carbohydrate that extends out from the page to the left of the hemiacetal carbon. The –OR group corresponds to the –O that is also connected to C5, and the –OH and –H groups are clearly visible. A hemiketal has the same structure, but the –H group is replaced by a second –R group (corresponding to the difference between a ketone and an aldehyde). In the fructose ring shown in Figure 5, that second –R group is the –CH₂OH group pointing down from the hemiketal carbon.

An important point to note here is that the achiral C=O carbon has now turned into a chiral center with four different substituents. In particular, the orientation of the substituents that aren't part of the ring is basically arbitrary. That is, in the structures shown in Figure 5, the –OH in the glucose points down while the –H points up and out, while in the cyclic fructose molecule, the –OH points up and the –CH₂OH points down—but this is entirely arbitrary and the molecule could be arranged in the opposite configuration.

The different possible orientations of these substituents correspond to what are known as different anomers of cyclic carbohydrates. In the structures shown above (Haworth projections), the structures in which the –OH points down are known as alpha (α) anomers, and those in which the –OH points up are known as beta (β) anomers. Figure 5 shows the α-anomer of glucose and the β-anomer of fructose. Combining this information with what we previously discussed about pyranoses versus furanoses, we could refer to the structures in Figure 5 as α-glucopyranose and β-fructofuranose. The β-anomers tend to be most common in solution. For example, an aqueous solution of glucose at equilibrium will be about one-third α-glucopyranose and two-thirds β-glucopyranose, with small amounts of the straight-chain and glucofuranose forms. The process of interconversion between the α- and β-anomers is known as mutarotation. Note that this interconversion does involve the breaking and reforming of covalent bonds.

Figure 6 below compares the α- and β-anomers of glucose to help you consolidate your understanding of this structural difference. Since this diagram is numbered, be sure to also review the numbering of the carbons.

**Figure 6.** α- and β-anomers of glucose

Since the term "anomer" is used to distinguish between these structures that differ in terms of the orientation of substituents at C1, C1 is known as the anomeric carbon.

Now that we've covered the structures of cyclic carbohydrates in isolation (as monosaccharides), let's move on to discuss how they combine with each other to form disaccharides, oligosaccharides, and polysaccharides.

# 3. Disaccharides and Polysaccharides

Monosaccharides can combine with each other to form groups of two carbohydrate molecules, known as disaccharides, and groups of many carbohydrate molecules, which are in turn known as polysaccharides.

The key mechanism through which monosaccharides combine with each other is known as a glycosidic bond. A glycosidic bond is formed when the anomeric carbon of one sugar reacts with a hydroxyl group in another sugar. This is a dehydration reaction, in which an $H_2O$ molecule is lost as the two monosaccharides condense to form a disaccharide; as such, it is similar to how peptide bonds are formed between amino acids, although the specific functional groups involved are different (an amide is formed in a peptide bond, whereas an ether [C–O–C] is formed in a glycosidic bond). Moreover, the formation of a glycosidic bond transforms the hemiacetal or hemiketal found at the anomeric carbon into an acetal or a ketal, because the –OH group that is characteristic of a hemiacetal/hemiketal is transformed into a second –OR group, which defines an acetal/ketal.

Disaccharides are important because we consume a considerable amount of carbohydrates in the form of disaccharides. There are three major disaccharides that you need to know for the MCAT: sucrose, lactose, and maltose.

Sucrose is also known as table sugar, and is formed by a combination of glucose and fructose. More specifically, in a sucrose molecule, a glycosidic bond is formed between C1 (the anomeric carbon) of the α-anomer of glucose and C2 of the β-anomer of fructose. This means that structurally, sucrose can be referred to in an abbreviated form as Glu(α1→β2)Fru, where the notation in parentheses provides information about the exact configuration of the glycosidic bond.

Lactose is a disaccharide found in milk. It is characterized by a β(1→4) glycosidic bond between galactose and glucose, and can therefore be abbreviated as Gal(β1→4)Glu. Lactose requires a specific enzyme, lactase, to be hydrolyzed. Lactase is expressed in all humans through early childhood to assist in the breakdown of breast milk, but then its expression is generally turned off. Throughout the evolution of human societies, several groups of people—notably including northern Europeans, as well as various isolated groups throughout Africa—who cultivated cows evolved the ability to express lactase throughout the life span. Humans who do not express lactase throughout their lifetime are susceptible to lactose intolerance; however, the terminology is slightly ironic, because evolutionarily speaking, it is lactose *tolerance* into adulthood that was the innovation.

Finally, maltose is formed by two glucose molecules joined by an α(1→4) glycosidic bond, such that it can be abbreviated as Glu(α1→4)Glu. It is produced when amylase breaks down the polysaccharide known as starch, which is formed by longer chains of glucose molecules. It is also present in a variety of food products, such as potatoes, pasta, and beer.

Polysaccharides consist of long chains of carbohydrates. Their most relevant function for the MCAT is energy storage, but they also play some important structural roles. The glucose polymer starch is one of the most important ways in which we consume carbohydrates; examples of starchy foods include potatoes, rice, and bread. In fact, starch is the major way in which green plants store energy. Starch is composed of two main subtypes of polymers: amylose and amylopectin. Amylose is a linear polymer of glucose molecules connected by α(1→4) glycosidic bonds; it composes about 20%-30% of starch. Amylopectin makes up the remaining 70%-80% of starch; it likewise contains glucose molecules connected by α(1→4) glycosidic bonds, but it has branches due to α(1→6) glycosidic bonds every 24-30 units. It is somewhat easier to break down than amylose.

Humans (as well as most other non-plant forms of life) store energy in the form of glycogen. In humans, glycogen is stored in liver and muscle cells. The glycogen stored in hepatocytes (liver cells) can be mobilized into the bloodstream to regulate blood glucose levels and provide cells with energy, while the glycogen used in muscle cells is generally broken down to power glycolysis. Structurally, glycogen is similar to amylopectin in that it contains chains of glucose molecules connected by α(1→4) glycosidic bonds, with intervening α(1→6) glycosidic bonds that create branches; the main difference is that glycogen is more heavily branched than amylopectin, with branches occurring every 8-12 units.

A polysaccharide known as cellulose plays a major structural role in the cell wall of plants. Like starch and glycogen, it is a polymer of glucose, but unlike them, it incorporates the β-anomer of glucose. More specifically, in cellulose, the glucose subunits are connected by β(1→4) glycosidic bonds. This seemingly small structural distinction makes a world of practical difference. Humans lack the necessary enzymes to digest cellulose. However, we do consume a considerable amount of cellulose contained in plants in our diet; in the context of nutrition, cellulose is referred to as insoluble fiber, and is excreted via defecation.

The must-know monosaccharides, disaccharides, and polysaccharides are summarized below in Table 1.

| MONOSACCHARIDES | | | | |
|---|---|---|---|---|
| Name | Type | Linear structure | Ring form | Notes |
| Glucose | Aldohexose | | | Main source of fuel for the organism |
| Fructose | Ketohexose | | | Produced by many plants/fruits, commonly used as a sweetener |
| Galactose | Aldohexose | | | Found in dairy products and sugar beets; can be rapidly converted to glucose |

| DISACCHARIDES | | | |
|---|---|---|---|
| Name | Composition | Ring form | Notes |
| Sucrose | Glucose + fructose | | Table sugar |

| Lactose | Glucose + galactose | | Lactose tolerance depends on continued expression of lactase |
| Maltose | Glucose + glucose | | Found in beer, cereal, pasta, and potatoes; produced by breakdown of starch |

| POLYSACCHARIDES | | |
|---|---|---|
| **Name** | **Composition** | **Notes** |
| Amylose | Linear chains of glucose linked by α(1→4) glycosidic bonds | A major component of starch (20%-30%); less easily digested than amylopectin |
| Amylopectin | Linear chains of glucose linked by α(1→4) glycosidic bonds + branching due to α(1→6) glycosidic bonds every 24-30 units | Comprises approximately 70%-80% of starch; broken down more easily than amylose |
| Starch | ~20%-30% amylose, ~70%-80% amylopectin | Major energy store produced by most green plants; most common form of carbohydrate in most diets |
| Glycogen | Linear chains of glucose linked by α(1→4) glycosidic bonds + branching due to α(1→6) glycosidic bonds every 8-12 units | Similar to amylopectin, but more branched; synthesized in liver and stored primarily in liver cells and muscle cells; how the body stores glucose to be used |
| Cellulose | Linear chain of glucose units linked by β(1→4) bonds | Produced by many plants; not digestible by humans; often referred to as dietary fiber |

**Table 1.** Structure and properties of important carbohydrates.

In addition to these must-know carbohydrates, there are a few other biologically relevant polysaccharides that you may have heard of. Peptidoglycan, which is a major constituent of bacterial cell walls, is a polymer composed of carbohydrates that have been modified with amino acids. Chitin is a polysaccharide composed of *N*-acetylglucosamine (a glucose derivative) molecules connected by β(1→4) glycosidic bonds. Chitin is a major component of cell walls in the exoskeletons of crustaceans (such as lobsters and crabs), insects, and fungi. You aren't responsible for knowing the structures of peptidoglycan and chitin to the same extent that you should be familiar with the polysaccharides in Table 1, but you may see them mentioned, and it is worth being generally aware that they are polysaccharides. These examples help underscore the fact that carbohydrates contribute to the structure of organisms as well as serving as sources of energy.

# 4. Stereochemistry of Carbohydrates

As we have seen to some extent already, the stereochemistry of carbohydrates poses several unique challenges due to the presence of multiple chiral centers, the fact that monosaccharides can exist in both linear and cyclic forms, and the fact that they can be connected to each other in multiple ways. This information is often presented piecemeal in biochemistry textbooks and MCAT prep books, but in order to consolidate this information, it's worth reviewing the stereochemistry of chemistry in one place. In this section, we'll work through the stereochemistry of carbohydrates systematically, starting with the absolute configuration of linear monosaccharides and then proceeding to cover cyclic monosaccharides, before finally reviewing the terminology used to describe glycosidic bonds that connect monosaccharides to each other.

There are a few options that we have to discuss the absolute configuration of monosaccharides from a stereochemical perspective: (1) the optical rotation of light (*d/l* or +/−); (2) the *R/S* system of absolute configuration that you have studied in organic chemistry and must know inside and out for the MCAT; or (3) a historically important system based on comparing longer-chain carbohydrates to the three-carbon substance glyceraldehyde (D/L).

Let's turn first to the classification of carbohydrates based on the optical rotation of light (*d/l* or +/−). This system is very rarely used, because the direction in which a compound rotates plane-polarized light must be determined empirically; that is, there is no one-to-one relationship between the direction in which light is rotated and the structure of the compound. However, you absolutely do need to know for the MCAT that enantiomers have the property of rotating plane-polarized light in opposite directions, and it is important to recognize that this can be applied to the analysis of carbohydrates.

The *R/S* system of absolute configuration can be applied to carbohydrates in principle, but this happens only rarely in practice because it can be quite cumbersome. For example, the systematic IUPAC name for D-glucose is (2*R*,3*S*,4*R*,5*R*)-2,3,4,5,6-pentahydroxyhexanal, which is certainly accurate, but a major mouthful and is accurate to the point of being difficult to understand in everyday contexts. For this reason, a different system was developed for carbohydrates: the D/L system.

If you know one thing about the D/L system, *you must understand it is __not__ the same as the d/l system and does __not__ have anything to do with how light is rotated.* This is admittedly a very frustrating point of nomenclature in sugar chemistry, but the italicized *d* is a completely different thing than the small capital D. To understand this system, we first have to look at the Fischer projections of glyceraldehyde. As we've discussed before, glyceraldehyde is a simple three-carbon carbohydrate that only has a single chiral center, and therefore only two stereoisomers. The two possible Fischer projections of glyceraldehyde are shown below in Figure 7.

**Figure 7.** Enantiomers of glyceraldehyde.

Figure 7 shows which enantiomer is referred to as D-glyceraldehyde and which is referred to as L-glyceraldehyde. The key point here is realizing that it's pretty arbitrary: D-glyceraldehyde has the higher-priority substituent (the –OH) at the chiral carbon pointing right (recall that the letter *d* is associated with 'right' in Latin-derived terms like 'dextrorotatory'), while L-glyceraldehyde has the –OH pointing left. Other carbohydrates are defined as D or L based on a comparison with D-glyceraldehyde and L-glyceraldehyde. However, there's one final point of nomenclature-related hygiene we have to deal with here. Hexoses have four stereocenters, so which one is compared to glyceraldehyde? By convention, the stereocenter furthest from the aldehyde carbon—or, visually, the one at the bottom of the conventional Fischer projection—is used. That is, by definition, any carbohydrate in which the bottom-most –OH in the Fischer projection is pointing right is defined as D, while if the bottom-most –OH is pointing to the left, it is L-glyceraldehyde.

We might ask at this point: what about the other stereocenters? Well, for different arrangements of the other stereocenters, we have different names. As shown in Figure 8, there are eight different D-aldohexoses, corresponding to the three remaining chiral centers: allose, altrose, glucose, mannose, gulose, idose, galactose, and talose.

**Figure 8.** The eight D-aldohexoses.

Let's be bluntly honest: this system is convoluted, and the potential confusion with *d/l* notation can be frustrating. Nonetheless, let's step back and explore why scientists continue to use it. First off, it turns out that the overwhelming majority of carbohydrates in living organisms are D-isomers. Therefore, if not otherwise specified, you can assume that 'glucose' refers to D-glucose. Moreover, using this terminology to refer to the stereocenter furthest from the carbonyl carbon reduces the number of hexoses that have to get their own names

## MCAT STRATEGY > > >

You do *not* have to know all eight of the hexoses. The point of this figure is to underscore that all D-hexoses have the bottom-most –OH group pointing to the right in their Fischer projections, and that this is what it means to be D.

from 16 to eight, which is much more manageable. As we discussed above, the *d/l* systems and the *R/S* systems have problems of their own in handling carbohydrates, so it may be best to think of the D/L system as being the least bad of the various options.

The terms 'diastereomer' and 'enantiomer' can be applied to carbohydrates, just as they can be applied to chiral compounds in general. The key here is to remember that for a compound with multiple stereocenters, enantiomers refer to pairs in which the orientation of *all* the chiral centers are flipped. Therefore, the D/L isomers of each carbohydrate are enantiomers. Diastereomers refer to all other stereoisomers. The special term 'epimer' exists in sugar chemistry, and refers to pairs of carbohydrates that differ at only one stereocenter. Keeping all of these terms straight can be a real challenge, so let's review them more concretely by seeing how they apply to aldohexoses, which are a category comprising 16 (=2⁴) possible stereoisomers at four chiral centers.

> Each aldohexose has a single enantiomer, corresponding to the D/L-isomers. The fact that each aldohexose has only one enantiomer reflects the fact that there is only one other structure in which *all* of the stereocenters would have an opposite notation, and the fact that the enantiomers are D/L-isomers is because the principle of D/L orientation was built into how the aldohexoses are named (Fig. 8).
> Each aldohexose has four epimers. That is because there is one epimer for each stereocenter.
> Each aldohexose has 14 diastereomers. This number is obtained by starting from 16, subtracting 1 to account for the aldohexose itself (D-glucose is obviously not its own diastereomer) and subtracting 1 to account for its enantiomer (for D-glucose, that would be L-glucose). An important point to note here is that *epimers are diastereomers*, just very specific diastereomers.

## MCAT STRATEGY > > >

You can think of enantiomers as being like siblings and diastereomers as being like cousins. With this analogy, epimers are like close cousins—on one hand, they're close, but on the other hand, they're still cousins.

## MCAT STRATEGY > > >

It's unlikely that you'd get a question on the MCAT showing you a structure and asking you to determine whether it's β-D-glucopyranose, β-D-glucofuranose, α-D-glucopyranose, or α-D-glucofuranose (although it's conceivably possible); instead, the main payoff in studying this terminology is to help you cope with these terms more easily if they show up in a passage and to help pave the way for talking about glycosidic bonds.

In section 2, we discussed what happens when linear carbohydrates form cyclic rings. There are two basic things that you have to account for here: (1) whether a six-member or a five-member ring is formed, and (2) whether the –OH group at the anomeric carbon is pointing up or down. To review, six-carbon carbohydrate rings are known as pyranoses, and five-carbon carbohydrate rings are known as furanoses. If the –OH group at the anomeric carbon is pointing down, the anomer is defined as being an α-anomer, while if it is pointing up, it is a β-anomer. Refer back to Figure 6 to clarify this point if needed.

The point about pyranoses versus furanoses is just a relatively low-yield (but still fair game!) terminological point. However, it's worth making a special note of the α- and β-anomers for two reasons. First, this adds another '-mer' term to your arsenal, so you have to make sure that you can distinguish enantiomers, diastereomers, epimers, *and* anomers. Second, as we saw in section 3, α- and β-anomers can have different biological properties; for instance, the only major structural difference between amylose (which is digestible by humans) and cellulose (which isn't) is that amylose has α(1→4) glycosidic bonds and cellulose has β(1→4) glycosidic bonds.

We can combine all these points of terminology to come up with very specific names for carbohydrates.

For example, we could refer to the most common form of glucose in an aqueous (physiological) solution as β-D-glucopyranose.

A final point to note regarding the stereochemistry of monosaccharides is that hexoses can exist in various conformations, much like cyclohexane (a prototypical six-membered ring). To review, conformations are spatial arrangements that are interchangeable without breaking bonds (unlike anomers). Pyranoses exist in either a chair or a boat form, while furanoses exist in the envelope form. It is difficult to give general rules about which conformation will be favored; as a rule, the least sterically hindered form will be favored, but which form is the most/least sterically hindered will depend on which substituents may be present. These conformations are shown in Figure 9.

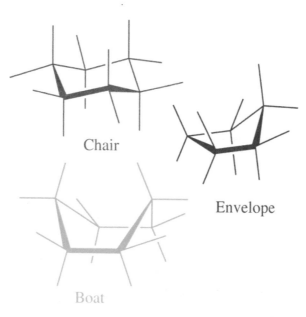

**Figure 9.** Conformations of hexoses.

Now that we've covered the stereochemistry of cyclic monosaccharides, disaccharides and polysaccharides are fairly straightforward. In theory, we can use the nomenclature that we used to discuss monosaccharides to specify every component in a disaccharide or polysaccharide, but that is very rarely done within the scope of MCAT-relevant science. Instead, the only thing we really need to review is the terminology used to refer to the glycosidic bonds that connect monosaccharides. We already saw this in section 3, in fact; to review, the α- and β-anomer status of each component is specified, and an arrow is used to indicate the numbers of the carbons involved in the bond. Thus, an α(1→4) is a bond between two α-isomers, in which C1 in the first monosaccharide (the anomeric carbon, which is involved in a glycosidic bond by definition) forms a glycosidic bond with C4 in the second monosaccharide.

**MCAT STRATEGY > > >**

The details of the conformations of hexoses are not as important as the points of nomenclature that can affect naming (i.e., D/L, α- vs. β-anomers, and pyranose vs. furanose), but you should be aware that the different conformations exist, much like how they exist for cyclohexane and its derivatives.

**> > CONNECTIONS < <**

Chapter 9 of Chemistry

## 5. Important Reactions

Both the formation and breakdown of glycosidic bonds are important physiologically. Since glycosidic bonds are formed via dehydration, it is not surprising that they are broken through hydrolysis. As with other physiologically

## MCAT STRATEGY > > >

The nomenclature of glycosidic bonds is often painful for students, as it can be confusing to keep track of which structures involve α(1→4) bonds versus α(1→6) bonds versus β(1→4) bonds. The key here is to learn the fundamentals thoroughly. If you know what α- and β-anomers are, and are familiar with carbon numbering, the nomenclature of glycosidic bonds becomes straightforward. If you skim through the fundamentals, though, you'll find yourself in the position of reading these terms without really understanding them, which makes you vulnerable to surprise questions on Test Day.

important bonds that are broken via hydrolysis, like peptide bonds, the hydrolysis of glycosidic bonds is carefully regulated through enzymes. We mentioned in section 3 that many adult humans lack lactase, which is the enzyme needed to break down lactose into its constituent monosaccharides. Additionally, humans (and most animals) lack the enzymes necessary to break down the β(1→4) bonds in cellulose. Thus, we can see that the hydrolysis of glycosidic bonds is necessary for carbohydrate processing and metabolism.

Carbohydrates also participate in some important reduction/oxidation reaction. Consider glucose, or any other aldose. Aldehydes in general can be oxidized to carboxylic acids, and this is particularly easy to accomplish for aldoses. Relatively straightforward oxidizing agents, such as $Ag^+$, $Cu^{2+}$, and $Fe^{3+}$, can be used to carry out this reaction. The resulting change in the oxidizing agent can be monitored to visualize the progress of such a reaction. For example, in the Tollen's test, the oxidation of an aldose is coupled with the reduction of $Ag^+$ to $Ag$, which precipitates to form a visually notable silver film. Benedict's reagent uses a similar principle, but involves copper(II) sulfate; the $Cu^{2+}$ ions in copper(II) sulfate are oxidized to $Cu^+$ ions, which form insoluble oxides and precipitate out. This can be visualized as a change from a blue solution to the formation of a red precipitate. Sugars that can participate in this reaction are known as reducing sugars, because they reduce the reagents that are used to monitor the reaction.

Reducing sugars and the reagents used to identify them are of historical importance in medicine, because these tests were previously used to identify the presence of glucose in urine to diagnose diabetes, although they have now been superseded by enzymatic techniques. They also provide an important window onto carbohydrate structure, and a way that the MCAT can connect carbohydrate structure to classic themes in general and organic chemistry.

As we extend this analysis into cyclic carbohydrates, disaccharides, polysaccharides, and ketoses, we need to remember the basic principle: if a sugar can be converted into an aldose, it's a reducing sugar.

Turning to cyclic carbohydrates first, any cyclic carbohydrate in which a hemiacetal is formed at the anomeric carbon is a reducing sugar, because the cyclic hemiacetal form exists in equilibrium with the linear aldose form. The linear aldose form can undergo oxidation, and then Le Châtelier's principle will push the reduction/oxidation reaction forward.

## MCAT STRATEGY > > >

The details of reducing sugars can be complicated, because this phenomenon involves synthesizing carbohydrate structure with redox chemistry, both of which are challenging topics. The key points you should focus on are (1) the point of the reaction and how it manifests; and (2) the fact that monosaccharides, maltose, and lactose are reducing sugars, while polysaccharides and sucrose are not.

Some disaccharides are reducing sugars as well. The principle here is that if an anomeric carbon is involved in a glycosidic bond, it cannot participate in a reduction/oxidation reaction, but if a free anomeric carbon is present, it can do so. Maltose and lactose are disaccharides with a free anomeric carbon, and are therefore reducing disaccharides. In theory, the same principle applies to polysaccharides, but there are so few terminal reducing anomeric carbons in polysaccharides that in practice, they are considered to be non-reducing.

Somewhat surprisingly, even ketose monosaccharides such as fructose are reducing sugars. This is due to keto-enol tautomerism. The resonance forms involved in the keto-enol tautomerism of ketoses include an aldose form, which can act as a reducing sugar. As with cyclic carbohydrates, Le Châtelier's principle will push the reduction/oxidation reaction forward.

# 6. Must-Knows

> Carbohydrates fit the formula $C_x(H_2O)_y$, and have a carbon backbone, a carbonyl group (C=O), and at least one hydroxyl group (–OH).
>   – If C=O is terminal → aldose, if not → ketose.
> Carbons numbered starting from the terminal C=O group or the end closest to it
> Crucial biological hexoses: glucose, fructose, galactose
> Pentose and hexoses can form cyclic forms (hemiacetals and hemiketals) via reaction of the carbonyl carbon (anomeric carbon) with C4 or C5, resulting in α- and β-anomers depending on the orientation of the –OH group pointing out of the ring.
>   – –OH group points down in α-anomers and up in β-anomers
> Disaccharides are formed by a glycosidic bond between two monosaccharides
>   – Glycosidic bond creates an acetal/ketal
>   – Sucrose: glucose + fructose, α1→β2 glycosidic bond
>   – Lactose: galactose + glucose, β(1→4) glycosidic bond
>   – Maltose: glucose + glucose, α(1→4) glycosidic bond
> Polysaccharides: long chains of carbohydrates
>   – Amylose: linear glucose chain with α(1→4) bonds
>   – Amylopectin: like amylose, but with α(1→6) branches every 24-30 units
>   – Starch (in foods): 20%-30% amylose + 70%-80% amylopectin
>   – Glycogen (energy storage in human): α(1→4) bonds with α(1→6) branches every 8-12 units
>   – Cellulose: indigestible fiber in plants; connected by β(1→4) bonds
> Stereochemistry
>   – Most common system is D/L system, based on orientation of D-glyceraldehyde – in linear Fischer projection, a D-carbohydrate is one with the bottom-most –OH group.
>   – Virtually all biological carbohydrates are D, and the use of the D/L system reduces the number of hexoses that need to be named from 16 to 8.
>   – Epimer = a pair of carbohydrates in which the orientation of only one chiral center differs; epimers are a special subset of diastereomers.
>   – Hexoses have 4 chiral centers and $2^4$ = 16 possible stereoisomers.
>   – Each hexose will have…
>     • One enantiomer (differing by D vs. L)
>     • Four epimers (one epimer for each stereocenter)
>     • 14 diastereomers
> Reducing sugars: terminal C=O in aldoses can easily be oxidized to carboxylic acids
>   – When an aldose is oxidized, something else gets reduced, making the aldose a reducing agent, more specifically known as a *reducing sugar.*
>   – Many redox reactions involving sugar can be monitored colorimetrically, allowing one to test for reducing sugars (Tollen's test, Benedict's reagent)
>   – Aldoses are reducing sugars, as are disaccharides where an element can be converted into a linear aldose. So are ketose monosaccharides, because they can tautomerize to aldoses.
>   – Sucrose is reducing; polymers like starch are effectively non-reducing, as only one end is reducing out of the hundreds to thousands of residues.

## Practice Passage

In portal systems, such as the liver and hypophyseal portals, blood is carried from one capillary bed to another without returning to the heart in between. The hepatic portal system allows nutrient-rich blood coming from the gastrointestinal tract and spleen to take an express path via the hepatic portal vein to the liver. The nutrients, which largely consist of monosaccharides absorbed by the first bed of capillaries, can be quickly processed and any ingested toxins can be filtered out.

Glycogen storage disease (GSD) type IV is a hereditary metabolic disorder resulting from enzymatic defects affecting glycogen processing, and can take a variety of forms. In the most common form, the progressive hepatic type, an affected baby is born with no apparent health defects but soon shows difficulty gaining weight and enlargement of the liver, leading to cirrhosis (i.e., scarring of the liver tissue) and hypertension (i.e., high blood pressure) in the hepatic portal. The disease is usually fatal within the first few years of life.

A two-month old girl born to healthy parents begins exhibiting such symptoms and is eventually diagnosed with GSD type IV. The child's father remembers that his brother died of a rare disease at the age of two, and quickly learns from his parents that this resulted from the same disease. The child's mother does not have any siblings.

1. Which of the following is NOT a metabolism-related or cardiovascular role performed by the liver?
   A. Breakdown of caffeine
   B. Insulin storage
   C. Bile production
   D. Angiotensinogen synthesis

2. As mentioned in the passage, to which organ does the other hypophyseal portal system circulate blood?
   A. Kidneys
   B. Heart
   C. Feet
   D. Brain

3. Which of the following sugars could NOT be oxidized to produce a dioic acid?

D-(-)-arabinose    D-(+)-xylose    D-(-)-lyxose    D-(-)-ribulose

   A. D-(-)-arabinose
   B. D-(+)-xylose
   C. D-(-)-lyxose
   D. D-(-)-ribulose

4. What type of inheritance does GSD type IV display, and if the same parents were to have a son, what is the likelihood that he will also suffer from GSD type IV?
   A. X-linked dominant; 100%
   B. Autosomal recessive; 25%`
   C. Autosomal recessive; 6.25%
   D. X-linked recessive; 50%

5. Which hexose shown below is the C-4 epimer of glucose?

A.

B.

C.

D.

6. Based on information provided in the passage, which of the following would be likely symptoms for someone born with the progressive, hepatic type of GSD type IV?
   I. Increased bone strength
   II. Toxin buildup in the brain
   III. Hepatomegaly
   A. I only
   B. I and II only
   C. II and III only
   D. I, II, and III

7. The structure of D-(-)-fructose is shown below.

```
    CH2OH
    |
    C=O
    |
HO—C—H
    |
 H—C—OH
    |
 H—C—OH
    |
    CH2OH
```

What is the correct structure of L-(-)-fructose?

```
       CH2OH                    CH2OH
       |                        |
       C=O                      C=O
       |                        |
   H—C—OH                   H—C—OH
       |                        |
  HO—C—H                    H—C—OH
       |                        |
  HO—C—H                    H—C—OH
       |                        |
       CH2OH                    CH2OH
A.                       B.

       HOCH2                    CH2OH
       |                        |
       C=O                      C=O
       |                        |
   H—C—OH                   HO—C—H
       |                        |
  HO—C—H                    HO—C—H
       |                        |
   H—C—OH                    H—C—OH
       |                        |
       HOCH2                    HOCH2
C.                       D.
```

## Practice Passage Explanations

In portal systems, such as the liver and hypophyseal portals, blood is carried from one capillary bed to another without returning to the heart in between. The hepatic portal system allows nutrient-rich blood coming from the gastrointestinal tract and spleen to take an express path via the hepatic portal vein to the liver. The nutrients, which largely consist of monosaccharides absorbed by the first bed of capillaries, can be quickly processed and any ingested toxins can be filtered out.

*Key terms: hepatic/hypophyseal portal system*

*Contrast: portal system = capillary pools into another capillary through veins w/o returning to the heart*

*Cause and effect: hepatic portal system shunts blood coming from the GI/spleen → liver → heart*

Glycogen storage disease (GSD) type IV is a hereditary metabolic disorder resulting from enzymatic defects affecting glycogen processing, and can take a variety of forms. In the most common form, the progressive hepatic type, an affected baby is born with no apparent health defects but soon shows difficulty gaining weight and enlargement of the liver, leading to cirrhosis (i.e., scarring of the liver tissue) and hypertension (i.e., high blood pressure) in the hepatic portal. The disease is usually fatal within the first few years of life.

*Key terms: GSD IV, cirrhosis, hypertension*

*Cause and effect: GSD IV = improper glycogen metabolism → symptoms (BP, liver) → death*

A two-month old girl born to healthy parents begins exhibiting such symptoms and is eventually diagnosed with GSD type IV. The child's father remembers that his brother died of a rare disease at the age of two, and quickly learns from his parents that this resulted from the same disease. The child's mother does not have any siblings.

*Key terms: GSD type IV genetics*

*Cause and effect: phenotypically normal parents → GSD IV daughter → dad is carrier*

1. B is correct. Insulin is stored in beta cells in the pancreas. The other three options, breakdown of caffeine, bile production, and angiotensinogen synthesis, are all well-established functions of the liver.
   A. The liver is responsible for the breakdown of toxins, which include caffeine and alcohol.
   C. Bile is produced in the liver before being transported to the gallbladder to be stored and concentrated.
   D. Angiotensinogen is the zymogen precursor to angiotensin, a peptide hormone that leads to vasoconstriction. It is produced in the liver.

2. D is correct. This requires the reader to know that the hypophyseal portal system, which is mentioned in the passage, connects the hypothalamus to the anterior pituitary in the brain, allowing for quick transport of hormones, which leads to rapid effects.
   A. A renal portal system is not present in humans, and is exclusively found in non-mammals.
   B. By definition, a portal system consists of two capillary beds, in which blood travels from the first capillary bed to the second without first returning to the heart. This is explicitly stated in the passage.
   C. There is no portal system that extends to the feet, nor would this be a logical explanation, as no organs that would necessitate such rapid transport of material via blood are present there.

3. D is correct. In order to produce 2 carboxylic acid groups, both ends of the sugar must be capable of being oxidized. Only an aldose can be oxidized on both ends. Choice D, D-(-)-ribulose, is a ketose. The ketone end will not be oxidized to a carboxylic acid, only the alcohol end will.

4. B is correct. This is a two-part question. Since both parents are healthy but clearly carry the gene leading to GSD type IV, the disease must be recessive. The key piece of information that points toward the disease being autosomal rather than X-linked is that the father is a carrier of the disease, but does not have it. If it were X-linked and he had an allele for the disease, he would present symptoms and likely not be alive today. This means the disease is autosomal recessive, and both parents must be heterozygous for the mutation leading to disease. The probability of two heterozygous parents producing a child homozygous for the mutation is ¼.
   A. If the disease gene were dominant, at least one of the child's parents would have had the disease.
   D. This answer implies that the female child has one copy of the disease gene from each parents. However, if this gene was on the X chromosome, her father would be affected by the disease since he only carries one X chromosome.

5. C is correct. Epimers are carbohydrates which differ in their configuration of a single chiral center. Here we want the one structure that differs from glucose at the 4$^{th}$ carbon.

6. C is correct. Enough information is stated in the passage to allow for the reasonable conclusion that both toxin buildup in the brain and hepatomegaly (enlarged liver) could occur as a result of GSD type IV and resulting cirrhosis. Bone strength may be decreased as a result of cirrhosis, but not enough information is given to conclude this. No evidence is provided that may allude to an increase in bone strength.
   A. As stated above, the passage does not provide any information that may allow a reasonable deduction to be made regarding bone strength, and if it had, it would point toward the possibility of decreased bone strength as a result of cirrhosis, not increased bone strength.
   B. Toxin buildup in the brain is a likely symptom for someone suffering from cirrhosis, as implied in the passage when it stated that one of the roles of the liver is to filter out ingested toxins. However, this answer is not correct because it excludes another correct answer.
   D. Since increased bone strength is not a likely symptom for someone born with progressive hepatic GSD type IV, as described above, this answer is not correct.

7. A is correct. D/L sugars are enantiomers. This means they are mirror images of each other, flipped at each and all of their chiral centers.

## Independent Questions

1. The structure of fructose is shown below:

   Which of the following is true of fructose?
   A. Fructofuranose is a ketose, while fructopyranose is an aldose.
   B. Elemental silver will be produced when fructose is present in a solution of Tollens' reagent.
   C. Fructofuranose is a pentose, while fructopyranose is a hexose.
   D. Fructose and glucose are stereoisomers.

2. In biological systems, glucose exists in equilibrium between two:
   A. anomers.
   B. structural isomers.
   C. enantiomers.
   D. polymers.

3. D-mannose is an epimer of D-glucose. If a solution of D-glucose has a specific rotation of +52°, what is the specific rotation of a solution of D-mannose?
   A. +52°
   B. -52°
   C. 0°
   D. It cannot be determined from the given information.

4. Which of the following is a disaccharide?
   A. Cellulose
   B. Galactose
   C. Ribose
   D. Sucrose

5. Glycogen storage disease type III (GSD-III) is the result of inadequate production of glycogen debranching enzyme, which cleaves α-1,6 glycosidic linkages at glycogen branch points. Glycogen phosphorylase, which cleaves α-1,4 glycosidic linkages, is unaffected by this condition. One would expect patients with GSD-III to:
   A. have greatly increased levels of circulating insulin.

   B. be unable to produce glucose by gluconeogenesis.
   C. develop liver abnormalities due to accumulated glycogen fragments.
   D. store more amylose as an alternative to glycogen.

6. The structure of glyceraldehyde, an important metabolic intermediate, is shown below:

   What is the absolute stereochemical configuration of the glyceraldehyde stereoisomer depicted above?
   A. (R)
   B. (S)
   C. (+)
   D. (-)

7. Compared to RNA, DNA exhibits much more physical flexibility in solution. This facilitates tight helical coiling and may partially explain the prevalence of DNA as genomic material. DNA is more flexible than RNA because:
   A. deoxyribose is a pentose, while ribose is a bulkier hexose.
   B. ribose has a hydroxyl substituent at C-2, which increases its steric bulk.
   C. ribose predominantly exists in the pyranose form when incorporated into a nucleotide.
   D. deoxyribose is a more energetically unstable enantiomer of ribose.

8. Glycolysis begins with the phosphorylation of D-glucose at its sixth position by the enzyme hexokinase. If a population of bacteria were raised in media containing L-glucose as the only carbon source, which of the following would be a likely result?
   A. Increased expression of downstream glycolytic enzymes
   B. Increased expression of enzymes that metabolize fructose
   C. Absence of any hexokinase activity
   D. Increased consumption of ATP by hexokinase

# Independent Question Explanations

1. B is correct. Tollens' reagent, like Benedict's reagent, is used to test for reducing sugars. Reducing sugars have free aldehyde groups that can be oxidized to carboxylic acids, with concomitant reduction of Tollens' reagent. Tollens' reagent contains an oxidized silver compound, which is reduced to elemental silver. Although fructose does not have an aldehyde group, in aqueous solution it can tautomerize to glucose and give a positive result. Therefore, fructose is considered a reducing sugar. Regarding choices A, C, and D, fructose, which includes fructose's isomers fructofuranose and fructopyranose, is a ketohexose, and fructose and glucose are not stereoisomers of each other.

2. A is correct. In aqueous solution, glucose readily undergoes mutarotation between its α and β anomers. By definition, anomers are a specific category of epimers, which are stereoisomers that differ at only one chiral center. These are not structural isomers because they have the same formula and connectivity (eliminate B). Enantiomers would require the α and β anomers to be mirror images, which is not the case (eliminate choice C). Finally, they are not polymers because polymers are larger molecules consisting of repeated subunits (eliminate choice D).

3. D is correct. Specific rotation is an experimental value. Generally, the specific rotation of a particular compound does not relate in any predictable way to that of another compound. The exceptions to this rule are enantiomers, which have equal but opposite specific rotation values, and racemic solutions, which have a specific rotation of 0°.

4. D is correct. Sucrose is a disaccharide of glucose and fructose. Cellulose is a large polymer that confers structural integrity to plant cell walls. Ribose and galactose are both monosaccharides.

5. C is correct. Since glycogen phosphorylase functions normally in GSD-III, linear glycogen segments are catabolized normally. However, small, branched fragments of glycogen cannot be broken down and slowly accumulate in the cytoplasm of affected liver cells. Gluconeogenesis would not be affected by defective glycogen metabolism. Circulating insulin would most likely be low due to persistent hypoglycemia. Animals do not synthesize amylose (a component of starch).

6. A is correct. The convention for drawing Fischer projections dictates that substituents branching horizontally from the vertical backbone of the molecule are directed out of the plane of the paper, toward the reader. Therefore, the hydrogen and oxygen atoms bonded to the chiral C-2 carbon atom are directed outward. The hydroxyl group has the highest priority, and the aldehyde carbon has the second highest priority. Moving around the molecule from highest priority downward, we travel counterclockwise, which typically denotes an S configuration. However, since our fourth-priority group (the hydrogen atom) points toward us, we must reverse this configuration. Our final answer should be R.

7. B is correct. Despite its relatively small size, the presence of the C-2 hydroxyl group does increase the steric bulk of ribose compared to deoxyribose. This reduces the flexibility of RNA compared to DNA. Both ribose and deoxyribose are pentoses (eliminate choice A), and they exist exclusively as furanoses when incorporated into nucleotides (eliminate choice C). Finally, if DNA was more energetically unstable, it would not help to explain why DNA is a prevalent genomic material (eliminate D).

8. C is correct. L-glucose does not exist in nature, and virtually no naturally-occurring enzymes are able to metabolize it. Since enzymes have chiral active sites, the ability of hexokinase to utilize D-glucose as a substrate does not mean that it would also be able to accept L-glucose. Since hexokinase would not work under these conditions, this eliminates D because it would not increase ATP consumption if it is not being used, and would eliminate A because glycolysis would not be able to proceed past the initial step if hexokinase activity was absent. Finally, although the bacteria may compensate by looking for other energy sources (answer choice B), such as fructose, the absence of hexokinase activity (answer choice C) more directly answers this question.

This page left intentionally blank.

# Non-Aerobic Carbohydrate Metabolism

## 0. Introduction

In this chapter, we'll move on from discussing general principles of biochemistry and the specific chemical properties of important biomolecules, and start putting these principles in motion by exploring how the body breaks down molecules to obtain energy and/or constituents for other pathways (catabolism) and how the body builds up larger molecules from smaller components (anabolism). The present chapter focuses on the non-aerobic metabolism of carbohydrates, starting with some general considerations about glucose as a source of energy and glucose transport, before proceeding to a discussion of glycolysis, gluconeogenesis, glycogenesis, glycogenolysis, and the pentose phosphate pathway. Finally, we will explore how these pathways are regulated.

This chapter and the next few chapters on metabolism contain a potentially overwhelming amount of detail. These topics are notoriously challenging for MCAT students, because they both contain a tremendous amount of details to master and illustrate fundamental, higher-level principles of biochemistry and regulation.

A perennial question students ask is: how much do I need to know about these pathways? This is a surprisingly difficult question to answer. On one hand, the MCAT *can* test you on the level of knowing specific enzymes. On the other hand, you shouldn't just jump to memorizing every single detail. You're also likely to get questions where having a bigger-picture knowledge of the pathway would be enough, and more importantly, having a bigger-picture perspective will help you make sense of and retain the smaller-scale details better.

With that in mind, we'd suggest using the following guidelines to prioritize what you understand about a given pathway:

1.  <u>What does it do? What's its physiological purpose?</u> This may sound really basic, but don't skip over it. It certainly sets the stage for understanding the pathway in more detail, and you'd be surprised how often just understanding what a certain pathway does in the big picture can allow you to eliminate one or two answer choices.

2.  <u>Where does it take place?</u> This will help you build up your own conceptual picture of how the cell operates. It is additionally helpful because eukaryotic cells divide up certain functions between the mitochondria and the cytosol, and understanding which steps take place where can help you obtain a better understanding of crucial

steps of a pathway. Additionally, though, it's possible that you could be asked point-blank about where a process happens, or indirectly in the form of a question that asks about the hypothetical outcomes if certain organelles were damaged. These are very "gettable" points if you take the time to focus on this information separately.

3. <u>What goes in and what comes out?</u> Knowing net reactants and products can directly allow you to get many questions on these topics right, and focusing on this also helps you solidify your understanding of how a pathway fits into the big picture of the body.

4. <u>Which steps are most important?</u> Look for irreversible steps and/or steps that are important for regulating the process, and take some extra time to make sure you understand what happens in those steps, which enzymes are involved, and why such steps are important.

5. <u>Regulation</u>. How is the pathway regulated? First answer this question from a big-picture physiological point of view. For example, is it upregulated when cellular energy stores are high or when they're low? Next, you might want to look at specific regulatory steps and mechanisms.

6. <u>Details</u>. Once you've got the big-picture points outlined above taken care of, now is the time to dive into the details of working through the pathways step by step.

7. <u>Review multiple times from different conceptual angles.</u> Metabolism is a very deep topic, in the sense that you can look at these pathways from several different angles and notice new things. It can also be overwhelming and counterproductive to attempt to learn everything at once. For this reason, we suggest walking through a pathway multiple times from multiple angles. For instance, one day you might set yourself the goal of following all the carbons in carbohydrate metabolism. The next day you might look at energetically favorable/unfavorable steps. The day after that, you might focus specifically on redox reactions. The fourth day, you might explore regulation – and so on and so forth. Doing so will help you build up your understanding from different perspectives, which will both lead to a deeper level of mastery and prepare you to encounter these topics on Test Day in the context of difficult passages.

# 1. Glucose and ATP as Energy Sources

Before delving into the details of carbohydrate metabolism, it's worth stepping back and making sure you have a clear idea of how energy works in the body overall. This sounds exceedingly basic, but it's something that often gets skipped over in Biology 101 in the rush to have students memorize the inputs and outputs of various pathways, and as always, for the MCAT it pays off to have a rock-solid understanding of the fundamentals in order to quickly and efficiently answer questions that give you new or surprising contexts for familiar information.

We tend to speak about energy differently on the level of the cell than on the level of tissues or the body as a whole. This is because ATP is only used to produce energy in the cell. (Very small amounts of ATP do circulate in the blood, but in that context ATP functions as a signaling molecule rather than as a source of energy; the details go beyond the scope of the MCAT). Although fatty acids and amino acids can also be used to produce energy, glucose is the main molecule that circulates in the body as a ready precursor for ATP synthesis. As we will see in the next chapter, oxygen is also needed in the body to get the maximum energy from glucose, so when we talk about the body as a whole or a set of tissues within the body, low levels of glucose/oxygen are associated with inadequate energy, while increased levels of glucose/oxygen are associated with adequate levels of energy. This is because cells turn glucose and oxygen into energy in the form of ATP. Further details of how ATP works as a source of energy are presented in Chapter 12, but the crucial point is that in tissues, glucose/oxygen are common proxies for the amount of available energy, whereas in cells, high levels of ATP mean that abundant energy is available, while low levels of ATP and high levels of ADP (or AMP) are indicators of insufficient energy.

So how *does* glucose provide energy? There are two basic strategies that recur throughout various pathways. The first is substrate-level phosphorylation. This essentially just means that a phosphate group is attached to a derivative of glucose and then transferred to a molecule of ADP to form ATP. In this context you can just think of the carbon skeleton derived from glucose as a staging area for phosphate as it is shuffled around the cell.

> > **CONNECTIONS** < <

Chapter 12 of Biochemistry

The second strategy is a little bit more involved, and is leveraged in aerobic metabolism in eukaryotes. Although aerobic metabolism is discussed more in Chapter 8, it's worth reviewing the basic principle here, because anticipating the subsequent steps of the Krebs cycle and the electron transport chain will help you understand the various steps of glycolysis better. Remember that our ultimate goal is to produce ATP, and this requires energy. This energy is obtained in the form of a proton gradient in the mitochondria that powers ATP synthase. In turn, this proton gradient is made by a structure known as the electron transport chain, which simultaneously transfers electrons to oxygen, reducing it to water, and pushes protons into the intermembrane space to create that gradient. Therefore, the energy used to power ATP synthase ultimately comes from molecules known as NADH and $FADH_2$ that carry electrons to the transport chain. NADH and $FADH_2$ are, in turn, created by redox reactions with various derivatives of glucose, and such steps are common in glycolysis and the citric acid cycle.

**MCAT STRATEGY > > >**

Metabolism can be a useful opportunity to review redox chemistry, because both topics have to do with energy production and shuttling electrons around. Students often study electrochemistry and metabolism in very different courses, but the MCAT may test you on the common ground between these two topics.

To summarize, the two main mechanisms through which glucose derivatives help create energy are:

1. **Phosphorylation**: phosphate groups are shuffled around to create ATP.

2. **Redox reactions**: the oxidation of a glycolysis/citric acid cycle intermediate is paired to the reduction of $NAD^+$ to NADH or FAD to $FADH_2$.

As you study metabolic pathways, keep an eye out for these two types of steps. You will find that most "important" reactions fall into one of these two categories, and the remaining reactions are generally reactions that add or remove a carbon, isomerizations, or preparatory reactions that set the stage for phosphorylation or a redox reaction.

## 2. Glucose Transport

Cells must be supplied with glucose in order for them to use it to make energy. Since the MCAT often asks you to link physiology and molecular biology, understanding how glucose gets to the cells that need it is a crucial piece of the puzzle.

There are two basic ways that glucose can enter the bloodstream: either through absorption from the small intestine (discussed in Chapter 10 of the Biology textbook) or from liver cells (hepatocytes) and cells in the renal cortex that produce glucose via gluconeogenesis or glycogenolysis. Once glucose is in the bloodstream, it needs to enter cells. Glucose is too polar to diffuse directly through the plasma membrane, so specialized glucose receptors are responsible for this task. In mammals, these receptors belong to the GLUT family. Currently, 14 receptors have been identified in this family. The four most important receptors are briefly presented below.

> GLUT1 is expressed throughout the body, and is responsible for constant low-level baseline glucose intake. It is expressed more often in response to low blood sugar levels and less often in response to high blood sugar levels, and is also especially common in fetal tissues and red blood cells. Interestingly, it is also upregulated in many forms of cancer.

> GLUT2 is expressed by liver cells, pancreatic beta cells, and some kidney cells. The distinctive feature of GLUT2 is that it is a bidirectional transporter that allows glucose to be transported both in and out of the cell. This is necessary in cells that carry out gluconeogenesis, because the newly generated glucose needs to be released. Pancreatic beta cells secrete insulin in response to circulating blood sugar levels, and this bidirectional transport pattern allows them to monitor blood glucose levels.

> GLUT3 is primarily expressed in neurons and the placenta. It is a high-affinity transporter, meaning that it will transport glucose effectively even when blood glucose levels are low. This is one of the ways that the body can prioritize especially important areas like the nervous system (and, interestingly, a gestating fetus) even in times of deprivation or starvation.

> GLUT4 is expressed in non-smooth muscle (skeletal and cardiac muscle) and in adipose tissues. It is regulated by insulin, and its basic job is to store glucose in skeletal muscle, cardiac muscle, and adipose tissue when a surplus of glucose is present in the blood. Insulin causes higher concentrations of GLUT4 receptors to be expressed in the plasma membrane, thereby increasing glucose uptake into cells and reducing blood sugar levels. Insulin is in turn stimulated by high blood glucose levels. Frequent high blood glucose levels leading to frequent insulin spikes can cause cells to become desensitized towards insulin, leading to a condition known as insulin resistance. Over time, increasingly severe insulin resistance can cause type 2 diabetes. In contrast, type 1 diabetes is caused by an autoimmune reaction that destroys the beta cells of the pancreas, which secrete insulin.

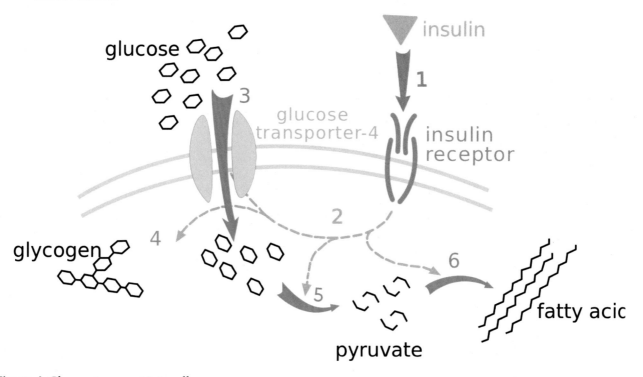

**Figure 1.** Glucose transport into cells.

Blood glucose levels are closely regulated by the hormones insulin and glucagon, with insulin acting to stimulate glucose uptake by cells in response to high blood glucose levels, and glucagon acting to increase blood glucose levels when they are low, primarily by upregulating gluconeogenesis. Blood glucose levels can also be increased by the steroid hormone cortisol and by the amino acid-derived hormones epinephrine and norepinephrine; these hormones are released in response to stress.

# 3. Glycolysis

Glycolysis is just about *the* most fundamental metabolic pathway. It is universal to all forms of cellular life, and its basic purpose is to allow cells to obtain some energy from glucose regardless of whether oxygen is present. Glycolysis takes place in the cytosol of cells.

The net equation for glycolysis is given below:

Glucose $+$ 2 NAD$^+$ + 2 ADP + 2 P$_i$ $\rightarrow$ 2 pyruvate + 2 NADH + 2 ATP + 2 H$_2$O

Let's begin our analysis of glycolysis by understanding how its major components contribute to the goal of liberating energy from glucose. In particular, let's work from left to right and match reactants with products.

The major outcome of glycolysis is that glucose is broken up, producing two molecules of pyruvate, a three-carbon alpha-keto acid that participates in multiple pathways in the body. Another important outcome is that NAD$^+$ gets converted to NADH. NAD$^+$/NADH (and the similarly functioning pair FAD/FADH$_2$) is an electron carrier. What does this mean? In the context of glycolysis by itself, it just means that NAD$^+$ and NADH are part of a redox reaction, such that NADH needs to be converted back to NAD$^+$ somehow for the process to continue. However, as we'll see in Chapter 8, the electron transport chain allows these electrons to be converted into energy in the form of ATP. Finally, let's consider ADP, P$_i$ (inorganic phosphate), and ATP. The cycle of ADP + P$_i$ $\rightarrow$ ATP is one of the basic ways that energy is cycled in the cell, and this process represents the direct energy payoff of glycolysis. As a reminder, ATP is considered to be the basic unit of energy within the cell because its breakdown to ADP + P$_i$ is highly exergonic – that is, it's a source of energy that can be coupled to make other, less favorable, reactions go forward.

However, the actual mechanism of glycolysis is considerably more complicated. It involves 10 major steps, and can be divided into an investment phase and a payoff phase. In the investment phase, 2 molecules of ATP are required (representing an energy investment). More specifically, this investment is made in order to break up glucose into two three-carbon molecules. Then, in the payoff phase, 4 molecules of ATP are generated through the conversion of these three-carbon intermediates to pyruvate, resulting in a net yield of 2 ATP per glucose.

Let's take a closer look at the steps of the investment phase. Especially important steps are noted in bold.

> **Step 1: glucose $\rightarrow$ glucose 6-phosphate (G6P).** This reaction is catalyzed by hexokinase (glucokinase in the liver), and consumes 1 ATP (the phosphate group is transferred from ATP to glucose). The point of this reaction is twofold. First, it traps G6P within the cell, because the cell membrane does not have receptors for G6P, and because it places a strong –2 charge on the molecule, ensuring that it cannot diffuse through the plasma membrane. Second, it maintains the concentration of glucose low, so glucose can keep being transported into the cell. The basic idea of this step is to add a phosphate group to glucose to separate it out from the remaining glucose in the cell.

> Step 2: G6P $\rightarrow$ fructose-6-phosphate (F6P). This is an isomerization reaction catalyzed by glucose 6-phosphate isomerase. It is easily reversible, and can simply be thought of as a small rearrangement necessary for subsequent steps.

---

**MCAT STRATEGY > > >**

Understanding the basic mechanism of diabetes (including how type 1 and type 2 diabetes differ) is very helpful for the MCAT, because it is a reasonably common topic in passages.

---

**MCAT STRATEGY > > >**

It is unlikely that you'll have a specific question that asks you to distinguish between (for instance) GLUT2 and GLUT4, but on a conceptual level, it's very much worth understanding that glucose must be transported and that there are several types of receptors that help carry this out in various circumstances.

---

> **Step 3: F6P → fructose 1,6-bisphosphate (F1,6BP).** This reaction is catalyzed by phosphofructokinase-1 (PFK1). This is probably the most significant step of glycolysis because it is the committed step (meaning that at this point, a glucose molecule now has no choice but to undergo glycolysis), it is the rate-limiting step, and it is the major target for the regulation of glycolysis. So, why is this reaction such a big deal? Probably the easiest way to think about this is to think ahead. Remember that the goal is to break up glucose into two identical three-carbon molecules. This means that each of the three-carbon intermediates must have its own phosphate group, so two phosphate groups need to be added to the six-carbon precursor. Moreover, having two highly negative phosphate groups destabilizes F6P, making it easier to cleave.
> **Step 4: F1,6BP → glyceraldehyde 3-phosphate (GADP) and dihydroxyacetone phosphate (DHAP).** This is catalyzed by fructose-bisphosphate aldolase, and is mostly worth noting because this is where the cleavage of a six-carbon carbohydrate (originally glucose) to three-carbon molecules happens.
> **Step 5: DHAP → GADP.** This is catalyzed by triosephosphate isomerase. This point of this step is to make sure that we have two *identical* three-carbon compounds for the payoff phase.

To summarize, in the investment phase we start with a molecule of glucose, put in 2 ATP, and get 2 units of GADP (a three-carbon glyceraldehyde with a phosphate group attached). Now we're ready for all that hard work to pay off! In the payoff phase, we have to be careful with the stoichiometry. Keep in mind that each of these reactions is carried out *twice* for every glucose molecule, because we've now broken down glucose into two identical smaller molecules.

> **Step 6: GADP → 1,3-bisphosphoglycerate (1,3BPG).** This is catalyzed by glyceraldehyde phosphate dehydrogenase (GAPDH). This reaction does two main things: it catalyzes the conversion of $NAD^+$ to NADH, and it loads up our carbon chain with another phosphate group (this time obtained from inorganic phosphate, or $P_i$).
> **Step 7: 1,3BPG → 3-phosphoglycerate (3PG).** This is catalyzed by phosphoglycerate kinase (PGK). In this step, a phosphate group is transferred from our three-carbon skeleton onto a molecule of ADP to create a molecule of ATP. This is the point where we start actively getting energy out of the process. It is also a regulatory point in the pathway.
> **Step 8: 3PG → 2-phosphoglycerate (2PG).** This step just rearranges the phosphate group. It is catalyzed by phosphoglycerate mutase.
> **Step 9: 2PG → phosphoenolpyruvate (PEP).** This step is catalyzed by enolase, and essentially is just another rearrangement.
> **Step 10: PEP → pyruvate.** This step is catalyzed by pyruvate kinase (PK). Similarly to step 7, in this step a phosphate group is transferred from our three-carbon skeleton to an ADP molecule, forming ATP. This is the second ATP-forming step, and can also be regulated. Note pyruvate serves as the final electron acceptor.

## MCAT STRATEGY > > >

As corny as it might sound, try to see glycolysis as a story. The sign of having studied glycolysis successfully is to be able to tell that story to someone else, starting with the basic logic of the process and filling in the details as necessary. Metabolic pathways are a great topic to work on in a study group for this reason. Remember that active learning and an ability to focus on the principles outweighs desperate memorization!

Let's step back and review the basic logic of glycolysis. On the most basic level, ATP is the currency of energy in the cell, and glycolysis works by shuffling around phosphate groups to generate more ATP. Two phosphate groups are pulled from ATP molecules in the investment phase, and two phosphate groups are added from cellular stores of inorganic phosphate ($P_i$) in the payoff phase. All four of these phosphate groups are ultimately added to ADP to form ATP, resulting in the overall formation of 4 ATP and the net formation of 2 ATP when we account for the investment phase. This process is accompanied by breaking the glucose molecule into two three-carbon molecules.

Glycolysis is illustrated below in Figure 2.

**Figure 2.** Glycolysis.

NADH needs to be converted back to NAD$^+$ for glycolysis to continue. As we'll see in Chapter 8, the electron transport chain provides one way for this to happen, but this requires oxygen. In the absence of oxygen, fermentation provides a way for NAD$^+$ to be regenerated. There are two main forms of fermentation that you should be aware of: ethanol fermentation and lactic acid fermentation.

Ethanol fermentation is used by yeast, and consists of two steps. In the first step, pyruvate loses a carboxylic acid functional group, becoming acetaldehyde ($CH_3CHO$) and carbon dioxide ($CO_2$). This step is catalyzed by pyruvate decarboxylase. In the next step, alcohol dehydrogenase turns acetaldehyde into ethanol in a reaction coupled to the conversion of NADH to NAD$^+$.

Lactic acid fermentation is simpler, as it is a one-step process. Pyruvate is converted to lactate (this term refers to the deprotonated form of lactic acid) by lactate dehydrogenase in a reaction that is also used to convert NADH to NAD$^+$. Lactic acid fermentation is carried out in muscle cells in humans, because muscle cells often use both aerobic and anaerobic respiration. Lactic acid fermentation is also widely used in culinary applications; it is used to produce products as diverse as yogurt and kimchi.

# 4. Gluconeogenesis

Now that we've explored how the body gets energy out of glucose, what happens if we need to reverse the process and *create* glucose? This is accomplished through a process known as gluconeogenesis, which in humans occurs primarily in the liver and to some extent in the adrenal cortex. A follow-up question might be why we would need to create glucose. Essentially, this is because the liver needs to regulate blood glucose levels, ensuring an adequate supply of glucose (which can then be converted into energy, or stored as glycogen) throughout the tissues of the body. In particular, it can be important to replenish the stores of glycogen in muscle cells after they have been depleted by intense activity.

Gluconeogenesis starts with pyruvate and ends with glucose. This observation might lead us to think that gluconeogenesis is just reverse glycolysis, but that's not quite correct. Glycolysis and gluconeogenesis actually do share some of the same enzymes and steps (although they occur in reverse), but they also differ at some crucial stages. There are two basic reasons for this. First, from a relatively nitty-gritty biochemical point of view, glycolysis contains some steps that are highly exergonic and essentially irreversible under biological conditions, so gluconeogenesis needs to find a way to bypass those steps. Second, from a higher-level point of view, glycolysis and gluconeogenesis need to be separated in order to prevent a futile cycle in which glucose is broken down to pyruvate and then pyruvate is built back up into glucose.

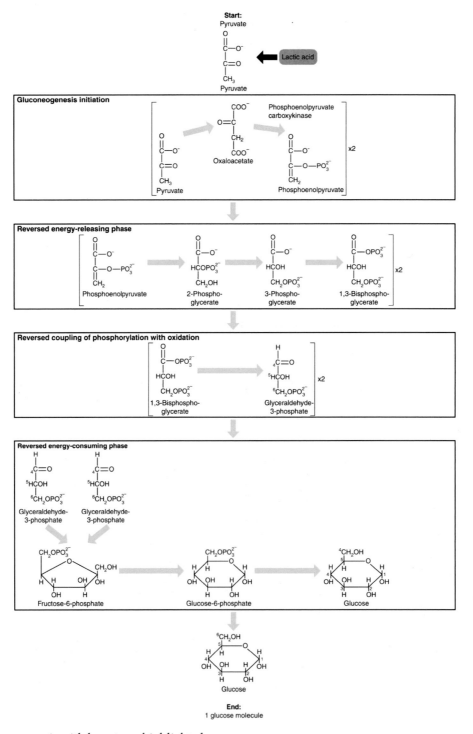

**Figure 3.** Gluconeogenesis with key stages highlighted.

The details go beyond the scope of the MCAT, but it is helpful to be aware that the body can obtain pyruvate from multiple sources, meaning that gluconeogenesis can be used to produce glucose from a variety of upstream substrates, including fatty acids and certain amino acids.

Let's look at the various ways that gluconeogenesis differs from glycolysis, starting with the pyruvate end of the pathway. The final step of glycolysis is the conversion of phosphoenolpyruvate (PEP) to pyruvate. This step is highly energetically favorable, so the first challenge in gluconeogenesis is to bypass it. In the mitochondria, pyruvate carboxylase converts pyruvate to oxaloacetate by adding a $COO^-$ group. Oxaloacetate is briefly converted to malate for transport out of the mitochondria, where it is then converted immediately back to oxaloacetate. At this point, in the cytosol, PEP carboxykinase converts oxaloacetate to PEP.

Once pyruvate is converted to PEP, gluconeogenesis follows the same stages of glycolysis, but in reverse, for several steps, until fructose 1,6-bisphosphate (F1,6BP). You may recall that the formation of F1,6BP was the committed step of glycolysis. Therefore, it is not surprising that it needs to be bypassed in gluconeogenesis. In gluconeogenesis, the enzyme fructose 1,6-bisphosphatase catalyzes the hydrolysis of the phosphate group on C1 of F1,6BP, resulting in fructose 6-phosphate (F6P). F6P is isomerized to glucose 6-phosphate (G6P).

The conversion of G6P to glucose is the final step where gluconeogenesis bypasses glycolysis. In glycolysis, an ATP is invested in putting the phosphate group onto glucose via hexokinase. This suggests, in and of itself, that this step cannot simply be reversed. Instead, in gluconeogenesis, glucose 6-phosphatase catalyzes a hydrolysis reaction in which G6P yields glucose and $P_i$.

The details of this process can seem overwhelming, but actually follow a fairly simple logic:

> The final stage of glycolysis must be bypassed by gluconeogenesis, both because it is irreversible and because the cell must avoid a futile cycle in which pyruvate from glycolysis is immediately converted back to PEP. This is why gluconeogenesis has a two-step pathway split up between the mitochondria and cytosol.
> The early stages of glycolysis where phosphate groups are added need to be bypassed by gluconeogenesis. These are irreversible steps, but you may also find it helpful to remember that these steps in glycolysis involve the investment of ATP (that's where the phosphate comes from!). It wouldn't make sense for gluconeogenesis to just reverse these steps, because doing so would mean creating ATP, which is the job of ATP synthase in the electron transport chain. Instead, gluconeogenesis bypasses these steps using enzymes that catalyze a simple hydrolysis reaction, splitting off a $P_i$ from the carbohydrate.

Gluconeogenesis and glycolysis are compared below in Figure 4, which highlights the differences between these two pathways. Recall that the upstream bypasses (involving glucose/G6P and F6P/F1,6,BP) involve differences in the mechanism of how phosphate groups are added and removed, while the downstream pathway involving the interconversion of PEP and pyruvate involves transport between the mitochondria and cytosol to avoid a futile cycle.

**MCAT STRATEGY > > >**

There are two keys to studying gluconeogenesis for the MCAT. First, be sure to understand the basic rationale for the process—namely, the fact that it happens in liver cells and provides a ready source of blood glucose when supplies are low. Second, understand *why* the crucial steps of glycolysis are bypassed (i.e., to bypass irreversible reactions, to avoid a futile cycle, and to transfer phosphate groups by hydrolysis).

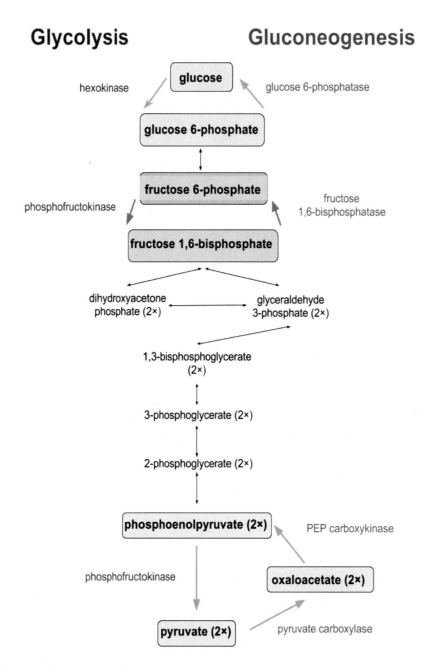

**Figure 4.** Glycolysis versus gluconeogenesis.

# 5. Glycogenesis and Glycogenolysis

Glycogen is a branched polymer of glucose that is used to store glucose, primarily in liver and muscle cells. Each glycogen molecule is formed around a core formed by the protein glycogenin, which serves as the base for glycogen synthesis. Glycogen is shown in Figure 5. As you can see, glycogen is a highly-branched molecule. Within each branch, glucose molecules are linked together by α(1→4) linkages, while separate branches are formed by α(1→6) linkages.

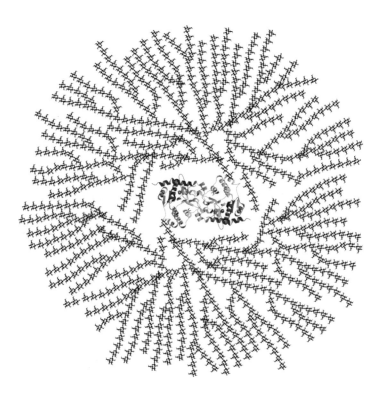

**Figure 5.** Glycogen.

Let's explore how glycogen is built up. This process is known as glycogenesis. The starting point for glycogenesis is glucose 6-phosphate (G6P), which corresponds to the second compound in the glycolysis pathway and the second-to-last compound in the gluconeogenesis pathway. G6P is turned to glucose 1-phosphate (G1P) by phosphoglucomutase. You can think of this step as essentially being a way to mark that a glucose molecule is being shunted towards glycogen synthesis. G1P is then converted to a compound known as UDP-glucose. UDP stands for uridine diphosphate, meaning that UDP-glucose is actually a nucleotide sugar. UDP-glucose donates glucose to a growing strand of glycogen via the action of glycogen synthase, which forms α(1→4) connections to existing glucose molecules. This means that glycogen synthase cannot create new branches. Instead, new branches (i.e., α(1→6) linkages) are created by an enzyme with an intuitive name: glycogen-branching enzyme. When a new glycogen molecule is created, the core protein glycogenin also helps catalyze the buildup of the first 8 glucose molecules, after which glycogen synthase can take over.

Releasing glucose molecules from glycogen is somewhat simpler. This process is known as glycogenolysis. The major step in glycogenolysis is catalyzed by glycogen phosphorylase. In this reaction, a substitution reaction takes place, in which a phosphate group is added to replace the α(1→4) linkage. This mechanism is known as phosphorolysis (analogous to hydrolysis), and results in G1P. G1P is then converted to G6P by phosphoglucomutase. Since G6P is part of the gluconeogenesis pathway, the mechanisms of gluconeogenesis essentially take over from here. The only additional thing to note is that glycogen phosphorylase – like glycogen synthase – only works on α(1→4) linkages. Glycogen debranching enzyme helps deal with α(1→6) linkages and the breakdown of glycogen branches.

## MCAT STRATEGY > > >

The key points about the glycogenesis mechanism are that glucose is shunted off from the glycolysis/gluconeogenesis pathway and 'marked' for glycogenesis by moving the phosphate group, and that branching and non-branching enzymes are added via different enzymes.

# 6. Pentose Phosphate Pathway

The final non-aerobic carbohydrate pathway that you must know for the MCAT is the pentose phosphate pathway. Unlike many of the metabolic pathways needed for the MCAT, the pentose phosphate pathway is not primarily about energy. Instead, the point of the pentose phosphate pathway is to shunt glucose 6-phosphate away from the glycolysis/gluconeogenesis pathway and use it to do other structurally important things. Namely, the pentose phosphate pathway converts $NADP^+$ into NADPH and converts glucose 6-phosphate into ribose 5-phosphate. These products are not necessarily the most commonly encountered molecules, so it's worth briefly reviewing their importance.

> > NADPH has two main functions: it serves as a reducing agent needed for the synthesis of lipids and nucleic acids, and it helps protect against damage from reactive oxygen synthesis by regenerating the antioxidant glutathione from its oxidized form.
> > Ribose-5-phosphate is used in nucleotide synthesis. Recall that DNA and RNA stand for deoxy*ribo*nucleic acid and *ribo*nucleic acid, respectively.

The pentose phosphate pathway is broken up into two stages: the oxidative phase and the non-oxidative phase.

In the oxidative phase, glucose 6-phosphate is first converted to 6-phosphoglucono-δ-lactone by glucose 6-phosphate dehydrogenase. This step produces 1 NADPH and is the rate-limiting step of the process. The next step converts 6-phosphoglucono-δ-lactone into 6-phosphogluconate, in a relatively minor step. The final major step is the cleavage of 6-phosphogluconate to form ribulose 5-phosphate and NADPH. A carbon is lost as $CO_2$. Once ribulose 5-phosphate is generated, it can easily be converted into ribose 5-phosphate. To summarize, the oxidative phase is notable for the following reasons: (1) the main products of the pentose phosphate pathway are generated in the oxidative phase; and (2) a carbon is lost as $CO_2$.

The issue at this point is that a cell might carry out the pentose phosphate pathway because it needs NADPH, not ribose 5-phosphate. Examples of this would include cells that actively produce lipids, such as liver cells, adipose tissue, mammary glands during lactation, the adrenal gland, and the gonads (the latter two because they produce high levels of steroid hormones), as well as cells that receive especially intense exposure to reactive oxygen species, such as erythrocytes and cells on the external surfaces of the eye. In contrast, ribose 5-phosphate is relatively more necessary in cells that are rapidly dividing, such as the bone marrow and skin, because they need the raw materials for rapid DNA replication.

> > CONNECTIONS < <
>
> Chapter 10 of Biochemistry

> MCAT STRATEGY > > >
>
> The pentose phosphate pathway is one of the least familiar pathways for many MCAT students. Therefore, on Test Day, investing the time in developing a solid big-picture understanding of its importance and major phases can really pay off if you see a question on it!

The non-oxidative phase allows cells that don't specifically need ribose 5-phosphate to process it in a way that feeds back into the glycolysis pathway and allows the oxidative phase to continue. More specifically, it involves multiple steps, through which the carbon skeleton of ribose 5-phosphate is rearranged, resulting in a net conversion of six five-carbon sugars (ribose 5-phosphate) to five six-carbon sugars (fructose 6-phosphate). Fructose 6-phosphate can be easily converted back into glucose 6-phosphate, which can re-enter glycolysis; additionally, glyceraldehyde 3-phosphate, which is another product of the non-oxidative phase, can also be shunted back into glycolysis.

**Figure 6.** Pentose phosphate pathway.

Figure 6 illustrates the pentose phosphate pathway. For the pentose phosphate pathway, focus your attention on understanding its general purpose, products, and the basic features of the oxidative and non-oxidative phases.

# 7. Regulation

Metabolic pathways are regulated through a complex set of interlocking mechanisms. The best way to tackle the regulation of metabolic pathways is by focusing on the high-level principles, which can be summarized as follows for the pathways discussed in this chapter:

> Glycolysis is upregulated when the cell needs more ATP. This can be signaled by relatively high concentrations of AMP/ADP, as well as by an abundance of extra inorganic phosphate ($P_i$).

> Glycolysis is downregulated when the cell doesn't need more ATP. This is most directly signaled by a high level of ATP, but is also indirectly signaled by abundant levels of NADH and by high levels of citrate (the product of the first step in the Krebs cycle, discussed in the next chapter).

> Glycolysis is also subject to negative regulation, in which certain products inhibit previous steps. Most notably, glucose 6-phosphate, the first product of glycolysis, inhibits hexokinase, which catalyzes the conversion of glucose to glucose 6-phosphate.

> Gluconeogenesis is upregulated when the body specifically needs more glucose and as an alternate pathway to handle surplus pyruvate/acetyl-CoA that builds up when downstream metabolic processes (in particular, the Krebs cycle) are saturated.

> Gluconeogenesis and glycolysis are regulated in tandem in ways that respond to hormonal signaling from outside the body (most notably, insulin and glucagon).

> Glycogen is how cells store excess glucose, so glycogen breakdown occurs when cells need more glucose for either gluconeogenesis or glycolysis, and glycogen synthesis is upregulated when the cell has a surplus of glucose.

With these principles in mind, let's explore how the regulation of these pathways is accomplished in more detail.

Glycolysis has three main regulatory points, and it's important to understand why these steps in particular are targeted for regulation.

The first regulatory point of glycolysis is the first step, in which hexokinase catalyzes the conversion of glucose to glucose 6-phosphate. This step is important because phosphorylating glucose essentially "marks" it as being targeted for some kind of metabolic pathway, although this reaction is reversible and it is not a committed step of glycolysis in particular. To review, glucose 6-phosphate can also be converted back to glucose via gluconeogenesis if conditions are appropriate, and can also be shunted towards glycogenesis or the pentose phosphate pathway. Hexokinase is negatively regulated by its product, glucose 6-phosphate, in order to keep the process balanced. An interesting complication, however, is that liver and pancreatic cells contain the isozyme hexokinase IV, also known as glucokinase. Glucokinase has a lower affinity for glucose and is *not* inhibited by glucose 6-phosphate, meaning that it can help liver and pancreatic cells respond specifically to the amount of glucose in the environment, rather than metabolizing glucose based on the intracellular need for ATP.

## MCAT STRATEGY > > >

Review the high-level principles of regulation until you have a solid understanding of them. These alone may be enough to answer MCAT questions related to this topic, and they certainly will allow you to eliminate incorrect answer choices. These principles also form a conceptual underpinning for the more detailed mechanisms of regulation discussed in this section.

The second main regulatory point of glycolysis is its committed step, in which phosphofructokinase-1 (PFK1) catalyzes the formation of fructose 1,6-bisphosphate from fructose 6-phosphate. PFK1 is downregulated by high levels of ATP and citrate, which signal that the cell is already producing enough energy, and is upregulated by high levels of AMP/ADP, which signal that the cell needs more energy. PFK1 also participates in the interwoven regulation of glycolysis and gluconeogenesis via the related enzyme PFK2 and its effector fructose 2,6-bisphosphate. We discuss this in greater detail below in the context of the jointly coordinated regulation of glycolysis and gluconeogenesis.

The final main regulatory point of glycolysis is its final step, in which phosphoenolpyruvate (PEP) is converted to pyruvate by pyruvate kinase (PK). PK is allosterically inhibited by high levels of ATP, as well as abundant acetyl-CoA and the presence of high levels of long-chain fatty acids in the cell. All of these are indicators that the cell has sufficient energy supplies and therefore doesn't need to process more glucose into ATP.

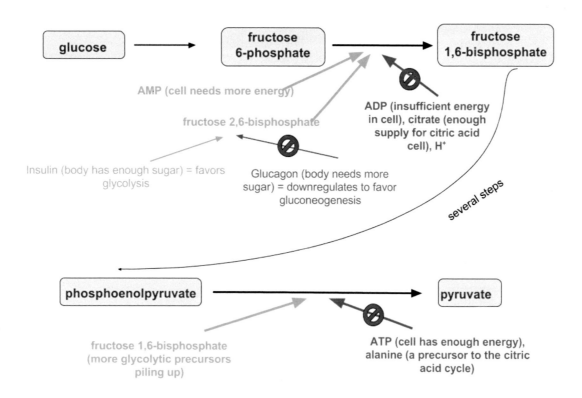

**Figure 7.** Glycolysis: crucial steps and regulation.

Turning to gluconeogenesis, its first step is likewise the first place it can be regulated. In the first step of gluconeogenesis, a two-step process converts pyruvate to PEP via oxaloacetate. Essentially, the cell faces a choice about what to do with pyruvate: it can either shunt it "upstream" through glycolysis or push it "downstream" by converting it into acetyl-CoA, which can then be fed into the Krebs cycle to produce energy. We will cover the details in subsequent chapters, but acetyl-CoA can be generated from several sources. The presence of abundant acetyl-CoA is an indicator that the cell doesn't need more, so the conversion of pyruvate to acetyl-CoA is downregulated, and the conversion of the excess pyruvate to PEP is favored.

The other major regulatory point of gluconeogenesis is the step in which fructose 1,6-bisphosphate is converted to fructose 6-phosphate, bypassing the rate-limiting step of glycolysis. This step in gluconeogenesis is catalyzed by fructose 1,6-bisphosphatase, which is inhibited by AMP. The corresponding enzyme in glycolysis (phosphofructokinase-1) is stimulated by AMP/ADP, so in this sense, the enzymes work together to ensure that when the cell needs more energy, glycolysis is favored over gluconeogenesis. So far, this is reasonably straightforward, and has essentially recapitulated the major themes we've seen repeated throughout this discussion: glycolysis is favored when the cell needs ATP, and gluconeogenesis is favored when it doesn't. However, this step gets more complicated, because this is the step in which the regulation of these pathways is influenced by the hormones glucagon and insulin.

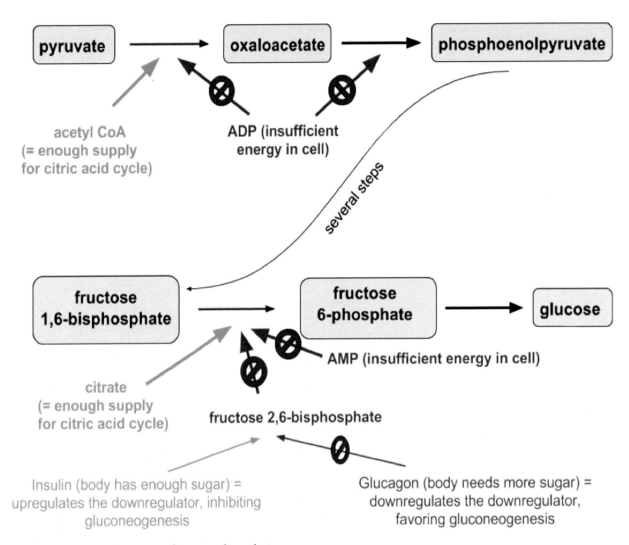

**Figure 8.** Gluconeogenesis: crucial steps and regulation.

In addition to AMP/ADP, the glycolytic enzyme PFK1 and the gluconeogenic enzyme fructose 6-phosphate are also allosterically regulated by a compound known as fructose 2,6-bisphosphate. Fructose 2,6-bisphosphate is *not* an intermediary in the glycolytic/gluconeogenic pathway (don't get it confused with fructose 1,6-bisphosphate!); instead it is a purely regulatory molecule. Fructose 2,6-bisphosphate allosterically regulates PFK1 to the point that PFK1 is virtually inactive under cellular conditions; therefore, it is essential for glycolysis to take place. Fructose 2,6-bisphosphate additionally inhibits the gluconeogenic enzyme fructose 6-phosphate. Therefore, high levels of fructose 2,6-bisphosphate favor glycolysis and lower levels favor gluconeogenesis.

The next question we have to ask is how fructose 2,6-bisphosphate is regulated. It is produced by an enzyme known as phosphofructokinase-2 (PFK2) and broken down by fructose 2,6-bisphosphatase; interestingly, although we use two different names to describe these functions, a single bifunctional enzyme actually carries out the activity of both PFK2 and fructose 2,6-bisphosphatase. Through a series of intermediate steps that goes beyond what you are required to know for the MCAT, glucagon promotes the activity of fructose 2,6-bisphosphatase and inhibits the activity of PFK2, thereby reducing the levels of fructose 2,6-bisphosphate and promoting gluconeogenesis. In contrast, insulin upregulates PFK2 activity to stimulate glycolysis.

Glycogen is regulated somewhat differently in liver and muscle cells, because it is used differently: in liver cells, the glucose stored in glycogen is primarily mobilized for gluconeogenesis when blood glucose levels are low, whereas in muscle cells, the glucose stored in glycogen is fed into glycolysis to generate the energy needed to support intense muscle contraction. In both liver and muscle cells, however, glycogen phosphorylase (the enzyme responsible for breaking down glycogen) is regulated both hormonally and allosterically.

Epinephrine is the main hormone that regulates glycogen phosphorylase in muscle cells; it induces a signaling cascade that activates glycogen phosphorylase and stimulates the release of glucose 1-phosphate, which is eventually shunted into the glycolytic pathway. In liver cells, in contrast, glucagon is the main hormone that triggers glycogen breakdown via glycogen phosphorylase. In contrast, insulin inhibits glycogenolysis via an intermediary known as phosphoprotein phosphatase 1.

The allosteric regulation of glycogen phosphorylase also differs slightly between muscle cells and liver cells. In muscle cells, Ca2+ (which is involved in muscle contraction; see Chapter 12 of the Biology textbook) upregulates glycogen phosphorylase, as does AMP, which is a sign of low energy. Essentially, both of these stimuli signal that the muscle needs more energy for contraction. In contrast, in liver cells, glucose allosterically inhibits glycogen phosphorylase. This is one mechanism through which glycogen breakdown is prevented when enough glucose is already available.

> **MCAT STRATEGY > > >**
>
> When it comes to glycogen metabolism and gluconeogenesis, you can think about the difference between liver and muscle cells as essentially being that liver cells respond to the needs of the entire organism, while muscle cells respond to the intracellular need to supply energy for contraction.

Glycogen synthesis, which is catalyzed by glycogen synthase, is somewhat simpler conceptually. Insulin upregulates glycogen synthase through a somewhat convoluted process: it inactivates a protein known as glycogen synthase kinase 3, which inhibits glycogen synthesis. In this case, two negatives make a positive, so insulin promotes glycogen synthesis. This makes sense on a higher-level conceptual level, as well. Insulin's most well-known effect is promoting the uptake of glucose by cells, and once that glucose is in the cell, it needs to do something with it. Some of it can be shunted into glycolysis, but the cell needs to store any extra supplies.

Figure 9 summarizes the regulation of all of the non-aerobic carbohydrate pathways discussed in this chapter.

> **> > CONNECTIONS < <**
>
> Chapter 12 of Biology

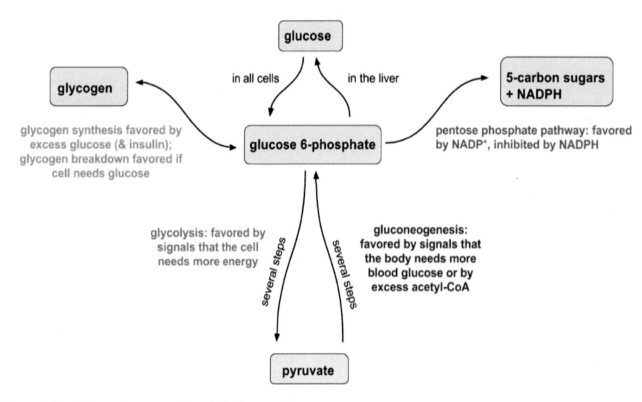

**Figure 9.** Regulation of non-aerobic carbohydrate pathways.

## 8. Must-Knows

> Glucose is energy currency within body/tissues, ATP is energy currency within the cell.
> ATP provides energy by coupling of highly-exergonic ATP → ADP + $P_i$ with reactions that require energy.
> Glucose → ATP in two main ways:
>   – Substrate-level phosphorylation (backbone used to move phosphate groups around, generating more ATP)
>   – Oxidation: redox reactions generate reduced forms of electron carriers NADH and $FADH_2$, which generate energy via electron transport chain (next chapter), which requires oxygen.
> Glycolysis: in cytosol in all forms of cellular life; no oxygen needed:
>   – Glucose + 2 $NAD^+$ + 2 ADP + 2 $P_i$ → 2 pyruvate + 2 NADH + 2 ATP + 2 $H_2O$
>   – Investment phase: 2 ATP invested, payoff phase: 4 ATP generated, net yield of 2 ATP.
> Key steps of glycolysis:
>   – Step 1: glucose → glucose 6-phosphate (G6P). Consumes ATP and prevents glucose from leaving cell; is a target of regulation.
>   – Step 3: fructose 1,6-bisphosphate. Consumes ATP, catalyzed by phosphofructokinase. It is the rate-limiting and committed step, and is heavily regulated.
>   – Step 10: Phosphoenolpyruvate → pyruvate. Also target of regulation.
> Gluconeogenesis: produces glucose in hepatocytes (for circulation in body) and muscle cells (for glycolysis).
>   – Bypasses committed steps of glycolysis: (1) pyruvate → oxaloacetate → phosphoenolpyruvate, different enzymes used for F1,6BP → F6P and G6P → glucose.
> Glycogen: polymer in hepatocytes/muscle cells that stores glucose molecules linked through α(1→4) linkages, while separate branches are formed by α(1→6) linkages.
>   – Glycogen synthesis: catalyzed by glycogen synthase, starts from G6P.

- Glycogen breakdown: catalyzed by glycogen phosphorylase
- Pentose phosphate pathway: G6P → NADPH and ribulose 5-phosphate (→ ribose 5-phosphate); NADPH is needed for lipid/nucleic synthesis and as antioxidant, ribose 5-phosphate is 5-carbon sugar used for nucleotide synthesis.
  - Oxidative phase: carbon is lost, NADPH + ribulose 5-phosphate produced; non-oxidative phase: carbons cycled to produce compounds that can enter citric acid cycle or regenerate fructose 6-phosphate.
- Main regulation principles: energy homeostasis and negative feedback.
  - ↑AMP/ADP = ↑glycolysis (cell needs energy); ↑ATP/NADH/citrate = ↓glycolysis (cell has enough energy)
  - Excess acetyl-CoA → ↑gluconeogenesis (cell has enough energy)
  - Glucagon = ↑gluconeogenesis and ↓glycolysis, insulin = ↑glycolysis and ↓gluconeogenesis

## Practice Passage

Carrageenan, agarose, and alginate are algae-derived polysaccharides that are used as food additives. Fermentation of dietary carbohydrates in the human gut is a critical process for the function of both the bacterial community and host cells. These carbohydrates cannot be digested by the enzymes encoded by the human genome. However, the genes encoding alginase and agarase, which, respectively, cleave agarose and alginate (Figure 1), have been found in *Bacteroides plebeius*, isolated from the microbiota of Japanese individuals.

**Figure 1.** Agarose (a) and alginate (b)

There are actually two types of agarase: α-agarase cleaves α-1,3-glycosidic bonds, while β-agarase cleaves β-1,4-glycosidic bonds. Some bacteria can only secrete one kind of lyase, and there are also bacteria that can secrete both. In order to analyze the enzyme hydrolyzing carrageenan, the products of hydrolytic degradation after 14 h were separated using gel filtration and determined with electrospray ionization collision-induced-dissociation mass spectrometry (ESI-CID-MS$^2$). The degradation products were identified mainly as 4-O-sulfate-d-galactose, κ-carratriose, κ-carrapentaose, and κ-carraheptaose.

**Figure 1.** Fragments generated from electrospray ionization collision-induced-dissociation mass spectrometry of neocarrabiose (a) and neocarradiitol (b)

Next, the degradation productions of alginate were analyzed. Part of the degradation solution after centrifugation was precipitated with 2 volumes of ethanol, twice, and then dried. Thirty milligrams of dried sample were co-evaporated by lyophilization, twice, with 1 mL of $D_2O$, to remove exchangeable protons before a final dissolution in 0.5 mL of $D_2O$ for NMR analysis. Based on the molecular weight from the negative-ion electrospray ionization mass spectrometry (ESI-MS) results (Table 1), fractions C1 to C4 were assigned as unsaturated alginate disaccharides, trisaccharides, tetrasccharide, and pentasaccharides, respectively.

**Table 1.** ESI-MS analysis of the fragments generated from alginate degradation

| Fraction | Found Ions (Charge) | Calculated Mol Mass (H Form) | Assignment | |
|---|---|---|---|---|
| | | | DP | Sequences |
| C1 | 351.05 (−1) | 351.06 | 2 | ΔNN |
| C2 | 527.08 (−1) | 527.09 | 3 | ΔNNN |
| C3 | 351.05 (−2), 703.11 (−1) | 704.13 | 4 | ΔNNNN |
| C4 | 439.06 (−2), 879.13 (−1) | 880.16 | 5 | ΔNNNNN |

N = β-D-mannuronic acid (M) or α-L-guluronic acid (G).

*Adapted from Li, M., et al. (2017). Degradation of Marine Algae-Derived Carbohydrates by Bacteroidetes Isolated from Human Gut Microbiota. Marine Drugs, 15(4), under CCBY 4.0*

1. Which of the following best describes the type of fermentation which occurs in human skeletal muscle?
   A. Homolactic
   B. Ketogenic
   C. Aerobic
   D. Catabolic

2. According to the passage, which disaccharide is most likely to be cleaved by α–agarase?

A.

B.

C.

D.

3. If ESI uses electrical energy to assist the transfer of ions from solution into the gaseous phase before they are subjected to mass spectrometric analysis, which amino acid will have ions enter the gaseous phase first?
   A. P
   B. K
   C. L
   D. F

4. In a follow up experiment, researchers analyzed the fermentation products of 10 different strains of bacteria. Which of the following was least likely to be found in the product solution?
   A. $CH_4$
   B. $CH_3CH(OH)COOH$
   C. $H_2$
   D. CH3COCOOH

5. Researchers hypothesized that fermentation-inhibiting drugs could be used as cancer treatment. Which of the following would best support this hypothesis?
   A. Cancer cells growth is much more rapid than accompanying angiogenesis in the tumor region.
   B. Cancer cells rapidly deplete local glucose stores in the tumor region.
   C. Metabolism of carbohydrates during tumorigenesis results in a hyperoxic tumor region.
   D. GLUT-1 expression by cancer cells negatively correlates with tumor aggressiveness and a poor prognosis.

6. When comparing the human eukaryotic fermentation path and yeast fermentation path, which enzyme is found only in one path?
   A. Pyruvate kinase
   B. Hexokinase
   C. Lactate dehydrogenase
   D. Phosphoglycerate mutase

7. Which of the following could explain why *Bacteroides plebeius* must undergo anaerobic carbohydrate metabolism?
   I. The cells lack a sufficient amount of any final electron acceptor to carry out cellular respiration.
   II. The cells lack genes to make appropriate complexes in the electron transport system.
   III. Their nuclei lack genes to make citrate synthase.
   IV. High cellular levels of $NAD^+$ inhibit glycolysis.
   A. II and III only
   B. I, III and IV only
   C. I, II, and III only
   D. II, III, and IV only

## Practice Passage Explanation

Carrageenan, agarose, and alginate are algae-derived polysaccharides that are used as food additives. Fermentation of dietary carbohydrates in the human gut is a critical process for the function of both the bacterial community and host cells. These carbohydrates cannot be digested by the enzymes encoded by the human genome. However, the genes encoding alginase and agarase, which, respectively, cleave agarose and alginate (Figure 1), have been found in *Bacteroides plebeius*, isolated from the microbiota of Japanese individuals.

*Key terms: algae-derived polysaccharides, alginase, agarase, microbiota, B. plebius*

*Contrast: human cells cannot digest these saccharides so gut flora do it, carry out fermentation*

**Figure 1.** Agarose (a) and alginate (b)

*Figure 1 shows both a β-link (a) and an α-link (b); alg has carboxylate groups*

There are actually two types of agarase: α-agarase cleaves α-1,3-glycosidic bonds while β-agarase cleaves β-1,4-glycosidic bonds. Some bacteria can only secrete one kind of lyase, and there are also bacteria that can secrete both. In order to analyze the enzyme hydrolyzing carrageenan, the products of hydrolytic degradation after 14 h were separated using gel filtration and determined with electrospray ionization collision-induced-dissociation mass spectrometry (ESI-CID-MS²). The degradation products were identified mainly as 4-O-sulfate-d-galactose, κ-carratriose, κ-carrapentaose, and κ-carraheptaose.

*Key terms: agarase, hydrolytic degradation, ESI-CID-MS*

*Contrast: α-agarase cuts 1,3; β-agarase cuts 1,4 links*

*Cause and effect: carrag. hydrolysis → 4 products*

**Figure 1.** Fragments generated from electrospray ionization collision-induced-dissociation mass spectrometry of neocarrabiose (a) and neocarradiitol (b)

*Figure 1 shows each molecule being subject to 2 cuts at the glycoside link*

Next, the degradation productions of alginate were analyzed. Part of the degradation solution after centrifugation was precipitated with 2 volumes of ethanol, twice, and then dried. Thirty milligrams of dried sample were co-evaporated by lyophilization, twice, with 1 mL of $D_2O$, to remove exchangeable protons before a final dissolution in 0.5 mL of $D_2O$ for NMR analysis. Based on the molecular weight from the negative-ion electrospray ionization mass spectrometry (ESI-MS) results (Table 1), fractions C1 to C4 were assigned as unsaturated alginate disaccharides, trisaccharides, tetrasccharide, and pentasaccharides, respectively.

### Key terms: alg degradation, fractions C1-C4, D₂O, fermentation

**Table 1.** ESI-MS analysis of the fragments generated from alginate degradation

| Fraction | Found Ions (Charge) | Calculated Mol Mass (H Form) | Assignment | |
|---|---|---|---|---|
| | | | DP | Sequences |
| C1 | 351.05 (−1) | 351.06 | 2 | ΔNN |
| C2 | 527.08 (−1) | 527.09 | 3 | ΔNNN |
| C3 | 351.05 (−2), 703.11 (−1) | 704.13 | 4 | ΔNNNN |
| C4 | 439.06 (−2), 879.13 (−1) | 880.16 | 5 | ΔNNNNN |

N = β-D-mannuronic acid (M) or α-L-guluronic acid (G).

### Table 1 reveals that not all alg degradation products were not uniform in size or charge

Adapted from Li, M., et al. (2017). Degradation of Marine Algae-Derived Carbohydrates by Bacteroidetes Isolated from Human Gut Microbiota. Marine Drugs, 15(4), under CCBY 4.0

1. A is correct. When lactic acid is the only fermentation product, the process is said to be homolactic, as is the case for the bacteria used in yogurt production and human skeletal muscle. However, many bacteria perform heterolactic fermentation, which produces a mixture of lactic acid, ethanol and/or acetic acid, and $CO_2$ as a result, because of their use of the branched pentose phosphate pathway instead of the standard pathway for glycolysis.

2. C is correct. The 2nd paragraph tells us that α-agarase cleaves 1,3 links while β-agarase cleaves 1,4 links. Only choice C shows a 1,3 link.
   A. Maltose is 2 molecules of glucose linked by an α-1,4-glycosidic bond.
   B. Sucrose has an α-1,2 linkage.
   D. This is a β-1,6 linkage.

3. B is correct. The easiest amino acid to ionize will likely be the one to transfer from solution to the gaseous phase. This is most likely going to be the amino acid which gives up or takes on protons the most easily. Of the choices given, only lysine (K) is an amino acid which has a readily available side chain to be protonated or deprotonated.

4. D is correct. The most common products of fermentation are lactic acid (B), ethanol, methane gas (A), hydrogen gas (C). Pyruvic acid (D) is a key intermediate in metabolic pathways that serves as a reactant in fermentation, not a product.

5.  A is correct. Cancer cells grow more rapidly than the blood vessels to nourish them; thus, as solid tumors grow, they are unable to obtain oxygen efficiently. Under these hypoxic (low $O_2$) conditions, glycolysis leading to lactic acid fermentation becomes the primary source of ATP. Glycolysis is made more efficient in hypoxic tumors by the action of a transcription factor, *hypoxia-inducible transcription factor (HIF-1)*. In the absence of oxygen, HIF-1 increases the expression of most glycolytic enzymes and several glucose transporters.
    B.  While this can happen, the cancer cells could can switch to alternative fuel sources (fats, amino acids, other hexoses) to produce the needed ATP.
    C.  This is the opposite of what occurs, and excess oxygen (hyperoxia) would not favor fermentation.
    D.  This would imply that the more aggressive (fast-growing) the tumor, the less dependent on glucose the cancer is.

6.  C is correct. Both alcoholic fermentation (yeasts) and lactic acid fermentation (human cells) are anaerobic fermentation processes that begin with the sugar glucose. Glycolysis requires 10 enzymes which degrade glucose → pyruvate and then an $11^{th}$ enzyme converts pyruvate to lactic acid. Alcoholic fermentation follows the same enzymatic pathway for the first 10 steps. The last enzyme of human fermentation, lactate dehydrogenase, is replaced by two enzymes in alcoholic fermentation. These two enzymes, pyruvate decarboxylase and alcoholic dehydrogenase, convert pyruvate into carbon dioxide and ethanol in alcoholic fermentation.
    A, B, D: These enzymes are part of the primary glycolysis pathway (steps 10, 1 and 8) and would be present in both pathways.

7.  C is correct. Cells are unable to carry out respiration due to multiple circumstances, both environmental and intrinsic. Aerobic respiration cannot take place if: I- the cell lacks a sufficient amount of any appropriate, final electron acceptor to carry out cellular respiration; II -the cell lacks genes to make appropriate complexes and electron carriers in the electron transport system or; III- the cell lacks the DNA to make one or more enzymes needed I the aerobic pathway (citrate synthesis is the first step in the Krebs cycle).
    IV: Recall that fermentation is a way for the cell to reproduce the $NAD^+$ required to carry out glycolysis (Pyruvate + NADH $\leftrightarrow$ lactic acid/EtOH/other + $NAD^+$). Thus, high $NAD^+$ levels would favor the anaerobic cycle of glycolysis + fermentation.

## Independent Questions

1. Glycolysis is a near-universal pathway of energy acquisition. This series of reactions can best be characterized as:
   A. the oxidation of glucose to carbon dioxide.
   B. the anabolism of glucose to pyruvate.
   C. the catabolism of glucose to acetyl-CoA.
   D. the oxidation of glucose to pyruvate.

2. By the end of the investment phase of glycolysis, each molecule of glucose has been converted to:
   A. two molecules of glyceraldehyde 3-phosphate, with a net loss of two ATP molecules.
   B. two molecules of glyceraldehyde 3-phosphate, with no net loss or gain of ATP.
   C. two molecules of pyruvate, with a net gain of two ATP molecules.
   D. two molecules of pyruvate, with a net gain of four ATP molecules.

3. Anaerobic respiration is considerably less efficient than aerobic respiration. Which of the following situations best characterizes why an organism would need to utilize anaerobic respiration?
   A. Sustained aerobic respiration has depleted the body's stores of $NAD^+$ and FAD.
   B. Lactic acid is present at excessively high levels and must be recycled by the liver to prevent damage to muscle tissue.
   C. Muscular demands for ATP have exceeded the rate at which aerobic respiration can produce it.
   D. When aerobic respiration is insufficient, cells require the ATP that is directly produced by lactic acid fermentation.

4. A facultative anaerobe is capable of undergoing which metabolic process(es) in the presence of oxygen?
   A. Fermentation only
   B. Aerobic respiration only
   C. Both fermentation and aerobic respiration
   D. Neither fermentation nor aerobic respiration

5. All of the following enzymes are used in gluconeogenesis, but not in glycolysis, EXCEPT:
   A. pyruvate carboxylase.
   B. glucose 6-phosphate isomerase.
   C. fructose 1,6-bisphosphatase.
   D. glucose 6-phosphatase.

6. Which enzyme plays the most direct role in breaking branched linkages during glycogenolysis?
   A. Glycogen phosphorylase, which breaks α (1→4) linkages
   B. Glycogen phosphorylase, which breaks α (1→6) linkages
   C. Glycogen debranching enzyme, which breaks α (1→4) linkages
   D. Glycogen debranching enzyme, which breaks α (1→6) linkages

7. The rate-limiting step of glycolysis involves phosphorylation and the expenditure of ATP. Which enzyme catalyzes this irreversible step?
   A. Hexokinase
   B. Phosphofructokinase-1
   C. Fructose-bisphosphate aldolase
   D. Pyruvate kinase

8. Glucokinase and hexokinase are two key enzymes that phosphorylate glucose to glucose 6-phosphate (G6P). However, these two enzymes have differing kinetics and regulatory mechanisms. Which of the following describes how these two enzymes are regulated to prevent excess glycolysis?
   A. Hexokinase binds glucose with a higher affinity and inhibits glucokinase at low glucose concentrations.
   B. Glucokinase is the preferred enzyme to phosphorylate glucose and inhibits hexokinase when glucose concentrations are low.
   C. Hexokinase is inhibited by high levels of G6P, while glucokinase is inhibited by low blood sugar.
   D. Both hexokinase and glucokinase are most active when blood sugar levels are high.

# Independent Question Explanations

1. D is correct. Glycolysis involves the breakdown (catabolism) of glucose to form two molecules of pyruvate, among other products. This process constitutes oxidation. (If you find it difficult to remember this, recall that the electron carrier $NAD^+$ is reduced during glycolysis, so *something* must be oxidized in turn.) Acetyl-CoA is produced later, during pyruvate decarboxylation, and carbon dioxide is formed during the Krebs cycle.

2. A is correct. The investment phase of glycolysis refers to the first five steps. By the end of these steps, the original glucose molecule has been converted into two three-carbon glyceraldehyde 3-phosphate molecules. As this is the "investment" phase, we must have used some ATP (specifically, two molecules), making choice A correct. ATP is not produced until the payoff phase, which refers to the last five steps of the overall pathway.

3. C is correct. The single most crucial reason for the use of anaerobic respiration is that it is capable of producing ATP at a rate significantly faster than oxidative phosphorylation. Thus, when tissue (especially muscle tissue) requires more ATP than aerobic respiration can produce, cells turn to anaerobic methods. We can also eliminate the remaining choices. While option A may be tempting, anaerobic respiration does nothing to regenerate stores of FAD. Choice B is incorrect because lactic acid is a product of fermentation, so anaerobic respiration would thus only serve to increase its levels in the body. Finally, regarding choice D, note that no ATP is directly produced by fermentation. Instead, fermentation merely allows glycolysis to continue.

4. C is correct. Remember the difference between a facultative anaerobe and an obligate anaerobe! A facultative anaerobe can undergo both anaerobic respiration (fermentation) and aerobic respiration, even in the presence of oxygen. In contrast, an obligate anaerobe would not be able to survive in the presence of oxygen and would be restricted to anaerobic processes.

5. B is correct. Glucose 6-phosphate isomerase, also known as phosphohexose isomerase, is involved in both glycolysis and gluconeogenesis. Its name helps give this away; it interconverts glucose 6-phosphate and fructose 6-phosphate, which is required for both processes and is not highly exergonic in either direction. The remaining three enzymes are used specifically in gluconeogenesis to bypass steps that are highly energetically favorable in the glycolytic direction.

6. D is correct. Branch points in glycogen consist of α (1→6) linkages. These linkages are broken by an enzyme aptly termed glycogen debranching enzyme. In contrast, straight-chain glycogen is held together by α (1→4) linkages, which are broken through the action of glycogen phosphorylase.

7. B is correct. The rate-limiting step of glycolysis is the phosphorylation of fructose 6-phosphate by the enzyme phosphofructokinase-1. This is also a key regulatory step because it is essentially irreversible, so it commits the glucose molecule to the glycolytic pathway. We can eliminate answer choice A because although it does add a phosphate at the expense of ATP, it is not the rate-limiting step in glycolysis. Answer choice C can be eliminated because fructose-bisphosphate aldolase does not utilize ATP in glycolysis. Answer choice D can be eliminated because pyruvate kinase creates ATP, not expends it.

8. C is correct. Hexokinase transports glucose into the cell and is inhibited by high levels of its own product – G6P. Thus, its regulation is dependent on how quickly G6P can be cleared from the cell. Glucokinase, which is active in liver and pancreatic cells, is not inhibited by G6P. Its activity is positively correlated with blood sugar. As a result, when blood sugar is low, glycolysis is slowed, and when blood sugar is high, glycolysis as catalyzed by glucokinase occurs more rapidly.

This page left intentionally blank.

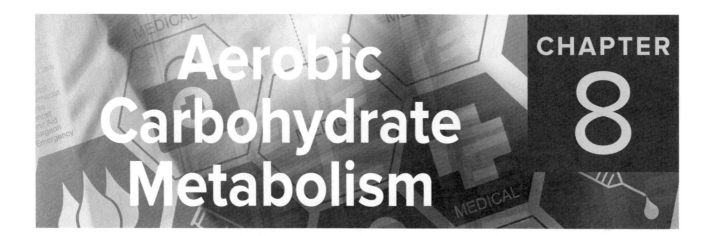

# Aerobic Carbohydrate Metabolism

## CHAPTER 8

## 0. Introduction

In this chapter, we'll turn to aerobic carbohydrate metabolism. The ability to engage in aerobic metabolism allows much more energy to be obtained from glucose (and other molecules that are broken down for energy), because it allows the electrons stored on the electron carrier molecules NADH and $FADH_2$ to be used for energy production via the electron transport chain and oxidative phosphorylation. As discussed previously in Chapter 7, there are two basic ways that we can get energy out of glucose: (1) use it as a substrate to shuffle around phosphate groups and form ATP, and (2) push it through a series of redox reactions in which glucose is oxidized and the reduced electron carriers NADH and $FADH_2$ are generated, and then do something useful with those electrons. In a nutshell, non-aerobic carbohydrate metabolism deals with part (1), and aerobic carbohydrate metabolism addresses part (2).

## 1. Citric Acid Cycle

The citric acid cycle, also known as the Krebs cycle or the tricarboxylic acid (TCA) cycle, is a major step in aerobic metabolism. If we're following the path of glucose in particular, we can think of the citric acid cycle as being the next step after glycolysis, but it's worth being aware that a large part of the importance of the citric acid cycle is that it is the crossroads of various metabolic pathways in the body (that is, non-carbohydrate precursors can be fed into it, and its intermediates can be siphoned off to use as building blocks for other classes of molecules). For the most part, the details about this go beyond the scope of the MCAT, but we'll pause to highlight some specific points in the citric acid cycle that you should be aware of from this perspective. The citric acid cycle does generate some ATP directly (through GTP), but its main value is that it generates several electron-carrying molecules that are fed into the electron transport chain to generate relatively huge amounts of ATP.

In eukaryotes, the citric acid cycle takes place in the mitochondrial matrix, while in aerobic prokaryotes it is carried out in the cytosol. Before entering the citric cycle, pyruvate (a three-carbon molecule) must be converted into acetyl-CoA, a molecule that consists of a short two-carbon chain (the "acetyl" group) connected to a sulfur atom, which is connected to a larger molecule known as coenzyme A (CoA). This takes place in the mitochondria, in a special area called the pyruvate dehydrogenase complex (PDC), and results in 1 NADH and 1 $CO_2$, which corresponds to the oxidative decarboxylation of pyruvate.

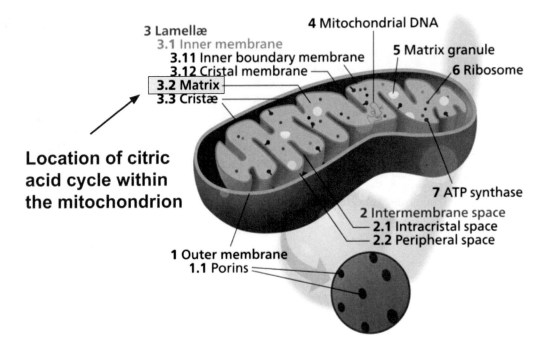

**Figure 1.** Citric acid cycle: location in the cell.

**Figure 2.** Acetyl-CoA.

There's a reason they call the PDC a "complex" – it is indeed a very complicated structure composed of multiple molecules. It contains three distinct enzymes that are physically linked with each other (pyruvate dehydrogenase being the most important for the MCAT, but pyruvate dehydrogenase is linked to dihydrolipoyl transacetylase and dihydrolipoyl dehydrogenase, which assist in some of the maneuvering involved with the coenzymes). It also requires the action of no fewer than five coenzymes: thiamine pyrophosphate (TPP), FAD, NAD, CoA, and lipoate. You don't have to worry about the details of all of the coenzymes, but it is useful to note that several of them (thiamine, FAD, NAD, and CoA) have components derived from B vitamins.

**Figure 3.** PDC and acetyl-CoA production.

Acetyl-CoA then enters the citric acid cycle. It is not only produced via glycolysis; as we will see in Chapter 9, acetyl-CoA is the end point of the beta-oxidation of fatty acids, and it can also be produced from amino acids. As such, it is useful to think of acetyl-CoA as being the main entry point to the citric acid cycle *overall*, not just for glucose. Each turn of the citric acid cycle generates 1 GTP (which you can think of as functionally equivalent to ATP), 3 NADH, 1 $FADH_2$, and 2 $CO_2$. As in glycolysis, NADH and $FADH_2$ are electron transporters that ultimately produce energy through the electron transport chain.

As we'll see below, the electron transport chain directly involves oxygen, but the citric acid cycle requires oxygen indirectly, even though oxygen is not a reactant or a product. This may seem contradictory at first, but you can make sense of this fact by recognizing that the main products of the citric acid cycle are the electron carriers NADH and $FADH_2$, not ATP (although some GTP is produced). In our discussion of glycolysis, we saw that fermentation can be used to regenerate $NAD^+$ in anaerobic conditions, but this doesn't work for the citric acid cycle – instead, the citric acid cycle is dependent on the exclusively aerobic electron transport chain to regenerate $NAD^+$ and FAD so the process can continue.

The basic idea of the citric acid cycle is that the two-carbon molecule acetyl-CoA joins with the four-carbon molecule oxaloacetate to form a six-carbon molecule known as citrate (this term is used for the deprotonated form of citric acid). Citrate then undergoes a series of redox and decarboxylation reactions to generate the products of the citric acid cycle. The final product is the four-carbon compound oxaloacetate, which joins with acetyl-CoA to start the process again.

> ### MCAT STRATEGY > > >
>
> It's worth highlighting the point that acetyl-CoA is the entry to the citric acid cycle. Because the citric acid cycle is most commonly presented as part of what can be thought of as the 'story of glucose,' it's easy to just think glucose → pyruvate → citric acid cycle → electron transport chain → ATP. That's not *wrong*, but it's not the whole story. Therefore, you should also try to cultivate the instinct of linking acetyl-CoA with entry into the citric acid cycle, because that will help you build links with other metabolic processes.

Let's review the steps of the citric acid cycle. As with glycolysis, the most important steps are noted in bold.

> **Pyruvate dehydrogenation complex**: Pyruvate is decarboxylated and CoA is added to the resulting two-carbon molecule, generating acetyl-CoA. This process also generates 1 NADH.

> **Step 1: oxaloacetate (4C) + acetyl-CoA (2C) → citrate (6C).** This process is catalyzed by citrate synthase. It is highly energetically favorable, and is essentially irreversible.

> Step 2: citrate (6C) → cis-aconitate (6C) → isocitrate (6C). This is sometimes given as two distinct steps, but it is best considered as a single step, because it is catalyzed by a single enzyme, aconitase. As suggested by the name *iso*citrate, this is a reversible isomerization step in which a hydroxyl group gets moved around.

> **Step 3: isocitrate (6C) → oxalosuccinate (6C) → α-ketoglutarate (5C).** Similarly to the previous step, some sources give this as two steps, but it is catalyzed by a single enzyme, isocitrate dehydrogenase, and it therefore makes sense to see oxalosuccinate as a short-lived intermediate. This is the first time in the citric acid cycle where we lose a carbon; the decarboxylation of oxalosuccinate results in 1 $CO_2$. This step also produces 1 NADH. It is rate-limiting and irreversible.

> **Step 4: α-ketoglutarate (5C) → succinyl-CoA (4C).** This is catalyzed by α-ketoglutarate dehydrogenase, and involves the release of 1 $CO_2$. Like step 3, this step involves the loss of a carbon from the skeleton of what was once citrate, produces 1 NADH, and is irreversible.

> **Step 5: succinyl-CoA (4C) → succinate (4C).** This reaction is catalyzed by succinyl-CoA synthetase, and allows 1 GTP to be synthesized (recall that GTP is functionally equivalent to ATP).

> **Step 6: succinate (4C) → fumarate (4C).** This redox reaction is catalyzed by succinate dehydrogenase. The oxidation of succinate is coupled with the reduction of FAD to $FADH_2$.

> Step 7: fumarate (4C) → malate (4C). This is a reversible hydration reaction catalyzed by fumarase.

> **Step 8: malate (4C) → oxaloacetate (4C).** Now we're back where we started! This reaction also produces 1 NADH. This reaction is also notable from the point of view of thermodynamics and regulation. Under standard conditions, it is extremely unfavorable ($\Delta G$ = +29.7 kJ/mol). So how does it move forward? The key here is Le Châtelier's principle. After this step is completed, the product oxaloacetate is immediately consumed in step 1 of the Krebs cycle, which is very favorable. Therefore, concentrations of oxaloacetate are kept very low, which pushes the reaction to the right.

## MCAT STRATEGY > > >

A well-known off-color mnemonic exists for the intermediates of the citric acid cycle: "can I keep selling sex for money, officer?" for citrate, isocitrate, α-ketoglutarate, succinyl-CoA, succinate, fumarate, malate, and oxaloacetate. On one hand, this is a good example of how racy mnemonics can be useful. But on the other hand, don't rely too heavily on mnemonics. No one on Test Day is going to make you stand up and rattle off a list of the intermediates of the citric acid cycle, and it's not *that* likely that you will run into a question that critically depends on knowing, for instance, that malate comes after succinate. Remember that the MCAT is all about *applying* your knowledge. Therefore, your first step should be to recognize all of the names and understand the logic of the process. Only then is it worth investing in memorizing the linear sequence of compounds.

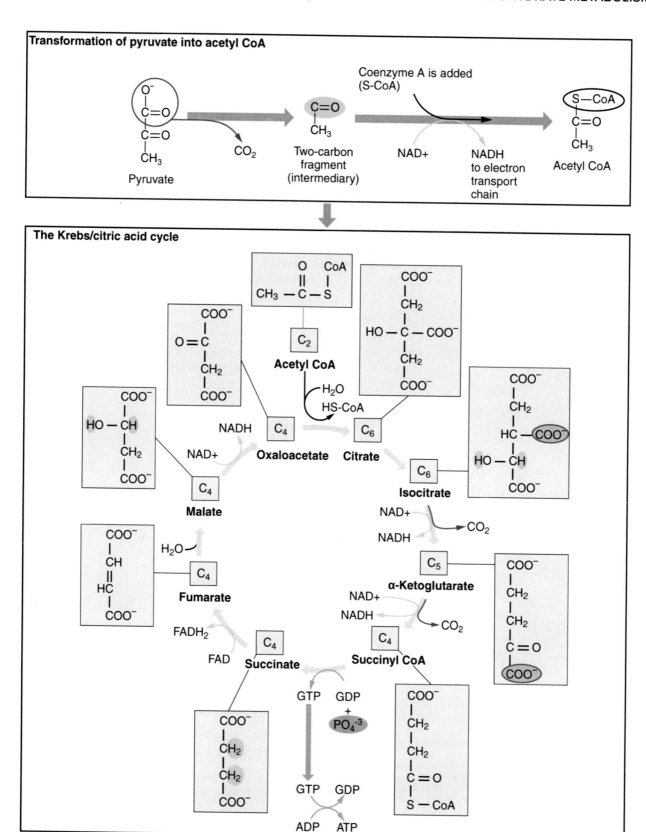

**Figure 4.** The citric acid cycle.

Figure 4 summarizes the citric acid cycle. Walk through the figure a few times, following where the carbon atoms are going, what kind of reactions are happening, and where the important products are produced.

## 2. Electron Transport Chain/Oxidative Phosphorylation

So far, we've generated some ATP (a net of 2 ATP from glycolysis and 2 GTP – one from each of the two pyruvate molecules produced from each glucose) from the glucose molecule that we started with, but the main action in terms of energy generation happens in the electron transport chain. The electron transport chain is located in the inner mitochondrial membrane in eukaryotes, and in the cell membrane of prokaryotes that carry out aerobic respiration. Its basic task is to get energy in the form of ATP from the electron carriers NADH and $FADH_2$, from which $NAD^+$ and FAD are regenerated.

Let's first review the fundamental logic of this process before plunging into the details. So how does this happen? A series of redox reactions transfers the electrons from $NADH/FADH_2$ to $O_2$, which is the final electron acceptor and is ultimately reduced to water. When NADH and $FADH_2$ are oxidized to $NAD^+$ and FAD, you can think of the hydrogens that are lost as being broken up into protons ($H^+$) and electrons. The electrons are passed on to reduce oxygen, and the protons are pumped into the intermembrane space. The resulting imbalance in charge is known as the proton gradient, and it is a way of storing electrochemical energy. This electrochemical energy – more specifically, the controlled flow of $H^+$ back into the mitochondrial matrix – is used to power the enzyme ATP synthase, which catalyzes the formation of ATP from ADP and $P_i$.

As shown in Figure 5, the electron transport chain involves four complexes embedded in the inner membrane, known as complexes I, II, III, and IV, as well as the electron carriers ubiquinone (Q) and cytochrome C.

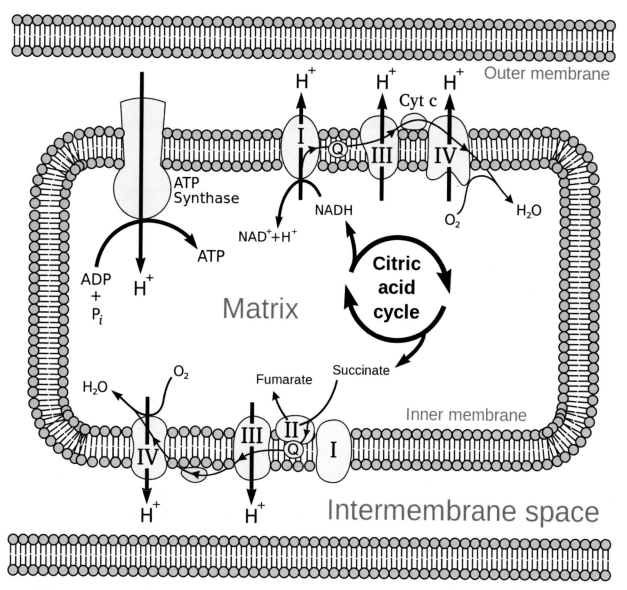

**Figure 5.** Electron transport chain.

The mechanism of the electron transport chain is complex, but can be thought of as similar to a series of electrochemical cells. On a mechanistic level, the 'transfer' of electrons is accomplished by them being handed from a carrier that 'wants' them relatively less to a carrier that 'wants' them relatively more. Translating this into electrochemical terms, this means that electrons are transferred from compounds with lower reduction potentials (corresponding to not really 'wanting' electrons that badly) to compounds with higher reduction potentials (corresponding to 'wanting' electrons more). In eukaryotic cells, the final electron acceptor is oxygen, which means that the reduction potential for $O_2 \rightarrow H_2O$ is higher than that of any of the other reduction half-reactions involved.

Complex I is also known as NADH dehydrogenase, and as the name implies, it converts NADH to $NAD^+$. In this reaction, the electron is transferred to the electron carrier ubiquinone (Q), with an overall reaction of $NADH + H^+ + Q \rightarrow NAD^+ + QH_2$. At the same time, four protons are transferred from the mitochondrial matrix into the

> > **CONNECTIONS** < <

**Chapter 8 of Chemistry**

intermembrane space; as such, complex I begins to generate the proton gradient that ultimately powers ATP synthase.

Complex II is notable because it specifically deals with FAD/FADH$_2$ and is a point of overlap with the citric acid cycle. Complex II consists of succinate dehydrogenase, which is a membrane-bound enzyme that catalyzes the conversion of succinate to fumarate in the citric acid cycle, generating FADH$_2$. In complex II, FADH$_2$ delivers more electrons to Q, generating QH$_2$.

In complex III, electrons get passed from QH$_2$ to the electron carrier known as cytochrome *c*, regenerating Q and resulting in the reduced form of cytochrome *c*. Note that Q carries two electrons, while cytochrome *c* carries one. The transfer of electrons from Q to cytochrome *c* is accompanied by the translocation of four protons into the intermembrane space per molecule of QH$_2$ (corresponding to a pair of electrons). On an interesting historical note, the structure of this complex was not fully characterized until the late 1990s.

## MCAT STRATEGY > > >

The complexes and electron carriers of the ETC are fair game for Test Day, but your first priority should be to understand the logic of the ETC and the idea that a series of spontaneous electron transfer reactions can be modeled as galvanic cells. As is almost always the case for the MCAT, be sure to focus on principles as well as memorization.

Complex IV is where the electron transport chain ends. Cytochrome *c* transfers electrons to O$_2$, reducing it to H$_2$O. Complex IV contains multiple subunits, such that the electron transfer is mediated through a series of steps, but the details are not relevant for the MCAT.

It's worth pausing briefly to review the electron carriers Q and cytochrome *c*, because they are valuable examples of how organic chemistry properties can be linked to biochemical functionality. The oxidized form of Q is technically known as ubiquinone, and the reduced form QH$_2$ is ubiquinol. The partially reduced form, which exists as an intermediate, is known as a ubisemiquinone, and is an example of a semiquinone. These molecules are discussed in greater depth in Chapter 10 of the General and Organic Chemistry textbook.

**Figure 6.** Oxidized and reduced forms of Q.

## > > CONNECTIONS < <

Chapter 10 of Chemistry

In contrast, cytochrome *c* is a much larger molecule. It is classified as a hemeprotein, which more specifically means that it is a protein (~12 kDa, which is relatively small for a protein but is huge compared to Q) that has a heme group, in which an iron atom is used to shuttle electrons. The mechanism of electron shuttling is for the iron atom to alternate between +2 and +3 oxidation states.

**Figure 7.** The heme group in cytochrome *c*.

Comparing and contrasting Q and cytochrome *c*, a common thread is that both molecules use redox reactions to shuttle electrons through the ETC. However, the details are different. Q has two carbonyl (C=O) groups that can be reduced to hydroxyl (–OH) groups, allowing it to carry two electrons, whereas the heme group on cytochrome *c* explains why it only carries a single electron.

At this point, let's step back and review what the electron transport chain accomplishes from the point of view of providing energy for the cell. The transfer of electrons from NADH/FADH$_2$ to oxygen is extremely exergonic, with $\Delta G$ values on the order of –200+ kJ/mol. Recall our analogy between the electron transport chain and a battery: the electron transport chain does actually generate energy! However, it generates energy in the form of localized electrochemical energy, which is not especially useful for the cell, because the cell needs a more transferable form of energy that can be stored and regulated – that is, ATP. Thus, the basic task that the cell faces at this point is how to leverage the electrochemical energy generated by the electron transport chain to form ATP.

The cell solves this problem in a simple and elegant way. It uses the energy generated by the energetically favorable redox reactions of the electron transport chain to push protons into the intermembrane space. The mechanisms of this are complex; some have yet to be fully established, and you certainly don't have to know them for the MCAT. The resulting proton gradient powers ATP synthase. ATP synthase is a complex enzyme with multiple subunits that interact closely with each other to capture the energy of the proton gradient as efficiently as possible. The details go beyond the scope of the MCAT, but the basic idea is that ATP synthase catalyzes ATP production and that the energy provided by the proton gradient is directly used to dislodge already-synthesized ATP from the enzyme to keep the process moving.

> **MCAT STRATEGY > > >**
>
> It's useful in your study process to demystify ATP production. Understanding that ATP synthase is a way of converting *local* energy into *storable, transportable* energy helps underscore the importance of the electron transport chain and oxidative phosphorylation for metabolism.

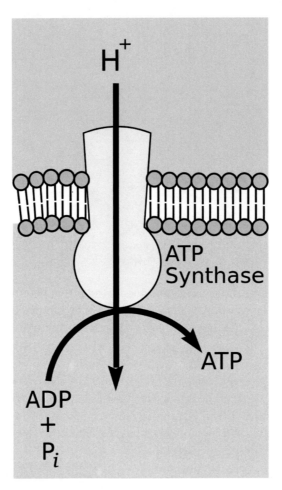

**Figure 8.** ATP synthase and proton pump.

The stoichiometry of the electron transport chain and oxidative phosphorylation is somewhat complex. Previously, it was estimated that each NADH produces 3 molecules of ATP and that each $FADH_2$ produces 2 molecules of ATP, with the difference being accounted for by which complexes in the electron transport chain they interact with and how many protons they cause to be pushed into the intermembrane space. More recent research has suggested that that a closer estimate would be 2.5 molecules of ATP per NADH and 1.5 molecules of ATP per $FADH_2$. The basic idea is that the electron transport chain is not a perfectly efficient process, meaning that some leakage and inefficiency do occur.

Nonetheless, with all of the above in mind, we can now calculate how many molecules of ATP are generated when a molecule of glucose is fully metabolized. This calculation is shown in Table 1.

| PROCESS | PRODUCT | RESULTING ATP |
|---|---|---|
| Glycolysis | 2 ATP | 2 |
| | 2 NADH | 5 |
| Pyruvate → acetyl-CoA (2× per glucose) | 2 NADH | 5 |
| Krebs cycle (2× per glucose) | 2 GTP | 2 |
| | 6 NADH | 15 |
| | 2 FADH$_2$ | 3 |
| Subtotal | | 32 |
| Energy needed to transport pyruvate into mitochondrion | | −2 |
| Total | | 30 |

**Table 2.** Energy generation from glucose.

As shown in Table 2, in eukaryotic cells each glucose produces about 30 units of ATP when fully metabolized. In other textbooks, you may have seen higher values (in the 36-38 range), but those values fail to adequately account for inefficiencies and leakage in the electron transport chain, and may also not consider the energy that is needed to transport pyruvate into the mitochondria.

# 4. Regulation

The regulation of the citric acid cycle and the ETC/oxidative phosphorylation is relatively simple compared to the intricate processes of regulation of nonaerobic carbohydrate metabolism that we discussed in the previous chapter. This may be surprising given the relative complexity of these processes, but it makes more sense in light of the fact that all of the machinery of metabolism works together simultaneously. The citric acid cycle and the ETC/oxidative phosphorylation are relatively late steps in the process of extracting energy from biomolecules, so *entry* into the citric acid cycle is very tightly regulated, but the cycle itself is regulated in a less complicated manner.

A basic rule governing both the citric acid cycle and oxidative phosphorylation is that they are upregulated when the cell needs more ATP, as reflected by a relatively high level of ADP present in the cell. Moreover, the citric acid cycle is also subject to negative feedback, in which certain products inhibit key upstream steps in the process.

The first regulatory step of the citric acid cycle is the production of acetyl-CoA, which is technically slightly upstream of the cycle itself. Pyruvate is converted to acetyl-CoA by the pyruvate dehydrogenase complex (PDC). This process is upregulated by high levels of AMP, CoA, and NAD$^+$, which are all signs that the cell needs to make more energy. It is downregulated by ATP and NADH, which are indicators that the cell has access to ample energy, as well as by acetyl-CoA, in a classic example of negative feedback. The final major negative

> **MCAT STRATEGY > > >**
>
> The ratio of ADP to ATP (or sometimes AMP to ATP) is used as an indicator of the energy status of the cell. If that ratio is high—that is, if there's a *relatively* high amount of ADP— then the cell must need more energy, and vice versa. For MCAT purposes, a 'high ADP-to-ATP ratio' is the same as *"needs more energy!"*

regulator of the PDC is the presence of high levels of fatty acids. This may seem counterintuitive at first, but this reflects the fact that fatty acids are metabolized to acetyl-CoA, so they can be seen as "potential" acetyl-CoA molecules that signify that there is no need for the PDC to be especially active.

The citric acid cycle is also regulated at three major exergonic steps. The initial step in the cycle, in which citrate is formed, is upregulated by high levels of ADP, and is downregulated by ATP and NADH, which are signals that the cell has ample energy, and by citrate and succinyl-CoA, which are the immediate and slightly downstream products of this reaction, respectively. The conversion of isocitrate to α-ketoglutarate and is downregulated by ATP and upregulated by ADP, and the formation of succinyl-CoA from α-ketoglutarate is downregulated by succinyl-CoA and NADH.

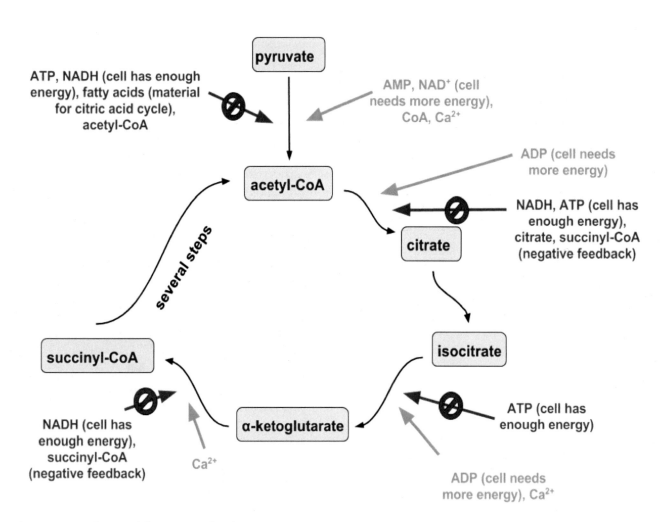

**Figure 9.** Regulation of the citric acid cycle.

The regulation of oxidative phosphorylation is even simpler in principle: it is upregulated (largely via upstream elements, such as the citric acid cycle and glycolysis) when a relatively large amount of ADP is present, indicating that the cell needs energy, and is slowed down when abundant ATP is present.

A range of substances have been discovered that interfere with the electron transport chain and oxidative phosphorylation. The most notable of these are cyanide and carbon monoxide, both of which interfere with cytochrome $c$ oxidase, the enzyme that transfers electrons to oxygen, which is the final electron acceptor. Without this step, the whole process breaks down. (Carbon monoxide is also deadly because it binds with hemoglobin, preventing it from binding with oxygen).

> **MCAT STRATEGY > > >**
>
> Cyanide poisoning is a classic example of a clinically relevant scenario in which ETC function is impaired, so if you see cyanide poisoning on the MCAT, immediately think of the ETC.

# 5. Must-Knows

> High-level points about aerobic metabolism:
>   - Requires oxygen; electron transport chain and oxidative phosphorylation require oxygen directly, but citric acid cycle depends on those processes, so requires oxygen indirectly.
>   - Citric acid cycle, electron transport chain, and oxidative phosphorylation occur in mitochondria of eukaryotes.
>   - Aerobic metabolism allows *much* more energy to be generated than is possible through glycolysis (2 ATP per glucose → ~30 ATP per glucose).
> Citric acid cycle:
>   - In eukaryotes, carried out in mitochondrial matrix.
>   - Pyruvate dehydrogenase complex (PDC) converts pyruvate to acetyl-CoA before entering citric acid cycle → 1 NADH generated.
>   - Net products of citric acid cycle per turn: 1 GTP, 3 NADH, 1 $FADH_2$, 2 $CO_2$.
>   - Stoichiometry: each glucose molecule → *2 turns* of citric acid cycle.
>   - Byproducts of other molecules (lipids, proteins) can enter into citric acid cycle, and intermediates of citric acid cycle are precursors for other metabolic processes, making it a metabolic crossroads in the body.
>   - Start of citric acid cycle: acetyl-CoA (2C) + oxaloacetate (4C) → citrate (6C); other key steps include step 3 [isocitrate (6C) → oxalosuccinate (6C) → α-ketoglutarate (5C] and step 4 [α-ketoglutarate (5C) → succinyl-CoA (4C)].
> Electron transport chain (ETC)/oxidative phosphorylation.
>   - In glycolysis/citric acid cycle, the direct formation of ATP via substrate-level phosphorylation only accounts for a small amount of the net energy. The electron carriers NADH and $FADH_2$ are the main sources of energy, but the ETC and oxidative phosphorylation are needed to make it happen.
>   - Principle of ETC: electrons transferred along series of carriers, moving from carriers with lower reduction potentials to those with higher electron potentials, similarly to a galvanic cell. Energy from ETC → pumps protons into intermembrane space, creating proton gradient.
>   - Complexes I, II, III, IV are embedded in inner mitochondrial membrane, and together with electron carriers Q and cytochrome $c$ are used in electron transfer.
>   - Oxygen is the final electron acceptor in the ETC, and is reduced to $H_2O$.
>   - Electrochemical energy of proton gradient is used to power ATP synthase, which attaches a phosphate group to ADP to form ATP.
> Regulation: ↑ATP, ↑products of citric acid cycle = ↓citric acid cycle; ↑ADP (showing that cell needs energy) = ↑citric acid cycle; ↑ADP = ↑ ETC/oxidative phosphorylation.

## Practice Passage

Glioblastoma multiforme (GBM) is an aggressive malignant primary brain tumor. The highly glycolytic nature of GBM reflects their propensity to metabolize glucose to lactic acid at an elevated rate, even in the presence of abundant oxygen. Their metabolism is characterized by efflux of lactic acid from the tumor microenvironment through transmembrane transporters known as monocarboxylate transporters (MCTs). Of the four known functional MCTs (MCTs 1–4) that transport lactate, all except MCT3 are currently known to be overexpressed in tumors.

Researchers analyzed the effects of MCT inhibition on glycolytic metabolism and GBM invasiveness, by treating U251-MG glioma cells engineered to express enhanced green fluorescent protein (EGFP) with α-cyano-4-hydroxy-cinnamic acid (ACCA), a membrane-impermeable small-molecule inhibitor of MCTs.

To test for invasion capacity of GBM when lactate transport is inhibited, cellular assays containing pyruvate, lactate, glucose, or glucose supplemented with ACCA were tested. After 120 hours, the fluorescence of the samples was quantified using a fluorescent plate reader and the invasive capacity was calculated. The results are shown in Figure 1.

**Figure 1.** Invasive capacity test results

Measurements of oxygen consumption upon application of ACCA or of digitonin, an agent that increases the permeability of plasma membranes to ACCA, were also carried out to determine the potential impact on mitochondrial respiration after *in vivo* application of ACCA. Figure 2 shows the results of the measurements.

**Figure 2.** Rate of oxygen usage in cell media

1. According to the data in Figure 1, comparison across brain slice cultures would reveal that U251-MG invasiveness:
    A. is not enhanced in glioma cells treated with ACCA and glucose versus untreated cells.
    B. is negatively correlated with the presence of lactate in the medium.
    C. is positively correlated with enhanced glycolytic flux.
    D. demonstrates that glioma invasiveness is decreased versus controls in glucose treated cells also treated with ACCA.

2. In addition to blocking lactate transport, the results in Figure 2 most strongly suggest which fact about the effect of ACCA on glioma cell respiration?
    A. Intracellular ACCA induces an increase in respiration due to the exposure of mitochondria to respiratory substrates.
    B. Intracellular ACCA blocks intracellular pyruvate entry into mitochondria.
    C. Extracellular ACCA acts to decrease $O_2$ permeability across the cell membrane.
    D. Extracellular ACCA interferes with glucose transport across the cell membrane.

3. Gliomas such as GBM arise from glial cells, which provide which of the following functions?
    I. Maintenance of the myelin sheath in the peripheral nervous system
    II. Secretion of cerebrospinal fluid
    III. Maintenance of the myelin sheath in the central nervous system
    A. I only
    B. III only
    C. I and III only
    D. I, II, and III

4. MCT4 participates in the astrocyte-neuron lactate shuttle that occurs between neurons and astrocytes during routine axonal firing. Given this, what is the most likely reason that researchers believe ACCA is a better candidate as a potential treatment for GBM than other small molecule inhibitors with greater affinity for MCTs?
   A. The relatively lower MCT affinity implies broader activity against all MCTs overexpressed in GBM.
   B. High-affinity inhibitors may be unable to disrupt the neuron-astrocyte lactate shuttle in GBM.
   C. Other small molecule inhibitors may have few adverse effects against the elevated glycolytic metabolism of GBM.
   D. ACCA is less likely to impact normal tissue while adversely affecting cells displaying elevated rates of glycolysis.

5. The researchers hypothesized that lactate can initiate a cascade of events that upregulate the expression of growth factors that enhance the invasive capacity of GBM. What alternative explanation for the increase in GBM invasiveness when lactate efflux is inhibited is NOT consistent with results from the passage?
   A. Efflux of lactate decreases an invasive GBM cell's capacity for aerobic metabolism in highly vascularized sites.
   B. The collapse of glycolytic metabolism degraded the cellular energy pool and the invasive capacity of GBM.
   C. Lactate efflux directly modulates the tumor microenvironment in such a way as to promote GBM invasiveness.
   D. Tumor lactate can upregulate expression of proteins that degrade the extracellular matrix in the tumor microenvironment.

6. The reactants used in the fold-invasion experiment are directly involved with:
   > I. aerobic respiration.
   > II. anaerobic respiration.
   > III. fermentation.
   A. I only
   B. II only
   C. II and III only
   D. I, II, and III

7. If the complete combustion of glucose yields 686 kcal of energy, and ATP hydrolysis yields 7.3 kcal, what is the approximate efficiency of complete aerobic respiration by cerebellar neurons unaffected by GBM?
   A. 20%
   B. 40%
   C. 60%
   D. 70%

## Practice Passage Explanations

Glioblastoma multiforme (GBM) is an aggressive malignant primary brain tumor. The highly glycolytic nature of GBM reflects their propensity to metabolize glucose to lactic acid at an elevated rate, even in the presence of abundant oxygen. Their metabolism is characterized by efflux of lactic acid from the tumor microenvironment through transmembrane transporters known as monocarboxylate transporters (MCTs). Of the four known functional MCTs (MCTs 1–4) that transport lactate, all except MCT3 are currently known to be overexpressed in tumors.

*Key terms: GBM, brain tumor, MCTs*

*Cause and effect: GBM = ↑glucose → lactic acid (even when O₂ available); expel excess LA via 4 MCTs*

Researchers analyzed the effects of MCT inhibition on glycolytic metabolism and GBM invasiveness, by treating U251-MG glioma cells engineered to express enhanced green fluorescent protein (EGFP) with α-cyano-4-hydroxy-cinnamic acid (ACCA), a membrane-impermeable small-molecule inhibitor of MCTs.

*Key terms: U251-MG glioma cells, EGFP, ACCA*

*Cause and effect: experiment: U251-MG glioma cells express EGFP, tx with MCT inhibitor ACCA, measure metabolism*

To test for invasion capacity of GBM when lactate transport is inhibited, cellular assays containing pyruvate, lactate, glucose, or glucose supplemented with ACCA were tested. After 120 hours, the fluorescence of the samples was quantified using a fluorescent plate reader and the invasive capacity was calculated. The results are shown in Figure 1.

*Key terms: fluorescent plate reader, invasion capacity*

*Cause and effect: control vs. GBM + reactant, and/or ACCA were measured after 120 hours for the invasive capacity*

**Figure 1.** Invasive capacity test results

*Figure 1 shows that adding the inhibitor in conjunction with glucose, leads to severely ↓cancer invasion; IC is elevated versus glioma cells treated with ACCA*

Measurements of oxygen consumption upon application of ACCA or of digitonin, an agent that increases the permeability of plasma membranes to ACCA, were also carried out to determine the potential impact on mitochondrial respiration after in vivo application of ACCA. Figure 2 shows the results of the measurements.

*Key terms: oxygen consumption, digitonin, mitochondrial respiration*

*Cause and effect: mitochondrial respiration was measured in cells after addition of ACCA or ACCA and digitonin, an agent that increase the permeability of the plasma membrane to ACCA*

**Figure 2.** Rate of oxygen usage in cell media

*Figure 2 shows O$_2$ consumption is approximately equal in the glucose-containing cellular media with and without ACCA, but is decreased in glioma cells treated with ACC when digitonin is added*

1. C is correct. Figure 1 shows U251-MG invasiveness is positively correlated to the presence of glucose in the growth medium, while ACCA treatment decreases lactic acid efflux, causing glioma cell invasiveness to decrease below the level shown with any other treatment. This suggests that a buildup of intracellular lactic acid, which is typically avoided by the characteristic efflux of lactic acid through MCTs described in the passage, inhibits glycolytic flux and thus glioma invasiveness.
   A, B: Figure 1 shows enhanced glial cell invasiveness relative to control (0.0) levels for ACCA-treated and lactate-supplemented media.
   D. Figure 1 shows that that glioma invasiveness is increased versus controls in glucose-treated cells also treated with ACCA.

2. B is correct. Figure 2 shows that rates of $O_2$ consumption by GBM cells in glucose-containing media are approximately equal with and without ACCA, but are decreased versus glioma cells treated with ACCA when digitonin (increases the permeability of ACCA to the plasma membrane), is also present. This suggests that ACCA inhibition occurs mostly when ACCA, which is otherwise membrane impermeable, is able to enter the cell following digitonin treatment. Therefore, the mechanism by which ACCA mediates its inhibition of aerobic respiration must occur intracellularly.

   A. ACCA decreases, rather than increases, mitochondrial activity as reflected by the changes in oxygen consumption by GBM cells shown in Figure 2.

   C, D: The mechanism by which ACCA mediates its inhibition of aerobic respiration must occur intracellularly.

3. D is correct. Glial cells are non-neuronal cells that maintain homeostasis, form myelin, and provide support and protection for neurons in the brain and peripheral nervous system. Oligodendrocytes are glial cells that coat axons in the central nervous system with myelin, while Schwann cells perform a similar function in the peripheral nervous system. Ependymal cells line the spinal cord and the ventricular system of the brain. These cells synthesize and secrete cerebrospinal fluid (CSF).

4. D is correct. If ACCA is a relatively lower affinity inhibitor of MCTs, it is less likely to interfere with normal neuronal function and specifically inhibit the metabolic function of cancerous cells displaying abnormally rapid glycolytic flux.

   A. lower MCT affinity does not necessarily imply broader activity against all MCTs.

   B. high-affinity inhibitors are more likely to disrupt the neuron-astrocyte lactate shuttle in GBM than a lower affinity inhibitor.

   C. high-affinity inhibitors are likely to disrupt all MCT-related functions to a greater extent than would a lower affinity inhibitor.

5. A is correct. When efflux of lactate is decreased in GBM due to ACCA/digitonin co-treatment, Figure 2 shows that oxygen consumption decreases, implying that aerobic metabolism had decreased. This implies that efflux of lactate maintains a basal state of aerobic activity in glioma cells either for reasons separate from or related to its promotion of glycolytic metabolism—it does not decrease the cancerous cells' capacity for aerobic metabolism.

   B, C, D: All of these statements are alternate explanations for the relationship between changes in lactate efflux and changes in GBM invasiveness as indicated by the data.

6. C is correct. The reactants used with the cancer cells were pyruvate, lactate, and glucose. Glucose/pyruvate are the initial and final products of glycolysis, an anaerobic process since none of its 10 steps involve the use of oxygen. However, upon finishing glycolysis, the cell must continue respiration in either an aerobic or anaerobic direction. Lactate is the result of anaerobic fermentation.

7. B is correct. Aerobic cell respiration (glycolysis + Krebs cycle + electron transport chain) produces 36 ATP/ glucose consumed. The ATP phosphate bond has an energy of 7.3 kcal; 36 ATP are produced during aerobic respiration for a total of at least 263 kcal. This efficiency is 263/686, or 39% of the available energy in glucose is transferred to ATP. Thus, aerobic respiration converts about 40% of the available energy of glucose into ATP.

## Independent Questions

1. Which key intermediate of the citric acid cycle connects it with gluconeogenic pathways?
   A. Acetyl-CoA
   B. Succinate
   C. Citrate
   D. Malate

2. Which of the following statements best summarizes the function of Complex I in the electron transport chain?
   A. Complex I receives electrons from NADH and results in the translocation of 4 protons across the inner mitochondrial membrane.
   B. Complex I oxidizes $FADH_2$ and does not contribute to the proton gradient.
   C. Complex I reduces ubiquinone, translocating 2 protons across the inner mitochondrial membrane.
   D. Complex I acts as an electron carrier intermediate, giving its electrons to cytochrome C.

3. Three molecules of acetyl-CoA enter the citric acid cycle, which proceeds through three full turns as a result. This process produces all of the following EXCEPT:
   A. three molecules that contain high-energy phosphodiester bonds.
   B. six NADH molecules.
   C. three $FADH_2$ molecules.
   D. six molecules of carbon dioxide.

4. What is the irreversible, rate-limiting step of the citric acid cycle?
   A. Production of citrate from oxaloacetate and acetyl-CoA
   B. Oxidative carboxylation of α-ketoglutarate
   C. Decarboxylation of oxalosuccinate, forming α-ketoglutarate
   D. Oxidation of malate to form oxaloacetate

5. Which of the following pairings of an ETC protein complex with the number of protons it contributes to the proton gradient is INCORRECT?
   A. Complex III – 4 protons
   B. Complex I – 4 protons
   C. Complex II – 0 protons
   D. Complex IV – 8 protons

6. An abundance of which of the following molecules would most likely be responsible for indirectly slowing the electron transport chain?
   A. NADH
   B. $FADH_2$
   C. ATP
   D. Vitamin B12

7. Uncoupling proteins (UCPs) are potent poisons that dramatically inhibit ATP production. These proteins function to increase the permeability of the inner mitochondrial membrane. Which component of the electron transport chain and/or oxidative phosphorylation is targeted by UCPs?
   A. Complex I
   B. The proton gradient
   C. The electron carriers NADH and $FADH_2$
   D. ATP synthase

8. The metal atom found in cytochrome $c$ is which of the following?
   A. Mg
   B. Ca
   C. Cu
   D. Fe

# Independent Question Explanations

1. D is correct. During gluconeogenesis, oxaloacetate in the mitochondria is converted to malate for export from the mitochondria. Cytosolic malate is then re-oxidized to oxaloacetate and converted to phosphoenolpyruvate. This step is almost always the rate-limiting step in gluconeogenesis. Malate is also a citric acid cycle intermediate. Note that acetyl-CoA is a reactant in the citric acid cycle, not an intermediate.

2. A is correct. Complex I, also known as NADH dehydrogenase, removes 2 electrons from NADH. These electrons are transferred to ubiquinone, or coenzyme Q. Complex I translocates 4 protons across the inner mitochondrial membrane as a result of this activity.

3. B is correct. Each turn of the citric acid cycle yields 1 GTP, 3 NADH, 1 $FADH_2$, and 2 $CO_2$. As such, three turns of the cycle should produce 3 GTP, 9 NADH, 3 $FADH_2$, and 6 $CO_2$. GTP, like ATP, contains high-energy phosphate bonds, eliminating choice A. Choice B is the only option that is listed inaccurately, as nine molecules of NADH will be produced, not six.

4. C is correct. The rate limiting step of the citric acid cycle is the generation of the five-carbon molecule α-ketoglutarate. This step is catalyzed by enzyme isocitrate dehydrogenase.

5. D is correct. Complex IV removes eight protons from the mitochondrial matrix; however, four of these protons are given to molecular oxygen along with four electrons, forming water. The other four protons are translocated across the membrane and contribute to the gradient. Remember that Complex II does not directly contribute to the gradient.

6. C is correct. ATP is a negative regulator of phosphofructokinase, which is the enzyme that catalyzes the rate-limiting step of glycolysis. By inhibiting the amount of pyruvate and thus acetyl-CoA and electron carriers such as NADH and $FADH_2$, abundant ATP also inhibits the electron transport chain. In general, ATP inhibits respiration, as large amounts of available ATP signal that the cell does not need to produce more.

7. B is correct. The electron transport chain is often said to be "coupled" to the production of ATP via the production of the proton gradient. Specifically, the ETC creates the gradient, which is then used to produce ATP via the flow of protons through ATP synthase. If the permeability of the inner mitochondrial membrane is increased by administration of a UCP, protons will be able to freely flow between mitochondrial compartments rather than being sequestered in the intermembrane space. As such, the proton gradient will be dissipated.

8. D is correct. Cytochrome *c* is a hemeprotein, which means that it contains a heme group. Heme contains iron (Fe). (The same group is found in hemoglobin.) Note that magnesium (Mg) is a cofactor involved in glycolysis.

This page left intentionally blank.

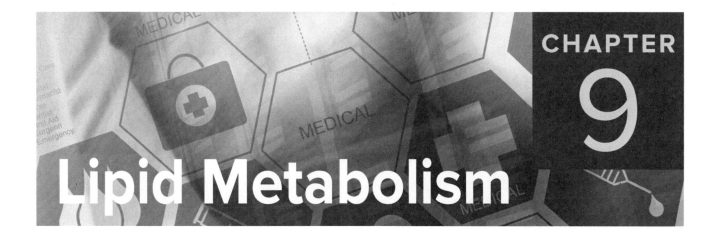

# CHAPTER 9

# Lipid Metabolism

## 0. Introduction

Lipids are a major source of energy for the body, and also play major roles as structural elements (for example, the lipids of the plasma membrane) and signaling molecules (for example, steroid hormones). In this chapter, we will first cover some details of fatty acid nomenclature, before discussing lipid transport. Then, we will discuss lipid catabolism, or the mechanisms through which lipids are broken down to provide energy. This will be followed by an overview of lipid anabolism, which refers to how lipids are built up from smaller constituents in the body, and finally a review of how lipid precursors are modified to generate important structural and signaling molecules.

The structural properties of the lipids that you have to be familiar with for the MCAT are presented in Chapter 1 of the Biology textbook (biomolecules), but a high-level review of the major categories of lipids you are responsible for will help provide context for this chapter.

> Fatty acids and triglycerides. Fatty acids are long-chain carboxylic acids, and triglycerides are formed when three fatty acids form ester linkages to a three-carbon glycerol backbone. The main function of fatty acids and triglycerides is to provide energy, although they also serve as precursors for the synthesis of other molecules.
> Fatty acid/triglyceride derivatives. This is a large category that includes phospholipids and sphingolipids. These molecules play structural and signaling roles.
> Cholesterol and its derivatives. Cholesterol has a characteristic four-ring structure and plays a major role in stabilizing the structure of the plasma membrane, where it contributes to fluidity in low temperatures and reduces fluidity in high-temperature conditions. Steroid hormones are derived from cholesterol, and play a major role in the endocrine system.
> Eicosanoids. These compounds are derived from arachidonic acid and have a characteristic structure involving a five-carbon ring and 20 carbons overall. The most important eicosanoids are a large family of signaling molecules known as prostaglandins, which have a diverse range of effects, including the modulation of inflammation. Additionally, thromboxanes are involved in clotting.

palmitic acid (a saturated fatty acid)

linoleic acid (an unsaturated fatty acid)

a sample triacylglycerol
(triglyceride) with two    saturated
fatty acid chain and one trans fatty
acid chain

**A.**

**examples of fatty acids and triacylglycerols**

a phosphatidylcholine (phospholipid)

a sphingomyelin

**B.**

**examples of phospholipids and sphingolipids**

cholesterol

estradiol

aldosterone

**C.**

**Cholesterol and some derivatives**

arachidonic acid

alprostadil (prostaglandin E1)

**D.**

**Arachidonic acid and some of its eicosanoid derivatives**

thromboxane

**Figure 1.** Representatives of various classes of lipids.

# 1. Fatty Acid Nomenclature and Properties

For cholesterol and cholesterol derivatives, eicosanoids, and terpenes/terpenoids, you can focus on being aware of the structure in general terms. That is, you should be able to visually distinguish these classes of molecules, but you are not responsible for extensive details about their structure or nomenclature. The situation is different for fatty acids, which do have important structural and nomenclature-related complexities that you must be aware of for the MCAT.

Fatty acids can either be saturated, if their aliphatic tail contains only C–C single bonds, or unsaturated, if at least one C=C bond is present. To remember which is which, it may be helpful to think of "saturated" as describing a situation in which the hydrocarbon tail has as many hydrogens as possible, meaning that only single bonds between carbon atoms are possible.

The nomenclature of fatty acids is somewhat tricky, and you should be aware of multiple nomenclature possibilities for the MCAT. First, fatty acids may have common names, such as linoleic acid. It may be worth familiarizing yourself with the common names of some especially common fatty acids, but doing so is not technically a requirement for the MCAT. However, you do have to be aware of some of the possibilities for describing where double bonds are present in unsaturated fatty acids, as summarized below:

> IUPAC nomenclature. For instance, palmitoleic acid could be referred to as (9Z)-hexadecanoic acid. This indicates that it has a total of 16 carbons, and a Z (or *cis*) double bond at carbon 9. In this nomenclature, carbons are counted starting at the carbonyl carbon.

> Omega (ω) notation. This notation counts from the *non-carbonyl* end of the fatty acid chain. Therefore, palmitoleic acid would be described as an ω-7 fatty acid, because the double bond begins on the seventh carbon. Considerable effort has gone into researching the relative composition of ω-3 and ω-6 fatty acids in food sources and their health impacts.

> Lipid numbering. This is a system in which the total number of carbons in a fatty acid is given, along with an indication of how many double bonds are present, such that an 18:3 fatty acid has 18 carbons and 3 double bonds. You may notice that this system is somewhat ambiguous, in that several compounds could fit this description. Unless otherwise stated, you can assume that the double bonds are present at three-carbon intervals along the chain. Aspects of other notations can be used to provide more information about the specific location of double bonds if needed. The basic point of lipid numbering is that it can be useful to quickly refer to how many double bonds exist in a molecule.

> Delta notation. The capital Greek letter delta (Δ) is sometimes used to identify the position/orientation of double bonds (the idea is that *d* stands for both *d*elta and *d*ouble). In this notation, carbons are counted from the carbonyl carbon, such that a $\Delta^9$ bond would be at the ninth carbon from the carbonyl end.

The presence of one or more double bonds in a fatty acid has a significant effect on its physical properties. Naturally occurring unsaturated fatty acids generally have *cis* bonds, which introduce a degree of bending into the chain. This is especially true for polyunsaturated fatty acids with *cis* bonds. Such acids do not stack readily on top of each other, meaning that they tend to have lower melting and boiling points than the corresponding saturated fatty acids. In the context of plasma membranes, unsaturated fatty acids tend to make the membrane more fluid. Small amounts of *trans* fatty acids are produced in nature, but they are mostly present in the human diet as a result of the industrial processing of vegetable oils. Partial hydrogenation of unsaturated vegetable oils results in trans fats, which are more stackable than *cis* fatty acids and therefore are more likely to be solids at room temperature. Trans fats have been consistently linked to heart disease, and have been banned in many countries. In the United States, they are expected to be phased out by 2018.

Some common fatty acids illustrating the above structural patterns are presented below in Figure 2.

## MCAT STRATEGY > > >

The effects of fatty acid saturation/unsaturation on melting temperature and membrane fluidity are a classic example of the kind of structure-function relationship that you should focus on for the MCAT.

## MCAT STRATEGY > > >

A key point to understand is that in naturally occurring fatty acids, more double bonds = more unsaturation = lower melting point = more fluidity. You should be able to quickly recognize that an 18:3 fatty acid will have a lower melting point than an 18:1 fatty acid, for instance.

**Figure 2.** Some common fatty acids.

# 2. Lipid Transport

The absorption of lipids in the digestive system is discussed in more detail in Chapter 10 of the Biology textbook. In this section, we will focus on how they are transported throughout the body and mobilized when the body needs to use lipids as a source of energy.

Lipids are packaged into chylomicrons in the small intestine, and are then released into lacteals, which drain into the lymphatic system. Ultimately, lipids are released into the bloodstream via the thoracic duct. Chylomicrons are mostly made up of triglycerides, but additionally contain apolipoproteins, which allow the hydrophobic lipids to be transported through the aqueous solution of the blood, as well as phospholipids and cholesterol. Chylomicrons deliver some triglycerides to cells, and their remnants are processed in the liver.

> > CONNECTIONS < <

Chapter 10 of Biology

The liver then produces very-low-density lipoprotein (VLDL), which is similar to chylomicrons in that it also transports triglycerides to other tissues. The triglycerides in question are those left over after chylomicrons are processed in the liver, as well as triglycerides that are produced de novo in the liver. After delivering triglycerides to the tissues, VLDL becomes intermediate-density lipoprotein (IDL). These are either returned to the liver or become low-density lipoprotein (LDL).

Unlike chylomicrons and VLDL, which primarily transport triglycerides, LDL primarily transports cholesterol. Essentially, this is because the triglycerides are offloaded to tissues first, such that by the time we work down the density scale to reach LDL, predominantly cholesterol remains. The job of LDL is to transport cholesterol to the tissues that need it. Finally, high-density lipoprotein (HDL) transports cholesterol, as well as other lipids, *away* from the tissues, to the liver for processing and excretion. Of note, cholesterol returned to the liver may be processed into bile.

In clinical contexts, you may have heard doctors or other healthcare providers describe LDL as "bad cholesterol" and HDL as "good cholesterol." From a strictly biochemical point of view, this is a misconception. LDL and HDL are *transporters*, not different types of cholesterol; moreover, there is only one type of cholesterol. The reason for this description is that LDL levels are directly associated with an increased risk of developing cardiovascular disease, whereas HDL levels show an inverse association with cardiovascular risk. Therefore, if a patient has a lipid profile that includes relatively low LDL levels and relatively high HDL levels, their situation with regard to future cardiovascular risk is relatively favorable. Referring to "bad cholesterol" and "good cholesterol" may be an approachable way to communicate with patients about their lab tests, for the MCAT—and in your future as a physician—you should know that cholesterol is just cholesterol and that lipoproteins are transporters.

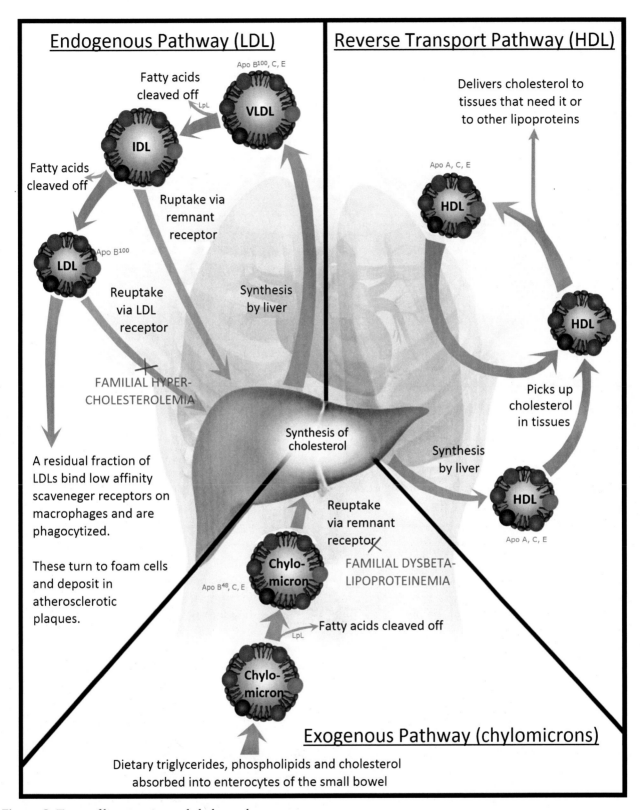

**Figure 3.** Types of lipoproteins and cholesterol transport.

In the body, fatty acids are primarily stored in adipocytes. When necessary, fatty acids are mobilized via the action of hormones. In particular, epinephrine and glucagon trigger the hydrolysis of triacylglycerols via an enzyme known as hormone-sensitive lipase. Once triacylglycerols are hydrolyzed, the resulting free fatty acids enter the bloodstream, where they are transported by the serum protein albumin.

# 3. Lipid Catabolism

Next, let's explore how lipids are metabolized to obtain energy. This is more or less synonymous with the catabolism of fatty acids, because other forms of lipids are not used to generate energy to any significant extent. With regard to obtaining energy from fatty acids, the same basic strategy is used as we saw with glucose in previous chapters. Specifically, fatty acids are broken down into acetyl-CoA, which can be fed into the citric acid cycle (similarly to the effects of glycolysis and the pyruvate dehydrogenation complex), and the electron carriers NADH and $FADH_2$ are generated, which produce energy in the electron transport chain. This process is known as beta-oxidation because the beta carbon of each fatty acid is oxidized to a carbonyl group (C=O). It occurs in the mitochondria in eukaryotic cells.

The basic logic of beta-oxidation is to chop up extended fatty acid chains into two-carbon units of acetyl-CoA. Each acetyl-CoA has a carbonyl carbon, whereas fatty acid chains contain only C and H, so the beta-oxidation process requires two high-level steps to be repeated: (1) convert the beta carbon to a carbonyl carbon and (2) chop up the fatty acid chain to release an acetyl-CoA molecule, at which point the process can be restarted.

Some preparatory steps have to take place before beta-oxidation can be initiated. Essentially, CoA has to be attached to the head of the fatty acid and the resulting compound (known as acyl-CoA) has to be moved to the mitochondria. If the fatty acid has a short enough chain, the acyl-CoA compound can diffuse directly, but if it is a long-chain fatty acid, something known as the carnitine shuttle is needed for transport into the mitochondria. The carnitine shuttle works in three steps: (1) an enzyme recognizes the acyl-CoA and swaps out CoA with carnitine, resulting in an acyl-carnitine complex; (2) the acyl-carnitine complex is transported into the mitochondria; (3) another enzyme removes carnitine and places a CoA back on, regenerating the original acyl-CoA compound.

Let's work through what happens in the simplest case of beta-oxidation: a saturated (single bonds only) fatty acid chain with an even number of carbons. We start with an acyl-CoA molecule with $n$ carbons and need to generate an acetyl-CoA molecule with 2 carbons and a new, shorter acyl-CoA molecule with $n - 2$ carbons. This happens in four steps, as shown in Figure 5:

> Step 1: Formation of a C=C double bond. This bond is formed between the alpha and beta carbons of the carbonyl group at the head of the acyl-CoA molecule. The enzyme responsible for this is acyl-CoA dehydrogenase. This is a redox reaction in which the oxidation of a C–C single bond to a C=C double bond is coupled to the reduction of FAD to $FADH_2$. The result of this process is known as a trans-$\Delta^2$-enoyl-CoA.
> Step 2: Add an –OH group to the beta carbon (or C3). This is a hydration reaction. Interestingly, this reaction is stereospecific, and only the L isomer is formed. The end product is known as a L-$\beta$-hydroxyacyl-CoA.
> Step 3: Oxidize the C–OH bond on the beta carbon (C3) to C=O. Like Step 1, this is a redox reaction in which the oxidation of the C–OH bond to a C=O bond is coupled to the reduction of $NAD^+$ to NADH.

> Step 4: The molecule is broken up. The thiol group of another CoA group carries out a thiolysis reaction targeting the beta-carbon. This results in an acetyl-CoA group detaching from the fatty acid chain and the formation of a new, shorter acyl-CoA chain.

**The beta carbon:**

**Figure 4.** Beta-oxidation.

This process continues until the fatty acid chain is completely oxidized. However, we might ask: what happens if we have to deal with an unsaturated fatty acid chain (i.e., one that already contains a double bond) or one that contains an odd number of carbons? Conceptually the answers are quite simple, although the mechanics are somewhat involved.

Let's first consider what happens if there's a double bond in the chain. If it's an odd-numbered *cis* bond (which we can note as $\Delta^3$, because by convention we use notation that refers to the structure that is present when the beta-oxidation process runs into this problem, not the absolute configuration of the double bond in the original fatty acid chain), an enzyme known as *cis*-$\Delta^3$-enoyl-CoA isomerase flips it to a $\Delta^2$ *trans* bond. This bond corresponds to what is created in step 1 of beta-oxidation anyway, so beta-oxidation can simply continue at this point.

If it's an even-numbered double bond ($\Delta^4$), which can occur in polyunsaturated fatty acids, an enzyme known as 2,3-dienoyl-CoA reductase creates a $\Delta^3$ double bond. At this point, we have a situation identical to what we discussed in the previous paragraph, meaning that cis-$\Delta^3$-enoyl-CoA isomerase can take over and the process can continue.

**Figure 5.** Beta-oxidation of unsaturated fatty acids.

Now what if there's an odd number of carbons in the fatty acid chain? Throughout most of the cycle, it doesn't matter. Only the final cleavage of the chain is affected by this. Instead of the final step resulting in two acetyl-CoA molecules (2 carbons + 2 carbons), it results in an acetyl-CoA molecule and a three-carbon substance known as propionyl-CoA (2 carbons + 3 carbons). Propionyl-CoA gets a carbon added to it by an enzyme known as propionyl-CoA carboxylase, and the resulting four-carbon compound is further rearranged by various enzymes to form succinyl-CoA, which then enters the citric acid cycle.

Finally, let's assess how much energy is created by oxidizing a fatty acid, limiting ourselves to the simple case of a saturated chain with an even number of carbons. Each oxidation step produces 1 FADH$_2$, 1 NADH, and 1 acetyl-CoA, except for the final step that creates an extra acetyl-CoA. The ATP equivalents are summarized in Table 1.

| REGULAR OXIDATION STEPS | | | FINAL OXIDATION STEP | | |
|---|---|---|---|---|---|
| Yield | ATP per molecule | Total ATP | Yield | ATP per molecule | Total ATP |
| 1 FADH$_2$ | 1.5 | 1.5 | 1 FADH$_2$ | 1.5 | 1.5 |
| 1 NADH | 2.5 | 2.5 | 1 NADH | 2.5 | 2.5 |
| 1 acetyl-CoA | 10 | 10 | 2 acetyl-CoA | 10 | 20 |
| Total | | 14 | Total | | 24 |

**Table 1.** Energy yield of beta oxidation.

The above table can be used to calculate a formula; if an even-numbered fatty acid chain contains $n$ carbons, there must be $(n/2) - 1$ oxidations. One of these is the final oxidation, so we have $(n/2) - 2$ regular oxidation steps and 1 final oxidation step. We also have to account for the loss of 2 ATP needed to activate the fatty acid molecules at the beginning of the process and turn them into acyl-CoA molecules. This results in the following formula:

$$\text{total ATP} = \left(\frac{n}{2} - 2\right) * 14 + 24 - 2 = 7n - 6$$

However, we do not necessarily recommend that you memorize that equation. If you do get a question about the energy output of beta oxidation, the rough conversion factor of estimating that a fatty acid chain of $n$ carbons will produce slightly less than $7n$ ATP will be enough to get the right answer.

The citric acid cycle is not the only destination for the acetyl-CoA generated by beta-oxidation. In the liver, additional acetyl-CoA can be used to generate ketone bodies. Basically, ketone bodies are a way for hepatocytes to package acetyl-CoA in a portable structure that can be secreted into the bloodstream and sent to tissues that need energy. Conceptually, this is pretty similar to gluconeogenesis, and you can actually think of ketone body production as a process that runs more or less in parallel with gluconeogenesis, but is particularly upregulated under different conditions.

> ## MCAT STRATEGY > > >
>
> A takeaway point here is that fatty acid metabolism produces a *lot* of ATP. This is because fatty acid hydrocarbon chains are highly reduced, so there are a lot of extra electrons that can be pulled away by the electron carrier $NAD^+$ during the oxidation of this molecule. On a broader level, this is why fats are the most calorie-dense nutrient (9 kcal/g compared to 4 kcal/gram for carbohydrates and proteins).

The first step in the generation of ketone bodies is for two acetyl-CoA molecules to be joined together to form acetoacetyl-CoA, a four-carbon molecule with a single CoA group. Another acetyl-CoA molecule is added to form a six-carbon compound known as β-hydroxy- β-methylglutaryl CoA, from which an acetyl-CoA compound is broken off, resulting in a four-carbon compound known as acetoacetate, which you can think of as essentially two joined-together acetyl-CoA molecules with the CoA groups removed.

Acetoacetate is one of the compounds known as a ketone body. It can be reversibly reduced to D-β-hydroxybutyrate, and can also be cleaved via acetoacetate decarboxylase to form acetone. Acetone is formed in relatively small quantities from acetoacetate, and is exhaled. Both D-β-hydroxybutyrate and acetoacetate are transported to tissues throughout the body; D-β-hydroxybutyrate is oxidized to acetoacetate, and acetoacetate is then converted into acetyl-CoA that can be fed into the citric acid cycle.

**Figure 6.** Ketogenesis.

The production of ketone bodies, also known as ketogenesis, is a normal part of healthy physiology, and is particularly likely to take place during periods of fasting, when glycogen stores are depleted. However, starvation and untreated diabetes mellitus can lead to the overproduction of ketone bodies. The basic idea here is that it is upregulated when acetyl-CoA molecules cannot enter the citric acid cycle. This takes place if the intermediaries of the citric acid cycle, especially oxaloacetate, have been siphoned off to gluconeogenesis. (Recall that oxaloacetate is involved in the first major step of gluconeogenesis, in which pyruvate is turned back into phosphoenolpyruvate via the intermediary of oxaloacetate).

The ketone bodies D-β-hydroxybutyrate and acetoacetate are both acidic, meaning that when present in the blood at an excessively high level, they can cause the blood pH to drop, resulting in a condition known as ketoacidosis. In patients with underlying diabetes, this condition is known as diabetic ketoacidosis. Ketoacidosis can be smelled on a patient's breath, because acetone accumulates to a noticeable level. Moreover, ketogenic diets have been developed that deliberately push metabolism in the direction of ketogenesis, although ideally not to the point of out-and-out ketoacidosis. One such diet has been used to help control epilepsy in children, and ketogenesis may also occur as part of low-carbohydrate diets such as the Atkins diet.

# 4. Lipid Anabolism

Next, let's analyze how lipids are synthesized. This is probably less of a must-know than beta-oxidation and ketone bodies, but is nonetheless a topic that the MCAT does expect you to be familiar with.

The synthesis of fatty acids is not quite beta-oxidation in reverse, although it may be tempting to think of it that way. Fatty acid synthesis takes place in the cytosol, and involves different enzymes and intermediates than those found in beta-oxidation. Fatty acid synthesis involves acetyl-CoA to some extent, but the most important intermediate is malonyl-CoA, a three-carbon compound generated by acetyl-CoA carboxylase. The first step of fatty acid synthesis is for an acetyl group and a malonyl group to become attached to the acyl carrier protein (ACP) subunit of fatty acid synthase. The acetyl and malonyl groups then condense, forming a four-carbon chain with the release of a $CO_2$ molecule. In this condensation reaction, steps of reduction, dehydration, and subsequent reduction remove the C=O that was initially on the acetyl-CoA molecule, forming a fatty acid-like thioester structure with a single C=O bond corresponding to what will ultimately be the head of the fatty acid. These reduction processes require NADPH, and are repeated six times to generate palmitate.

**Figure 7.** Fatty acid synthesis.

Interestingly, the fatty acid synthesis process itself results in only one fatty acid: palmitic acid, a 16-carbon saturated fatty acid that exists in its deprotonated form (palmitate) under physiological conditions. The body can make other fatty acids, but only by modifying palmitate in processes that are distinct from fatty acid synthesis itself. You should also note that fatty acid synthesis requires NADPH, which is generated by the pentose phosphate pathway. This provides a link between lipid metabolism and an often-overlooked area of non-aerobic carbohydrate metabolism.

## MCAT STRATEGY > > >

The pentose phosphate pathway is a perennial non-favorite of MCAT students because it often seems like a random add-on to non-aerobic carbohydrate metabolism, but in reality, it's a key linkage between the world of carbohydrates and the world of lipids. Be alert for these crossovers as you study metabolism, because you may be able to leverage them on Test Day if these topics come up in a passage or question.

## > > CONNECTIONS < <

Chapter 7 of Biochemistry

You should also be aware of the basics of how cholesterol is synthesized. Although cholesterol is obtained from the diet to some extent, it can also be synthesized de novo in the liver. Cholesterol synthesis is similar to fatty acid synthesis in that takes place in the cytosol and ultimately uses acetyl-CoA as the building block, but the similarities end there. In the first major step, the six-carbon compound mevalonate is formed: two acetyl-CoA molecules condense to form acetoacetyl-CoA, a third acetyl-CoA is added to form β-hydroxy-β-methylglutaryl CoA, and then a reduction coupled with NADPH yields mevalonate. This is the rate-limiting step of cholesterol synthesis.

Once mevalonate is formed, three units of ATP are invested to form one of two compounds known as activated isoprenes, which are five-carbon molecules with a double bond and two phosphate groups (if you're counting carbons, one carbon is lost as $CO_2$; don't worry about the rest of the stoichiometry here). You may note that there are two activated isoprene isomers, dimethylallyl pyrophosphate and $\Delta^3$-isopentenyl pyrophosphate, but the details are beyond our scope. Six isoprene units condense to form squalene. In turn, squalene passes through a series of steps, of which one requires NADPH, to form cholesterol. In fact, squalene can be processed to form a variety of related compounds known as sterols, many of which are present in plants, but for the purposes of the MCAT, cholesterol is its most important immediate derivative.

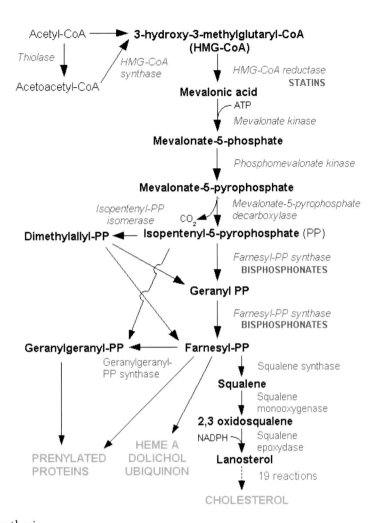

**Figure 9.** Cholesterol synthesis.

In addition to the synthesis of fatty acids and cholesterols from scratch (or, more precisely, from acetyl-CoA), you should be generally aware that lipids can be modified in a variety of ways. The details go beyond the scope of what you are expected to know for the MCAT, but it's worth being aware of these modifications in general terms in case they come up in a passage.

> Fatty acids/diacylglycerols are modified into phospholipids, predominantly in the smooth endoplasmic reticulum and inner mitochondrial membrane. The basic idea is that a diacylglycerol is formed, and the third "slot" on the glycerol backbone is occupied by a phosphate group that connects to the head of the phospholipid.

> Cholesterol is modified to form steroid hormones in the cells of endocrine organs.

> Arachadonic acid, a 20:4 polyunsaturated acid, is modified to form eicosanoids. The most prominent eicosanoids are prostaglandins, which have a range of effects including the modulation of inflammation, and thromboxanes, which are involved in the clotting cascade. The enzymes cyclooxygenase-1 (COX-1) and cyclooxygenase-2 (COX-2) are involved in early steps of this pathway, and are targeted therapeutically by non-steroidal anti-inflammatory drugs (NSAIDs), such as aspirin.

# 5. Must-Knows

> Major classes of lipids:
>   - Fatty acids/triglycerides: FAs = long-chain carboxylic acids; triglycerides/triacylglycerols formed by 3 FAs esterified to a 3-carbon glycerol backbone. Main role is to provide energy.
>   - Phospholipids/fatty acid derivatives: large category including phospholipids and sphingolipids; play structural/signaling roles.
>   - Cholesterol and its derivatives: four-ring structure. Cholesterol contributes to fluidity of plasma membrane; steroid hormones are derived from cholesterol.
>   - Eicosanoids: derived from arachidonic acid; have 20 carbons and a 5-carbon ring; prostaglandins modulate inflammation and thromboxanes are involved in clotting.
> Fatty acid nomenclature: main issue is how to denote presence of double bond(s).
>   - IUPAC/normal nomenclature: start numbering from carboxylic C at head.
>   - ω (omega) notation: start numbering at end; ω-3 has a double bond at third C from the end, may have other double bonds as well.
>   - More double bonds = more unsaturation = lower melting/boiling point = greater contribution to fluidity of membrane.
> Beta oxidation: fatty acid broken down into acetyl-CoA (2-carbon) units in the mitochondria.
>   - Acetyl-CoA products are fed into the citric acid cycle or used to produce ketone bodies in the liver. Ketone bodies are formed in the liver and sent to provide energy to other cells, where they are broken back down into acetyl-CoA (think of ketone bodies as an acetyl-CoA delivery service).
>   - If fed into citric acid cycle, a fatty acid chain of $n$ carbons → $7n - 6$ ATP.
>   - Carnitine shuttle moves activated FAs into the mitochondria.
>   - Four major steps:
>     - A C=C double bond is formed between C2 and C3, and FAD → $FADH_2$.
>     - An OH group is added to C3.
>     - C–OH → C=O at C3, coupled with $NAD^+$ → NADH.
>     - Molecule is broken up, generating acetyl-CoA and a shorter acyl-CoA.
>   - Ketone body formation upregulated in starvation and untreated diabetes.
> Fatty acid synthesis: acetyl-CoA is the ultimate building block, but malonyl-CoA (a three-carbon compound generated by carboxylating acetyl-CoA) is the intermediate that transfers two-carbon units to an extending chain. FA synthesis takes place in cytosol.
> Cholesterol synthesis: built from mevalonate → repeating isoprene units → squalene → cholesterol; mevalonate is limiting step.
> Cholesterol/triacylglycerol transport:
>   - Chylomicrons: least density; first transporters of triacylglycerols to tissue
>   - Very-low-density lipoprotein (VLDL): transport triacylglycerols from liver to tissue
>   - Intermediate density lipoprotein (IDL): remnants of VLDL
>   - Low-density lipoprotein (LDL): transport cholesterol to tissue; high levels associated with risk of cardiovascular disease
>   - High-density lipoprotein: transport cholesterol *from* tissue to liver; high levels are cardioprotective.

This page left intentionally blank.

## Practice Passage

Ketogenesis and ketolysis are central metabolic processes activated during fasting periods. The nuclear receptor peroxisome proliferator activated receptor α (PPARα) is one of the key transcription factors which regulate ketogenesis. PPARα is an important element in the metabolic network, where it participates in signaling driven by the nutrient sensor AMP-activated protein kinase (AMPK), and triggers fatty acid oxidation and ketogenesis. Ketogenesis takes place in hepatocyte mitochondria, whereas ketolysis involves utilization of ketone bodies, primarily β-hydroxybutyrate (bHB), in the mitochondria of peripheral tissues (Figure 1).

**Figure 1.** Metabolism of ketone bodies

The rate of ketogenesis depends on the velocity of HMG-CoA synthesis. This reaction is performed in three steps:

1. Cleavage of acetyl-CoA with formation of a covalent bond between the acetyl moiety and the thiol group of catalytic cysteine (acetyl-SH-Enzyme) with the release of free CoA-SH

2. Binding of acetoacetyl-CoA with acetyl-SH-Enzyme and formation of HMG-CoA (Enzyme-S-HMG-CoA)

3. Hydrolysis of the HMG-CoA-Enzyme intermediate with the release of HMG-CoA and free Enzyme-SH

Ketone body supply and metabolism is particularly important in the brain. In brain tissue ketolysis accounts for about 65% of the energy supply during starvation, and the rest comes from glucose derived from various sources (Figure 2). Fatty acid oxidation, on the other hand, is not a source of ATP for neurons, because it takes place exclusively in astrocytes. Oxidation of long-chain fatty acids in mitochondria is controlled at the level of their transport. Only fatty acids of eight or fewer carbon atoms can freely enter into mitochondria.

**Figure 2.** Energy substrates for neurons during fasting

Besides PPARα, there are other transcription factors capable of impacting ketogenesis either positively or negatively. Positive regulators include: CREB, COUP-TF while in opposition to these transcription factors is the hepatocyte nuclear factor 4 (HNF4). On the systemic level, ketogenesis is also regulated by monitoring the utilization of ketone bodies by peripheral tissues. During fasting, the main membrane transporter responsible for ketone body absorption, MCT1, is expressed at high levels, which enables efficient import and ketolysis. Diabetic ketoacidosis, the decrease in blood pH caused by excessive ketolysis, causes over 100,000 hospital admissions per year.

*Adapted from Grabacka, M., et al. (2016). Regulation of Ketone Body Metabolism and the Role of PPARα. International Journal of Molecular Sciences, 17(12), 2093 under CCBY 4.0*

1. According to the passage, what is the most likely effect of AMPK?
   A. AMPK blocks the expression of MCT1 in astrocytes.
   B. AMPK blocks anabolic processes such as protein and fat biosynthesis.
   C. AMPK decreases the concentration of ketone bodies in the cell.
   D. AMPK increases the rate of fatty acid oxidation in neurons.

2. In diabetes mellitus type I, insulin levels are most likely to cause:
   A. no change in MCT1 mRNA expression.
   B. decreased MCT1 mRNA expression.
   C. increased levels of β-hydroxybutryate.
   D. no change in β-hydroxybutryate levels.

3. Increased activity of which enzyme will most directly lead to production of MCT1?
   A. Acyl-CoA dehydrogenase
   B. Pyruvate kinase
   C. Hexokinase
   D. Pyruvate dehydrogenase

4. Which of the following fats will result in the greatest energy production in astrocyte mitochondria?
   A. Caproic acid ($C_6H_{12}O_2$)
   B. Caprylic acid ($C_8H_{16}O_2$)
   C. Capric acid ($C_{10}H_{20}O_2$)
   D. Behenic acid ($C_{22}H_{44}O_2$)

5. Patients fasting for 24 hours prior to surgery often report to their surgery with low blood glucose levels. Which of the following is most likely true in such a patient?
   A. AMPK1-triggered fat oxidation inhibits gluconeogenesis.
   B. AMPK1-triggered fat oxidation produces pyruvate.
   C. AMPK1-triggered fat oxidation produces glycogen.
   D. AMPK1-triggered fat oxidation favors gluconeogenesis.

6. What is the rate-limiting step of ketogenesis?
   A. Step 1
   B. Step 2
   C. Step 3
   D. Steps 2 and 3

7. According to data in Figure 2, which of the following molecules is responsible for the lowest proportion of ATP production in neurons?

## Practice Passage Explanations

Ketogenesis and ketolysis are central metabolic processes activated during fasting periods. The nuclear receptor peroxisome proliferator activated receptor α (PPARα) is one of the key transcription factors which regulate ketogenesis. PPARα is an important element in the metabolic network, where it participates in signaling driven by the nutrient sensor AMP-activated protein kinase (AMPK), and triggers fatty acid oxidation and ketogenesis. Ketogenesis takes place in hepatocyte mitochondria, whereas ketolysis involves utilization of ketone bodies, primarily β-hydroxybutyrate (bHB), in the mitochondria of peripheral tissues (Figure 1).

*Key terms: ketogenesis, ketolysis, PPAR, AMPK, nutrient sensor, ketone bodies*

*Contrast: genesis = liver mito; lysis = periphery*

*Cause and effect: fasting → ↑AMP → PPARα → FA oxidation/ketogenesis*

**Figure 1.** Metabolism of ketone bodies

*Figure 1 shows the complex ketogenic/ketolytic pathways, save detailed analysis for later*

The rate of ketogenesis depends on the velocity of HMG-CoA synthesis. This reaction is performed in three steps:

1. Cleavage of acetyl-CoA with formation of a covalent bond between the acetyl moiety and the thiol group of catalytic cysteine (acetyl-SH-Enzyme) with the release of free CoA-SH

2. Binding of acetoacetyl-CoA with acetyl-SH-Enzyme and formation of HMG-CoA (Enzyme-S-HMG-CoA)

3. Hydrolysis of the HMG-CoA-Enzyme intermediate with the release of HMG-CoA and free Enzyme-SH

*Key terms: HMG-CoA synthesis, three steps*

Ketone body supply and metabolism is particularly important in the brain. In brain tissue ketolysis accounts for about 65% of the energy supply during starvation, and the rest comes from glucose derived from various sources (Figure 2). Fatty acid oxidation, on the other hand, is not a source of ATP for neurons, because it takes place exclusively in astrocytes. Oxidation of long-chain fatty acids in mitochondria is controlled at the level of their transport. Only fatty acids of eight or fewer carbon atoms can freely enter into mitochondria.

*Key terms: ketone supply, brain, FA oxidation, astrocytes*

*Cause and effect: brain primarily uses ketones during fasting; FA oxid. limited to ≤ 8 carbons*

- β-hydroxybutyrate
- Acetoacetate
- Glucose from ketone bodies
- Glucose from lactate and pyruvate
- Glucose from glycerol (lipolysis)
- Glucose from aminoacids (proteolysis)

**Figure 2.** Energy substrates for neurons during fasting

Besides PPARα, there are other transcription factors capable of impacting ketogenesis either positively or negatively. Positive regulators include: CREB, COUP-TF while in opposition to these transcription factors is the hepatocyte nuclear factor 4 (HNF4). On the systemic level, ketogenesis is also regulated by monitoring the utilization of ketone bodies by peripheral tissues. During fasting, the main membrane transporter responsible for ketone body absorption, MCT1, is expressed at high levels, which enables efficient import and ketolysis. Diabetic ketoacidosis, the decrease in blood pH caused by excessive ketolysis, causes over 100,000 hospital admissions per year.

*Key terms: positive regulators, negative regulators, ketone transporter MCT1, ketoacidosis*

*Contrast: CREB/COUP = ↑ketogenesis; HNF4 = ↓ketogenesis*

*Cause and effect: fasting → ↑MCT1 → ↑ketone import/lysis*

*Adapted from Grabacka, M., et al. (2016). Regulation of Ketone Body Metabolism and the Role of PPARα. International Journal of Molecular Sciences, 17(12), 2093 under CCBY 4.0*

1. B is correct. The first paragraph tells us that AMPK is an important activator of metabolic pathways activated by AMP. The body monitors energy levels via AMP:ATP ratio. If this ratio gets too high, catabolic energy-releasing processes should be upregulated and energy consuming, anabolic process will be downregulated.
   A. MCT1 plays a direct role in ketone import and ketolysis, a catabolic process. Thus, AMPK1 is more likely to increase MCT1 activity.
   C. AMPK increases FA oxidation, which will result in ketogenesis (Figure 1).
   D. The third paragraph tells us that neurons cannot utilize FA for energy.

2. C is correct. Type I DM is a lack of insulin secretion. Without insulin to inhibit FA transport and drive glucose into the cell, cells will have to increasingly rely on fatty acids and other molecules for fuel generation via the Krebs cycle. This will likely cause an increase in MCT1 expression and increased concentrations of ketone bodies, such as β-hydroxybutryate.

3. A is correct. The passage tells us that MCT1 is involved in absorption of ketone bodies, which is most likely to be needed when fatty acids are being oxidized. Only choice A is a fatty acid oxidation enzyme.
   B, C D: These are all enzymes of glycolysis and the Krebs cycle, not fatty acid oxidation.

4. B is correct. According to paragraph 3, only fatty acids of eight or fewer carbon atoms can freely enter into mitochondria for oxidation inside the astrocytes. The more carbon atoms in the fat, the more acetyl-CoA molecules will be produced and thus the more ATP that will be generated.

5. D is correct. During starvation, the cell will rely on several sources for energy. First it will consume its glycogen stores and then switch to gluconeogenesis. Fatty acids can be oxidized to propionyl-CoA, a precursor for succinyl-CoA, which can then be converted to pyruvate and enter gluconeogenesis. Being unable to effectively oxidize fatty acids will limit gluconeogenesis, which maintains blood glucose levels in a fast.
   B.  While this is true, it would not explain the low glucose levels.
   C.  While glycogen synthesis would reduce glucose levels, it is not triggered by fatty acid oxidation.

6. B is correct. Paragraph 2 says the rate of ketogenesis depends on the velocity of HMG-CoA synthesis. Of the 3 steps shown, only step 2 mentions the formation of HMG-CoA.

7. C is correct. According to Figure 1, the largest proportion (55%) comes from β-hydroxybutyrate, and then we go clockwise around the circle, with ketone bodies the lowest (2%). Choice C is acetone, one of the 3 ketone bodies commonly produced by the cells. We do not need to know the identity of ketone bodies for the exam, but we are expected to recognize the other three biological molecules given.
   A.  This is β-hydroxybutyrate, which Figure 2 says accounts for 55% of the brain's energy.
   B.  This is pyruvate, which Figure 2 says accounts for 17% of the brain's energy.
   D.  This is glycerol, which Figure 2 says accounts for 8% of the brain's energy.

## Independent Questions

1. Suppose a pharmaceutical researcher has discovered a molecular inhibitor of acyl-CoA dehydrogenase, an enzyme involved in fatty acid oxidation. The researcher subsequently discovers that this inhibitor does not readily diffuse through lipid membranes, but rather enters the cell via endocytosis together with large lipoprotein complexes. Is this molecule likely to be an effective pharmaceutical agent?
   A. Yes, because fatty acids are primarily broken down in the cytoplasm.
   B. Yes, because fatty acids are primarily synthesized in the cytoplasm.
   C. No, because fatty acids are primarily broken down in the mitochondria.
   D. No, because fatty acids are primarily synthesized in the mitochondria.

2. One product of triglyceride catabolism is glycerol, which is converted to glyceraldehyde 3-phospate, a glycolytic intermediate. Triglyceride catabolism also yields free fatty acids. During periods of extended fasting, free fatty acids are converted to:
   A. ketone bodies, which may be utilized by neurons via the TCA cycle.
   B. ketone bodies, which may be utilized by neurons via glycolysis.
   C. glucogenic amino acids, which may be utilized by neurons via the TCA cycle.
   D. glucogenic amino acids, which may be utilized by neurons via glycolysis.

3. A large number of plant species synthesize and secrete fatty acid derivatives that prevent the loss of water from their leaves. These fatty acid derivatives are known as:
   A. sterols.
   B. prostaglandins.
   C. waxes.
   D. starches.

4. Phospholipids are the primary components of the plasma membrane. A phospholipid molecule generally consists of a glycerol backbone:
   A. covalently bound to two fatty acids and a phosphate group.
   B. covalently bound to one fatty acid and two phosphate groups.
   C. covalently bound to three fatty acids, one of which is phosphorylated at its omega position.
   D. covalently bound to three phosphate groups, which are bound to three fatty acids via ester linkages.

5. Apoptotic cells exhibit phosphatidylserine (PS) on the outer surface of their plasma membranes, which acts as a signal to macrophages. Which of the following is most likely true of PS?
   A. PS is able to move freely between the inner and outer leaflets of the plasma membrane.
   B. Enzymatic activity is required to transfer PS between the inner and outer leaflets of the plasma membrane.
   C. Enzymatic activity is required for PS to move laterally within the inner leaflet of the plasma membrane.
   D. PS is sufficiently large that it spans both leaflets of the plasma membrane in healthy cells.

6. Fatty acid synthesis is accomplished by fatty acid synthase, a large enzymatic complex with multiple active sites and a long acyl carrier arm that moves the growing fatty acid between these active sites. This type of synthetic mechanism:
   A. increases catalytic efficiency by limiting substrate diffusion.
   B. reduces catalytic efficiency by limiting substrate diffusion.
   C. increases enzymatic promiscuity by limiting available substrates.
   D. reduces enzymatic promiscuity by limiting available substrates.

7. Which of the following is most likely to serve as the transport molecule that carries cholesterol toward skeletal muscle cells?
   A. VLDL
   B. Chylomicrons
   C. HDL
   D. LDL

8. The structure of tamoxifen, a drug used in the treatment of breast cancer, is shown below.

It is believed that tamoxifen acts by structurally mimicking an endogenous signaling molecule. Which of the following is the most likely pharmacological target of tamoxifen?
   A. Insulin receptors
   B. T-cell receptors
   C. Glycine receptors
   D. Estrogen receptors

# Independent Question Explanations

1. C is correct. The inhibitor in question interferes with fatty acid oxidation, which is the process by which fatty acids are broken down, not synthesized (choices B and D are wrong). Fatty acid oxidation occurs in the mitochondria, which is a membrane-bound organelle. If this inhibitor does not freely diffuse through lipid membranes, it is unlikely to enter the mitochondria in concentrations sufficient to affect its pharmacological target.

2. A is correct. Fatty acids are broken down into ketone bodies, which can freely diffuse across the blood-brain barrier and enter neurons. Ketone bodies are then converted to acetyl-CoA, which enters the TCA cycle directly (choice A). Ketone bodies cannot be converted to glucose (the main glycolytic reactant), making choice B incorrect. Regarding choices C and D, glucogenic amino acids are a subset of amino acids that are readily converted to glucose. Although amino acids are converted to glucose during times of extended fasting, these amino acids are generated by the breakdown of proteins rather than fatty acids.

3. C is correct. Waxes were not mentioned directly in this chapter, so it may be necessary to use process of elimination here. (Note that waxes were referenced in Chapter 1 of the Biology MCAT Review book.) Starches are derived from carbohydrates, not fatty acids (eliminate choice D). Prostaglandins and steroids are signaling molecules (eliminate choices A and B). Biological waxes are composed of long-chain fatty acids esterified to long-chain alcohols. Consequently, they are very hydrophobic and used by many plants and animals as a form of waterproofing.

4. A is correct. There are many types of phospholipids, but this family of molecules generally consists of a glycerol backbone esterified to two fatty acid molecules at two of its hydroxyl groups. The third glycerol hydroxyl group is bound to a single phosphate group.

5. B is correct. Phospholipids have charged phosphate heads that present a sizeable energetic penalty for passing through the hydrophobic membrane core. Generally, enzymatic activity is required to permit phospholipids to move between the inner and outer leaflets. According to the fluid mosaic model, phospholipids are able to freely diffuse laterally within the same leaflet. Phospholipids do not span the plasma membrane, and the question stem implies that the presence of PS on the outer membrane only occurs during apoptosis (and thus not in healthy cells).

6. A is correct. Enzymatic promiscuity refers to the case in which a single enzyme can exercise catalytic effects on a wide variety of structurally diverse substrates. This effect is not relevant to the consideration of fatty acid synthase, which has highly specific substrates. By preventing intermediates from diffusing away and having to diffuse back into the next active site, fatty acid synthase is able to more efficiently conduct the sequential reactions necessary to form a complete fatty acid.

7. D is correct. LDL, or low-density lipoprotein, is the major transporter of cholesterol to the tissues of the body. HDL also transports cholesterol, but it brings it to the liver, rather than to other tissues like skeletal muscle. Chylomicrons and VLDL primarily transport triglycerides.

8. D is correct. We can use process of elimination here. Insulin is a relatively large peptide hormone, which does not resemble the small organic molecule depicted (eliminate choice A). T-cell receptors recognize proteins, not small molecules (eliminate choice B). Glycine is a single amino acid with a structure much smaller than tamoxifen (eliminate C). Estrogen contains aromatic rings, so since tamoxifen contains multiple aromatic rings, it could feasibly mimic estrogen in the body.

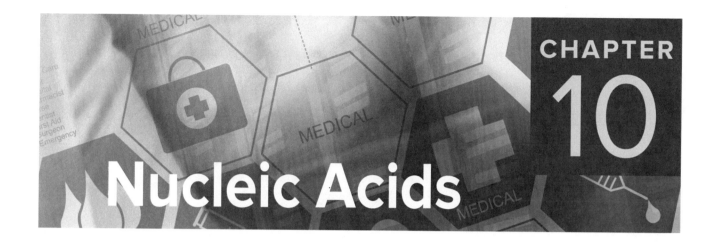

# CHAPTER 10

# Nucleic Acids

## 0. Introduction

Nucleic acids are the smallest class of biomolecules that you will encounter in terms of the absolute number of structures that you need to familiarize yourself with, but they are tremendously important because they are the means through which biological information is passed from generation to generation and within the cell. Structurally, the nucleic acids deoxyribonucleic acid (DNA) and ribonucleic acid (RNA) are polymers of smaller units known as nucleotides. However, as we will see in this chapter, individual nucleotides also play some important roles in the cell, so don't automatically limit yourself to thinking of DNA and RNA when you hear the term!

DNA and RNA recur again and again in MCAT biology, making appearances in chapters on cell biology and genetics, as well as being perennial favorites for passages and questions on Test Day. In fact, they are discussed, in greater or lesser detail, in four full chapters of the Biology textbook. The reason why they are so important is that the polymeric sequence of nucleotides in nucleic acids encodes genetic information. That information is transmitted across generations and in the process of gene expression is used to synthesize proteins.

> > CONNECTIONS < <

Chapter 3 of Biology

Since genetics is directly discussed in a third of the entire Biology textbook, we may ask ourselves: what more do we have to learn from the point of view of biochemistry? Essentially, the point of studying nucleic acids from a biochemistry perspective is to solidify your understanding of the structure of nucleic acids and how that structure contributes to their functionality. The basic concept of structure-function mapping underpins all the material covered in this chapter.

MCAT STRATEGY > > >

This chapter is relatively short but sweet. The material contained in it may be superficially familiar because it is at least briefly discussed in many different biology classes. However, the MCAT can test you directly on very specific aspects of the structure of nucleic acids, so take the time to review it thoroughly.

# 1. Nucleotides and Nucleosides

A nucleotide is composed of a nitrogenous base (also sometimes referred to as a nucleobase), a pentose sugar, and a phosphate group. The term 'nucleoside' is also used to refer to the smaller structure formed by just a nitrogenous base plus a pentose sugar, with no phosphate group. Be sure to understand that these structures are not synonymous!

There are two basic differences between DNA and RNA. The first is that ribose is used in RNA (*ribo*nucleic acid) and deoxyribose is present in DNA (*deoxyribo*nucleic acid). This is illustrated below in Figure 1, which shows how deoxyribose is missing the −OH group present at carbon 2.

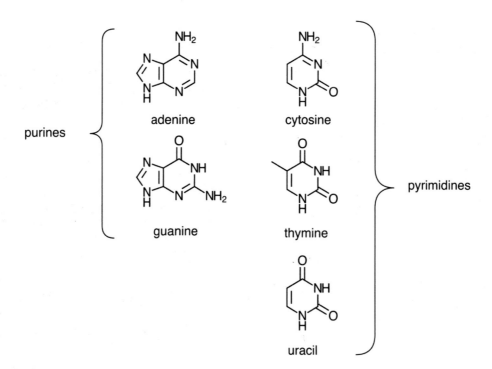

**Figure 1.** Ribose versus deoxyribose.

The second major difference between DNA and RNA has to do with the nitrogenous bases that make them up. There are five nitrogenous bases: adenine (A), cytosine (C), guanine (G), thymine (T), and uracil (U). T occurs in DNA only, whereas U occurs in RNA only. Nitrogenous bases are classified as purines, which have two-ring structures, and pyrimidines, which have one-ring structures. A and G are purines, while C, T, and U are pyrimidines.

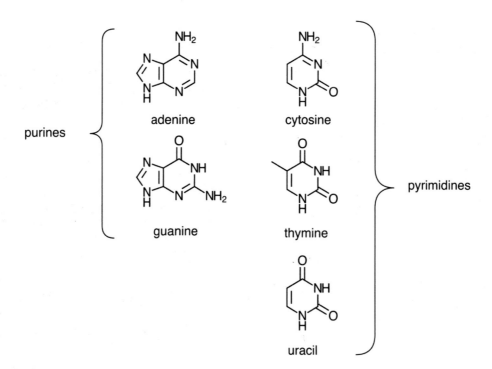

**Figure 2.** Nitrogenous bases.

You should become quite familiar with the structure of the nitrogenous bases. Knowing which are purines and which are pyrimidines is an absolute must, and you should also study the individual structures of each molecule at least on the level of being able to match the structure to the name. A particularly important fact to note is that U is simply a demethylated version of T. An additional observation that may help you organize your structural knowledge of these molecules is that adenine and guanine differ based on the presence of an amine group (adenine) versus a carbonyl group (guanine). Analogously, cytosine can be distinguished from the other pyrimidines because it is the only one to have a primary amine group.

Now that we've covered the pentose sugar and nucleobase components of nucleic acids, let's move on to the phosphate component of nucleotides. Structurally, phosphate groups ($PO_4^{3-}$) are quite simple, but they make a major contribution to how nucleic acids fit together. Phosphate groups interact with the 3' and 5' carbons of the pentose sugar to form phosphodiester bonds. Understanding the structure here is important; the 3' carbon is the one that has a downward-pointing hydroxyl group on the left side of the nucleotide as usually portrayed, and the 5' carbon is the one sticking up on the left.

Under certain circumstances, more than one phosphate group can be attached; such molecules are known as nucleoside diphosphates or nucleoside triphosphates, depending on whether two or three phosphate groups are attached. A major example of this is adenosine triphosphate, which may be familiar to you as ATP. The structure of ATP is shown below in Figure 3. GTP has an identical structure, but with G as the nucleobase instead of A. This similarity explains why ATP and GTP are considered to be rough equivalents when discussing the production of energy through various metabolic processes.

**Figure 3.** ATP.

In nucleoside monophosphates, it is possible for a single phosphate group to attach to both the 3' and 5' carbons, resulting in a cyclic configuration. One of the most well-known examples of this is 3',5'-cyclic adenosine monophosphate (cAMP), which is an important intracellular signaling molecule.

**Figure 4.** cAMP.

In linear polymers of nucleotides, such as RNA and DNA, phosphate groups bind with the 3' carbon of one nucleotide and the 5' carbon of another. These bonds are referred to phosphodiester bonds because they contain two C–O–P bonds. They join nucleotides together in a linear string, the directionality of which can be referred to as 5' to 3' (in one direction) or 3' to 5' (in the other direction). Figure 5 shows this as exemplified by RNA.

**Figure 5.** RNA strand.

As we've already mentioned, in addition to the standard examples of RNA and DNA, there are some important cyclic nucleotides (like cAMP and the related molecule cGMP) and nucleotide derivatives, such as ATP and GTP. Several important cofactors for enzymatic reactions include nucleotides, such as FAD, FMN, NAD, NADP⁺, and CoA. You certainly don't have to know the structures of these molecules, but having a sense that nucleotides play a broader role than being the constituents of RNA and DNA can be useful.

## 2. Base Pairing, Double Helix, Watson-Crick Model

As a general rule, RNA molecules are single-stranded and DNA molecules are double-stranded, although some exceptions to this generalization exist (most notably in viruses; additionally, single-stranded DNA can be formed through denaturation, as discussed in section 3, and small interfering RNA [siRNA] contains double-stranded RNA sequences). Additionally, DNA-RNA hybrids can occur, most notably as a temporary step in eukaryotic gene transcription. The fact that nucleic acids can form paired strands is absolutely critical to their role in transmitting information in biological systems, and in turn, this ability is due to base pairing.

Base pairing is caused by the formation of hydrogen bonds between complementary nucleotides. Cytosine (C) pairs with guanine (G), while adenine (A) pairs with thymine (T) in DNA and with uracil (U) in RNA. Two hydrogen bonds are formed between A and T, and three are present between C and G. A result of this is that sequences in which C and G bases predominate require higher temperatures for the strands to denature (or separate). Another important point to note is that purines pair with pyrimidines and vice versa. The specificity of complementary base pairing allows one strand to serve as a template for another; this property is integral to DNA replication and the transcription of DNA into mRNA.

> **MCAT STRATEGY > > >**
>
> Knowing the base pairing rules is an absolute must for Test Day! If they're not already a reflex, practice until they become one.

The regularity of the base pairing rules leads to an interesting generalization that is known as Chargaff's rule. This rule can be formulated in two ways. More generally, purines and pyrimidines will be present in a cell at a 1-to-1 ratio. This is because purines always pair with pyrimidines, and vice versa. More specifically, the fact that C pairs with G and A pairs with T means that the amount of C in a cell's genome will equal the amount of G, and the amount of A will equal that of T. This means that you can use information about one nucleotide to infer information about the others. For instance, if we know that 15% of a cell's DNA is T, then we can infer that 15% must be A. The remaining 70% must be equally divided between C and G, so the overall composition will be 15% T, 15% A, 35% C, and 35% G.

> **> > CONNECTIONS < <**
>
> Chapter 3 of Biology

Double-stranded DNA has an antiparallel orientation: that is, if the 5' → 3' direction of one strand runs "up" the page, the 5' → 3' of the other strand runs "down" the page. Figure 6 shows the structure of double-stranded DNA, including both base pairing and the sugar-phosphate backbone.

**Figure 6.** DNA structure.

Figure 6 shows the hydrogen bonds between nitrogenous bases, which is the mechanism of base pairing. This also helps contribute to the stability overall structure of the DNA molecule, although its stability is also enhanced by hydrophobic base-stacking interactions. That is, nitrogenous bases interact with each other in two ways: through hydrogen bonding with nitrogenous bases in the opposite strand, and through hydrophobic interactions with adjacent bases in the same strand.

When examining the structure of DNA, voids, also known as grooves, can be seen. These grooves are adjacent to the base pairs and differ in size. The wider groove is referred to as the major groove, while the narrower groove is referred to as the minor groove. These grooves serve as a binding site for transcription factors, usually at the sides of the bases exposed through the more accessible major groove.

Double-stranded DNA is also characterized by curves, and the twisting of the polymer results in a structure that is famously known as the double helix. This structure—along with other key features of DNA such as base pairing and its implications for information transmission—was elucidated by James Watson and Francis Crick, building on the work of Maurice Wilkins and Rosalind Franklin, in 1953. Watson and Crick discovered a conformation of DNA that is now known as B-DNA. In B-DNA, the double-helix is right-handed, has approximately 10.5 base pairs per turn, and extends approximately 34 Å per 10 base pairs. It is the most common form of DNA, and is what you probably envision when you imagine the double helix. In addition to the outer structure provided by the phosphodiester bonds, hydrophobic stacking interactions between the nitrogenous bases contribute to the stability of the double helical structure.

A-DNA is most probably a dehydrated form of B-DNA that can also be formed by DNA-RNA hybrid helices. It is right-handed, like B-DNA, and can be thought of as "tighter," with 11 base pairs per turn and 23 Å per 10 base pairs. A conformation known as Z-DNA can be found in DNA that has been methylated (usually because of epigenetic regulation); it displays a left-handed helical geometry, and is "looser," with 12 base pairs per turn but 38 Å per 10 base pairs.

**A-DNA**
"tighter" helix

**11 base pairs/turn**
**23 Å/10 base pairs**

**B-DNA**
most common

**10.5 base pairs/turn**
**34 Å/10 base pairs**

**Z-DNA**
"looser" helix

**12 base pairs/turn**
**38 Å/10 base pairs**

**Figure 7.** A, B, and Z DNA.

A DNA segment that is overwound or underwound is referred to as being positively or negatively supercoiled, respectively. Such supercoiling is a function of torsional strain in the molecule. As mentioned above, in a relaxed double-helical segment of B-DNA, the two strands complete a cycle of rotation about the helical axis once every 10.5 base pairs. Additional twisting or unwinding causes supercoiling, and thus, strain. Under physiological conditions, DNA is usually negatively supercoiled. This conformation makes unwinding of the double helix—a requirement of transcription—more energetically favorable.

## 3. Hybridization, Denaturation, and Reannealing

Hybridization is the process in which complementary base pairs combine. As we discussed in section 2, the driving force behind hybridization is the hydrogen bonds that form between A and T (or U in cases of RNA hybridization) and between C and G. Perfectly complementary strands of DNA, RNA, or short stretches of nucleic acids, known as oligonucleotides, will bind one another readily. However, a single inconsistency between the nucleotides positioned along either of the two strands will decrease the energetic favorability of the strands' annealing. While strands that are not perfectly congruous will still very often anneal, they will do so—to an extent determined by their complementarity—with decreasing avidity.

The degree of sequence similarity between two base-paired strands may be quantified by measuring the temperature at which the strands anneal. In the reverse process, heating of annealed strands imparts the energy required to overcome the hydrogen bonds between the nitrogenous bases of the annealed strands. This process of thermal denaturation is also referred to as melting, and can cause the reversible dissociation of the base-paired complex. Once the hydrogen bonds are overcome, the strands of the double helix unwind as the hydrophobic stacking interactions between the bases become insufficient to maintain the base-paired complex. The temperature at which half of the DNA strands of a sample are present in their single-stranded (ssDNA) state is defined as the melting temperature ($T_m$) of the nucleic acid. The $T_m$ depends on the length and the nucleotide sequence of a molecule. Denaturation can also cause the dissociation of complementary strands by chemical means, using denaturants as urea.

In addition to being a metric of how dissimilar annealed strands are to each other, DNA denaturation can be a useful analytical tool for determining certain other properties of annealed strands. In particular, since C-G base-pairing is generally stronger than A-T base-pairing because C and G form 3 hydrogen bonds rather than 2, the melting point of annealed strands containing more C and G than A and T will be higher. This is shown in Figure 8, which contains a schematic portrayal of how altering a DNA sequence to include more CG content will raise the melting temperature.

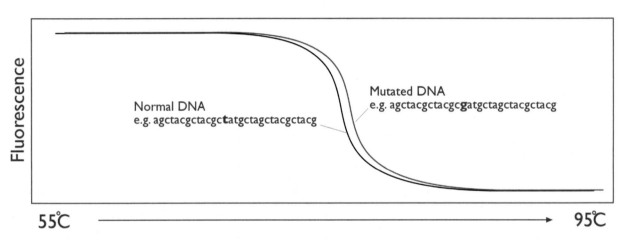

**Figure 8.** Melting temperature and CG content.

The annealing of complementary base pairs in separate strands can be seen in the binding of a DNA probe or a primer to a DNA strand during a polymerase chain reaction (PCR). In PCR, DNA is repeatedly heated to a temperature above its melting point, and then allowed to cool, in a process known as thermal cycling. During the cooling process, DNA strands become templates for DNA polymerase enzymes to selectively amplify target DNA within regions flanked by primers specific to the start and end points of the replicated regions. The end result is to tremendously amplify a DNA sequence.

## > > CONNECTIONS < <

### Chapter 6 of Biology

Figure 9 presents a schematic of PCR showing the importance of denaturation and annealing in this process. For more details about PCR and other forms of biotechnology involving DNA, consult Chapter 6 of the Biology textbook.

## Polymerase chain reaction - PCR

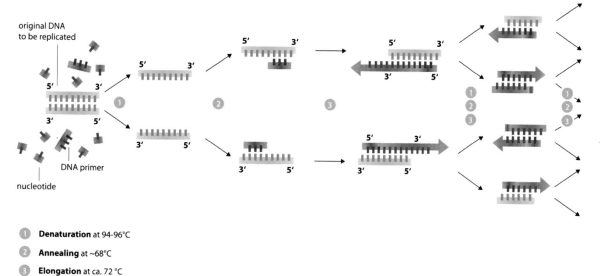

- **①** **Denaturation** at 94-96°C
- **②** **Annealing** at ~68°C
- **③** **Elongation** at ca. 72 °C

**Figure 9.** PCR.

## 4. Must-Knows

> Nucleotide: nitrogenous base + pentose sugar + phosphate group
- Nucleo*side*: just nitrogenous base + pentose sugar
- Nitrogenous bases: purines (A, G) and pyrimidines (C, U, T)

> DNA vs. RNA (structurally):
- RNA is almost always single-stranded, DNA is almost always double-stranded
- Pentose sugar is different; RNA has ribose, and DNA has *deoxy*ribose, which is missing the –OH group at carbon 2.
- T in DNA corresponds to U in RNA.

> Base pairing
- In DNA, bases pair in opposite strands. A pairs with T, C pairs with G. Hydrogen bonds are formed between paired bases (2 between A and T, 3 between C and G).
- In RNA, U pairs to A in DNA.
- Chargaff's rule: 1-to-1 ratio of purines and pyrimidines, %A = %T, %C = %G.

> Phosphate-sugar backbone of DNA/RNA
- Formed by 5' to 3' phosphodiester bonds
- Polar phosphate and sugar molecules face out, relatively hydrophobic nitrogenous bases are on the inside.

> Other nucleotides
- Adenosine triphosphate (ATP): main form of cellular energy
- Cyclic adenosine monophosphate (cAMP): crucial intracellular signaling molecule
- Cofactors like FAD, FMN, NAD, $NADP^+$, and CoA.

> Double helix
- Strands have antiparallel orientation: one runs 5' to 3', the other 3' to 5'.
- Three conformations: B-DNA, A-DNA, Z-DNA
  - B-DNA: most common form. Right-handed, 10.5 base pairs per turn, 34 Å per 10 base pairs
  - A-DNA: dehydrated form of B-DNA, 'tighter,' 11 base pairs per turn and 23 Å per 10 base pairs

> > CONNECTIONS < <

Chapter 6 of Biology

- Z-DNA: found in methylated DNA, left-handed helical geometry, is 'looser' with 12 base pairs per turn but 38 Å per 10 base pairs.
  - In physiological conditions, DNA is usually negatively supercoiled, which helps unwind the double helix for transcription (mediated through enzymes)
> Hybridization: the process in which complementary base pairs combine.
  - Denaturation (melting): breaking up annealed (=joined) strands through heating
  - The melting temperature ($T_m$), at which half of the double-stranded sequences have been denatured, is a rough indicator of relative A-T vs. C-G content.
  - C-G-rich sequences have a higher $T_m$ because C-G pairs have 3 hydrogen bonds, while A-T pairs have two.
  - Denaturation and subsequent hybridization have been leveraged in polymer chain reaction (PCR), which is used to tremendously amplify small amounts of a genetic sequence given primers.

This page left intentionally blank.

## Practice Passage

In the last decade, one helical junction has emerged as important throughout functional RNAs: the kink turn, abbreviated as k-turn (Figure 1b). k-turns are found in dsRNA, most often comprising a three-nucleotide bulge followed on the 3' side by successive G•A and A•G pairs. The duplex axis is kinked about the loop, minor groove to minor groove, to include an angle close to 50°, forming a tight kink in the duplex RNA.

**Figure 1.** tRNA structure and the sequence of standard, simple k-turns

Frequently, one of the component helices is a relatively short stem–loop, the loop of which interacts with some kind of receptor at a remote location in the RNA. For example, the k-turns found in the ribosome make such contacts with transfer RNA (tRNA, Figure 1a) and the U4 snRNA in the B-complex of the spliceosome cycle that precedes the tri-snRNP complex has a k-turn.

The ribosomal k-turn Kt-7 of the archaeon *H. marismortui* illustrates common k-turn structure. The helix to the 5' side of the bulge is normally Watson–Crick base paired and is called the C (canonical) helix, while that containing the G•A pairs is called the NC (non-canonical) helix. Loop nucleotides are labelled L1, L2… from the 5' end and the remaining nucleotides are given positive numbers in the 3' direction through the NC helix and negative numbers in the 5' direction through the C helix. Those on the bulged strand have a suffix b and those on the non-bulged strand have a suffix n. Research suggests four empirical rules governing k-turn folding behavior.

**Rule 1** Watson–Crick pairs plus G•U all fold weakly or not at all, with G•C and C•G being especially bad (U4 k-turn follows this rule). This rule supersedes all subsequent rules.

**Rule 2** The presence of 3n = G confers an ability to fold in $Mg^{2+}$ ions (Natural HmKt-7 follows this rule).

**Rule 3** The presence of 3b = C confers an ability to fold in $Mg^{2+}$ ions.

Due to their role in the formation of RNA structures, k-turns are important in the functions of cellular RNA. tRNA molecules have multiple levels of structure. Probably the single-most important role of k-turns is to mediate tertiary interactions; often one of the arms is involved in a loop-receptor interaction of some kind. Many k-turns are also the targets of specific protein binding. During the biogenesis the ribosome (Figure 3), k-turns will initially be relatively flexible, allowing the exploration of conformational space. However, the formation of successful tertiary contacts will begin to reduce this flexibility.

**Figure 2.** Human ribosomal structure (nt = nucleotides)

*Adapted from Huang, L., et al. (2016). The Kink Turn, a Key Architectural Element in RNA Structure. Journal of Molecular Biology, 428, 790–801 under CCBY 4.0*

1. Which of the following best explains the finding that in archaea such as *H. marismortui*, translation can begin before transcription has finished?
   A. *H. marismortui* have ribosomes on their nuclear envelope and need not transport mRNA before translation.
   B. *H. marismortui* have no endoplasmic reticulum and exclusively use bound ribosomes for translation.
   C. *H. marismortui* lack a nucleus and thus need not transport the mRNA before translation.
   D. *H. marismortui* have circular DNA which allows transcribed mRNA easy access to ribosomes.

2. Which of the following RNA structural elements is shown directly in Figure 1?
   I. Primary structure
   II. Secondary structure
   III. Tertiary structure
   A. I only
   B. II only
   C. III only
   D. I and II only

3. According to the passage, what is the approximate total length of human rRNA?
   A. 6500 nucleotides
   B. 7000 nucleotides
   C. 7500 nucleotides
   D. 8000 nucleotides

4. During sedimentation analysis, which of the following best explains why the 60S and 40S subunits together do not result in a 100S ribosome?
   A. The volume of the ribosome is smaller than sum of the volumes of each subunit.
   B. Buoyant force on the ribosome is smaller than the sum of the buoyant forces on each subunit
   C. Drag force on the ribosome is smaller than the sum of the drag forces on each subunit
   D. The gravitational force on the ribosome is greater than the sum of the gravitational forces on each subunit

5. Which of the following best describes the production pathway for a plasma membrane-bound protein, starting with the production of the mRNA?
   A. Nucleus → cytoplasm → ribosome → endosome
   B. Nucleus → RER → Golgi → secretory vesicle
   C. Nucleus → cytoplasm → ribosome → RER → Golgi
   D. Nucleus → cytoplasm → RER

6. Which of the following RNA molecules forms the most stable, long-term RNA-protein structure?
   A. mRNA
   B. rRNA
   C. tRNA
   D. snRNA

## Practice Passage Explanations

In the last decade, one helical junction has emerged as important throughout functional RNAs: the kink turn, abbreviated as k-turn (Figure 1b). k-turns are found in dsRNA, most often comprising a three-nucleotide bulge followed on the 3' side by successive G•A and A•G pairs. The duplex axis is kinked about the loop, minor groove to minor groove, to include an angle close to 50° forming a tight kink in the duplex RNA.

*Key terms: helical junction, kink turn; bulge, duplex axis, 50°*

*Cause and effect: bulge → GA/AG → minor-minor interaction → 50° kink*

**Figure 1.** tRNA structure and the sequence of standard, simple k-turns

Frequently, one of the component helices is a relatively short stem–loop, the loop of which interacts with some kind of receptor at a remote location in the RNA. For example, the k-turns found in the ribosome make such contacts with transfer RNA (tRNA, Figure 1a) and the U4 snRNA in the B-complex of the spliceosome cycle that precedes the tri-snRNP complex has a k-turn.

*Key terms: component helices, ribosome, U4 snRNA, spliceosome*

*Cause and effect: k-turns are commonly found at receptor sites*

The ribosomal k-turn Kt-7 of the archaeon *H. marismortui* illustrates common k-turn structure. The helix to the 5' side of the bulge is normally Watson–Crick base paired and is called the C (canonical) helix, while that containing the G•A pairs is called the NC (non-canonical) helix. Loop nucleotides are labelled L1, L2… from the 5' end and the remaining nucleotides are given positive numbers in the 3' direction through the NC helix and negative numbers in the 5' direction through the C helix. Those on the bulged strand have a suffix b and those on the non-bulged strand have a suffix n. Research suggests four empirical rules governing k-turn folding behavior.

*Key terms: Kt-7, archaeon, canonical, non-canonical, loop nucleotides*

*Cause and effect: nomenclature for k-turns is given; GA = NC; 5'→3'> 0; 3' → 5' C, < 0*

**Rule 1** Watson–Crick pairs plus G•U all fold weakly or not at all, with G•C and C•G being especially bad (U4 k-turn follows this rule). This rule supersedes all subsequent rules.

**Rule 2** The presence of 3n = G confers an ability to fold in $Mg^{2+}$ ions (Natural HmKt-7 follows this rule).

**Rule 3** The presence of 3b = C confers an ability to fold in $Mg^{2+}$ ions.

*Cause and effect: Rule 1 trumps 2/3; U4 = rule 1; HmKt-7 = rule 2*

Due to their role in the formation of RNA structures, k-turns are important in the functions of cellular RNA. tRNA molecules have multiple levels of structure. Probably the single-most important role of k-turns is to mediate tertiary interactions; often one of the arms is involved in a loop-receptor interaction of some kind. Many k-turns are also the targets of specific protein binding. During the biogenesis the ribosome (Figure 3), k-turns will initially be relatively flexible, allowing the exploration of conformational space. However, the formation of successful tertiary contacts will begin to reduce this flexibility.

*Key terms: RNA structure, tertiary interactions, protein binding, flexibility*

*Cause and effect: k-turns drive tertiary interactions, which make rRNA less flexible, more rigid*

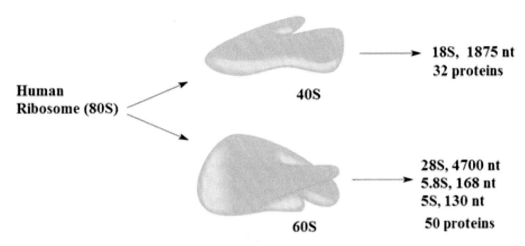

**Figure 2.** Human ribosomal structure

*Figure 2 provides nucleotide (nt) count for the individual components of the human ribosome*

*Adapted from Huang, L., et al. (2016). The Kink Turn, a Key Architectural Element in RNA Structure. Journal of Molecular Biology, 428, 790–801 under CCBY 4.0*

1. C is correct. This question asks us to determine what about prokaryotes (e.g. archaea) allows them to move quickly from transcription of DNA to translation of the transcribed mRNA before it is completely finished being transcribed. Eukaryotes lack this ability because transcription occurs in the nucleus and mRNA needs to be transported to the cytoplasm or the ER to be translated. Prokaryotes have no nucleus and thus the mRNA can interact with ribosomes directly and quickly.

   A, B: Prokaryotes have no nucleus, and do not have an ER so their ribosomes would actually be free ribosomes, not bound ribosomes (which would mean ER-bound in this context).

   D. The structure of the DNA is not related to the location advantage that prokaryotes have for moving from transcription to translation.

2. D is correct. The primary structure is the sequence of base pairs. Secondary structure is the interaction of base pairs to create hairpin loops and other structures. Tertiary structure is the folding of the molecule that gives it an L-shape.

   III: The three-dimensional folding of tRNA is not directly shown, though it is discussed in the passage.

3. B is correct. We need only add the nucleotide (nt) totals from each of the rRNA subunits that make up the large and small subunits. 1900 + 4700 + 170 + 130 = 6900 nucleotides.

4. C is correct. During sedimentation analysis, a tube with sucrose solution is covered with a layer which contains the sample molecules of interest. The tube is then centrifuged (spun at high speed) for several hours; the sucrose gradient remains stable. Depending on the sizes/molecular weights of the macromolecules in the sample, they migrate through the gradient at different rates: lighter molecules will move less quickly than denser molecules. Each molecular type will eventually form a discrete band at its isopycnic point, where its density equals that of the sucrose gradient. The volumes of the subunits are additive which means that the buoyant force on subunits is additive. The masses are additive so the gravitational force is additive as well. This means that the only remaining force, drag must not be additive. This is the drag force. The drag force has the most to do with the shape of the falling particle, which will change when the subunits come together.

   A. The volume of the ribosome is equal to the sum of the volumes of each subunit.

   B. $F_{buoyant}$ on the ribosome is equal to the sum of the buoyant forces on each subunit because $F_{buoyant}$ depends on volume.

   D. The $F_{gravity}$ on the ribosome is equal to the sum of the gravitational forces on each subunit because $F_{gravity}$ depends on mass.

5. C is correct. mRNA is transcribed in the nucleus, exported to the cytoplasm, where it is bound by a ribosome. It will then code for a signal sequence that will cause it to be transported to the RER and then to the Golgi to be moved to the cell's plasma membrane. When presented with problems that involve ranking or ordering, identify the extreme portions of the answer first. This can allow you to reach the answer with less effort.

   A. mRNA will not go to an endosome, a membrane-bounded compartment inside eukaryotic cells. This serves as a compartment of the endocytic membrane transport pathway from the plasma membrane to the lysosome.

   B. mRNA will not go directly to the RER from the nucleus.

   D. mRNA will not go to the RER without being bound by a ribosome.

6. B is correct. rRNA and proteins combine to form the nucleoprotein called a ribosome. The ribosome serves as the site and carries the enzymes necessary for protein synthesis. Thus, rRNA forms most of the structure of ribosomes.

   A. mRNA is synthesized from DNA and carries the code into the cytoplasm where protein synthesis occurs. Afterwards the mRNA will be degraded once it is not needed.

   C. tRNA reads the mRNA code and carries the amino acid to be incorporated into the assembled protein. On one end the amino acid is attached. On the opposite end, a specific base triplet, called the anticodon, is used to read the codons on the mRNA.

   D. Small nuclear RNA (snRNA) is a small RNA species confined to the nucleus. snRNAs are involved in splicing and other RNA processing reactions.

## Independent Questions

1. Phosphodiester bonds connect monomers of which of the following biomolecules?
   A. Polypeptides
   B. Polysaccharides
   C. Nucleic acids
   D. Polyamines

2. Which of the following statements correctly describes a structural or functional difference between DNA and RNA?
   A. The sugar found in DNA contains more -OH groups.
   B. DNA is capable of a greater diversity of functions.
   C. RNA is less likely to be single-stranded.
   D. RNA is capable of catalyzing reactions.

3. If the percent composition of adenine in a sample of double-stranded DNA is 34%, what is the percent composition of cytosine?
   A. 16%
   B. 17%
   C. 32%
   D. 34%

4. Compare an A-T base pairing with a C-G base pairing in double-stranded DNA.
   A. An A-T base pairing contains three phosphodiester bonds, while a C-G base pairing contains only two.
   B. An A-T base pairing contains only two phosphodiester bonds, while a C-G base pairing contains three.
   C. An A-T base pairing contains three hydrogen bonds, while a C-G base pairing contains only two.
   D. An A-T base pairing contains only two hydrogen bonds, while a C-G base pairing contains three.

5. All of the following are true of the sugar found in ribonucleosides EXCEPT:
   A. it is a pentose.
   B. it is a furanose.
   C. it has a formula of $C_5H_{10}O_5$.
   D. it contains the 3' -OH group that deoxyribonucleosides lack.

6. What is the difference between traditional PCR and RT-PCR?
   A. The two techniques use different polymerase enzymes.
   B. RT-PCR does not use primers.
   C. The two techniques use different templates.
   D. RT-PCR does not amplify DNA.

7. Imagine that a nucleotide and a nucleoside are subjected to gel electrophoresis. Compared to the nucleotide, where would the nucleoside be found on the gel at the conclusion of the procedure?
   A. It would be closer to the negative pole.
   B. It would be closer to the positive pole.
   C. The two molecules would travel the same distance along the gel.
   D. It would depend on the identity of the nucleotide and the nucleoside.

8. The mRNA codon that corresponds to aspartic acid is GAC. What is its complementary anticodon?
   A. 5' CUG 3'
   B. 5' GTC 3'
   C. 3' CUG 5'
   D. 3' CTG 5'

# Independent Question Explanations

1. C is correct. Phosphodiester bonds connect individual nucleotide monomers to form nucleic acid polymers, such as DNA or RNA. Polypeptides are composed of amino acids joined by peptide bonds and polysaccharides are composed of monosaccharide monomers joined by glycosidic linkages. Polyamines are molecules with two or more primary amino groups, but they do not necessarily contain phosphodiester bonds like nucleic acids.

2. D is correct. While DNA is used primarily for transmitting genetic information, RNA is capable of a greater diversity of functions (eliminate choice B). One of these is the ability for ribozymes, which are composed of RNA, to catalyze chemical reactions. DNA cannot act as a catalyst. Note also that ribose, the sugar found in RNA, contains one more -OH group than deoxyribose, the sugar present in DNA. DNA is typically double-stranded, meaning that RNA is more (not less) likely to be single-stranded.

3. A is correct. Based on Chargaff's rules, the percent of adenine in a sample of double-stranded DNA must be equal to the percent of thymine. Thymine, then, must make up 34% of this sample. Adenine and thymine together, then, comprise 68% of the total sample, leaving 32% for cytosine and guanine. Since the amounts of cytosine and guanine also must be equal to each other, 16% of the sample must consist of cytosine.

4. D is correct. The two complementary strands in the DNA double helix are held together by hydrogen bonds, not phosphodiester bonds (eliminate choices A and B). In an A-T base pairing, adenine and thymine are held together by only two hydrogen bonds, in comparison with the three that connect cytosine with guanine.

5. D is correct. This question overlaps with what you may have already read about carbohydrates. Ribonucleosides contain ribose, while deoxyribonucleosides contain deoxyribose. Ribose does contain a 3' -OH group, but so does deoxyribose; it is the 2' -OH group that deoxyribose lacks. This makes choice D untrue

and the correct answer to this NOT question. The remaining answers are accurate. Ribose contains five carbons, making it a pentose. Its structure includes a five-membered ring where four atoms of the ring are carbon and one is oxygen, as is typical for furanoses. Even if you do not have the formula of ribose memorized, you should know that it contains five carbons and that most carbohydrates have a formula of $C_m(H2O)_n$; ribose is no exception, making $C_5H_{10}O_5$ a logical formula for it to have.

6. C is correct. Traditional PCR simply aims to amplify a DNA sequence, while RT-PCR first reverse-transcribes an RNA template and then amplifies the resulting DNA. Thus, the templates are different for these techniques (DNA in PCR and RNA in RT-PCR). Both techniques use primers and a thermostable DNA polymerase, typically *Taq* polymerase. Note that RT-PCR is a technique used to detect low levels of RNA.

7. A is correct. A nucleotide consists of a sugar, a nitrogenous base, and one or more phosphate groups (one phosphate group in DNA and RNA). In contrast, a nucleoside lacks any phosphate groups. As such, a nucleotide will be more negatively charged than a nucleoside and will be found closer to the positive pole. The nucleoside, then, will be located closer to the negative pole.

8. C is correct. Unless otherwise specified, mRNA is written in the 5' to 3' direction. This mRNA codon, then, has a sequence of 5' GAC 3'. The complementary anticodon thus must have a sequence that can be written either 3' CUG 5' or 5' GUC 3'. This corresponds to choice C. Note that options B and D can be eliminated immediately because anticodons are composed of RNA, which does not contain thymine.

# Biological Membranes

**CHAPTER**

**11**

## 0. Introduction

Biological membranes are arguably at the core of life. All forms of life are dependent on having some way of separating what is happening inside the organism from the external environment. In larger organisms, that role can be carried out by larger organs like the skin, but if we take a closer look, we will always find that separation from the environment is accomplished through membranes (and cell walls in organisms like plants and bacteria).

A recurring theme throughout physiology—and therefore, much of MCAT biology—is that cells must closely regulate what enters them and what they secrete. On a mechanistic level, this function is carried out by the plasma membrane, which provides an effective diffusion barrier between the cell and its surroundings, permitting only the entry and exit of those ions for which it is selectively permeable. In addition to their role as a barrier to diffusion, cell membranes are involved in other important cellular processes, such as adhesion and signaling.

## 1. Fluid Mosaic Model and Membrane Structure

The structure of the plasma membrane is commonly described in terms of the fluid mosaic model, which states that biological membranes are two-dimensional, fluid structures within which lipid and protein molecules diffuse freely. The predominant structural component of the cell membrane is the lipid bilayer, which is composed of two layers of amphipathic phospholipids that spontaneously arrange so that the hydrophobic "tail" regions are isolated from the surrounding aqueous (i.e., polar) environment, causing the more hydrophilic "head" regions to associate with the intracellular (cytosolic) and extracellular faces of the resulting bilayer. A continuous, spherical lipid bilayer is formed by this process. Lipid bilayers are formed primarily in response to hydrophobic interactions, but van der Waals forces, electrostatic and noncovalent interactions, and hydrogen bonding contribute to their formation as well. A consequence of this structure is that very small and nonpolar molecules can diffuse easily through the cell membrane, whereas large and polar molecules must be transported, through mechanisms discussed in more detail below.

You should be aware of two main structural factors that affect the stability of the plasma membrane. The first are lipid rafts, which are held together by large amounts of cholesterol and contain relatively high concentrations of sphingomyelins. They can diffuse within the lipid bilayer, and their main functions include contributing to the fluidity of the membrane and helping to regulate signaling processes. In general, cholesterol helps modulate the fluidity of the plasma membrane at a range of temperatures. At high temperatures—including physiological temperature—cholesterol decreases membrane fluidity by impeding the diffusion of phospholipids within the bilayer, while at low temperatures, cholesterol increases membrane fluidity via essentially the same mechanism (i.e., preventing phospholipid tails from clustering together). The second major factor you should be aware of in this regard is the fact that unsaturated fatty acid tails in the phospholipids promote fluidity by preventing the tails from stacking, as can occur with saturated fatty acid tails. This is shown in Figure 1.

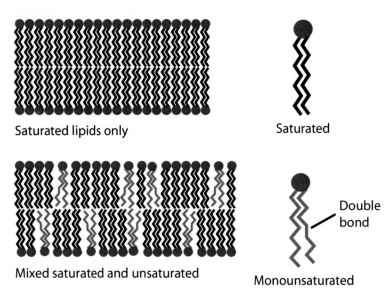

**Figure 1.** Phospholipid bilayer with effects of saturated versus unsaturated fatty acid tails.

Phospholipids are mobile in the horizontal direction, as shown in Figure 1; that is, they can move around relatively freely within a single layer of the bilayer membrane. It is possible for phospholipids to shift from one side of the membrane to another (i.e., from facing the cytoplasm to facing the extracellular space), but this is energetically costly and is catalyzed by enzymes known as flippases.

There are a total of three main classes of lipids that are present in the plasma membrane: phospholipids, the predominant component of the lipid bilayer that we discussed above; sterols, as exemplified by cholesterol; and glycolipids. Glycolipids are a diverse class of lipids that share essentially the same large-scale structure as phospholipids: a hydrophobic tail that is located inside the membrane, and a hydrophilic head that is located outside of the membrane. As the name implies, glycolipids involve a carbohydrate moiety that modifies the lipid. In general, they are involved with cell signaling and adhesion properties. Depending on whether the lipid has a glycerol or sphingosine backbone, a glycolipid can be classified as either a glyceroglycolipid or a sphingolipid. For the MCAT, you are not responsible for knowing extensive details about individual glycolipid molecules, but you should know how they are structured in general and that they both play a role in the structure of the membrane and are involved in communication and adhesion.

Figure 2 below illustrates the major classes of lipids that are present in the plasma membrane. Focus on understanding the high-level structural features of these molecules—for example, the interplay between hydrophilic and hydrophobic areas—and how they contribute to the structural integrity and function of the membrane. Some additional structural facts that you should be aware of is that the fatty acid chains in phospholipids and glycolipids usually contain an even number of carbon atoms (typically between 16 and 20 carbons). Although the fatty acid chains may be saturated or unsaturated, unsaturated fatty acid chains in the bilayer membrane are nearly always found in the *cis* orientation.

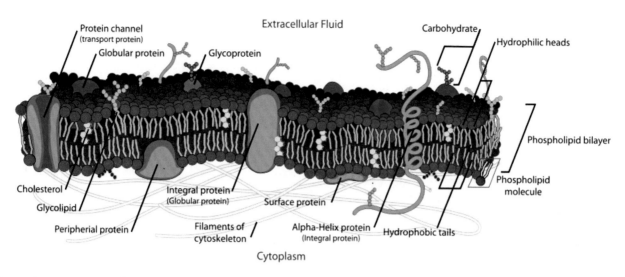

Figure 2. Structures in the bilayer membrane.

In addition, the interior and exterior surfaces of the plasma membrane contain embedded proteins, which are closely rooted in the interior of the membrane but do not span it, and membrane-associated proteins, which are held in place by non-covalent interactions with other structures present on the surface of the plasma membrane. The plasma membrane is also traversed by many different types of proteins, including membrane receptors and transport proteins (channels and pores), as well as proteins that facilitate cellular recognition, such as antigens. The three main classes of membrane proteins are summarized below:

> Transmembrane (integral). This category includes membrane-spanning proteins with (1) a hydrophilic cytosolic domain that interacts with the interior of the cell; (2) a hydrophobic membrane-spanning domain that anchors it to the cell membrane; and (3) a hydrophilic extracellular domain that interacts with the extracellular environment. This is a very common and important class of membrane proteins. Well-known examples include proton pumps, ion channels, and G protein-coupled receptors.

> Peripheral. These proteins are transiently attached to integral membrane proteins or are associated with peripheral regions of the lipid bilayer. They tend to interact with the biological membrane only transiently before resuming their function within the cytoplasm. This category includes some enzymes and hormones.

> Lipid-anchored. Lipid-anchored proteins are covalently bound to single or multiple lipid molecules that anchor the protein within the membrane without the protein contacting the membrane. There is one major example of this type of protein that you should be aware of: G proteins. Note that G proteins are distinct from G protein-coupled receptors; G proteins are intracellular membrane-bound structures that help coordinate the signaling cascade initiated by G protein-coupled receptors.

> > CONNECTIONS < <

Chapter 3 of Biochemistry

For proteins destined for insertion or association with the plasma membrane, an N-terminus signal sequence directs the newly synthesized proteins to the endoplasmic reticulum, where they are inserted into the lipid bilayer. Once inserted, the proteins are then transported to their final destination in vesicles, which eventually fuse with the target membrane.

Much like lipids, proteins can be glycosylated. This refers to the addition of oligosaccharide chains to a peptide chain. The most common biochemical types of glycosylation are O-glycosylation, in which a glycosidic bond is formed to the oxygen atom present in serine and threonine side chains, and N-glycosylation, in which the oligosaccharide binds to a nitrogen on the side chain of asparagine. Many important proteins throughout the body are actually glycoproteins, or at least are glycosylated to some extent. Examples relevant to the plasma membrane include the major histocompatibility complex and the antigens involved in the ABO blood type system. As these examples suggest, membrane glycoproteins are often involved in cell recognition and communication processes.

Material is incorporated into, or removed from, the cell membrane (notably its protein and lipid content) through multiple means. When intracellular vesicles fuse with the membrane during exocytosis, not only are the contents of the vesicle excreted, but they also incorporate the vesicle's membrane components into the cellular membrane. In contrast, membrane material may be lost when the membrane forms blebs around extracellular material that pinch off to become vesicles, in a process known as endocytosis. Moreover, there is a constant low-level exchange of molecules between the lipid phase of the membrane and the aqueous phases of the intracellular and extracellular environments.

A final point that you should be aware of regarding the structure of the plasma membrane has to do with the terminology associated with some ways of simulating its structural features under laboratory conditions. The basic idea here is that the bilayer structure is so fundamental to life that it is important to be able to simulate and replicate it. Lipid vesicles or liposomes are lipid bilayers enclosing a spherical space. These laboratory-derived structures are used by researchers to deliver material to target cells and to test cell membrane permeability with respect to substances of interest by measuring their rate of efflux or influx across the vesicle or liposome. They are formed by first suspending a lipid in an aqueous solution, then agitating the mixture, resulting in a vesicle. The structure of a cell membrane can be simulated even more closely by embedding proteins in the membrane. This can be accomplished by solubilizing the desired proteins in the presence of detergents and attaching them to the phospholipids in the liposome.

Be sure to note that a liposome is not the same thing as a micelle. A micelle is an aggregate composed of a single layer of lipids in aqueous solution, where the hydrophilic head region is in contact with the solvent, while the hydrophobic tail region is sequestered in the center of the micelle. The shape and size of a micelle are a function of the molecular geometry of its surfactant molecules and solution conditions, such as surfactant concentration, temperature, pH, and ionic strength. Liposomes and micelles are contrasted in Figure 3.

## MCAT STRATEGY > > >

The structure of the plasma membrane is complicated, and you do have to be aware of its components in a fair amount of detail for the MCAT, but don't lose sight of the fact that the basic logic of the structure is simple. The interior of the plasma membrane is a hydrophobic wall that separates two aqueous solutions, and the exterior is polar in order to interface with those solutions (the cytoplasm and the rest of the body). This simple layered structure has various modifications and things poking out of it to allow the communication and transport processes that are mandatory for life.

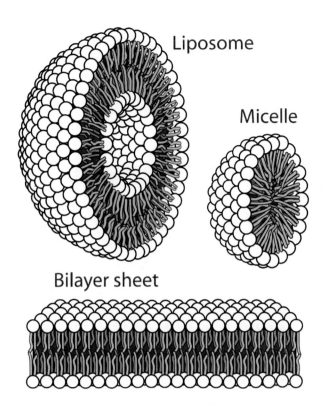

**Figure 3.** Liposomes and micelles.

## 2. Membrane Function

The basic function of biological membranes is to separate the cell from its surrounding environment. This sounds simple, but it actually reflects a delicate and intricate balance that is closely regulated, because in a very real sense, the life or death of a cell depends on whether it can appropriately regulate what enters and exits it. There are four main methods through which substances cross the lipid membrane: osmosis, passive transport (including simple diffusion and facilitated diffusion), active transport (which can be subdivided into primary active transport and secondary active transport), and exocytosis and endocytosis.

Simple diffusion refers to the tendency for solutes to diffuse down their concentration gradient; that is, from an area of high concentration to an area of low concentration. This process is important biologically in the sense that it is absolutely fundamental to life, but is also atypical in that it does not occur for very many substances. The reason for this is that not very many molecules can just diffuse across the cell membrane—those that do tend to be small or nonpolar— but some of the molecules that engage in simple diffusion are absolutely crucial for physiological function, with typical examples including gases such as oxygen and carbon dioxide. In general, gases can freely diffuse through the plasma membrane, and the plasma membrane is also slightly, but meaningfully, permeable to small uncharged polar molecules, such as water, ethanol, and urea.

Osmosis is a special form of simple diffusion that *only applies to solvents*. For the purposes of the MCAT, this virtually always means water. Do not fall for any answer choice that states or implies that a solute is moving during osmosis, and be extremely careful before choosing an answer choice that implies that anything besides water is moving during osmosis. Theoretically, osmosis can occur with other solvents, but this is unlikely to appear on the MCAT. Osmosis takes place when you have a physical setup in which water can diffuse through a barrier but solutes cannot. If both solutes and water could diffuse, then the concentration of solute would just equalize through simple diffusion. This is essentially the case for cells, although as always in biology the full story is somewhat more complex than the story you have to know for the MCAT (in particular, simple diffusion/osmosis is not the only way that water can cross the plasma membrane and the membrane is permeable to some solutes). If you have such a physical setup, in which only water can diffuse, it will travel through the membrane until the concentration of solutes is equalized.

**Figure 4.** Osmosis.

Imagine a cell with a certain concentration of solutes inside of it (remember that the cytosol is essentially an aqueous solution). If it is placed in a solution that has an equal concentration of solute, we would say that the solution in question is isotonic. If the solution has a lower concentration of solutes than the cell, the solution is hypotonic, and if it has a higher concentration of solutes it is hypertonic. When a cell is placed in an isotonic solution, nothing happens in terms of net osmosis. When a cell is placed in a hypotonic solution, the solution is too watery and the cell is too solute-y. Remember that solute cannot move out of the cell in this setup. Therefore, water must move from the solution into the cell in order to equalize the concentration of solute, causing the cell to swell and potentially to burst. When a cell is placed in a hypertonic solution, we have the opposite problem: the solution is too solute-y and the cell is too watery. Therefore, water will move from the cell into the solution in an attempt to equalize the solute concentration. This will cause the cell to lose water and shrink.

**Figure 5.** Hypertonic, isotonic, and hypotonic solutions.

Now let's consider what happens if you build an experimental setup in which one side of the membrane has a certain concentration of solute (let's say 1 M glucose) and the other side of the membrane has no solute at all, as illustrated in Figure 6. Based on what we've discussed so far, we would predict that osmosis would act to equalize the concentrations of solute – but that's physically impossible without *all* the water transferring to the side of the membrane that has solute. In fact, we don't observe anything of the sort: instead, the water level on the side with solute rises to a certain extent and then we reach equilibrium. Equilibrium is reached when the hydrostatic pressure of the water becomes large enough that it prevents more net osmosis from occurring. This pressure is known as the osmotic pressure, and can be expressed in the following equation according to van 't Hoff's law:

## MCAT STRATEGY > > >

Do not allow any question wording to confuse you on this point: isotonic, hypotonic, and hypertonic refer to properties of the *solution* relative to a cell placed in that solution.

## CLINICAL CONNECTIONS > > >

Osmosis explains why saline is infused into patients to maintain hydration, not distilled water. Instilling pure water into the bloodstream would make the blood a hypotonic solution, with potentially catastrophic consequences.

**Equation 1.**
$$\Pi = MRT$$

Semipermeable membrane

**Figure 6.** Osmosis experiment.

In this equation, $M$ is the concentration of solutes, R is the ideal gas constant, and $T$ is the temperature in Kelvin. Be careful with $M$: it refers to the total concentration of solute particles, which means that you have to be sure to account for the behavior of compounds that yield multiple particles in solution (for example, NaCl dissolves into Na⁺ ($aq$) and Cl⁻ ($aq$)). For this reason, you may sometimes see this formula as $\Pi = iMRT$, where $i$ refers to the van 't Hoff constant, which is the number of particles that result from a substance being placed into solution (for example, it would be 1 for glucose and 2 for NaCl). The bottom line is that it doesn't really matter for the MCAT which formula you use, but it does matter that you understand that osmotic pressure depends on the total quantity of particles of solutes present, even if they are different chemically. This makes osmotic pressure a colligative property, much like boiling point elevation/depression.

> > **CONNECTIONS** < <

**Chemistry chapter 5**

Passive transport encompasses both simple diffusion and facilitated diffusion. Facilitated diffusion takes place with molecules that are too big to undergo simple diffusion through the plasma membrane. For this reason, it is necessary to use a transmembrane channel to transport these molecules. More specifically, facilitated diffusion refers to the process of spontaneous passive transport of ions or molecules across a biological membrane via specific transmembrane integral channels. These channels are gated, meaning that they open and close, and thus regulate the flow of ions or small polar molecules across membranes, sometimes against the osmotic gradient. Larger molecules are transported by transmembrane carrier proteins that change their conformation as the molecules are carried across.

There are some specific subcategories of channels involved in facilitated transport that you should be aware of. One such category is aquaporins, also known as water channels, which are transmembrane proteins that selectively conduct water molecules in and out of the cell while preventing the passage of ions and other solutes. This may seem counterintuitive, given the amount of time that we invested above into explaining how osmosis is responsible for transporting water across the plasma membrane. It is indeed the case that water crosses the plasma membrane through osmosis, but only to a limited degree. This makes sense biochemically, because the hydrophobic inner layer of the plasma membrane does indeed constitute a significant barrier to water flow. Therefore, cells deploy aquaporins when they need to move large amounts of water into or out of the cell. Ion channels are another important category. As the name implies, they transport ions, and are generally extremely specific for a single ion. For example, most potassium channels are characterized by a 1000:1 selectivity ratio for potassium over sodium, although potassium and sodium ions have the same charge and differ only slightly in their radius.

Passive transport, which includes the subcategories of simple diffusion, osmosis, and facilitated transport, does not require the input of chemical energy. Passive transport is a spontaneous process that is "powered" by the increase in entropy associated with transport (remember that all things being equal, increased entropy is equivalent to thermodynamic favorability). The rates of simple diffusion and osmosis are regulated by the concentration gradient down which particles are flowing and by the degree to which the plasma membrane is permeable to the molecule in question. However, the rate of facilitated diffusion is not linear. Because the transport mechanism relies on molecular binding between the cargo and the membrane-embedded channel or carrier protein channels, the rate of facilitated diffusion depends on the enzyme activity of the carrier protein or channel. Therefore, the rate of transport can be saturated (like enzyme activity), unlike free diffusion, in which the rate of diffusion is only dependent on the concentration gradient across a membrane.

Even though facilitated diffusion is a form of passive transport and therefore does not require the input of chemical energy, it is subject to regulation, unlike osmosis and simple diffusion. Gated carrier proteins—many of which are classified as uniporters, which bind and facilitate the transport of a single molecule at a time—open in response to a stimulus. There are several ways in which the opening of ion channels is regulated, but the most important ones that you should be aware of for the MCAT are ligand-gated channels and voltage-gated channels.

Ligand-gated channels open and close in response to the binding of a ligand molecule, such as a neurotransmitter. You can think of these as essentially behaving like transmembrane receptors, in that the binding of a ligand causes a response; the only real difference is that ion channels are a specific kind of transmembrane protein structure that is classified separately. Ligand-gated ion channels are involved in the propagation of signals in response to external stimuli; examples include ion channels that open and close in response to mechanical forces. Another example can be found in sensory neurons, which contain ion channels that open and close in response to stimuli such as light, temperature, and pressure.

As the name implies, voltage-gated channels open and close in response to the voltage across the membrane. There is a mechanistic difference between voltage-gated sodium and calcium channels on one hand, and voltage-gated potassium channels on the other. Voltage-gated sodium and calcium channels are made up of a single polypeptide with four homologous domains. Each domain contains six membrane-spanning alpha helices, one of which is the voltage-sensing helix. It contains many positive charges, meaning that a high positive charge outside the cell repels the helix, keeping the channel in its closed state. Depolarization of the cell interior causes the helix to move, inducing a conformational change that allows ions to flow through the channel (the open state). The basic logic of potassium channels is similar, but they are composed of four separate polypeptide chains, each comprising a single domain. During transmission of a neuronal signal from one neuron to the next, calcium is transported into the presynaptic neuron by voltage-gated calcium channels. Potassium leak channels, also regulated by voltage, then help to restore the resting membrane potential after impulse transmission.

In active transport, unlike passive transport, energy is consumed (most typically in the form of ATP) to move a solute against a concentration or electrochemical gradient. An important distinction exists between the mechanisms of primary active transport and secondary active transport. In primary active transport, energy is used directly to transport a solute against its gradient, whereas in secondary active transport, the energy stored in an electrochemical gradient established via primary active transport is used to facilitate the movement of a solute.

Most enzymes that perform primary active transport are members of the transmembrane ATPase family. The name of these enzymes alone tells you that they are transmembrane proteins that catalyze the hydrolysis of ATP to release energy. More specifically, they couple the movement of solutes to ATP hydrolysis. The most important example is known as the sodium-potassium pump (more formally, $Na^+/K^+$-ATPase, which is a mouthful to say but very concisely summarizes its function). This enzyme helps to maintain the cell potential across membranes by exchanging $Na^+$ for $K^+$ across a membrane, moving both ions against the transmembrane concentration gradients established by the pump. More specifically, for every ATP molecule hydrolyzed, three $Na^+$ ions are transported *out* of the cell and two $K^+$ ions are transported *in*. This helps maintain the charge imbalance between the exterior and interior of the cell, because even though both ions have a +1 charge, there is a net imbalance, as a charge of +3 is moved out of the cell while a charge of +2 is moved in. Moreover, this is connected to the general fact that the intracellular concentration of $K^+$ is maintained at a level higher than the $K^+$ concentration in the extracellular environment, and vice versa for $Na^+$—that is, the $Na^+$ concentration outside the cell is higher than the $Na^+$ concentration inside the cell.

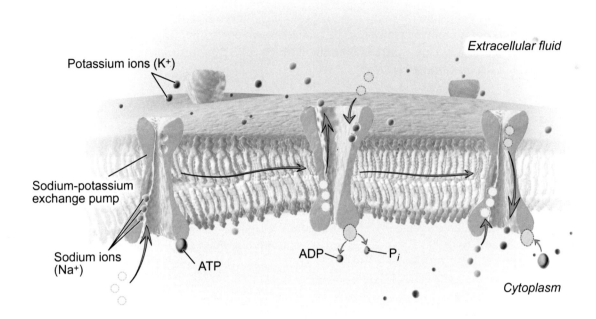

Potassium ions (K⁺)

Extracellular fluid

Sodium-potassium
exchange pump

Sodium ions
(Na⁺)

ATP

ADP

P$_i$

Cytoplasm

# The Sodium-Potassium Exchange Pump

**Figure 7.** Sodium-potassium pump.

Primary active transporters can also be powered by redox reactions or by energy harnessed from the photons of incident light. An important example of the former possibility is provided by the enzymes of the mitochondrial electron transport chain that use the energy released from redox reactions to translocate protons across the inner mitochondrial membrane against their concentration gradient.

In secondary active transport, also known as coupled transport or co-transport, energy is also used to transport molecules across a membrane; however, in contrast to primary active transport, the energy-releasing reaction is not directly coupled to this movement. Instead, it relies upon the electrochemical potential difference created across membranes by active transport. This point may become clearer if we analyze it more concretely by exploring the subcategories of transporters involved in secondary active transport: antiporters and symporters.

Antiporters pump two species of ions or other solutes in opposite directions across a membrane. One of these species is allowed to flow from high to low concentration (in a process that is functionally equivalent to facilitated diffusion), which yields the entropic energy that drives the transport of the other solute from a low-concentration region to a region of higher concentration. An example is the sodium-calcium exchanger, which allows three Na⁺ ions to flow down their concentration gradient, which was previously established by a primary active transport mechanism, into the cell, while transporting one Ca²⁺ ion out.

In contrast, symport uses the 'downhill' movement of one solute species from high to low concentration to move another molecule in the same direction, but *against* its concentration gradient, from low concentration to high concentration. An example is the glucose symporter SGLT-1, which is present in the small intestine, kidneys, heart, and brain humans. SGLT-1 co-transports one glucose (or galactose) molecule into the cell concomitantly with the transport of two Na⁺ ions. As we discussed above, the sodium-potassium pump is used to maintain a higher concentration of Na⁺ outside the cell than inside the cell, so when given the chance, Na⁺ will flow spontaneously into the cell, down its gradient.

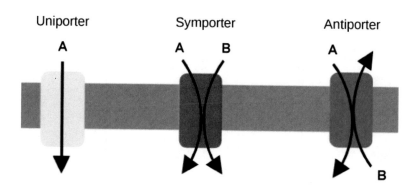

**Figure 8.** Uniporter, symporter, and antiporter mechanisms.

Finally, endocytosis and exocytosis can be used to bring substances into a cell or release them from a cell, respectively. Endocytosis is an energy-using process by which cells absorb molecules by engulfing them. Biologists often subdivide endocytosis into pinocytosis and phagocytosis. In pinocytosis, cells engulf liquid substances, while in phagocytosis, they engulf solid particles. The basic pathway of endocytosis involves recognition of a target molecule at the plasma membrane, followed by invagination and the formation of a vesicle on the inside of the cell.

One important role of endocytosis is the uptake of physiologically important molecules, such as low-density lipoprotein (LDL), growth factors, antibodies, and other proteins. This is accomplished via clathrin-mediated endocytosis, which involves small vesicles that have a coat composed mainly of the cytosolic protein clathrin. Clathrin-coated vesicles are found in nearly all cells and form domains of the plasma membrane termed clathrin-coated pits. Clathrin-coated pits, in turn, concentrate large extracellular molecules that are receptor-specific for the endocytosis of their ligands.

> ### MCAT STRATEGY > > >
>
> Knowing common Greek roots can help differentiate between pinocytosis and phagocytosis. Pinocytosis means something like 'cell drinking,' and you can associate *pino*cytosis with drinking a *pina* colada. In contrast, phagocytosis means 'cell eating'. The *phag-* root, meaning 'eat,' appears frequently in biology. Macrophages—or 'big eaters'—in the immune system are classic examples.

Phagocytosis is the process by which cells bind and internalize larger materials, such as cellular debris, micro-organisms, and in some specialized cell types, other apoptotic cells. These processes involve the uptake of larger membrane areas than is possible in clathrin-mediated endocytosis.

## Endocytosis

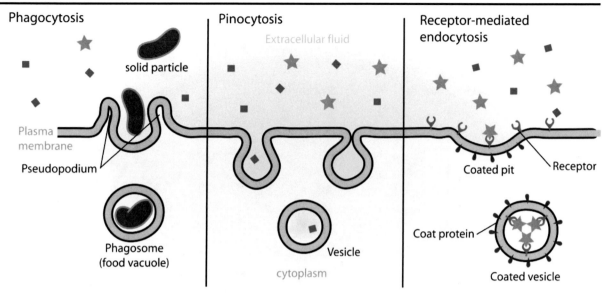

**Figure 9.** Mechanisms of endocytosis.

So far, we've just been focusing on what happens at the membrane itself, but we also need to account for what happens once molecules are internalized. The endocytic pathway of mammalian cells consists of distinct membrane components that internalize molecules from the plasma membrane and recycle them back to the surface (in early endosomes) or sort them for degradation (in late endosomes and lysosomes). Particularly relevant highlights of the endocytic pathway include early endosomes, which pass the molecule of interest on to late endosomes and recycle material back to the plasma membrane, and lysosomes, which are the final component of the endocytic pathway. Lysosomes are the principal hydrolytic compartment of the cell, function to break down cellular waste products and macromolecules, and are highly acidic by physiological standards, with a pH of 4.8.

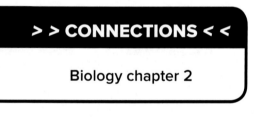

> > CONNECTIONS < <

Biology chapter 2

Exocytosis can be thought of as endocytosis in reverse. In other words, the membrane of an intracellular vesicle can be fused with the plasma membrane, extruding its contents to the surrounding medium. These membrane-bound vesicles contain soluble proteins that will be secreted into the extracellular environment, as well as membrane proteins and lipids that become components of the cell membrane.

There are two main types of exocytosis. Constitutive exocytosis is performed regularly by all cells to release material to the extracellular matrix or to deliver membrane proteins to the membrane. In contrast, non-constitutive (or regulated) exocytosis is mediated by $Ca2+$ signaling and is used to release vesicles with specific content into the extracellular space (or, in the case of neurons, into the synaptic cleft).

**Figure 10.** Exocytosis.

# 3. Must-Knows

> Plasma membrane is described in terms of the fluid mosaic model: biological membranes are two-dimensional, fluid structures within which lipid and protein molecules diffuse freely.
>  — Stability is affected by cholesterol-rich lipid rafts. Cholesterol is a fluidity buffer that increases fluidity at low temperatures and decreases it at high temperatures.

> Primary structure of cell membrane: lipid bilayer of amphipathic phospholipids with hydrophilic (polar) heads and hydrophobic (nonpolar) tails.
>  — Only very small and nonpolar molecules can diffuse easily through the cell membrane
>  — Large and polar molecules can only enter the cell via transport through complex and carefully regulated mechanisms

> Glycolipids are like phospholipids but with a polar carbohydrate moiety that interacts with substances outside of the cell; they often contribute to signaling and adhesion processes.

> Main classes of membrane proteins:
>  — Transmembrane (integral): membrane-spanning proteins with hydrophilic cytosolic and extracellular domains and a hydrophobic membrane-spanning domain. Examples include proton pumps, ion channels, and G protein-coupled receptors.
>  — Peripheral: only transiently attached to integral proteins or peripheral regions of lipid bilayer; examples include some enzymes and hormones.
>  — Lipid-anchored: covalently bound to membrane lipids without actually contacting the membrane directly; primary example is G proteins.

> Membrane transport mechanisms:
>  — Simple diffusion: some molecules, like small gases, can directly diffuse through the membrane.
>  — Osmosis (a type of simple diffusion that is limited to solvent motion; usually water for the MCAT): water will move in or out of cell to attempt to equalize concentrations of solute. Key point: in osmosis, the *solvent* moves through a semipermeable membrane, not the solute.
>  — Facilitated diffusion: still passive transport (no energy necessary), but a transmembrane channel is needed because the molecule is too big for simple diffusion. Often found with ions, and also water via aquaporins.
>  — Primary active transport: energy is used directly to move a solute against its gradient.
>  — Secondary active transport: the energy stored in an electrochemical gradient established via primary active transport is used to facilitate the movement of a solute.
>  — Endocytosis: used to ingest larger materials; exocytosis: used to release hormones, membrane proteins and lipids, and other materials, under close regulation.

# Practice Passage

Eukaryotic cells achieve intracellular homeostasis by adopting a compartmentalized organization, which minimizes the variations resulting from extracellular fluctuations. The plasma membrane ensures a mechanical protection, but also allows exchanges with the medium through transporters and receptors, as a form of very selective permeability (Figure 1).

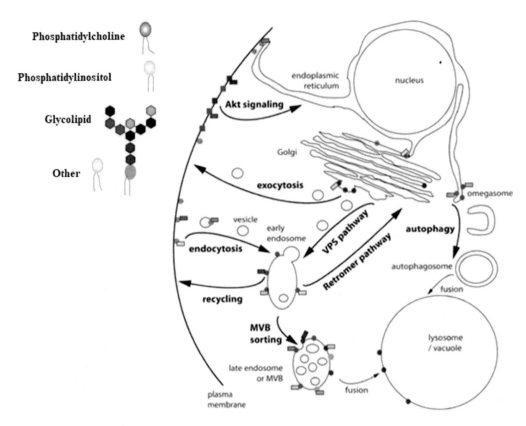

**Figure 1.** Intracellular localization of the different phosphoinositides and the membrane trafficking pathways

The membrane is composed of 4 phospholipids that are assembled at the endoplasmic reticulum: phosphatidylcholine (PC), phosphatidylethanolamine (PE), phosphatidylserine (PS), and phosphatidylinositol (PtdIns). Sphingomyelin is also an important membrane phospholipid. The lipid bilayer of membranes also has an asymmetric phospholipid composition between the inner and the outer leaflet, which partly results from the vertical diffusion between the two leaflets by a flip-flop mechanism with a low intrinsic rate. This asymmetry is compensated by the presence of proteins called flippases. PtdIns are the starting point of the phosphoinositide (PPIn) metabolism and are ubiquitous in eukaryotic cells in various proportions according to the type of membrane. Indeed, PPIn are all metabolized directly or sequentially from PtdIns.

The lipid kinase Vps34 (vacuolar protein sorting 34), catalyzes the phosphorylation of PtdIns. The kinase is activated via its binding to Vps15, which is anchored to membranes. This Vps34-Vps15 complex further recruits additional effectors to regulate either endosomal trafficking (via Vps38-Vps30 proteins) or autophagy (via Atg14-Vps30). Interestingly, it has been shown that the positive regulation of Vps34 by Vps15 is stimulated by the direct interaction between the C-terminal region of Vps15 constituted by seven repeats of the WD domains and the Gα subunit Gpa1.

*Adapted from De Craene, J.-O. et al. (2017). Phosphoinositides, Major Actors in Membrane Trafficking and Lipid Signaling Pathways. International Journal of Molecular Sciences, 18(3), 634 under CCBY 4.0*

1. Which of the following aspects of the cell membrane is regulated by sterol composition?
   I. Integrity
   II. Rigidity
   III. Lateral diffusion
   IV. Transverse diffusion
   A. I and IV only
   B. II and III only
   C. II and IV only
   D. I, II, III and IV

2. Which residues are most likely responsible for positive regulation of Vps34 by Vps15 and Gpa1?
   A. ST
   B. PP
   C. FD
   D. LK

3. If the exocytotic machinery of the cell in Figure 1 is damaged, what is the most likely effect on the movement of water?
   A. Intracellular water accumulates in the nucleus
   B. Excess water accumulates in the cytoplasm
   C. Excess water accumulates in the Golgi complex
   D. Extracellular water accumulates in the nucleus

4. Neurodegenerative deafness and dystonia syndrome is caused by a 6-nucleotide deletion (301-306) in the gene coding for the ion transport protein Tim8. The protein is unable to properly function most likely due to a change in:
   A. primary structure.
   B. secondary structure.
   C. tertiary structure.
   D. quaternary structure.

5. Which of the following membrane compositions is the direct result of the greatest level of flippase activity?

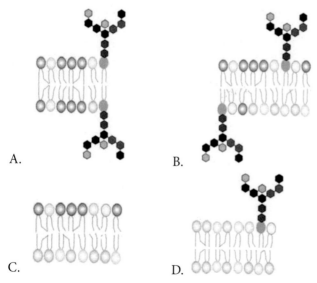

A.

B.

C.

D.

6. All of the following are freestanding principal components of eukaryotic membranes EXCEPT:
   A. Proteins
   B. Steroids
   C. Carbohydrates
   D. Phospholipids

7. Which of the following is NOT assembled in the endoplasmic reticulum?
   A. Proteins
   B. Lipids
   C. PtdIn
   D. Sphingomyelin

## Practice Passage Explanations

Eukaryotic cells achieve intracellular homeostasis by adopting a compartmentalized organization, which minimizes the variations resulting from extracellular fluctuations. The plasma membrane ensures a mechanical protection, but also allows exchanges with the medium through transporters and receptors, as a form of very selective permeability (Figure 1).

*Key terms: intracellular homeostasis, selective permeability*

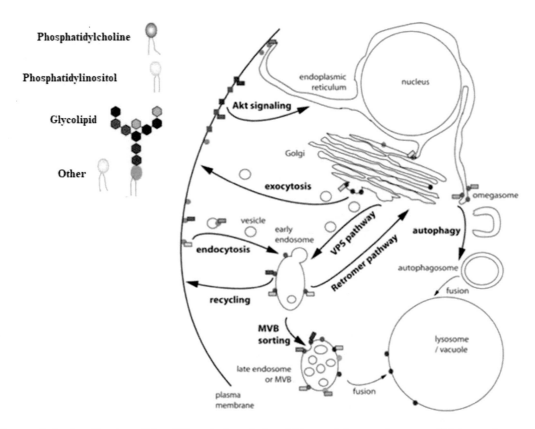

**Figure 1.** Intracellular localization of the different phosphoinositides and the membrane trafficking pathways

*Figure 1 shows multiple pathways we should recognize, save detailed analysis for later*

The membrane is composed of 4 phospholipids that are assembled at the endoplasmic reticulum: phosphatidylcholine (PC), phosphatidylethanolamine (PE), phosphatidylserine (PS), and phosphatidylinositol (PtdIns). Sphingomyelin is also an important membrane phospholipid. The lipid bilayer of membranes also has an asymmetric phospholipid composition between the inner and the outer leaflet, which partly results from the vertical diffusion between the two leaflets by a flip-flop mechanism with a low intrinsic rate. This asymmetry is compensated by the presence of proteins called flippases. PtdIns are the starting point of the phosphoinositide (PPIn) metabolism and are ubiquitous in eukaryotic cells in various proportions according to the type of membrane. Indeed, PPIn are all metabolized directly or sequentially from PtdIns.

*Key terms: 4 phospholipids, sphingomyelin, flippases*

*Cause and effect: PPIn → PtdIns → ?; PO$_4$-lipid membrane composition is asymmetric, flippases help correct this*

The lipid kinase Vps34 (vacuolar protein sorting 34), catalyzes the phosphorylation of PtdIns. The kinase is activated via its binding to Vps15, which is anchored to membranes. This Vps34-Vps15 complex further recruits additional effectors to regulate either endosomal trafficking (via Vps38-Vps30 proteins) or autophagy (via Atg14-Vps30). Interestingly, it has been shown that the positive regulation of Vps34 by Vps15 is stimulated by the direct interaction between the C-terminal region of Vps15 constituted by seven repeats of the WD domains and the Gα subunit Gpa1.

*Key terms: lipid kinase, Vps34, activated, positive regulation, additional effectors*

*Contrast: endosomal vs. autophagy activity of 34/15 complex*

*Cause and effect: Vsp34 binds to Vsp15 → complex $PO_4$-ylates PtdIns; regulates by other complexes; 15/34 binding involves WD residues*

*Adapted from De Craene, J.-O. et al. (2017). Phosphoinositides, Major Actors in Membrane Trafficking and Lipid Signaling Pathways. International Journal of Molecular Sciences, 18(3), 634 under CCBY 4.0*

1. D is correct. Because of the way cholesterol is shaped, part of the steroid ring is closely attracted to part of the fatty acid chain on the nearest phospholipid. This helps slightly immobilize the outer surface of the membrane and make it less soluble to very small water-soluble molecules that could otherwise pass through more easily. Without cholesterol, cell membranes would be too fluid, not firm enough, and too permeable to some molecules (RN I and II are true). Therefore, the answer must be choice D.
III, IV: Sterols modulate the fluidity/integrity of the membrane, which is essential for the lateral diffusion of molecules in the bilayer. Lateral diffusion refers to the lateral movement of lipids and proteins found in the membrane. Transverse diffusion or flip-flop involves the movement of a lipid or protein from one membrane surface to the other (i.e. into or out of the cell).

2. D is correct. The final paragraph tells us that positive regulation of Vps34 by Vps15 is stimulated by the direct interaction between the C-terminal region of Vps15 constituted by seven repeats of the WD domains and the Gα subunit Gpa1. WD stands for tryptophan and aspartic acid, a hydrophobic and acidic/negative group, respectively. Thus, we would expect hydrophobic and basic/positive residues to most strongly interact with the WD on Vps15. Choice D contains leucine (hydrophobic) and lysine (basic) residues.

3. B is correct. Exocytotic mechanisms are responsible for exporting material/solutes out of the cell. If this path is damaged/lost, then excess material will build up inside the cell, raising the solute levels inside the cell. This would cause excess solute to remain in the cell, and extracellular water would move down its concentration gradient and enter the cell.

4. C is correct. A protein's biological function is tied to its shape/configuration, and its function can be lost due to many factors. Given that the problem is a loss of just 6 sequential nucleotides (2 codons), it is unlikely that a 2 amino acid loss would cause enough of a change in primary structure (AA sequence) to lead to a loss of transport function. The same is true for the hydrogen bonds between nearby peptides. The most likely explanation is that loss of these two residues led to a loss of some aspect of the protein's 3-dimensional structure that prevents proper ion transport.
   D. Not all proteins are composed of multiple subunits, and we have no evidence that Tim8 has quaternary structure.

5. A is correct. What does flippase have to do with membrane composition? Paragraph 2 tells us that the membrane bilayer has an asymmetric phospholipid composition between the inner and the outer leaflet, which is corrected by proteins called flippases. Thus, we would expect the greatest flippase activity to result in the most symmetrical membrane (i.e. the membrane with the inner and outer layers most closely matching).

6. C is correct. The principal components of the plasma membrane are lipids (e.g. phospholipids, cholesterol, and phosphatids), steroids, and proteins. While there are carbohydrate groups, they are only present when attached to some of the lipids and proteins.

7. D is correct. Most proteins (rough ER) and lipids (smooth) are assembled in the endoplasmic reticulum. The passage also tells us that phosphatidylinositol (PtdIn) are assembled there as well. In addition, the ER synthesizes ceramide and cholesterol. The Golgi lumen is the site of synthesis of sphingomyelin (SM).

## Independent Questions

1. A graduate student synthesizes phospholipid liposomes that mimic the properties of the plasma membrane. Two fluorescent transmembrane proteins are inserted into the membrane a very short distance apart, such that their fluorescent tags are directed into the lumen of the liposome. Examination of the outer liposomal surface six hours later most likely shows that:
   A. the two proteins are located in their original positions and fluorescence cannot be seen on the outer liposomal surface.
   B. the two proteins have drifted laterally within the membrane and fluorescence cannot be seen on the outer liposomal surface.
   C. the two proteins are located in their original positions and fluorescence can be seen on the outer liposomal surface.
   D. the two proteins have drifted laterally within the membrane and fluorescence can be seen on the outer liposomal surface.

2. Amino acid sequencing of a novel membrane signaling protein yields the following partial sequence: LTFIPVAIW. This segment is most likely part of:
   A. a transmembrane domain.
   B. a cytoplasmic site.
   C. an unstructured extracellular domain.
   D. a helical domain.

3. Some species of methanogenic archaea can survive under anaerobic conditions by reducing carbon dioxide to methane and water. In this reaction, hydrogen gas acts as the reducing agent. Which of these metabolites is LEAST likely to passively diffuse through an archaeon's cell membrane?
   A. Carbon dioxide
   B. Methane
   C. Water
   D. Diatomic hydrogen

4. Examination of a certain peripherally associated membrane protein reveals that the protein can be stripped from the extracellular surface and isolated by washing the relevant bacterial cells with a concentrated salt solution. Which of the following mutations in the membrane-associated domain would most likely disrupt the association of this protein with the plasma membrane?
   A. Glutamate to alanine
   B. Aspartate to glutamate
   C. Lysine to arginine
   D. Valine to glycine

5. At high temperatures, cholesterol stabilizes biological membranes due to:
   A. electrostatic interactions with phospholipid head groups.
   B. van der Waals interactions with phospholipid tails.
   C. covalent interactions with membrane proteins.
   D. steric interactions that disrupt phospholipid clustering.

6. A significant energy barrier is associated with the passage of ions through the hydrophobic core of the plasma membrane. Which of the following would be most consistent with the structure of an ion channel that rapidly and specifically conducts potassium from the cytoplasm to the extracellular fluid?
   A. The cytoplasmic face of the channel has many exposed hydrophobic residues.
   B. The cytoplasmic opening of the channel is lined with positively charged residues.
   C. Ions initially pass through a short hydrophobic channel and reach a central cavity filled with water.
   D. Ions are coordinated by negatively charged amino acids during their entire journey through the channel.

7. GLUT2 is a transmembrane protein that allows glucose to move down its concentration

gradient. It is known that GLUT2 must undergo a conformational change to accomplish this. Transport of glucose by GLUT2 is best categorized as:

A. secondary active transport.
B. primary active transport.
C. facilitated diffusion.
D. enzyme transport.

8. Endocytosis is initiated when certain cargo molecules bind to extracellular receptors. The cargo is then internalized and the endosome is trafficked to its intracellular destination. Cargo that enters the cell in this way might include:

A. steroid hormones.
B. urea.
C. fructose.
D. insulin.

## Independent Question Explanations

1. B is correct. According to the fluid mosaic model, transmembrane proteins are able to freely diffuse within the membrane, so it is unlikely that the two proteins would still be found in their original positions after several hours (eliminate choices A and C). Generally, proteins do not spontaneously reverse their orientation within the membrane, so it is most likely that the fluorescent tags would remain internally directed and not visible on the outer liposomal surface.

2. A is correct. With the exception of threonine, every amino acid in the given sequence is hydrophobic. It is therefore likely that this segment is part of a transmembrane domain, meaning that it passes through the nonpolar lipid bilayer. With regard to choice D, note that alpha helices generally do not contain proline, which appears in the middle of the given sequence.

3. C is correct. All four metabolites are small, uncharged molecules. However, water is the only one of the given choices with a permanent dipole moment, which makes it unable to freely diffuse through the hydrophobic core of the lipid bilayer. Since this is a LEAST question, water (choice C) is our answer.

4. A is correct. Concentrated ionic solutions disrupt electrostatic interactions, which suggests that these interactions are involved in the protein's association with the membrane surface. Electrostatic interactions involve charged amino acids, such as glutamate or lysine. Conversion of a charged amino acid (glutamate) to a neutral amino acid (alanine) would likely weaken the association between the plasma membrane and this protein.

5. B is correct. At high temperatures, cholesterol increases membrane stability through attractive van der Waals interactions with neighboring lipids. This prevents the membrane from becoming excessively fluid. In contrast, at low temperatures, its steric bulk increases membrane fluidity by preventing tight packing of phospholipid tails.

6. C is correct. Potassium channels contain a central cavity filled with water. This local polar environment reduces the energetic penalty incurred by passage through the membrane core. The ions briefly pass through a hydrophobic section near the entrance of the channel, which facilitates rapid conduction by reducing attraction between the ions and the channel walls. Uninterrupted coordination between potassium ions and charged residues would greatly decrease conduction speed. Hydrophobic residues are generally not exposed in solution, and positively charged residues would repel potassium ions.

7. C is correct. No energy is required to move glucose down its concentration gradient, but a transport protein is needed to permit passage through the plasma membrane. These are characteristics of facilitated diffusion.

8. D is correct. Steroids may pass directly through lipid membranes, which would make their uptake by endocytosis unnecessary and their containment in vesicles difficult (eliminate choice A). Small, polar molecules such as urea and fructose generally cross the cell membrane via transmembrane proteins (eliminate choices B and C). Insulin is too large to utilize a transport protein and is thus the only feasible answer choice. In fact, endocytosis of insulin and its receptor is the mechanism by which insulin is internalized for degradation by its target cells.

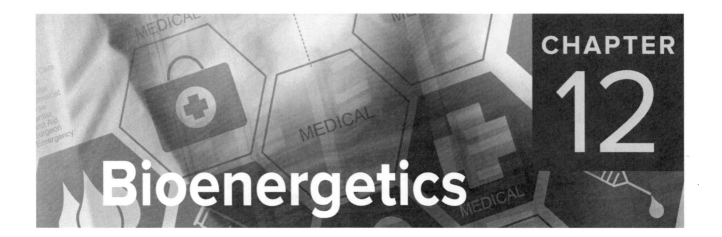

# Bioenergetics

## 0. Introduction

Bioenergetics has been lurking in the background of much of this textbook—in that it's at least implicit in any discussion of how biological pathways are regulated and which behaviors of biomolecules are spontaneous—but as the final step in our study of MCAT biochemistry, it's time for us to put all the pieces together. In this chapter, we'll review the key concepts of bioenergetics, and then move on to a discussion of biological energy sources. After this, we'll build connections with the all-important concept of regulation by first discussing principles of regulation, and then discussing some examples in depth of how important pathways are regulated.

## 1. Key Concepts of Bioenergetics

Living organisms obtain energy from organic and inorganic substrates using different strategies. Autotrophs can produce ATP from the energy contained in light by photosynthesis. Heterotrophs—a category that includes humans—use ingested organic materials as their primary energy source. Other, more unusual organisms, known collectively as lithotrophs, can obtain energy from the oxidation of sulfur- and nitrogen-containing compounds. Regardless of the materials from which organisms harvest energy, the process is not perfectly efficient, as there are variable energetic costs associated with the transfer and transformation of energy as it is obtained and used biologically.

Gibbs free energy (G) describes the maximum amount of non-PV work that can be performed within a closed system in a completely reversible process at a constant temperature and pressure. It is an indication of the total amount of chemical potential energy available in a system, and reflects the overall favorability of the reaction that it describes. A critical equation relates the change in Gibbs free energy, or $\Delta G$, to the important thermodynamic parameters of change of enthalpy (or heat) during reaction ($\Delta H$), temperature (T), and change of entropy ($\Delta S$):

**Equation 1.** $$\Delta G = \Delta H - T\Delta S$$

A reaction with a negative $\Delta G$ will be spontaneous, and such reactions are known as exergonic. This essentially means that they release energy that can be used to perform work in their surroundings. In contrast, a reaction with a positive $\Delta G$ is not spontaneous, and such reactions are known as endergonic. Endergonic reactions require work to be put into them to make them go forward. Free energy diagrams for exergonic and endergonic reactions are shown below in Figure 1.

**Figure 1.** Exergonic and endergonic reactions.

In MCAT biochemistry, you are more likely to be asked to think about ΔG in qualitative terms—that is, on a conceptual level—than to perform calculations with it, but if you do ever need to use this equation quantitatively, be sure to remember that the temperature must be expressed in Kelvin.

A crucial, but often overlooked, fact about ΔG is that it refers to the *maximum* free energy that can be produced. This clearly leads to the question of how to analyze the *actual* free energy that takes place under various conditions. The quantity ΔG°, known as the standard free energy change, was defined to do this. It refers to the free energy that occurs if the concentration of reactants and products is 1 M.

Both ΔG and ΔG° can be related to temperature and the concentrations of products and reactants as follows. Equation 2 applies at equilibrium, where the ratio of products to reactants is given by $K_{eq}$, while Equation 3 applies when a reaction is not at equilibrium, at which point the reaction quotient $Q$ gives the ratio of products to reactants:

**Equation 2:**  $\Delta G° = -RT\ln K_{eq}$

**Equation 3:**  $\Delta G = \Delta G° + RT\ln Q$

## MCAT STRATEGY > > >

One of the unfortunate realities of dealing with ΔG vs. ΔG° is that many textbooks are not careful about making this distinction in other chapters, because it's often not that important in context to specify whether we're talking about standard or nonstandard conditions. On one hand, this practice simplifies discussions in other chapters, but on the other hand, it sets the stage for some confusion in bioenergetics. The key takeaway point is just that ΔG° is what we use when we care about specifying standard concentrations.

A consequence of Equations 2 and 3 is that ΔG° is only an accurate predictor of reaction spontaneity under standard conditions. A reaction with a positive—and therefore unfavorable—ΔG° can proceed spontaneously to produce products if Q, which is the ratio of products to reactants at a given time—is sufficiently small to make the magnitude of the negative RTlnQ term sufficiently great to 'outweigh' ΔG°. This kind of discrepancy between ΔG and ΔG° is quite common in cellular conditions. One example is the conversion of glucose 6-phosphate to fructose 6-phosphate in the second step of glycolysis. This reaction has a positive ΔG°, but concentrations of fructose 6-phosphate are kept very low in the cell, because fructose 6-phosphate is immediately shunted off to further steps in glycolysis. This concept may remind you of Le Châtelier's principle, and rightly so. Essentially, what we've been talking about in terms of the discrepancy between ΔG° and ΔG is a more formalized and quantitative way of applying Le Châtelier's principle (as well as including a *T* term) in biochemical contexts.

Another important property of Gibbs free energy is that the ΔG values for individual reactions that are linked sequentially by common intermediates are additive. Two reactions have a common intermediate when they occur sequentially, such that the product produced by one reaction serves as the reactant of a second reaction. For biochemical pathways through which substrates must pass sequentially, the additive property of free energy changes allows for the possibility that the overall free energy of a pathway is negative, even while some of its steps have positive free energy changes. This allows cells to drive thermodynamically unfavorable reactions by coupling exergonic and endergonic reactions. This strategy of coupling favorable and unfavorable reactions is very common in the cell, and some version of this strategy is usually used to drive ATP-powered reactions, in which the energetically favorable hydrolysis of ATP is coupled to some other reaction that would otherwise not be spontaneous.

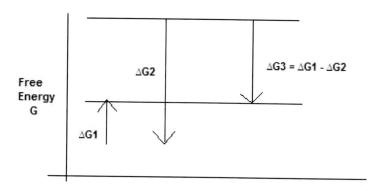

**Figure 2.** Gibbs free energy change of coupled reactions.

For the most part, the MCAT will ask you to apply these concepts qualitatively, although you may be asked to calculate the cumulative ΔG of a coupled pair of reactions based on their individual ΔG values. On one hand, the terms covered in this section may be familiar to you from your previous biology and biochemistry coursework, but on the other hand, some of these concepts can be tricky and there is definitely room for misinterpretations to emerge. The following simple guidelines will help you structure your studying for this content area:

> ΔG vs. ΔG°: ΔG° is a standardized measure of energy favorability (under standard conditions that include 1 M concentrations of products and reactants); ΔG is applicable under nonstandard conditions, and refers to the maximum possible free energy under constant temperature and pressure.

> ΔG or ΔG° < 0 indicates that a process is thermodynamically favorable. This corresponds to a $K_{eq}$ > 1, which simply means having more product than reactant at equilibrium.

> Concentration of products versus reactants will affect which way the reaction goes. Qualitatively, we think of this in terms of Le Châtelier's principle. Quantitatively, we can express this idea using ΔG = ΔG° + RTlnQ.

> ΔG values are additive for coupled reactions.

**MCAT STRATEGY > > >**

Note that we have said *nothing* about kinetics (rate) in this section. Be sure to strictly compartmentalize issues of rate and thermodynamics/equilibrium.

## 2. Biological Energy Sources

Next, let's turn more specifically to the question of how the body gets energy. At first glance, this may seem like a tremendously broad subject area, given the range of macronutrients and reactions that we've discussed in this textbook. However, it turns out that there are really only two high-level strategies for obtaining energy:

1. High-energy bonds

2. Redox reactions

At a *really* high level of abstraction, you could argue that high-energy bonds are the only real strategy the body uses, because as we will see, the main point of redox reactions as a biological energy source is to set the stage for forming high-energy bonds that are then directly used to power reactions. However, it's worth focusing on redox reactions specifically, because doing so can provide important insights into processes like glycolysis, the citric acid cycle, the electron transport chain, and beta-oxidation of fatty acids—that is, the entire core of MCAT metabolism.

The primary example of a high-energy bond that is used to power other reactions in the cell is adenosine triphosphate (ATP), which is essentially the energy currency of the cell. ATP contains three phosphate groups connected to each other by phosphoanhydride bonds. The hydrolysis of these phosphoanhydride bonds yields either adenosine diphosphate (ADP), if one bond is hydrolyzed, or adenosine monophosphate (AMP), if two bonds are hydrolyzed. For the most part, we can use the hydrolysis of ATP to ADP + $P_i$ (inorganic phosphate) as the prototype for how these reactions work. The idea is simple: the hydrolysis of ATP to ADP + $P_i$ is extremely energetically favorable, so it is used to power other reactions. The next question we can ask is *why* it is so energetically favorable.

The phosphoanhydride bonds in ATP are considered high-energy because their hydrolysis release a large amount of energy. This pattern is due to several features related to the structure of ATP. First, ADP and $P_i$, the products of the hydrolysis of a single ATP phosphoanhydride bond, have greater resonance stabilization than does ATP. Second, at physiological pH, the triphosphate unit of ATP carries four negative charges that are in close proximity to each other. This results in considerable repulsion, which can be minimized by hydrolysis. Finally, ADP and $P_i$ are more stabilized by hydration than is ATP, because additional negatively charged groups are made available to interact with and bind water following hydrolysis.

> **MCAT STRATEGY > > >**
>
> The high-energy properties of ATP, and the fact that they are largely due to charge-related properties, are yet another indication of why it is so important to 'follow the charge' for MCAT biochemistry.

**Figure 3.** Hydrolysis of ATP to ADP + $P_i$.

The hydrolysis of ATP can simply yield ADP + $P_i$, but in some contexts, the coupling mechanism is noteworthy. For instance, the phosphate group can be transferred to another molecule. The prototypical example of this is the conversion of glucose to glucose 6-phosphate in the first step of glycolysis. The direct reaction is thermodynamically unfavorable ($\Delta G° = +13.8$ kJ/mol), but it is coupled to the exergonic cleavage of ATP ($\Delta G° = -30.5$ kJ/mol), so that the overall reaction is favorable ($\Delta G° = -16.7$ kJ/mol). It is also worth noting that ATP can bind to certain proteins, inducing conformational changes that catalyze the hydrolysis of ATP and the release of energy.

Although we've been using ATP as the prototypical example of a high-energy bond, you should be aware that it is not the only high-energy bond used in cellular settings. Guanine triphosphate (GTP) is a similar high-energy nucleotide triphosphate that is used for energy in certain biosignaling and protein synthesis processes, via a similar mechanism of hydrolysis. Another important high-energy intermediate is acetyl-CoA, which contains a high-energy thioester bond, and reduced coenzymes such as NADH.

**Figure 4.** Acetyl-CoA

The hydrolysis and regeneration of ATP occurs continuously in the cell. How ATP is regenerated is not an obvious question; we've been talking a lot about how energetically favorable it is to hydrolyze ATP, which implies that it is energetically unfavorable to form ATP. That is indeed the case—so how does the cell do it? It turns out that there are a couple different ways that ATP can be formed, despite the fact that doing so is quite endergonic.

For most students, the most familiar mechanism of ATP formation is oxidative phosphorylation, which is preceded by the electron transport chain in the mitochondria. As discussed in chapter 8, the point of the electron transport chain is to store energy in the form of a charge gradient caused by an asymmetry in proton concentration. This energy is harnessed by ATP synthase to phosphorylate ADP, producing ATP. Additionally, there are some reactions in which ATP is produced by the very same mechanism that allows ATP itself to be used for energy: reaction coupling. Yet again, glycolysis provides a great example of this phenomenon. In the payoff phase, ATP synthesis is coupled to the even more exergonic cleavage of phosphoenolpyruvate (PEP). Another pathway is found in cells that have an extremely high ATP usage rate, most often cells found in nervous and skeletal system tissue. Such cells can utilize phosphocreatine as a reserve from which they can quickly regenerate ATP. Phosphocreatine can be synthesized from ADP and creatine by the enzyme creatine kinase. Under physiological conditions, with nearly equal concentrations of reactants and products, phosphocreatine and ADP can be reversibly converted to creatine and ATP.

## > > CONNECTIONS < <

### Chapter 8 of Chemistry

## MCAT STRATEGY > > >

The mnemonic OIL RIG (oxidation is loss, reduction is gain) is very helpful for remembering the basic meaning of oxidation and reduction. Be sure to invest some time into solidifying your knowledge of this terminology; this is *not* something you want to worry about on Test Day.

The fact that oxidative phosphorylation via the electron transport chain is the most familiar and important mechanism of ATP synthesis underscores the importance of redox reactions. In redox reactions—or, more formally, oxidation/reduction reactions—electrons are transferred. The compound that gains an electron (or electrons) is reduced, and the compound that loses an electron (or electrons) is oxidized. For more details about oxidation and reduction, see Chapter 8 of the Chemistry and Organic Chemistry textbook; in this chapter, we're going to take a closer look at how redox reactions tie into biochemistry and energy production.

The basic idea here is fairly simple. In metabolic pathways, electrons are transferred from nutrient molecules to electron carriers ($NAD^+$/NADH and FAD/$FADH_2$), which take them to the electron transport chain, where a series of redox reactions takes place, with $O_2$ as the final electron acceptor (in a reaction in which $O_2 \rightarrow H_2O$). These redox reactions in the electron transport chain also transport protons into the intermembrane space of the mitochondria, and the resulting proton gradient powers ATP synthase. In previous chapters, we've discussed each step of the process in detail, so below we will take a closer look at some of the key chemical machinery at play.

## MCAT STRATEGY > > >

By Test Day, you should be able to deliver a short explanation of how electron transfer powers ATP synthesis by heart; this principle is fundamental to understanding metabolic processes and is tested frequently.

Let's start with some basic principles of electrochemistry. Given the importance of electron transport in this chapter, we need to find some way to talk about whether a substance is relatively more or less likely to give or accept electrons. The concept of standard reduction potential is how we do this. For a given reduction half-reaction (and it's important that we make sure we're talking about a reduction half-reaction in this context, not its reversed oxidation counterpart), the standard reduction potential ($E°_{red}$, often just abbreviated as $E°$ if the context is clear) is essentially a measure of how much a compound "wants" to be reduced—that is, to gain electrons.

More formally, $E°_{red}$ is the potential difference at equilibrium, under standard conditions, of an electrochemical cell in which the cathode reaction is the half-reaction in question and the anode is a standard hydrogen electrode. The standard reduction potential for hydrogen is defined as zero. In general, for electrochemical cells, we can apply the equation $E°_{cell} = E°_{cathode} - E°_{anode}$, so you can think of the definition of the standard reduction potential as being a special case of this phenomenon in which $E°_{anode}$ is set to equal zero by convention. You may occasionally run into something called the oxidation potential, which refers to the same exact concept but in reverse, such that $E°_{red} = -E°_{ox}$.

Let's step back and take a look at how this can be applied in a practical context. If we're given two reduction half-reactions—$Cu^{2+}(aq) + 2e^- \rightarrow Cu(s)$ ($E° = +0.34$ V) and $Cd^{2+}(aq) + 2e^- \rightarrow Cd(s)$ ($E° = -0.40$ V)—what will actually happen in a spontaneous cell, and what will the overall reduction potential of that galvanic cell be? This may at first seem daunting, but let's work through this conceptually first. In order to predict what will happen spontaneously in a qualitative way, we need to figure out which ion— $Cu^{2+}$ or $Cd^{2+}$—'wants' to be reduced, or to gain electrons, more. This corresponds to having a higher reduction potential, so we can straightforwardly predict that $Cu^{2+}$ will be reduced to Cu, which means that Cd will be oxidized to $Cd^{2+}$. Our next task is to try to quantify how favorable this reaction will be. The way to do this is to combine an expression for how much $Cu^{2+}$ 'wants' to be reduced with an expression for how much $Cd^{2+}$ 'wants' to be oxidized. For $Cu^{2+}$, we just need the reduction potential (+0.34 V). For $Cu^{2+}$, we need the oxidation potential, which has the same magnitude as the reduction potential, but the opposite sign (+0.40 V). We add these together and get the total cell potential of +0.70 V.

There are three equations that can be used to describe this line of reasoning:

**Equation 4A:**
$$E°_{cell} = E°_{cathode} - E°_{anode}$$

**Equation 4B:**
$$E°_{cell} = E°(\text{reduced species}) - E°(\text{oxidized species})$$

**Equation 4C:**
$$E°_{cell} = [\text{larger } E°] + [-\text{smaller } E°]$$

Don't let these equations daunt you: they're actually just three different ways of looking at the same thing. You could also use a 'verbal' equation in which $E°_{cell}$ is defined as the reduction potential of the reduced species plus the oxidation potential of the oxidized species, which the reasoning we presented in the previous paragraph.

The reason why all of this matters is that the redox reactions in the electron transport chain can be modeled as a series of galvanic cells, in which electrons are transferred from substances with lower $E°$ values to substances with higher $E°$ values. Oxygen is the final acceptor of electrons, and the $E°$ value for the reduction half-reaction $\frac{1}{2}O_2 + 2H^+ + 2e^- \rightarrow H_2O$ is 0.82 V, which is relatively quite high.

Next, let's take a closer look at the most common electron carriers: nicotinamide adenine dinucleotide (NAD+/NADH) and flavin adenine dinucleotide (FAD/FADH$_2$). Nicotinamide adenine dinucleotide exists in an oxidized form (NAD+) and a reduced form (NADH), allowing it to donate or accept electrons during redox reactions, depending on the state in which it is found. In reactions involving NAD+, two electrons are removed from two hydrogen atoms present in a reactant, producing a hydride ion (H−) and a proton (H+). The proton is released into solution, the reactant is oxidized, and the electrons from the hydride are transferred to NAD+, reducing it to NADH. During the reduction, one electron from the hydride is transferred to the positively charged nitrogen of the nicotinamide ring of NAD+, while a second is transferred to a ring carbon. The

> **MCAT STRATEGY > > >**
>
> Don't let your eyes glaze over here. You will save yourself a lot of hassle if you invest the energy necessary to really recognize that Equations 4A, 4B, and 4C are equivalent. If you can explain all three versions to a study buddy, you'll know that you're on the right track for this aspect of electrochemistry.

reduction of NAD⁺ can be readily reversed, when NADH reduces another molecule and is returned to its oxidized state, NAD⁺, allowing the compound to be recycled during electron transfer.

**Figure 5.** NAD⁺ and NADH.

Like NAD⁺/NADH, flavin adenine dinucleotide exists in two forms: its fully oxidized, quinone form (FAD), which can accept two electrons and two protons to become FADH$_2$, which is its fully reduced hydroquinone form. FADH$_2$

> > **CONNECTIONS** < <

**Chapter 10 of Chemistry**

can then be oxidized to a semireduced form (semiquinone) FADH by donating one electron and one proton. It can then be oxidized again, returning to FAD. You should study the structures shown in Figure 6, because FAD/FADH/FADH$_2$ is an excellent example of the molecules known as quinones, hydroquinones, and semiquinones, which are actually testable organic chemistry content.

**Figure 6.** FAD and FADH$_2$.

# 3. Regulation of Metabolic Pathways

Now that we've taken a close look at how energy is produced and harnessed on the cellular level, we need to zoom out and take a more integrative look at how energy-producing (and energy-consuming) processes are regulated on the level of the body. In previous chapters, we've analyzed how specific metabolic pathways (such as glycolysis, gluconeogenesis, and beta-oxidation) are regulated, but the end of the Biochemistry textbook is an excellent place to try to synthesize these threads and get a sense of how the puzzle pieces of human metabolism fit together.

As always, you should have some basic principles of regulation in the back of your mind as you approach this material. One important point is that metabolic pathways are carefully regulated and balanced to maintain a metabolic steady state; that is, although we must be able to upregulate and downregulate various processes in response to external stimuli or biorhythms, it is also essential for metabolic parameters to be maintained within ranges compatible with life. For instance, our blood pH is very closely controlled; if the pH of the blood falls outside of the narrow range of 7.35-7.45, we are in major trouble and must receive intense medical treatment. Blood sugar levels can vary to a much greater extent—to some extent, the hyperglycemic states characteristic of diabetes mellitus can be asymptomatic—but extreme hypoglycemia and hyperglycemia can both be deadly in the short term. On the smaller-scale level, negative feedback regulation of pathways helps accomplish this goal by preventing pathways from spiraling out of control and producing too much product, while on the larger-scale level, balanced hormonal regulation is key to maintaining homeostasis and responding appropriately to stimuli. In this section, we'll discuss the effects of the hormones that are most important for regulating metabolism: the glucose-regulating hormones insulin and glucagon (note, however, that these hormones have other effects as well), with additional reference to the stress-response hormones epinephrine and norepinephrine.

> > **CONNECTIONS** < <

Chapter 7 of Biology

Insulin is released by the beta cells of the pancreas and its main effect is stimulating glucose uptake by target cells. More specifically, it is released upon the entry of glucose into pancreatic beta cells through the GLUT2 glucose transporters. As glucose enter the Krebs cycle within the beta cells, the ATP-to-ADP ratio within the cell increases. This increased ratio leads to the closure of an ATP-sensitive potassium channel and the buildup of intracellular potassium ions, which in turn leads to depolarization and the opening of voltage-gated calcium cells within the membrane of beta cells. The entry of calcium ions triggers a signaling cascade that results in the release of additional calcium ions from the endoplasmic reticulum. The resulting significant increase in the intracellular calcium concentration causes the release of previously stored insulin from secretory vesicles. Other substances known to stimulate insulin release include the amino acids arginine and leucine, parasympathetic release of acetylcholine, the digestive enzyme cholecystokinin (CCK), and the gastrointestinally derived hormones glucagon-like peptide-1 (GLP-1) and glucose-dependent insulinotropic peptide (GIP). Release of insulin is strongly inhibited by the stress hormone norepinephrine, leading to increased blood glucose levels during stressful situations as part of the so-called 'fight-or-flight' response.

**MCAT STRATEGY > > >**

You absolutely must know on Test Day that insulin release is stimulated by high blood glucose levels via glucose-sensing mechanisms in pancreatic beta cells, and that the 'fight-or-flight' response induces elevated blood glucose levels. It is also worth being aware that insulin can be involved in other signaling pathways; although it is unlikely that you will see specific discrete or pseudo-discrete questions on CCK, GLP-1, and GIP, it is possible that these or similar molecules could be introduced in passages, at which point some general previous familiarity will help you navigate a challenging passage.

In insulin-responsive tissues, including skeletal muscle and fat cells, insulin binds with insulin receptors, triggering an intracellular signaling cascade that promotes the recruitment of insulin-sensitive glucose transporters (GLUT4 receptors). The presence of more GLUT4 transporters in the plasma membrane promotes the uptake of glucose into the target cells, which has the effect of reducing blood glucose levels.

In addition to stimulating glucose absorption, insulin exerts a range of other effects on human metabolism. Insulin upregulates the synthesis of glycogen in the liver and muscle (a process known as glycogenesis). This makes sense, because by definition, insulin acts when the blood has a surplus of glucose that needs to be dealt with, and glycogen is a major way that cells can store glucose for future use. The details of how glycogenesis is regulated on the molecular level are fairly involved, and are presented in Chapter 7.

> > **CONNECTIONS** < <

### Chapter 7 of Biochemistry

Insulin also decreases the endogenous synthesis of glucose from non-sugar substances by suppressing gluconeogenesis, most likely through its negative regulation of the enzyme pyruvate carboxylase. This is in accordance with the same basic idea of insulin being a way to deal with a surplus of glucose. If a surplus of glucose is present in the body, then cells certainly don't need to produce more of it.

Interestingly, insulin also affects lipid and amino acid metabolism. It promotes the storage of lipids by increasing the rate of triglyceride synthesis via an insulin-mediated increase in the absorption of fatty acids from circulating lipids, which are released from lipoproteins in the blood by insulin-sensitive lipoprotein lipase, into fat cells. Those fatty acids are then re-esterified within adipose tissue to form triglycerides. Insulin also opposes the breakdown of fatty acids by downregulating lipolysis. In terms of amino acid regulation, increasing concentrations of circulating insulin reduces proteolysis (the breakdown of proteins) and increases the uptake of amino acids. The effects of insulin on lipid metabolism in particular can be thought of as stemming from the fact that a glucose surplus (the immediate stimulus for insulin release) reflects an energy surplus, meaning that insulin will downregulate the usage of fatty acids for metabolism and promote their storage for future energy needs.

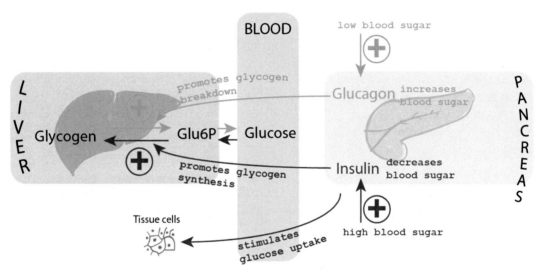

**Figure 7.** Effects of insulin and glucagon.

Diabetes mellitus results from the dysregulation of insulin, either through an autoimmune attack on the pancreatic beta cells, in type 1 diabetes, or through insulin resistance—that is, a more gradual breakdown of the degree to which target cells respond to insulin signaling—in type 2 diabetes. Individuals with type 1 diabetes are dependent upon the administration of exogenous insulin, because they no longer produce the hormone in sufficient quantity to properly regulate blood glucose levels. Patients with type 2 diabetes are generally initially treated with dietary modifications and/or anti-hyperglycemic medications, but they may eventually require insulin treatment as well.

Glucagon is essentially the opposite of insulin. It is synthesized by alpha cells of the pancreas, and is secreted in response to low concentrations of glucose in the blood stream. Glucagon induces a compensatory increase in blood sugar levels by causing the liver to convert stored glycogen into glucose, facilitating its release into the bloodstream, and by promoting gluconeogenesis. The exact mechanism through which gluconeogenesis is regulated by glucagon is quite intricate, and is presented in Chapter 7. It should be noted that both of these effects are the exact opposite of those of insulin. As a result, glucagon antagonizes insulin's action on blood glucose levels, meaning that glucagon and insulin form a feedback system that ensures blood glucose homeostasis if properly regulated.

Glucagon—as well as epinephrine, norepinephrine, growth hormone, and cortisol—promote lipolysis (the breakdown of triglycerides) by activating protein kinase A, which activates hormone-sensitive lipases found in adipose tissue. The hydrolysis of stored lipids by hormone-sensitive lipase releases free fatty acids and glycerol into the bloodstream. These mobilized free fatty acids may then be taken up by cells and metabolized to produce energy, while glycerol can enter the citric acid cycle after its conversion to glycerol 3-phosphate by glycerol kinase in the liver and kidneys. Again, this effect of glucagon is the opposite of the effect of insulin on lipid metabolism.

You might ask: why end the Biochemistry textbook with a discussion of hormonal signaling? The idea is that a tremendous amount of biochemistry has to do—in one way or another—with obtaining energy from nutrients and with regulating that process in a way that allows the tremendously complex systems of our body to remain in homeostasis and to respond appropriately to external stimuli. In fact, the analysis of the opposing effects of insulin and glucagon that we presented above touches on subjects from every single chapter in this textbook. Most obviously, it is interrelated with carbohydrate metabolism (Chapters 7 and 8), but in order to understand carbohydrate metabolism, you have to understand carbohydrate structure (Chapter 6). These hormones also affect lipid metabolism (Chapter 9). Insulin also affects the uptake of amino acids (Chapter 2), and the effects of these hormones are mediated by enzymes (Chapter 3) and non-enzymatic proteins such as transmembrane receptors (Chapter 4). Protein analysis (Chapter 5) comes into play because we have to have hands-on techniques for understanding how protein structures influence their functions. Biological membranes (Chapter 11) are the site where much of the action takes place in terms of glucose transport and signaling, and the material discussed in sections 1 and 2 of this chapter (Chapter 12) is relevant for understanding why nutrients function as energy sources. Last but not least, even nucleic acids (Chapter 10) are relevant, because the proteins necessary for all of these processes must be encoded and expressed properly for the whole system to work.

**MCAT STRATEGY > > >**

A mnemonic for remembering which is which in the insulin/glucagon pair is to remember that glucagon is released when <u>gluc</u>ose is <u>gone</u>.

**MCAT STRATEGY > > >**

The kind of integrative reasoning sketched out here is not just some random nice-sounding stuff to put at the end of a chapter (or a textbook) – it's actually an example of how you should try to train yourself to see the interconnections between the various subject areas you have to study for the MCAT, because the MCAT loves to test interconnections. On Test Day, if you can immediately assess (for example) the effects of altering the protein structure of an insulin receptor on blood glucose levels, you will be at a significant advantage. You can't possibly predict everything they could ask about, but focusing on interconnections ahead of time will help you develop the skills needed to react quickly and accurately on the spot.

# 4. Must-Knows

> Gibbs free energy of reactions:
  - $\Delta G < 0$: spontaneous, reaction releases energy that can be used for work
  - $\Delta G > 0$: non-spontaneous, reaction requires energy input
  - Relationship to equilibrium constant (and ratio of products to reactants at equilibrium): $\Delta G° = -RT\ln K_{eq}$
  - Relationship to non-standard conditions: $\Delta G = \Delta G° + RT\ln Q$
> Key regulatory concept: $\Delta G$ of linked reactions is additive. Therefore coupling favorable and unfavorable reactions is commonly used to drive energetically unfavorable reactions in the cell.

> Two main strategies for obtaining energy:
>    – High-energy bonds: most common example is ATP; hydrolysis of ATP to ADP + $P_i$ is extremely energetically favorable, largely (but not exclusively) due to accumulation of negative charges in triphosphate group. Other examples include GTP and acetyl-CoA, which has a high-energy thioester bond.
>    – Redox reactions: Electrons are transferred via redox reactions into the electron transport chain, which uses a series of redox reactions to pass electrons to the final electron acceptor of oxygen and set up a proton gradient. The electrochemical energy in the proton gradient is used to power ATP synthase.
>       • Most important electron carriers: $NAD^+$/NADH and FAD/FADH/$FADH_2$
> Regulation: metabolic pathways are carefully regulated and balanced to maintain a metabolic steady state
> Example of regulation: insulin and glucagon
>    – Insulin: released by the beta cells of the pancreas, stimulates glucose uptake by target cells
>       • Also upregulates glycogenesis, suppresses gluconeogenesis, promotes storage of lipids by increasing triglyceride synthesis and decreasing lipolysis, reduces protein breakdown and increases amino acid uptake
>    – Glucagon: synthesized by alpha cells of the pancreas, and is secreted in response to low concentrations of glucose in the blood stream. Basically the opposite of insulin.
>       • Triggers glycogenolysis (breakdown of glycogen to form glucose)
>       • Promotes gluconeogenesis (another way to get glucose into the blood)
>       • Promotes lipolysis as another way for cells to produce energy
>    – Diabetes mellitus: dysregulation of insulin
>       • Type 1: autoimmune attack on pancreatic beta cells
>       • Type 2: mediated via insulin resistance (target cells no longer respond to insulin as they should)

This page left intentionally blank.

## Practice Passage

Mitochondrial dysfunction and oxidative stress are associated with Huntington's disease (HD), a late-onset, neurodegenerative disease that causes death of select neurons in the brain. It is suggested that mitochondrial dysfunction links the genetic mutation to the neurological sequelae.

To assess any differences in tricarboxylic acid cycle (TCA) activity, experiments were performed with cultured human lymphoblasts from 20 healthy subjects and 30 HD patients. Since stress is required to reveal compromised metabolism, the cells were stressed in two ways. First, cells were deprived of serum. The second stressor was the addition of cyanide, an irreversible inhibitor of complex IV, to cells in serum-free media. The variables of interest were determined under normal basal conditions, following serum deprivation and following cyanide treatment (Figure 1).

**Figure 1.** Cellular response to stress

In the next phase of the experiment, for each cell line, three flasks were maintained in serum-containing media and six were maintained in serum-free media. Aliquots of the cells were stained with trypan blue, which only stains dead cells. Live and dead cells were counted manually under a standard light microscope. The average cell death was determined to be the percent death for that specific cell line for that particular experiment. The average change in cell death was induced by removal of serum for 54 hours and additional death induced by addition of 1 mM NaCN for 6 hours, after 48 hours of serum-deprivation (Figure 2).

**Figure 2.** Specific activities of TCA enzymes in Huntington's disease

Finally, two TCA enzymes were chosen and the effect of cyanide on their activity was measured (Figure 3). PET studies reveal that glucose metabolism is decreased in the caudate nuclei and putamen of brains from HD patients compared with normal subjects. Brain lactate is increased in HD, suggesting decreased metabolism through the tricarboxylic acid (TCA) cycle, the main pathway for converting glucose to reducing equivalents (NADH) for production of ATP.

**Figure 3.** Serum-deprivation and cyanide stress enzymatic changes

(Note: $*P < 0.05$; $**P < 0.01$; error bars represent standard errors of the mean)

*Adapted from Naseri, N. N., et al. (2016). Novel Metabolic Abnormalities in the Tricarboxylic Acid Cycle in Peripheral Cells From Huntington's Disease Patients. PLoS ONE, 11(9, under CCBY*

1. If experiments show that Htt proteins are able to block the oxidation of nicotinamide adenine dinucleotide, which of the following will be observed in HD patients?
   A. Increased transfer of electrons from complex II to complex III
   B. A decrease in NADH
   C. Decreased transfer of electrons from complex II to complex III
   D. Increased NADH/NAD⁺ ratio

2. If western blots were performed to determine the protein levels of TCA enzymes, which plot would best represent the effect of Huntington's disease on MDH expression?

3. The effect of increased NADH on the pyruvate dehydrogenase complex is best described as:
   A. competitive inhibition.
   B. feedforward inhibition.
   C. positive feedback.
   D. noncompetitive inhibition.

4. Given the purpose of the study, which of the following reasons would NOT justify the choice of lymphoblast as the cell type used in the experiment?
   A. Huntingtin protein is found in peripheral cells.
   B. Lymphoblasts provide a readily available tissue source from HD patients
   C. The lymphoblasts are transformed in the experiment, and they are not neurons.
   D. Lymphoblast cultures can be rapidly expanded to make many measurements under the same conditions.

5. Which of the following correctly describes the equilibrium between glucose-6-phosphate and fructose-6-phosphate in step 2 of glycolysis?
   A. $K_{eq} = 0$
   B. $\Delta G = 1$
   C. $\Delta G = 0$
   D. $K_{eq} = 1$

6. Which of the following metabolic intermediates has twice the carbon mass of glyceraldehyde-3-phosphate?
   A. Oxaloacetate
   B. Citrate
   C. Acetyl-CoA
   D. Ribose

7. Which of the following best explains the disparity between the change in cell death after introduction of cyanide in HD cells versus normal cells?
   A. HD causes a reduced reliance on oxidative phosphorylation in cells.
   B. HD causes an increased reliance on oxidative phosphorylation in cells.
   C. HD has no effect on oxidative phosphorylation in cells.
   D. Htt protein acts as an irreversible inhibitor of complex IV

# Practice Passage Explanations

Mitochondrial dysfunction and oxidative stress are associated with Huntington's disease (HD), a late-onset, neurodegenerative disease that causes death of select neurons in the brain. It is suggested that mitochondrial dysfunction links the genetic mutation to the neurological sequelae.

*Key terms: HD, mitochondrial dysfunction*

*Cause and effect: HD → mito changes → neurological pathology*

To assess any differences in tricarboxylic acid cycle (TCA) activity, experiments were performed with cultured human lymphoblasts from 20 healthy subjects and 30 HD patients. Since stress is required to reveal compromised metabolism, the cells were stressed in two ways. First, cells were deprived of serum. The second stressor was the addition of cyanide, an irreversible inhibitor of complex IV, to cells in serum-free media. The variables of interest were determined under normal basal conditions, following serum deprivation and following cyanide treatment (Figure 1).

*Key terms: TCA, cell stress, cyanide*

*Cause and effect: serum removal and/or cyanide → measure TCA changes*

**Figure 1.** Cellular response to stress

*Figure 1 lower plots show that serum removal significantly increased cell death in both types; while adding cyanide actually decreased the death rate in HD cells compared with healthy cells*

In the next phase of the experiment, for each cell line, three flasks were maintained in serum-containing media and six were maintained in serum-free media. Aliquots of the cells were stained with trypan blue, which only stains dead cells. Live and dead cells were counted manually under a standard light microscope. The average cell death was determined to be the percent death for that specific cell line for that particular experiment. The average change in cell death was induced by removal of serum for 54 hours and additional death induced by addition of 1 mM NaCN for 6 hours, after 48 hours of serum-deprivation (Figure 2).

*Key terms: trypan blue, cell count, average cell death, change in cell death*

*Cause and effect: serum removal → NaCN → cell death → measure trypan blue stain*

**Figure 2.** Specific activities of TCA enzymes in Huntington's disease

*Figure 2 shows that only 2 enzymes, pyruvate dehydrogenase complex and malate dehydrogenase, were significantly changed by HD; PDHC is a rate-limiting enzyme in TCA so the theory of HD → decreased metabolic TCA activity is supported*

Finally, two TCA enzymes were chosen and the effect of cyanide on their activity was measured (Figure 3). PET studies reveal that glucose metabolism is decreased in the caudate nuclei and putamen of brains from HD patients compared with normal subjects. Brain lactate is increased in HD, suggesting decreased metabolism through the tricarboxylic acid (TCA) cycle, the main pathway for converting glucose to reducing equivalents (NADH) for production of ATP.

*Key terms: PET, caudate nuclei, putamen*

*Cause and effect: HD → ↓glucose metab; ↑lactate indicates ↓TCA*

**Figure 3.** Serum-deprivation and cyanide stress enzymatic changes

*Figure 3 shows that aconitase ↓ in the presence of oxidative stressors in both healthy and HD cell lines; serum-deprivation ↑ICDH activity in healthy cells but not in HD cells*

(Note: $^*P < 0.05$; $^{**}P < 0.01$; error bars represent standard errors of the mean)

*Adapted from Naseri, N. N., et al. (2016). Novel Metabolic Abnormalities in the Tricarboxylic Acid Cycle in Peripheral Cells From Huntington's Disease Patients. PLoS ONE, 11(9, under CCBY*

1. D is correct. Nicotinamide adenine dinucleotide, or NAD, is an important redox cofactor in cellular metabolism. If the oxidation of this molecule is blocked, it means the cell is unable to convert NADH to $NAD^+$. Thus we would expect a buildup of NADH, which would not allow normal electron transport chain activity and thus, lower cellular respiration overall.
   A, C: The path of electrons through the ETC in eukaryotes is NADH → Complex I → Q → Complex III → cytochrome c → Complex IV → $O_2$.

2. C is correct. According to Figure 2, MDH levels were significantly reduced in HD patients compared to healthy controls. Thus, the western blot should show smaller bands for the HD columns compared to the control columns. Only choice C shows a smaller band for HD in all 3 trials.

3. D is correct. The synthesis of acetyl-CoA by the pyruvate dehydrogenase complex is a key irreversible step in the metabolism of glucose. The pyruvate dehydrogenase complex is inhibited by the immediate products, NADH and acetyl-CoA. This is known as negative feedback, feedback inhibition, or allosteric inhibition. Noncompetitive inhibition is when the inhibitor binds to an allosteric site on the enzyme, altering its activity. The pyruvate dehydrogenase complex is also regulated by covalent modification by kinase and phosphatase enzymes.
   A. A competitive inhibitor only binds to the active site of the enzyme. Neither NADH nor acetyl-CoA bind to the active site of pyruvate dehydrogenase.
   B. In feedforward inhibition, and upstream cell or molecule cell activates an inhibitory cell/molecule is downstream. This is a way of shutting down or limiting excitation in a downstream neuron/reaction.
   C. Positive feedback is when a downstream product serves to increase an upstream process.

4. C is correct. The study was intended to examine the relationship between HD and mitochondrial changes in brain tissue. Brain tissue is primarily composed of neurons and other neural cell types. The selection of lymphoblasts would be justified by several reasons. If huntingtin protein is found in peripheral cells, measuring the variables of interest in peripheral tissue has many advantages. Lymphoblasts provide a readily available tissue source from HD patients and controls that contain the patients' genetic material. Existing repositories of HD lymphoblasts allow for the selection of homogenous cell populations in which many critical variables can be controlled including age, sex and clinically relevant CAG repeat lengths. Furthermore, lymphoblasts can be rapidly expanded in culture to make many measurements under exactly the same conditions.

5. C is correct. For all systems at equilibrium, the change in state functions, such as $\Delta S$, $\Delta H$, $\Delta T$, and $\Delta G$ will all equal zero, since the forward rate = the reverse rate at equilibrium. $K_{eq}$, the ration of products to reactant at equilibrium, has no specific value, as it depends on the system and the temperature of the system.

6. B is correct. This question is asking us about glycolysis, the Krebs cycle and ribose. We should recognize glyceraldehyde as a 3-carbon intermediate in glycolysis. Thus, to answer this question, we must identify which molecule has 6 carbons in it. Citrate is formed from the combination of oxaloacetate ($C_4H_4O_5$) with acetyl CoA, forming a 6-carbon compound.
   A. Oxaloacetate is a 4-C compound.
   C. Acetyl-CoA is a 2-C compound.
   D. Ribose is a 5-C sugar.

7. A is correct. Examining Figure 1, we see that HD cells have a negligible change in death after introduction of the ETC inhibitor cyanide, compared with healthy cells. If cyanide, which inhibits complex IV of the oxidative phosphorlyation chain, shifted mRNA levels of TCA cycle-related genes in healthy cells to the same levels as in cyanide-treated HD cells, then cyanide-treatment mimics an HD-like cellular response in TCA cycle-related genes in healthy cells. Thus, blocking oxidative phosphorlyation would have a weaker effect on HD cells than on normal, healthy cells, accounting for the difference in cell death in response to cyanide treatment. This would strongly suggest that HD results in a markedly reduced reliance on oxidative phosphorylation compared to healthy cells.

# Independent Questions

1. Many globular proteins can fold spontaneously in aqueous solution without the need for molecular chaperones. Of the following, which is the greatest contributor to the change in free energy associated with protein folding?
   A. Increased entropy
   B. Reduced entropy
   C. Increased enthalpy
   D. Reduced enthalpy

2. The course of a simple reaction is depicted below.

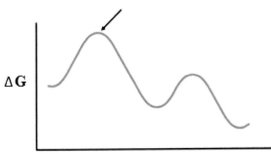

   **Reaction progress**

   The labeled point on the diagram corresponds to which of the following?
   A. A reaction intermediate
   B. A transition state
   C. A catalyst
   D. A substrate

3. Many cellular reactions are coupled to ATP hydrolysis because ATP hydrolysis is associated with a value of ΔG that is:
   A. less than zero, making the reaction spontaneous.
   B. greater than zero, making the reaction spontaneous.
   C. less than zero, making the reaction nonspontaneous.
   D. greater than zero, making the reaction nonspontaneous.

4. Alzheimer's dementia features the accumulation of a misfolded variant of a constitutively expressed protein called amyloid beta (Aβ). It has been discovered that the misfolded variant is actually much more stable than the normal Aβ protein and has an identical primary structure. Despite its low-energy state, misfolded Aβ does not normally form because:

   A. the enzyme responsible for its synthesis is expressed at very low levels in healthy cells.
   B. the gene coding for the misfolded variant is normally repressed.
   C. a high activation energy barrier normally prevents Aβ from folding into the more stable conformation.
   D. the conversion from normal Aβ to misfolded Aβ is not spontaneous.

5. Which of the following glycolytic enzymes does NOT participate in gluconeogenesis?
   A. Aldolase, which catalyzes a reaction with ΔG = -1.3 kJ/mol
   B. Phosphoglycerate kinase, which catalyzes a reaction with ΔG = +2.6 kJ/mol
   C. Phosphofructokinase, which catalyzes a reaction with ΔG = -22.2 kJ/mol
   D. Enolase, which catalyzes a reaction with ΔG = -6.6 kJ/mol

6. Enzymes facilitate biochemical reactions by all of the following methods EXCEPT:
   A. enabling extremely high local substrate concentrations.
   B. orienting the substrates in order to facilitate the formation of bonds.
   C. stabilizing unfavorable interactions that occur during the transition state.
   D. reducing the difference in free energy between the substrate(s) and product(s).

7. The establishment of a proton gradient across the inner mitochondrial membrane is a nonspontaneous process. In animal cells, the proton gradient is established by directly coupling the movement of protons to:
   A. ATP hydrolysis.
   B. the oxidation of water.
   C. the decarboxylation of pyruvic acid.
   D. the oxidation of NADH to NAD⁺.

8. Which of the following cellular conditions would most likely increase glycolytic enzyme activity via allosteric regulation?
   A. High [glucose 6-phosphate]
   B. High [AMP] and low [ATP]
   C. High [pyruvic acid]
   D. Low [glucose]

## Independent Question Explanations

1. A is correct. The change in enthalpy during protein folding is negligible. Hydrogen bonds with solvating water molecules are exchanged for internal hydrogen bonds between amino acid residues, which does not cause a significant change in enthalpy (eliminate choices C and D). The primary driving force behind protein folding is the increased entropy made possible by the sequestration of hydrophobic residues in the protein core. Hydrophobic residues in solution force solvent molecules to form a tight, highly ordered cage around them, which is entropically unfavorable.

2. B is correct. Transition states are high-energy systems that exist transiently before either reverting back into reactants or forming products. They correspond to peaks in the reaction coordinate diagram. Transition states differ from reaction intermediates in that they cannot be isolated. Valleys in the diagram indicate reaction intermediates, which are relatively stable chemical species formed during certain steps of multistep reactions.

3. A is correct. A value of ΔG < 0 is always associated with a spontaneous reaction, eliminating choices B and C. ATP hydrolysis is driven by the energetically favorable liberation of free phosphate groups, which are stabilized by multiple resonance contributors that do not exist when incorporated into a phosphodiester bond. Thus, ATP hydrolysis has a negative ΔG value and is spontaneous.

4. C is correct. Since we do not need to know specifics about the structure of amyloid beta, we must use our reasoning here. If Aβ is constitutively expressed and shares the same primary structure as its misfolded variant, the gene for misfolded Aβ must be the same as that for normal Aβ. Therefore, the synthesis of Aβ cannot depend on activation of the Aβ gene (choice B is wrong). Regarding choice A, enzymes can *catalyze* the synthesis of proteins, but this only speeds up the reaction; the protein would still form to some degree even without the enzyme present. In addition, we would not typically say that an enzyme is "responsible" for the synthesis of a protein, as it is ribosomes that actually synthesize proteins (eliminate choice A). If the misfolded variant has lower free energy than normal Aβ, then a change from normal to misfolded Aβ would be spontaneous (eliminate choice D). In fact, misfolded Aβ normally does not form because the activation energy required is very high, making option C correct.

5. C is correct. The reaction catalyzed by phosphofructokinase involves such a significant change in free energy that it is essentially irreversible under cellular conditions. As a result, the reverse reaction is not used during gluconeogenesis. The step is bypassed entirely by a different enzyme.

6. D is correct. The change in free energy of a reaction is a thermodynamic value that depends only on the chemical identity of the reactants and products. Enzymes can only alter reaction kinetics, not thermodynamics.

7. D is correct. Complex I catalyzes the oxidation of NADH (formed during the TCA cycle) to $NAD^+$ with the concomitant translocation of protons across the inner mitochondrial membrane. Do not fall for option A; the movement of protons back into the matrix is coupled with ATP *production*, but the formation of the proton gradient is not coupled to ATP *hydrolysis*.

8. B is correct. Elevated [AMP] and low [ATP] indicate inadequate ATP production. Upregulation of glycolytic activity is one mechanism to correct an ATP shortage (B is correct). Regarding choice C, pyruvic acid is the principal product of glycolysis. One would expect high levels of pyruvic acid to *decrease* glycolytic activity via negative feedback. For option A, note that G6P functions as an allosteric inhibitor of hexokinase in order to prevent unchecked glucose phosphorylation. Finally, low [glucose] in itself does not increase glycolytic enzyme activity in an allosteric fashion.

# IMAGE ATTRIBUTIONS

## Chapter 1

**Fig 1:** https://commons.wikimedia.org/wiki/File:DNA_Structure%2BKey%2BLabelled.pn_NoBB.png by Zephyris under CC-BY-SA 3.0

**Fig 2:** https://commons.wikimedia.org/wiki/File:ATPanionChemDraw.png by Smokefoot under CC BY-SA 4.0

**Fig 3:** https://commons.wikimedia.org/wiki/File:Figure_07_04_02.png CNX OpenStax under CC BY 4.0

**Fig 4:** https://commons.wikimedia.org/wiki/File:0303_Lipid_Bilayer_With_Various_Components.jpg by OpenStax under CC BY 4.0

## Chapter 2

**Fig 3:** https://commons.wikimedia.org/wiki/File:Protein_structure_(full).png by Thomas Shafee under CC BY 4.0

**Fig 4:** https://commons.wikimedia.org/wiki/File:Process_of_Denaturation.svg by Scurran 15 under CC BY-SA 4.0

**Fig 5:** https://commons.wikimedia.org/wiki/File:Titration_alanine.jpg by Laghi.I under CC BY-SA 4.0

**Fig 6:** https://en.wikipedia.org/wiki/File:Titration_Curves_of_20_Amino_Acids_Organized_by_Side_Chain.png by Lvwarren under CC BY-SA 3.0

## Chapter 3

**Fig 1:** https://en.wikipedia.org/wiki/File:Activation2_updated.svg by Jerry Mann under CC BY-SA 3.0

**Fig 2:** https://commons.wikimedia.org/wiki/File:Enzyme_structure.svg by Thomas Shafee under CC BY-4.0

**Fig 3:** https://en.wikipedia.org/wiki/File:Inducedfit080.png by paint under CC BY-SA 3.0

**Fig 4:** https://en.wikipedia.org/wiki/File:Inducedfit080.png by paint under CC BY-SA 3.0

**Fig 5:** https://en.wikipedia.org/wiki/File:105_Negative_Feedback_Loops.jpg by OpenStax under CC BY-4.0

**Fig 7:** https://en.wikipedia.org/wiki/File:Michaelis_Menten_curve_2.svg by Thomas Shafee under CC BY-4.0

**Fig 8:** https://commons.wikimedia.org/wiki/File:Lineweaver-Burke_plot.svg by Pro bug catcher under CC BY-SA 3.0

## Chapter 4

**Fig 2:** https://commons.wikimedia.org/wiki/File:Actin_filament_atomic_model.png by Thomas Splettstoesser under CC BY-SA 4.0

**Fig 3:** https://commons.wikimedia.org/wiki/File:Microtubule_structure.png by Thomas Splettstoesser under CC BY-SA 4.0

**Fig 5:** https://en.wikipedia.org/wiki/File:Cytoplasmic_dynein.svg by Delldot under CC BY 3.0

**Fig 6:** https://commons.wikimedia.org/wiki/File:Actin_myosin_filaments.png CC BY-SA 3.0

**Fig 7:** https://commons.wikimedia.org/wiki/File:Sarcomere.svg by Boumphreyfr under CC BY-SA 3.0

**Fig 9:** https://en.wikipedia.org/wiki/File:Mono-und-Polymere.svg by Martin Brandli under CC BY-SA 2.5

**Fig 10:** https://en.wikipedia.org/wiki/Ligand-gated_ion_channel#/media/File:Ion-Channel_Receptor.svg by Isaac Webb under CC BY-SA 3.0

**Fig 12:** https://en.wikipedia.org/wiki/File:GPCR_cycle.jpg by Repapetilto under CC BY-SA 3.0

## Chapter 5

**Fig 2:** https://commons.wikimedia.org/wiki/File:SizeExChrom.png by Takometer under CC BY 2.5

**Fig 4:** https://commons.wikimedia.org/wiki/File:Coomassie3.jpg by Yikrazuul under CC BY-SA 3.0

**Fig 5:** https://en.wikipedia.org/wiki/File:Coomassie-2D-Gels.jpg by Caspardavid under CC BY-SA 3.0

**Fig 6:** https://en.wikipedia.org/wiki/File:ELISA_diagram.png by Cavitri under CC BY 3.0

## Chapter 6

**Fig 3:** https://en.wikipedia.org/wiki/File:DRibose_Fischer.svg by Christopher King under CC BY-SA 3.0

**Fig 5:** https://commons.wikimedia.org/wiki/File:DGalactose_Fischer.svg by Christopher King under CC BY-SA 3.0

**Fig 6:** https://commons.wikimedia.org/wiki/File:Formation_of_hemiacetals.png by Kupirijo under CC BY-SA 3.0

**Fig 12:** https://en.wikipedia.org/wiki/File:DAllose_Fischer.svg by Popnose under CC BY-SA 3.0

**Fig 13:** https://en.wikipedia.org/wiki/File:DAltrose_Fischer.svg by Christopher King under CC BY-SA 3.0

**Fig 14:** https://en.wikipedia.org/wiki/File:DGlucose_Fischer.svg by Christopher King under CC BY-SA 3.0

**Fig 15:** https://en.wikipedia.org/wiki/File:Mannose.svg by Christopher King under CC BY-SA 3.0

**Fig 16:** https://en.wikipedia.org/wiki/File:DGulose_Fischer.svg by Christopher King under CC BY-SA 3.0

**Fig 17:** https://en.wikipedia.org/wiki/File:DIdose_Fischer.svg by Christopher King under CC BY-SA 3.0

**Fig 18:** https://en.wikipedia.org/wiki/File:DTalose_Fischer.svg by Christopher King under CC BY-SA 3.0

## Chapter 7

**Fig 2:** https://commons.wikimedia.org/wiki/File:Gluconeogenesis_pathway.png by Unused0026 under CC BY-SA 3.0

**Fig 3:** https://en.wikipedia.org/wiki/File:Pentose_Phosphate_Pathway.png by GdenBesten under CC BY-SA 3.0

## Chapter 8

**Fig 2:** https://commons.wikimedia.org/wiki/File:Pyruvate_dehydrogenase_multienzyme_complex.jpg by Speck0319 under CC BY 3.0

**Fig 5:** https://commons.wikimedia.org/wiki/File:2507_The_Krebs_Cycle.jpg by OpenStax under CC BY-3.0

## Chapter 9

**Fig 1:** https://commons.wikimedia.org/wiki/File:Lipoprotein_metabolism.png by Npatchett under CC BY-SA 3.0

**Fig 4:** https://en.wikipedia.org/wiki/File:HMG-CoA_reductase_pathway.png under CC BY-SA 3.0

## Chapter 10

**Fig 5:** https://commons.wikimedia.org/wiki/File:DNA_chemical_structure.svg by Madprime under CC BY-SA 2.5

**Fig 6:** https://commons.wikimedia.org/wiki/File:Dnaconformations.png by Mauroesguerroto under CC BY-SA 4.0

**Fig 7:** https://commons.wikimedia.org/wiki/File:Polymerase_chain_reaction.svg by Enzoklop under CC BY-SA 3.0

## Chapter 11

**Fig 4:** https://commons.wikimedia.org/wiki/File:Osmosis.svg by YassineMrabet under CC BY-SA 3.0

**Fig 6:** https://en.wikipedia.org/wiki/File:0307_Osmosis.jpg by OpenStax under CC BY 4.0

**Fig 7:** https://commons.wikimedia.org/wiki/File:Blausen_0818_Sodium-PotassiumPump.png by BruceBlaus under CC BY 3.0

## Chapter 12

**Fig 1:** https://en.wikipedia.org/wiki/File:Endergonic_Reaction.svg by Provenzano15 under CC BY-SA 3.0

**Fig 2:** https://en.wikipedia.org/wiki/File:Exergonic_Reaction.svg by Provenzano15 under CC BY-SA 3.0

**Fig 4:** https://commons.wikimedia.org/wiki/File:ADP_ATP_cycle.png by Meussig under CC BY-SA 3.0

**Fig 8:** https://commons.wikimedia.org/wiki/File:Blood_glucose_control.png by C. Muessig under CC BY-SA 3.0

This page left intentionally blank.

# INDEX

micelle 248–249
Michaelis-Menten 60–68
microfilament 79–80
microtubule 80
mitochondria 175–176
mitosis 79
mixed inhibitor 66
monosaccharide 124–128
mRNA 27, 30, 229
myoglobin 69
myosin 78–81
N-terminus 30
NADH 5, 273–274
negative feedback 9–11, 58–59, 184–185, 275–276
neurotransmitter 85–87
noncompetitive inhibitor 64–67
norepinephrine 23, 148, 275, 277
nucleic acid 225–228
nucleoside 226
nucleotide 226
osmosis 249–252
osmotic pressure 251–252
oxidative phosphorylation 180–185
oxidoreductase 57
paper chromatography 103
PCR 232
pentose phosphate pathway 156–157
pepsin 34
peptide hormone 7
pH 35–38

phagocytosis 255
phosphatase 68
phosphate 3, 7, 147, 227
phosphodiester 228, 230
phospholipid 7, 199, 246
pinocytosis 255
plasma membrane 7, 245–256
polarity 6, 103–104
polypeptide 30
polysaccharide 129–130
positive feedback 10, 59, 285
probe 232
prohormone 68
proline 23, 30
prostaglandin 199, 213
prosthetic 69
purine 226–227
pyrimidine 226–227
pyruvate 149–152
quaternary structure 31
salt bridge 31
saturated fat 201, 207
saturation 61
second messenger 7, 88
secondary active transport 254
secondary structure 30–31
secretory vesicle 275
separations 101–108
size-exclusion chromatography 105
sodium potassium pump 253–254
sphingolipid 199, 246

sphingomyelin 245
spontaneous 252, 255, 267–269, 273
steroid hormone 7–8, 213
Strecker synthesis 40–41
Substrate 55
substrate-level phosphorylation 147
sucrose 125, 129
sugar-phosphate backbone 229–230
supercoil 231
synthase 3
terpene 201
tertiary structure 31–32
thin-layer chromatography 103
thymine 226
tight junction 84
transferase 57
triacylglycerol 199–201
triglyceride 199–201
tyrosine 23, 58
ubiquinone 180–182
uncompetitive inhibitor 65–66
unsaturated fat 201, 207–208
uracil 226–229
urea 33, 232
voltage gated channel 253
water 34
western blot 107
Z-DNA 230–231
zymogen 68